WHO RUNS CONGRESS?

Other Books by Mark Green

With Justice for Some (1971, edited with Bruce Wasserstein)

The Closed Enterprise System (1972, with Beverly C. Moore, Jr., and Bruce Wasserstein)

The Monopoly Makers (1973, editor)

Corporate Power in America (1973, edited with Ralph Nader)

The Other Government: The Unseen Power of Washington Lawyers (1975)

Verdicts on Lawyers (1976, edited with Ralph Nader)

Taming the Giant Corporation (1972, with Ralph Nader and Joel Seligman)

WHO RUNS CONGRESS?

**Third edition completely revised
and updated by
MARK GREEN**

**with
Michael Calabrese
Lynn Darling
Bruce Rosenthal
James M. Fallows
David R. Zwick**

Introduction by Ralph Nader

The Viking Press   New York

Copyright © Ralph Nader, 1972, 1975, 1979
All rights reserved
First published in 1979 by The Viking Press
625 Madison Avenue, New York, N.Y. 10022
Published simultaneously in Canada by
Penguin Books Canada Limited

LIBRARY OF CONGRESS CATALOGING IN PUBLICATION DATA
Green, Mark
Who runs Congress?
Includes index.
1. United States. Congress. I. Title.
JK1061.G68 1979 328.73 79-15017
ISBN 0-670-76492-2

Printed in the United States of America
Set in Times Roman

To Deni and Jenya

Acknowledgments

Many friends and colleagues helped create and shape the three editions of *Who Runs Congress?* The original 1972 edition grew out of the fertile editorial guidance of Jean Highland and Judy Knipe of Bantam Books, and Dick Grossman, Tom Stewart, and Julie Colmore of Grossman Publishers. Doug Cassell contributed to the epilogue, "Taking on Congress: A Primer for Citizen Action." In addition, Joan Claybrook, Robert Fellmeth, Michael Pertschuck, and Harrison Wellford gave us valuable insights and comments. Production and research assistance were provided by Craig Kubey, Anne Uttermann, Pauline Postotnik and Elayne Butwinick.

The second edition in 1975 contained sections written by Lynn Darling and Bruce Rosenthal. Typing the manuscript and chasing down elusive facts were Pam Meyer, Cecelia Kelly and Steve Koch.

Significantly contributing to the researching and writing of the current edition was Daniel Becker of Congress Watch. Staffers Tim Winslow, Judy Trott and Bart Laws patiently helped in the research and production of the book, and Gene Karpinski participated in updating parts of the epilogue.

Finally, two people deserve special note. Oscar Dystel of Bantam Books perceived a need for citizens to better understand Congress in the early 1970s, and helped launch us. And of course there is Ralph Nader, without whom this book couldn't exist. In this effort as in so many others, he exemplifies what Felix Frankfurter used to call the highest office in a democracy—the office of citizen.

Mark Green
Washington, D.C.
July 1, 1979

Contents

Introduction
by Ralph Nader

Since 1972, when the first edition of this book was published, Congress has reformed many of its procedures and, at the same time, diminished much of its substance. This seeming paradox may surprise those observers who believe that improved legislative procedures alone can produce more well-conceived and fairer legislative results. For those who have *experienced* the dynamics of organized power groups acting on the Congressional process, however, the failure of procedural improvements to thwart special interest demands or advance public interest values confirms again that the roots of Congressional behavior lie more in the economy than in the polity.

On the procedural side, both the House of Representatives and the Senate have opened up more of their committee meetings to the public. Some of the stifling rules have been liberalized or abolished. The ethics committees of both Houses are more active, though some observers of Koreagate-type scandals would say "not active, enough." Disclosure of the legislators' finances has increased. The vast power of committee heads has been curtailed and is now shared with either committee members or all party members, such as the House Democratic Caucus. Substantial turnovers, largely through retirements, have brought in a larger number of legislators who do not have an ingrained history of special interest affiliation. The new lawmakers participate more aggressively, and Congress is asserting more of its authority vis-à-vis the executive branch.

In contrast, on the substantive side, Congress has been a disaster area in a period of crises and emergencies.

Fluctuating between paralysis, callousness, and venality, Congress as a whole has managed to avoid passage of responsive legislation to meet the problems of energy, tax, health insurance, consumer abuse, inflation, and unemployment. These are priorities set by Congress itself. Moreover, the legislature spent considerable effort hamstringing enforcement efforts by the few regulators who took their legal mandates seriously—as the Federal Trade Commission did. And, however unconstitutional or unwise they are, legislative vetoes and sunset bills have blossomed profusely in the post-Watergate era. Most of the legislative recommendations of the Senate Watergate Committee languished.

The Congress did react to reports of government waste and consumption by establishing Inspector General's offices in federal departments. But, against daily disclosures of a major corporate crime epidemic, the only response by Congress was a law designed to restrain foreign bribery by U.S. corporations. Against serious safety and economic problems in the nuclear industry, Congress has disregarded the many reports of its own investigative arm, the General Accounting Office, and done nothing. Against daily disclosures of consumer abuses and severe imbalances of representation before federal regulatory agencies, the House of Representatives in 1978 defeated a bill to establish a small consumer protection office. Against the proven effectiveness of earlier auto safety technology in the prevention of highway casualties, Congress has reacted sourly to modest government attempts, under the 1966 auto safety law, to require newer safety systems for motor vehicles that would improve on earlier successes. Against a major corporate merger movement most members of Congress have remained indifferent. Repeatedly, Congress has been whooping through major corporate subsidy legislation, involving billions of dollars, while impeding or defeating measures in auto, drug, pesticide, and food safety.

Some members of Congress have wisely recognized the need to champion the empowerment issues—rights and mechanisms that strengthen the ability of citizens to shape their government and advance their legitimate interests. Passage of the National Consumer Cooperative Bank bill in 1978 may prove a landmark step in strengthening consumers through its provision of credit and technical assistance to cooperatives in food, housing, health, repair, energy, and other areas.

Other pending legislation includes consumer class action and standing to sue bills, designed to overturn several U.S. Supreme Court decisions that restrict important procedural rights. Also in the hopper is a bill to reimburse the expenses of needy citizens who can participate significantly in rule-making governmental procedures such as those before the Food and Drug Administration.

A malaise of multiple dimensions is sweeping over Capitol Hill. One dimension is dismay. Failures of past programs to solve social problems have led to the "nothing-seems-to-work" attitude. The growing number of record votes, microissues, and special pleaders have produced a weariness that is leading many members of Congress to resign from office. When South Carolinian Mendel Davis, a young Representative from a safe district, announced in 1979 his retirement, he said it was chiefly because he was tired of "special interest groups from all sides."

There is more to the malaise than mood, however. The rise of the "Imperial Presidency," capped by the Watergate scandal, wounded Congressional pride. The result was a series of antagonisms against "big government and bureaucracy," fueled by an active corporate propaganda machine. Give a legislator a serviceable slogan and a Pandora's box of mischief can ensue. Unable to focus on general policy making, Congress now wants to exercise veto power over many regulations and standards (but not business subsidy decisions) issued by federal agencies under regular administrative procedures. The growing arrogance of Congress (some call it the "Imperial Congress") has become highly self-indulgent. Large salary increases for themselves and other perquisites are approved in a time of national inflation. In addition, Congress exempts itself explicitly from numerous laws it passed that give people employment, health, and citizen rights. Congress does not set a good example for the rest of the nation.

Other structural changes affecting Congressional performance involve the near total breakdown of Democratic party discipline on Capitol Hill. Time and time again, young legislators say "what can the Party do for me?" They build their own political base, promptly service constituent letters and requests, fly back home frequently for ceremonies and appearances, and feed off the burgeoning political action committees (PACs) of corporations for campaign financing. Party campaign treasuries mean less and less, and the absence of a mass based party apparatus to help them get out the vote completes the reality of party impotence that legislators are sensing. As they build their own organization they need the party less and less. And, such individuation of the electoral process is reflected in the inability of the House and Senate leadership to tie legislative programs to voting support from party members. On several occasions I have seen Speaker Tip O'Neill beseech young Democratic members of the House to vote for a bill. They shrugged him off almost mockingly and voted the other way. Speaker O'Neill must be nostalgic for the days of Speaker Sam Rayburn and the Texan's stable of usable sanctions against such rebellions. The problem of party strength is compounded by a president who is unable or unwilling to assert vigorous political leadership. As one Democrat put it: ". . . I am more popular than he is in my district. What can he do for me? What can he do to me?"

Looming over Capitol Hill are the omnipresent and relentless demands of corporate power. It is the strongest shaping force working on the Congress. both as an institution and as a collection of mostly quite susceptible legislators. The thousands of corporate lobbyists, law firms, and trade associations in Washington are closely coordinated with their business members and clients throughout the country. Their objectives are to shield corporate misbehavior from the rule of law and to turn Congress and the executive branch into a bustling bazaar of bonanzas. These bonanzas take the form of subsidies, tax privileges, protection from competition, inflated government contracts, and other assorted windfalls.

Lacking a comprehensive program for reform of the political economy, some members of Congress bemoan the loss of public consensus and the growth of single issue politics. However, there is a leadership gap in the Congress that bears a significant responsibility. The positions of Senate Majority leader or House Speaker, for example, do not have to consign their holders to being arbiters of House disputes and mere managers of legislative traffic. Unfortunately, Speakers and Majority leaders these days are not identified with leadership of strong legislative programs.

The seeds for new party movements may be found in the present conditions of party disintegration.

The fundamental necessity of a knowledgeable and involved citizen action process streaming regularly toward Congress from all over the country and from Washington-based centers is an axiom which receives continuous proof. For example, after the most intense experience with the executive lawlessness of Watergate, the Congress saw some of its members draw up a list of reforms in 1974 following the conclusion of those celebrated hearings. They remain on the shelf of Congressional disinterest. To any close observers of Congress, such withdrawals are not surprising. After all, some veteran members of Congress knew about the secret war in Laos and did nothing, in violation of their oath to uphold the Constitution. They knew much about the lawlessness of the CIA and did nothing, again in violation of their oath to uphold the Constitution.

With 435 members in the House and 100 members in the Senate, the Congress presents diverse characteristics among legislators and their staff. Many use their office to enrich themselves, such as Rep. Robert Sikes and Senator Russell Long. Others are models of probity, such as Rep. Bob Eckhardt and Senator Gaylord Nelson. Many work for special interests to secure their reelection resources or massage their egos and lust for power. One such ego, Rep. Mike McCormack, who boasts of being the only scientist in Congress, dutifully does the work of the nuclear power industry. Some will take a stand on issues that they believe are right, such as former Rep. Michael Harrington, notwithstanding the political liabilities. It is at the staff level, however, that public scrutiny is at its minimum. Special interests long ago learned that gifts, free trips, cash, and women lavished on key committee or other Congressional staff can result in the desired behavior by the boss without much risk of exposure. The decades-long wining and dining of Nick Zapple by the communications industry helped turn this powerful aide to Senator John Pastore's Communications Subcommittee into a bastion of defense and offense for the industry in the Senate.

Whatever their diversity, the members of Congress are not very representative of the American people. Almost one third of the Senate are millionaires. Almost half the Congress is composed of lawyers, who make up less than one-third of 1 percent of the population. Blue-collar workers may get to Congress, but usually as tourists passing through the guided tours. Women and minority groups are, for the most part, severely underrepresented. This institution will order over $400 billion of your money to be spent this year and use or refuse to use vast amounts of your power to affect your way of living and our relations with other nations. That is enough reason for this book.

In a democracy, ultimate governmental power is supposed to reside in the people. And in the interest of practicality and expertise, the people delegate much of the daily exercise of this power to elected legislatures, which on the national level means Congress. But delegation requires vigilance, and, lacking vigilance, delegation becomes abdication. One of the objectives of this volume is to make more people care about what they've lost to Congress so that they can take more of it back for the good of themselves, their fellow citizens, and their children. Less than half the adults polled back in 1965 knew the name of their member of Congress. Only 35 percent of the electorate voted in the November 1978 Congressional elections. As a result, without the participation of the people, Congress has surrendered its enormous authority and resources to special interest groups, waste, insensitivity, ignorance, and bureaucracy.

Although Americans do not spend much time doing something about Congress, they spend far more time worrying about their personal problems—taxes, school, health, pollution, energy, war, traffic, housing, inflated prices, crime, injustice, poverty, corruption. They worry about a steady slippage in the quality of American life—not about Congress. Yet these are the problems and abuses that Congress has the power to help them with—that is what Congress is *supposed* to be for. Its laws affect the price of meat and gasoline; decide how clean the environment is to be; permit or encourage warfare; feed massive military expenditures; shape huge government bureaucracies (which it alone can create); and affect the size and quality of the economy.

Congress is the great American default. Of the three branches of government, the executive and judicial may get away with being insulated from the citizenry, but Congress is potentially the branch most exposed to democratic demand. And so turning Congress around *for* the people is the most practical and immediate priority in improving the executive and judicial branches as well. The stakes are now so apparent and so mounting that accomplishing this transformation *by* the people must be viewed as an *obligation,* not just a right, of citizenship. This citizenship must be ingrained as part of the daily work and fun of America.

There should be little disagreement over the assertion that ours is a society of unparalleled material wealth and skill, increasingly unable to solve, diminish or forestall problems to which wealth and skill should be responsive. This gnawing paradox is a signal fact of contemporary American life—one with worldwide repercussions. As unemployment remains high, our cities are still deteriorating; malnutrition and disease stalk millions of impoverished citizens; pollution is increasing faster than GNP; the narcotics trade eats at the human fiber; government and corporate corruption and waste are bursting out all over; bureaucracy has become the opiate of the people; consumer fraud accelerates hand in hand with Big Business domination of the economy and much of government; rank-and-file disgruntlement with labor leadership deepens; and housing, rapid transit, energy, and medical care seem to defy even a focused effort at resolution. At the same time, the law stands mocked or manipulated by the powerful. Consequently, the poor and middle class, who are given little access and less compassion by the legal system, view it with increasing contempt.

If we cannot reduce our spreading crises, with all our wealth and talent, we are entitled to ask: What remains to meet the challenge of achieving the necessary changes? One answer is the U.S. Congress. Like the nerve center of a traffic control system, Congress stands potentially as both reflector and initiator of operational democratic responses and solutions. The word *potentially* is used deliberately—as both an expression of hope and of realistic possibilities—even though Congress in its past and in its present has been a continuous underachiever.

What does the public think of Congress? There is, to be sure, a widespread cynicism about "politicians," along with the feeling that nothing can be done about them beyond mere endurance. At times, three major impressions of Congress prevail: that it is something to be manipulated by special interest groups or bureaucracies; that it is something to be ridiculed, or ignored, because it is an ornament; or that it is hopelessly beyond reach.

I believe that an institution—which yearly distributes several hundred billion tax dollars; which is possessed of broad constitutional powers to advance the well-being of Americans and, to some degree, the rest of the world; which can assess or air a nation's problems openly; which can secure the information to plan for the future intelligently; and which can be run by the American people—can be a prime lever for change and justice in our country.

Nothing compares with the Congress as the initiating hope of reclaiming America. By reclaiming the Congress, America revolutionizes itself. For in so doing there is a required build-up of citizenship, expertise, and stamina such as this country has never seen. It is the right and duty of every citizen to strive for such development. And it should not have to be the equivalent of reaching for the stars.

Traditionally, the political system in this country has led Americans to look to the presidency for inspiration and leadership. But the Congress can be an even more effective leader and shaper and receiver of democratic values and action. For some of Washington's old hands, such an aspiration might be taken as a bad joke, if not an explicitly bizarre goal. But it is not as bizarre as it sounds when one considers the number of flexible and decentralized options that are open to Congress. The constitutional authority given to Congress accords it an importance that far transcends the indentured status or chronic inaction presently woven into its fabric by its insulated surroundings.

The personal stake of every citizen in Congress is obvious. Only Congress takes twenty-five cents out of every dollar earned by the worker, supposedly to achieve a better society.

Who Runs Congress? offers some initial practical advice on what *you* can do about reclaiming it for American citizens. The rest is up to you—your sense of justice, your faith in people, your energy and imagination. If you want to do something about it, start now. It is the mark of our nation's fingertip potential, unprecedented in world history, that we are a generation of Americans who have to give up little in order to achieve much of lasting endurance for the earth's people. Two centuries of delegation have worn their course. It is time to grasp the labors of daily citizenship and assume more closely the responsibility of government.*

Washington, D.C.
July, 1979

---

*Please turn to the last pages of this volume which describe how you can obtain useful materials to assist you in monitoring and contributing to Congressional policies on the important issues of the eighties.

WHO RUNS CONGRESS?

1

Who Owns Congress?

Congress is the best money can buy.

—Will Rogers

The influence of big money on government has been a theme of critics ever since the founding of the Republic. Were it not for the sordid tales of bribery and payoffs regularly floating out from behind the Capitol Curtain, scandal columnists might long ago have gone on unemployment compensation. But for all their titillating impact, the crudest forms of bribery are vastly overshadowed as a corrupting influence by a much more sophisticated and widespread practice. Instead of going into the congressman's pockets, the money is put in the campaign coffers for the next (or sometimes the previous) election.

Of course, when a big campaign contribution is given in return for an assurance of receiving special treatment, it doesn't matter what the transaction is called. It's still nothing more than good old-fashioned graft in a very thin disguise. But who needs to extract a promise from a politician if spending enough money at election time can put a "reliable" man or woman into office? Or better yet, if spending enough money at primary election and nominating time can ensure that *all* the surviving candidates by the time the general election rolls around are "reliable."

Expensive Merchandise

Part of the problem is inflation. Like meat, some members of Congress have risen in price. As the cost of U.S. Prime, political influence has soared, casual buyers have fled the market and left it to the truly rich or the cor-

1

porate purchasers. Expenses weren't always so high. In the election campaign of 1846, friends of Abraham Lincoln collected a fund for his first try for Congress. The $200 they scraped together would barely cover one week's phone bills for a modern candidate. But at the end of the campaign, Lincoln returned $199.25 of it. The rest had gone for his one campaign expense, a barrel of cider for local farm hands.

Honest Abe might have spent the rest of his life splitting rails if he'd tried the same thing much later. The turning point for campaign expenses came with the Civil War. As the newly powerful corporate empires began to buy political favors—and as the politicians of the time showed themselves willing to be bought—competition pushed the prices up. The mounting expense, however, did not curb demand, since the companies saw the hard business advantage of friendly politicians. In 1903, a Standard Oil agent (who was himself a member of Congress), screening a "loan request" from a senator, wrote to the company's vice president John Archbold, "Do you want to make the investment?"

The return on such investments was a Congress increasingly populated with men like Senator Boies Penrose. Penrose was a Pennsylvanian, a Republican, and a devoted glutton. (He weighed 350 pounds and kept in condition with meals like the following: one dozen oysters, pots of chicken gumbo, a terrapin stew, two ducks, six kinds of vegetables, a quart of coffee, and several cognacs.) But his deepest allegiance was to the welfare of Corporate America. He candidly explained his philosophy of economy and life to a group of his business beneficiaries: "I believe in a division of labor. You send us to Congress; we pass laws under . . . which you make money; . . . and out of your profits you further contribute to our campaign funds to send us back again to pass more laws to enable you to make more money." A good operating guideline, he once confided to an associate, was to work on "legislation that meant something to men with real money and let them foot the bill"—as when Archbold of Standard Oil gave him $25,000 on one proven occasion.

Today's politicians can afford neither Penrose's candor nor his appetite, but his mottoes live on. Former Oklahoma senator Fred Harris fondly recalls his baptism in this old style of campaign spending when, in the 1954 Oklahoma Senate race, incumbent oil millionaire Robert Kerr squared off against another oil millionaire, Roy Turner. Harris, who worked for Turner, says:

> Some [people] wanted to be county or town campaign managers for whichever candidate would pay the most. An unprincipled preacher offered to bargain away supposed influence with his unsuspecting congregation. An Avon saleswoman was willing to consider—for a price—adding a pitch for a candidate to her usual sales promotion to regular-route customers. And there were the ubiquitous importunings of hundreds of poll haulers and hangers-on. They wanted everything from $25,000 to carry a county to a half-pint of whiskey to make the day. From fifty dollars for "gas and expenses" to get to the district church conference, to a thousand dollars to pay back taxes to keep a weekly newspaper publishing. . . .
>
> One young man in the Turner headquarters had as his principal duty running to the Federal Reserve Bank every day as soon as it opened to bring back a thousand or so dollars in cash to be doled out to those who came in declaring that victory in their counties required a little money "to put on a barbecue" or "to hire some woman to pick up old folks on election day."

But Darwin rules in politics as in nature, and the richest survive. Turner ran out of money midway through the campaign and had to quit. Kerr kept his seat.

If Turner were running his campaign in 1978, the daily money deliveries would have to be closer to ten thousand than to one. As election techniques have risen from barbecues and preacher-bribing to the higher technologies of media advertising, costs have soared, putting extraordinary demands on members of Congress. Former Democratic national finance chairman Joseph Cole estimated that candidates can spend up to half of their time seeking campaign funds. "Campaign financing is a curse," said Senator Hubert Humphrey, who had been through enough campaigns to know. "It's the most disgusting, demeaning, disenchanting, debilitating experience of a politician's life.

It's stinky, it's lousy. I just can't tell you how much I hate it."

But they do it, for there are the inevitable campaign costs—especially the cost of television advertising.

When saturation campaigns of one-minute spots took over from more primitive forms of publicity, election funding became a truly big business. As recently as 1952, when Eisenhower first ran for the presidency, the total spent in federal election campaigns was "only" $140 million, according to the Citizens Research Foundation. Over the next twelve years, the total rose slowly; in 1964, it was an estimated $200 million. But only four years later, in the 1968 campaigns, the figure had risen by 50 percent, to $300 million—due largely to electronic electioneering, as thirty-second and sixty-second TV spots demonstrated that nearly *any* well-financed candidate could get elected, not that the *best* candidate could get elected.

Instead of becoming more restrained, however, recent election campaigns have accentuated the need for public financing of congressional campaigns. While there were ten million-dollar candidates in 1976, there were sixteen in 1978. Probably the most stunning display of waste and extravagance in congressional history was the 1978 campaign of the Senate's "6 million dollar man"—Jesse Helms of North Carolina. By spending ten times the $650,000 he used to get elected the first time around in 1972, Helms outspent his opponent 30 to 1 and more than doubled the previous spending record of $3 million set by ketchup magnate Senator H. John Heinz (R.-Pa.) in 1976. According to *Congressional Quarterly,* half of Helms's expenses went to pay for nationwide direct mail solicitations done by Richard Viguerie, the logistical general behind the New Right political movement.

Heinz still holds one record, however—he spent more money on himself than any candidate for public office in history. While Helms collected 80 percent of his receipts in outside contributions of less than $100, Heinz "loaned" his campaign $2,465,000. Alex Seith loaned himself $600,000 of his wife's wealth in a losing effort against incumbent Senator Charles H. Percy (R.-Ill.); John W. Warner of Virginia wrote checks totaling $616,000 to finance his campaign; and Minnesota businessman Bob Short, who once moved baseball's Washington Senators to

Texas, spent $1 million of his own money trying to get himself traded to the more prestigious club in Washington.

Overall in 1978. according to the *New York Times*, the average Senate candidate spent $920,000 and the average House candidate $108,000. All candidates for these federal offices spent about $150 million, up from $100 million just two years before. A Congress Watch analysis of expenditures found that winners outspent losers 4 to 1 and that Senate candidates who outspent their opponents won 85 percent of the seats contested.

As costs have risen to the point where even the millionaires must borrow, so too rises the certainty that politicians must turn to rich special interests for help. President Eisenhower, in an era of what now looks like small-change campaigns, was appalled by the "outrageous costs of getting elected to public office." Later, Robert Kennedy agreed that "we are in danger of creating a situation in which our candidates must be chosen from among the rich [like the Kennedys] . . . or those willing to be beholden to others."

Labor and Business in the Political Marketplace

Who "owns" the politicians?

A look at campaign fund sources shows that major contributors fall into several categories—business and professional groups, organized labor, and other ideological organizations. Most of these groups contribute funds through political fundraising affiliates. According to a Common Cause study, the largest business contributors in 1976 congressional races were the American Medical Association ($1,780,879), dairy interests ($1,362,159), and oil, natural gas, and coal firms ($809,508).

Labor unions became an important funding force in the 1950s, when the AFL-CIO set up a political action arm, the Committee on Political Education (COPE). Aside from COPE, the committee list now includes the Teamsters' DRIVE, the United Auto Workers' Good Government Fund, and many others. Together they contributed $8.1 million to congressional races in 1976.

Although union contributions may be a necessary counterweight to big-business spending, the tactics some unions use to collect their funds give the working class a bad name. One of the more notorious examples is the Seafarers International Union (SIU). The SIU has long been a big giver; in 1968, its 80,000 members came up with more than three times as much campaign money as the 1.4 million United Auto Workers. Much of the more than $600,000 collected that year was spread among friends of the maritime industry in Congress, where it oiled the way for a series of lush subsidies to the U.S. merchant fleet, totaling close to $1 billion a year.

But along the way, there had been technical troubles. In 1970, eight of the union's officers were indicted for making illegal contributions of $40,000. (The charges were dismissed in 1972 on the grounds that the Justice Department had delayed in pressing the case.) Also, while the source of the large funds was supposed to be "voluntary" contributions from union members, grumblers claimed that the word was used in a sense no one outside the SIU would recognize. As an aid to voluntarism, some SIU members said, "goon squads" show up at collection time, a charge denied by union spokesmen. According to Jerry Landauer of the *Wall Street Journal,* the SIU systematically collects from all crewmen on a U.S. ship—including foreigners, whose interest in American politics is presumably slight.

In 1974, together with the Maritime Engineers' Beneficial Association, the SIU sent $333,300 into the campaign chests of members of Congress who supported legislation to require that at least 20 percent of oil imports be shipped in U.S. tankers manned by U.S. crews. The biggest contributions were bestowed upon those who meant the most to the legislation, the chairmen of the Merchant Marine subcommittees in the Senate and the House: Senator Russell B. Long (D.-La.), $20,000; and Rep. Frank M. Clark (D.-Pa.), $17,600. (When an earlier chairman, Edward A. Garmatz [D.-Md.], was asked about accepting such large contributions from interests within his committee's jurisdiction, he responded, "Who in the hell do they expect me to get it from, the post office people, the bankers? You get it from the people you worked with, who you helped some way or another. It's only natural.") Of the 141 contributions made by the two unions in 1974, all but 4 went to supporters of the oil import bill. The bill did pass Congress but was vetoed by President Gerald Ford.

Undaunted, and habituated to their free-spending ways, maritime interests gave $449,000 to 215 members of Congress in 1976—including $102,563 to 29 of 40 members of the House Merchant Marine and Fisheries Committee —in an effort to get new cargo preference legislation passed. This time, however, they overplayed their hand. Even though they had the support of President Carter and the bill called for U.S. ships transporting only 9.5 percent of imported oil, the House voted 257–165 against the maritime interests. Extensive publicity about their lavish contributions persuaded many congressional beneficiaries that a yes-vote would be imprudent.

Campaign collectors in the business and professional community are delighted when exploits like the SIU's come to light. Together with the well-publicized contributions from COPE and DRIVE, the union horror stories are just the thing to spur businessmen to greater spending sacrifices for *their* favorite candidates. It is a tribute to the determination of business fundraisers that the money continues to roll out in response to the union threat.

It is difficult to total up the business contributions as exactly as those from labor. Unlike the unions, who typically trumpet each dollar they collect from the members and pass on to the candidate, business interests are far more hidden—to the extent of employing mysterious names. For example, if you'd like to know what role the railroads play in political gift-giving, you will have to look for the Civic Trust 80 (Santa Fe Railroad) and the Fund for Effective Government (Union Pacific Railroad of New York). Two companies that do their best to get their name across to the marketing world remain hidden in the political arena: the Coca-Cola Company fund calls itself the Non-Partisan Committee for Good Government (which gave $68,200 to federal candidates in 1976) and General Electric goes by the name Non-Partisan Political Committee (it gave the most of any corporate "political action committee," $104,235, in 1976). In Texas, where legend says everything is big, a group of political fund-giving Texas businessmen go by the name Big 50 Political Action Committee, and a loose group of Georgia business-men call themselves—the Loose Group.

There are other comparisons to be made between corporate and labor contributors. Where seafaring men might use a goon squad, Texaco uses an interoffice memorandum. "We must as individual citizens support those candidates who understand and appreciate the validity of our position," intones a letter from Texaco's vice president for public relations and personnel. It closes with a request that employees contribute $5 per month or $60 for the entire year. Sterling Drug, Inc., applying a means test, asks its 525 executives who earn more than $15,000 per year to give at least one-half of 1 percent of salary, up to a ceiling of $200. "Specifically, we're asking for a *voluntary* contribution from you," the letter says, "for a political fund to be allocated to those legislators . . . whose . . . election is *important* to our industry and to *Sterling Drug, Inc.*" (emphasis in original). The volunteer donor—eager to help his industry's patrons, and curious about the use of his money—might ask the company who the important legislators are. Upholding the best professional traditions of confidentiality, Sterling refuses to tell.

Other corporations, more considerate of their workers, may add "bonuses" to executive paychecks with the understanding that the money will be passed on to a candidate. Still others—like the Union Oil Company and the Cleveland-based defense firm Thompson-Ramos-Woolridge (TRW)—avoid the middleman by simply deducting an arranged amount for "campaign contributions" from the paychecks of cooperating employees. The Public Affairs Council, whose members include two hundred corporate titans, is so struck by the plan that it is working for the day when the nation's thousand biggest companies will all have automatic campaign funding.

Like labor, business has not kept out of legal trouble. In fact, investigations and admissions have uncovered a virtual corporate crime wave in the giving of campaign funds to candidates in the 1972 and 1974 elections. Scores of corporate heads and corporations have pleaded guilty to violations of campaign finance laws. The business list includes such blue-chip companies as American Airlines, Braniff Airlines, 3M, Goodyear Tire and Rubber, and Gulf Oil—firms where corporate executives diverted corporate funds for political use.

These revelations do not lead to the conclusion that the door has been slammed shut on illegal corporate contributions. First, those who were indicted or admitted guilt probably represent only a handful of the corporations and executives, small and large firms alike, who made illegal contributions. Second, the sentences given to violators were hardly effective deterrents. In most cases, individuals who earned tens of thousands of dollars a year were fined $1,000. In the only case involving a jail term, two corporate executives of the Associated Milk Producers, Inc., were each fined $10,000 and sentenced to four months in jail.

But however much business spent on congressional races in these years pales in comparison to 1978 and to expected amounts in the 1980s. The reason is the rise of the Political Action Committees, or PACs as they are called.

Due to seemingly minor changes in the 1974 and 1976 campaign acts and to Federal Election Commission rulings (discussed later), many corporations began to set up separate PACs to raise money from shareholders, executives, and even (twice a year) employees. Unlike individuals, who cannot contribute more than $1,000 to any federal candidate or $25,000 to all candidates, PACs can give a candidate up to $5,000 for a primary and/or a run-off and/or a general election; and there is no limit on their overall contributions. The method of fundraising is not very taxing. Texasgulf, Inc.'s solicitation letter to their shareholders is representative of the approach: "You may be dismayed, as we are, by the massive and growing federal budget and the continuing high level of inflation . . . Much of this has occurred because corporations and their shareholders have not been able to participate in politics as effectively as labor unions, environmentalists and other more narrowly focused pressure groups."

In 1974 there were less than 100 corporate PACs; by 1978, over 800. In 1976 they spent $5.8 million on congressional races; in the 1977–78 period, $17.7 million, a 200 percent increase. What is stunning is not how many more business PACs there are but how many more there can be. By 1979 only a third of the *Fortune* 500, and only a fifth of the 1,000 largest industrial firms, had created them. Since there are only so many international unions, but there are thousands of large companies, the trajectory of PAC giving is clear. "This is just the incubation period," warns Fred Wertheimer of Common Cause. "Within the next four to six years, corporate PACs will completely dominate congressional campaigns and Congress will represent special interests rather than their constituencies." Already PACs have attempted to convert money into influence. Senator Charles McC. Mathias reports that shortly before a crucial and close Judiciary Committee vote, he received this message from a corporate PAC (later identified as Bristol-Myers), "You tell Mathias if he doesn't vote my way on Illinois Brick, he won't get any of my PAC money."

Despite the conservative ethos dominant in corporate PACs, at least 40 percent of their money in 1978 went to Democrats. They gave five times as much money to Democratic incumbents as to Republican challengers (though they gave eleven times as much to Republican incumbents as to Democratic challengers). These numbers infuriate Republican ideologues and get their Democratic counterparts nervous. "Corporate managers are whores," fumed ultraconservative Rep. Robert F. Dornan (R.-Calif.). "They don't care who's in office, what party or what they stand for. They're just out to buy you." Senator Paul Laxalt (R.-Nev.), a leading Senate conservative, complained that "We found that our 'friends,' the *Fortune* 500, were playing both sides. When you push water for them as long as we have, that's a little hard to swallow." On the other hand, Democrats are nervous that a big-business community which arguably already controls the Republican party lock, stock, and cash register is insinuating itself into the "people's party." With beachheads in both parties, the political hegemony of business can be assured. "These PACs are influencing a lot of Democrats," confirmed a Democratic member on House Ways and Means. "You're seeing people from mainstream Democratic districts, elected with labor support, who are now voting with business."

But politicians cannot ignore what corporate PACs have to offer. "Did candidates come to us?" asked Bernadette Budde, manager of the $125,000 Business and Industry PAC. "I called this place the doctor's office because we had them lined up waiting to come in."

Wise Shoppers

Special interest investors, who would not dream of pouring their money into dud stocks, are equally careful when it comes to choosing their legislative portfolio. A freshman legislator with a seat on a dull committee won't cost much, but won't yield much return, either. The logical result is that the money goes to the men who rule Congress—the members of the key committees, the party leaders of each of the houses, and the committee chairmen. In 1976, all PACs gave an average $21,700 to House chairmen. In 1978 that figure jumped to $45,000.

Also following this guideline, the political arm of General Foods—the "North Street Good Government Group" —did not squander its money on Armed Services Committee members. Instead, it aimed at three men whose influence on questions crucial to General Foods equaled that of a hundred other congressmen combined: three powerful members of the House Agriculture Committee. The bankers' group, BankPAC, similarly excludes anyone not on committees which affect the banking industry. So, for example, banking and other financial interests in 1976 gave $91,725 to fifteen of seventeen members of a House subcommittee with jurisdiction over banking matters. Medical interests gave $49,550 to eleven of thirteen members of the House Commerce Health subcommittee.

For congressmen who happen to be in key positions and share the business perspective, these arrangements can ease many of their problems—congressmen like Joel Broyhill, for example. A study by Public Citizen's Tax Reform Research Group showed that 65 percent of Broyhill's 1972 campaign contributions came from outside his Virginia district, with an even larger percentage of his 1974 contributions coming from such sources. The key to Broyhill's success was his position as third-ranking Republican on the powerful Ways and Means Committee. Of Broyhill's net worth of $3.8 million, about $2.5 million came from real estate investments. Along with his other investments in banks, savings and loan companies, realty trusts, and a family-owned insurance company, Broyhill made sure during his twelve-year tenure on Ways and Means that the Internal Revenue Code would benefit . . . real estate developers, builders, and investors.

Broyhill's intermingling array of family interests, business partners, and campaign contributors held the mortgages and received the rents of much of the suburban housing and most of the apartment complexes in his congressional district in northern Virginia, according to Public Citizen. Instead of a congressman, Broyhill's constituents had a landlord diligent on behalf of those business friends who invested in him as their special interest guardian. But in 1974, weary of their congressman's favoritism to special interest groups, Broyhill's constituents retired him into the business world he could only previously serve part-time.

Broyhill may have been a gross example. But given the needs of the corporate economy, the impact of government regulations on business, and the vulnerability of politicians to financial persuasion, it takes little imagination to see how campaign contributions can influence the activity of Congress. In 1955, for example, the Texas oil industry noted that congressional proposals to change the industry's tax subsidies had not been killed as quickly as usual. Anxious to set things right, the president of the Texas oil trade association told his fellows that "it seems only fair to tie a few strings to the contributions we make to political organizations and candidates." When, in 1958, the oil depletion tax loophole was up for its biennial round of criticism in Congress, a staff member of the Democratic senatorial campaign committee went to see some candidates from the Western states. "I was informed that if I could get some of these fellas out West to express their fealty to the golden principle of 27.5 percent [depletion allowance], there might be a pretty good piece of campaign change involved," he later told Ronnie Dugger of the *Texas Observer*.

In each case, the contributions would obviously have a purpose—to get those sympathetic to the oil lobby into Congress and to convince those already there to remain loyal to oil. But the bargain need not be stated that baldly. "Don't kid yourself about the 'no-strings attached' to a contribution," one congressional staffer with long experience in the wilderness of fundraising has said. "There's always a string attached. It may not be a black string, but it's a string, and some day it's going to get pulled."

These invisible links may swell to chainlike dimensions when the contributions pull a candidate out of a predicament like the one former representative Edward A. Garmatz of Maryland nearly succumbed to in 1966. As primary election time approached, polls showed him doing badly. Then the Seafarers International Union appeared to rescue him. The $17,000 in publicly reported contributions from the SIU for Garmatz was the largest amount of money any representative got from any reported source that election year. Garmatz sailed through, and then found himself in a position to help out his contributors in his capacity as chairman of the Merchant Marine and Fisheries Committee, which doles out the subsidies to the shipping companies that hire the SIU. In 1968, 90 percent of Garmatz's funding came from shipping interests. In 1970, the industry raised a reported $37,000 for him, even though he was unopposed for reelection.

Men in the position of Garmatz often point to the old chicken/egg question: Do they do what they do because of the campaign contributions they received? Or do they receive the contributions because they do what they do? As one House staff aide noted, "There are some guys around here who honestly *believe* that industry is getting screwed by the consumers." When contributions make the difference between a career in Congress and another twenty years tending the small-town car dealership or law firm, the answer is that the distinction doesn't really matter.

Even when their contributions are not likely to be decisive, contributors often spread money for good will with whoever ends up in office. Thus if Tweedledee and Tweedledum are running a close race, a little butter may be applied to both. Several firms, for example—Braniff, First International Bancshares, Houston Oil, and Mineral Corp. —gave over $1,000 to both Senate candidates from Texas in 1978.

If those good-will contributions succeed in buying nothing else, they inevitably purchase that vague but crucial commodity—*access* to an elected official. "We're not trying to buy votes," says a money handler for the oil industry. "We're trying to buy an entrée to talk about our problems." Stanley J. McFarland, chief lobbyist for the National Education Association, explains that access "doesn't mean that we own them, of course. But the door is sure opened a little wider for us to get in and present our problems." Thus will politicians make room on their appointment schedules for potential or past contributors. As one congressional aide explained, "I'd always tell the

Old Man, 'You don't want to know where it [the money] comes from, but if I tell you to see a guy, you'd better damn well see him.' "

More than dramatic payoffs and scandals, it is this entrée that twists the direction of government policy. Reporter James Polk has described the "fraternal" atmosphere that springs from these cordial talks; politicians naturally begin to "understand" their patrons' problems better than they otherwise might. Few congressmen would admit that they can be "bought," but their protest is like that of a free-living woman who decides she might as well take money for what she enjoys, but insists she is not a prostitute. With their more sympathetic view, they can open up the range of government favors to private interests: subsidies, lucrative contracts, tax exemptions, toothless regulatory laws, restraints on overeager regulating agencies, protective tariffs, foreign policies to protect private investment. Those who suffer when the favors are passed out—the taxpayers, the purchasers of overpriced goods—never get a chance to sit down with the politicians in the same chummy atmosphere.

A Case of Milk

A striking example of the corrupting influence of special interest campaign contributions involved nothing more complicated than a quart of milk. Early in 1971, the dairy industry demanded that the government raise the guaranteed price it paid farmers for "manufactured milk"—raw milk used to make many dairy products. The increase they wanted would raise retail food prices by hundreds of millions of dollars, at a time when inflation was beginning to worsen. It would also, U.S. Department of Agriculture officials predicted, lead to serious milk surpluses piling up in government warehouses—an extra burden on a strained federal budget.

Weighing these disadvantages and finding no cost justification for an increase, Secretary of Agriculture Clifford Hardin announced on March 12, 1972, that the price would not go up. But not for long. Dairy representatives swung into action, and by March 25—less than two weeks later—the administration had caved in. Citing "new evidence," Secretary Hardin announced a 6 percent price

boost, just what the milk men had asked for. The cost of
the decision to the American eater, who spends one out
of every seven food dollars on dairy products, was an
estimated $500 to $700 million per year (one cent extra
per quart, plus large increases in other dairy prices).

What did the milk men have going for them that the
housewife didn't? They've got a lot of pure homogenized
Grade A cash, milked from consumers in inflated prices.
Like the shrewd John Archbold of Standard Oil, they invest their money wisely; by putting it into politics, they
earn the legal right to bilk the consumer of more money,
a small portion of which they can again invest in politics.
The dairymen hit on the tactic several years earlier, when
—as William A. Powell, president of Mid-America Dairymen, explained in a letter to one of his organization's
members—they learned "that the sincere and soft voice
of the dairy farmer is no match for the jingle of hard
currencies put in the campaign funds of the politicians by
the vegetable fat interests, labor, oil, steel, airlines, and
others."

The obvious remedy was to make sure the farmers could
match the other jingles with an ample jingle of their own.
In their first two years of political fundraising, they put
together a war chest of $1 million. More than $500,000
of this they sunk in the congressional elections of 1970.

The investment paid off. Within a week of Hardin's
first announcement, the industry had drafted a bill that
would have taken the price decision out of the Agriculture
Department's hands by making an increase mandatory.
In the House, 116 members—50 of whom had received
dairy contributions—jumped on the milk wagon as co-
sponsors. There were twenty-nine sponsors in the Senate,
including even consumer advocate (and Wisconsin's) Gaylord Nelson. Twelve of these senators had run in 1970—
eight of them with dairy contributions.

But another dairy beneficiary, the Nixon administration,
beat Congress in making the move. Helping enamor Richard Nixon was thousands of dollars the farmers sent to
his election fund. Of this, $35,000 was a down payment,
funneled into Republican campaign committees only days
before Hardin announced the price rise. The rest was paid
out in installments, stretching several months past "de-

livery." The first of these, a $45,000 installment, was paid on April 5, just four days after the new price went into effect.

What happened just before Hardin's turnabout announcement is revealing. The first big contribution was on March 22. It got quick results. The next day, President Nixon invited sixteen dairy and farm representatives to the White House. Their audience with the president—the ultimate in purchased political access—lasted nearly an hour, twice as long as scheduled. The meeting with the president was later described by William Powell, president of the Mid-America Dairymen, in a letter to one of his members:

> We dairymen as a body can be a dominant group. On March 23, 1971, along with nine other dairy farmers, I sat in the Cabinet room of the White House, across the table from the president of the United States, and heard him compliment the dairymen on their marvelous work in consolidating and unifying our industry and our involvement in politics. He said, "You people are my friends, and I appreciate it."
>
> Two days later an order came from the U.S. Department of Agriculture increasing the support price of milk. . . . We dairymen cannot afford to overlook this kind of economic benefit. Whether we like it or not, this is the way the system works.

The only thing unusual about the dairy campaign was the publicity it received. Fresh off the farm, the dairymen at first made the "mistake" of filing a candid set of financial reports. An amazed Democratic campaign hand told Frank Wright of the *Minneapolis Tribune,* "My God, we've been doing that sort of thing for years, and we've never, never had it reported so publicly." The milk men's efforts at concealment may have been a bit rough around the edges, but they had learned their basic lesson well: they paid their money and patiently waited for the dividends.

After the 1972 election, the dairy co-ops continued their monetary influence-peddling. Between election day 1972 and May 31, 1974, one of every seven members of the Senate and House had received a dairy contribution. But by 1974 the walls began to crash in on the cooperatives.

The publicity revealed not only their massive influence but also cast a shadow of illegality on some of the campaign donations: $222,450 in illicit corporate donations arranged by the former special counsel of the American Milk Producers, Inc. (AMPI), David L. Parr; $330,000 in illegal corporate contributions over a six-year period arranged by former AMPI general manager Harold S. Nelson. AMPI was fined $35,000 and Parr and Nelson were each fined $10,000 and sent to jail for four months.

The scandal, though, barely slowed the milk lobby down. In 1976 they spent $1.4 million—or more than the AFL-CIO and the oil industry; indeed, only the American Medical Association gave more money. Among other recipients, Democratic contender Jimmy Carter got $11,000 in his presidential bid. Between January, 1975, and July, 1978, dairy groups gave $381,651 to forty-six members of the House Agriculture Committee.

The Struggle for Reform

To all, except perhaps the big givers and big takers, the problem of money in politics should by now be glaring. So why hasn't something been done, the average citizen might wonder. To appreciate, fully, the roadblocks to reform and its likelihood of success, a review of the past half century is revealing.

The scripture of modern politics, the Federal Corrupt Practices Act of 1925, had deficiencies so obvious that Lyndon Johnson called it "more loophole than law." For a start, the law did not even apply to primaries—where so much of the spending goes on, particularly in one-party states. For everything after the primaries, Senate candidates were required to file spending reports with the secretary of the Senate, and House candidates with the clerk of the House. Just how seriously the law was taken is indicated by a few of the filed reports. In his 1968 Senate reelection campaign in South Dakota, George McGovern's total expenditures were "none." The explanation was that the candidates must only report funds used with their "knowledge and consent." McGovern's executive assistant George Cunningham kept McGovern in blissful ignorance by being "very careful to make sure that Senator McGovern never saw the campaign receipts."

Another clause provided that all donors of $100 or

more must list their names and addresses. Witty contributors then made as many $99.99 donations as they wanted to various campaign committees working for the same candidate. The most important loophole in the 1925 law, however, was its provision that campaign committees would have to report their contributors only if the committee operated in two or more states. There was ample office space in the District of Columbia for thousands of campaign committees, and *none* of them had to report their activities. Along with the cherry trees, another rite of election-year springs in Washington was the flowering of campaign committees for candidates all over the country. To give one illustration among many: James Buckley took in $400,000 in 1970 toward his New York Senate seat through a series of false-front D.C. committees. More receptive to the spirit of the law than many deadpan candidates, Buckley's staff invented names like "Committee to Keep a Cop on the Beat," "Neighbors for Neighborhood Schools," and "Town Meeting Preservation Society" for their groups. "We made a game of it," staffer David Jones said.

Figuring that even a good joke may get stale after forty-seven years, the public pressured Congress to enact a new law, which was signed by President Nixon in February, 1972. The saga of this reform actually began a decade before, when the Commission on Campaign Costs, appointed by President John F. Kennedy in 1962, reported that "individuals and organizations providing substantial gifts at critical moments can threaten to place a candidate in moral hock." The eventual Federal Election Campaign Act extended coverage to financing of primaries, runoff and special elections, party caucuses, and nominating conventions. A candidate could no longer feign ignorance of funds spent by others on his behalf.

But Congress, determined to have the last laugh, relented at the last minute and left in a few saving provisions. The least subtle of these was the "grace period" —the two-month delay between the bill's passage in February and the date when candidates would first have to report contributions. With a joyous, free-for-all spirit not seen since the Oklahoma Land Rush, candidates from all parties scrambled to pack their campaign chests before the April 7 deadline. Led by President Richard Nixon—

whose chief fundraiser, Maurice Stans, and others openly exhorted (some say extorted) businessmen to get their money in on time*—many congressmen lost all inhibitions in their eagerness to make the most of the remaining time. The only barrier was fatigue: one lobbyist, hand presumably sore from reaching for his wallet, complained to Arizona Rep. Sam Steiger that he had to attend 162 fundraising parties between February 23 and April 7.

With such freewheeling times behind them, private interests still have to rely in the future on the bill's more restrained loopholes. The 1972 act made a minor revision of the $99.99 clause by providing that only contributions of "more than" $100 must be reported—contributions identified by name, address, occupation, and principal place of business. This at least gave voters a fighting chance to find out who was contributing to campaigns and identify any possible special interests; unfortunately, sizable contributions could still be, and have been, poured into campaign coffers immediately prior to election day, or weeks or months after the election, giving the voter no opportunity to view a contributor list before he or she casts a ballot.

The disclosure provision proved very embarrassing for many members of Congress when it became clear their campaigns were being heavily financed by individuals and groups seeking to influence a legislator's performance. So Congress weakened the provision in 1974, requiring only "identification" of contributors—a phrase vague enough to shield most special interest givers under their more accustomed secrecy. Congress has not figured out what to do about the clause allowing the public to look at the reports, but takes some comfort in knowing that the public is in a race with the clock. As a matter of practice, the reports are kept on file and publicly available in the House and Senate for only one election term—two years in the House—before they vanish.

Other evasions of at least the spirit of campaign spending laws were available to determined business contributors. They could deploy a company lawyer as a broker:

---

*Common Cause reported that the Stans group raised as much as $10 million before April 7 for Nixon's landslide reelection. On Capitol Hill, Senator John G. Tower (R.-Tex.) raised $398,000 for himself; Senator John J. Sparkman (D.-Ala.), $157,000; and Senator Carl T. Curtis (R.-Neb.), $180,000, to name a few.

the company paid him "legal fees," which he then passed on to a grateful politician. More directly, a group could support its candidate by paying him an appropriate honorarium for a good speech (as could any other interest group, for that matter). In 1977, senators reported speaking fees totaling over $1 million, despite a $25,000 annual ceiling per senator—fees which can be veiled contributions. Senator Herman Talmadge (D.-Ga.), chairman of the Senate Agriculture Committee and a member of a health subcommittee of Senate Finance, received honoraria of $1,000 or more from the Poultry and Egg Assoc., Dairymen, Inc., the Farm and Industrial Equipment Institute, the AMA, and the Health Industry Manufacturers. Senator Jake Garn (R.-Utah), who sits on the Senate Banking Committee, received $25,000 in speaking fees, mostly from banking groups.

Payments also come "in kind." Some companies and labor unions keep men on the payroll to lend as campaign workers to deserving candidates. Boeing, recognizing a politician who had earned its support, did just that for Senator Henry Jackson during his unsuccessful run for the presidency in 1972. The American Milk Producers, Inc. did the same for Wilbur Mills's 1972 presidential race. Others give special discounts on or offer free services or products ranging from air travel to hotel rooms to printing presses. Companies can donate computer time to a candidate, or conduct expensive polls and give away the results.

The effect of all these twisting and hidden paths is, as might be expected, to thoroughly deter attempts to find who's sending money to whom. Journalist Walter Pincus, working with the Nader Congress Project in 1971, discovered how tangled the threads could be when he tried to survey campaign reports from eight states and the District of Columbia. At the end of his labors, he had turned up undercover spending programs run by General Electric, U.S. Steel, Procter and Gamble, Union Carbide, and other corporations totaling more than $1 million. But piecing together the evidence required a detective effort that would do credit to Scotland Yard. To track down one small item —a secret Union Carbide fund of at least $20,000—six researchers had to spend ten weeks looking through reports filed by individual candidates and cross-checking names of hundreds of contributors with lists of corporate

executives. Small wonder that few members of the public
know what firms and groups are supporting which politicians.

Also, whatever good the campaign reform act tried to
accomplish was in large measure undermined by its inadequate enforcement procedures. Congress avoided calling in
any outside supervisors or creating a scrupulous watchdog
agency. The guardians of the new law were instead the
same old crew that had "enforced" the old law: the House
clerk, the Senate secretary, and the Justice Department.
The clerk and the secretary are paid employees of Congress; over the years they have shown their reluctance to
come down on their masters.

Nor did the final stage of the enforcement process, the
Justice Department, inspire much optimism. Those who
watched this crack organization at work against ITT
and other corporate suspects were not surprised by its initial performance in regulating campaign finance. For
years, the law was openly and massively violated, yet Justice never acted.

Then in 1968, newly elected House Clerk W. Pat Jennings surprised everyone by sending a list of violations
from the 1968 campaign over to the Justice Department.
President Nixon's new attorney general, John Mitchell,
fresh from firsthand experience with campaign contributors during his year as Nixon's campaign manager, was
fascinated by Jennings's list; he and his colleagues at Justice kept it so close that it seemed to have disappeared.
Jennings, slow to get the message, sent other lists in 1969
and 1971—each time with the same result.

The 1972 act received roughly similar treatment. One
day after President Nixon signed it into law, Ralph Nader
and his organization, Public Citizen, tried to sting Justice
into action by filing a lawsuit demanding strict enforcement. Their complaint included a ninety-two-page list of
hundreds of unprosecuted campaign finance violations (for
example, candidates who had waited to file until after the
election, "thus defeating the purpose of preelection disclosures," or who had failed to file reports at all).

In June, 1972, Common Cause asked the clerk of the
House to investigate ninety-one candidates from Alabama,
Indiana, Ohio, Pennsylvania, and the District of Columbia
who had ignored the reporting requirements of the new

law. As of September, 1972, the Justice Department had never prosecuted a single candidate for breaking the campaign finance laws. (In 1974, the prosecutions of campaign finance violators were carried out by the Watergate Special Prosecutor's office, not the Justice Department.)

A final change in the 1972 law had little immediate consequence, but was a time bomb of explosive potential. The act modified the flat ban on the use of corporate and union treasuries. It allowed the establishment of a separate fund—a political action committee, or PAC—to make campaign contributions. But the ban still applied to entities with government contracts. And since so many companies had government business, they shied away from the contributions game. Help would be forthcoming.

The Federal Election Campaign Act of 1974 continues to illustrate Congress's inability to devise anything more than minor campaign reforms in a corrupt system. To be sure, there were some improvements: a $1,000 limit was placed on the amount an individual could contribute to any one candidate for the presidency, the Senate, or the House in each primary or general election race. This law not only sets a limit, but forbids an individual to contribute to numerous separate committees all supporting the same candidate. A $5,000 limit was placed on contributions from special interest groups, but national and local affiliates of an interest group can still make separate contributions. There was also a ceiling on what candidates could spend, but that restriction was later declared an unconstitutional abridgement of free speech by the Supreme Court in *Buckley v. Valeo*, on the theory that in this instance money was tantamount to speech.

The 1974 act, in a crucial provision, extended its predecessor by saying that a corporation could create PACs and contribute regardless of whether it held government contracts. It seems that organized labor, anxious about its own political gifts since many unions held government manpower contracts, led the move to delete the government-contract string. One student of this development observed that "labor pulled the business chestnuts out of the fire." For it was only after this change in the law, later upheld by the Federal Election Commission, that corporate PACs became a major political force.

Congress left one final gap in the 1974 law through

which special interest contributions will continue to flow unabated. As early as 1907, Theodore Roosevelt suggested that public tax funds should pay for campaigns. It would cost taxpayers pennies apiece, the reasoning went, but save consumers scores of dollars apiece in reduced special interest legislation. Recent public opinion polls have indicated that two-thirds of the American people prefer public financing of federal elections instead of private contributions from individuals and special interest groups. In 1974 the Senate Watergate Committee recommended that public funds should be used to finance elections. But members of Congress said "No." While instituting a system of public financing for presidential primaries and elections, Congress refused to include itself in a system by which challengers would be publicly provided equal funds to run against incumbents. Legislation to provide public funding narrowly failed to pass the 95th Congress. So much for principle when it collides with self-interest. Yet until Congress institutes the public financing of congressional campaigns as the best way to cleanse the epidemic of purchased politicians— or at least until it establishes free and equal access to television, radio, and the mails for bona fide candidates— the jingle of corruption and veiled bribery will continue to be heard in its halls. Until then the Golden Rule of politics will prevail—he who has the gold, rules.

2

Who Influences Congress?

Suppose you go to Washington and try to get at your government. You will always find that while you are politely listened to, the men really consulted are the men who have the biggest stake —the big bankers, the big manufacturers, the big masters of commerce. . . . The government of the United States at present is a foster child of special interests.

—Woodrow Wilson

Representative government on Capitol Hill is in the worst shape I have seen in my 16 years in the Senate. . . . We're elected to represent all the people of our states or districts, not just those rich or powerful enough to have lobbyists holding megaphones constantly at our ears.

—Senator Edward Kennedy

When the dairy industry was looking for its 1971 price rise, it had the advantage of having warmed up dozens of congressmen with campaign contributions. If the milk men had done no more, the quart of milk might simply have risen with the consumer price index. Only through *lobbying*—direct persuasion of legislators—was the industry able to convert its half-million line of credit with Congress into a half-billion extra income. As Congress is being bombarded by big money, the lobbyists act as the special interest's infantry. The dairy case is again illustrative.

With the bad news of Agriculture Secretary Hardin's initial decision not to grant the price increase, six full-time Washington lobbyists swung into action. In addition to lining up sponsors for the bill they had quickly drafted,

24

they worked at "getting friendly senators and representatives to file statements with the Department of Agriculture supporting our position," as one of them put it. The number of statements that came in was, according to a department source, "very substantial." Meanwhile, letters from producer co-ops across the country poured into Congress and the White House. Reaping the obvious financial rewards, the president quickly succumbed.

News of a lobbying coup like the milk men's understandably leaves the public with a sour taste, but, in its broadest sense, "lobbying" is anything but sinister. A lobbyist is, by definition, anyone who works to influence decisions by public officials—including a concerned citizen who writes his congressman urging a vote for stricter air pollution laws. This right to "petition the Government for a redress of grievances" is firmly grounded in the Constitution's First Amendment. But the way the armies of special interest agents have largely monopolized these guarantees has made "lobbyist" synonymous with corruption, shiftiness, and improper influence.

As might be supposed, the lobbyists first got their name from hanging around the lobbies of government buildings, waiting to launch their pitch for government favors. By the middle of the nineteenth century, high-paid panhandlers swarming all over Congress prompted James Buchanan to write to Franklin Pierce: "The host of contractors, speculators, stock-jobbers, and lobby members which haunt the halls of Congress all desirous . . . on any and every pretext to get their arms into the public treasury, are sufficient to alarm every friend of the country."

By 1950, lobbyists had so increased their strength in Washington that the House Select Committee on Lobbying Activities declared lobbying "a major industry." Then there were an estimated 2,000 lobbyists—and today there are an estimated 15,000 (or thirty for each member of Congress), spending $2 billion a year. Eighty percent of the nation's thousand biggest corporations already have representatives in Washington. In 1977, fifty trade and professional associations moved to Washington, D.C., which now surpasses New York City as the headquarters for such groups. Why Washington, D.C.? the head of the American Trial Lawyers Association was asked. "You don't see many datelines from Boston," he said.

The power of many lobbyists who have worked in Washington through the years is legendary. Wayne B. Wheeler, the legislative counsel for the Anti-Saloon League during the days of its prohibition successes, "controlled six Congresses, dictated to two presidents . . . and was recognized by friend and foe alike as the most masterful and powerful single individual in the United States," said his administrative assistant, who would watch him maneuver. While no single individual today approaches that power, the combined grip of the various lobbies on Congress remains tight.

Apart from whatever power they may have to generate election-time assistance (financial or otherwise), the lobbies derive their strategic advantage by controlling the flow of information in and out of Congress. By this, lobbyists serve two functions; they take and they give. They constitute, in effect, an informal intelligence network that can pick up advance and often confidential information, and use it to good advantage. When lawyer-lobbyist Thomas Corcoran was asked why he was so successful, he said, "I get my information a few hours ahead of the rest." Or in the words of Bernard Falk, president of the National Electrical Manufacturers Association, "Information flow is terribly important. We didn't come here to change the world; we came to minimize our surprises."

As any industrialist can tell you, he who controls the source of supply can control the product. During the "energy crisis" in 1973–74, for example, the government continued to rely heavily on, of all disinterested observers, the oil companies and their lobbyists for data on oil and gas supplies; tough subpoenas for cost data were never issued by interested committees—but then, congressional committees have rarely been eager to demand information from our giant corporations. This reliance by public authority on private interests is a consequence of congressional weakness. As former New York representative Allard Lowenstein complained,

> How much can anyone do with limited staff and all the mail and what-not to cope with? If you aren't independently wealthy, you can't have a staff that is capable of putting things together much beyond what you can come up with from the sources available to

everyone—the executive departments, the lobbies, the staffs of congressional committees, the Library of Congress. That's one reason why the lobbies are so influential. They have people who are able to spend all their time collecting data on why pollution is good for River X. What congressmen can match that?

None can. That's why congressmen so often have to depend on the superior manpower of the lobbies to suggest solutions to problems, draft legislation, provide the evidence for it, help develop legislative strategy, persuade the rest of Congress to go along, and even raise the problems in the first place. With the lobbies' pressure bearing in from all sides, Congress ends up, for the most part, responding to the heaviest push. It's true, as Senator John Kennedy once said, that lobbyists are "in many cases expert technicians and capable of explaining complex and difficult subjects in a clear, understandable fashion," which makes them all the more persuasive.

But there is one catch. "Each is biased," as Kennedy noted. He compared the procedure to "the advocacy of lawyers in court which has proven so successful in resolving judicial controversies." But while organized, special interest lobbies push hard in Washington, unorganized interests—the public, the taxpayer, the consumer—typically go unrepresented in the court of Congress. Who, for example, presented expert data on behalf of the American housewife when the dairymen were ramming through their price increase in less than two weeks? Information inundation of Congress by those with particular interests has created a kangaroo court.

A Who's Who of Lobbying

Despite the lobbies' awesome impact on the law, the public retains only a cloudy picture of who the lobbyists are and what they do. For the economic interests who run the lobbies have hidden behind vague, institutional titles like the sugar lobby and the highway lobby. What follows are specific descriptions of major lobbying influences in Washington:

BUSINESS ORGANIZATIONS. "The defenders of American business had it pretty easy in 1955," lamented the National Association of Manufacturers in its magazine *Enterprise* in the mid-1970s. "There were, in those days, no self-ordained public-interest lobbyists to cope with; and the Eisenhower Administration in league with the conservative leadership of Congress championed the interests of business whenever those interests were threatened." To the nostalgic executive, political conditions may never seem quite as favorable as during the quiescent 1950s. Still, the record of the big-business lobbies in the 95th Congress (1977–78) led consumer critics to call it "the Corporate Congress" and *Fortune* magazine to conclude that "the business community has become the most effective special interest lobby in the country. Suddenly, business seems to possess all the primary instruments of power—the leadership, the strategy, the supporting troops, the campaign money—and a new will to use them."

Recent evidence, indeed, supports the view that major business lobbies appear to be able to exercise a de facto veto over measures they oppose. If business lobbies don't object, reform measures can become law; if they do, they can't. A united business community defeated the labor law reform bill, consumer protection agency, consumer class actions, and tax reforms; a largely uninterested big-business community allowed airline deregulation, a bank for consumer cooperatives, and civil service reform to pass.

The leading general-membership business lobbies responsible for this record are the U.S. Chamber of Commerce and Business Roundtable. Operating out of a marble and limestone palace near the White House, the Chamber's $20 million budget, 70,000 corporate members, more than 1,300 professional and trade associations, and 2,500 local Chamber affiliates give it unusual leverage in Washington. It sends out a weekly newsletter, *Congressional Action,* to each of its members, describing the substance and timing of upcoming legislation. Its legislative department follows up with "Action Calls"—requests to their 1,200 local Congressional Action committees (with some 100,000 members) to contact their congressmen. These communications ultimately reach 7 million people sympathetic to its causes, says the Chamber.

Finally, the Chamber operates a backup communication process for critical bills or surprise votes. It activates its field force of Chamber representatives spread throughout the country. In each congressional district, field representatives develop personal contacts called key resources people (in Chamber jargon, KRPs). KRPs have close personal relationships with their representative or senator, whether from their college fraternity, law firm, country club, or church.

With networks such as these, it is not entirely surprising that, in a Congress supposedly controlled by Democrats, the Chamber won 63 percent of the bills it lobbied in the 95th Congress. Indeed, one former Chamber official—the late Carl Madden—said that "the Chamber thinks it does *better* under the Democrats," since the membership knows it has to stick together more than when a Republican administration can do their work for them.

A less militant and less visible counterpart to the Chamber is the Business Roundtable. Founded in 1972 and with a $2 million budget, it is a group of 190 chief executive officers (CEOs) of the nation's largest corporations. While groups like the Chamber issue alarms to their memberships, the Roundtable emphasizes the personal visit from a prominent CEO, the supportive study, the legal analysis. While few lobbyists can get direct access to a senator, no one in Congress is likely to turn away a Thomas Murphy of General Motors or an Irving Shapiro of Du Pont, the heads of their respective firms and recent heads of the Roundtable. As one congressional aide observed, "A visit from a CEO has an unbelievable impact, as perhaps it should. It shows a commitment."

Consequently, in a short time the Roundtable has become an influential, more genteel version of the Chamber. It has helped defeat the consumer protection office, negotiate a compromise Arab-boycott bill, and weaken the 1976 antitrust improvements act. All this despite the fact that its members almost never testify in public hearings, preferring instead to deal with staff and officials behind the scenes. In fact, the Business Roundtable won't even issue a list of who its 190 members are. It is the most influential secret lobby in Washington.

INDEPENDENT BUSINESS LOBBYISTS. These lobbyists, retained for their expertise or entrée on particular bills, are
an important part of the lobbying process. One of the
flashiest, if not most influential, of business's advocates
on Capitol Hill is Charls Walker, deputy secretary of
the treasury under President Nixon and founder of his
own "economic consulting" firm.

He has a large stable of blue-chip clients such as General Electric, Ford, Du Pont, Bethlehem Steel, and Procter
and Gamble. The telephone, three-martini lunch, chauf-
fered Cadillac limousine, flip-chart, and personal association are his primary tools of trade. He dines or plays golf
regularly with cabinet secretaries, senators, journalists, and
banking and business leaders. He claims to phone Russell
Long, Senate Finance Committee chairman, two or three
times weekly before breakfast. It didn't hurt his efforts on
the energy bill to be godfather to Energy Secretary James
Schlesinger's youngest child and close family friends with
the chairman of the House ad hoc energy committee, Rep.
Thomas (Lud) Ashley (D.-Ohio).

Walker claims that much of his influence comes simply
from understanding the motivations and professional problems of key legislators. "You got to understand what motivates the politician. Dummies, even in this town, think
that politicians just want to be reelected," Walker told
Elizabeth Drew of the New Yorker. "But what motivates
a Lud Ashley? He doesn't want to run for President of
the United States, or for senator or governor. He's a
House man. He takes extreme pride in doing a good
legislative job. So if I'm talking to Lud I'm talking merits."
Like a good attorney, Walker marshals only the facts that
best suit his case. There is a difference, however, between
being selective and being wrong; to mislead a congressman
or his staff is potentially suicidal to a lobbyist's reputation
and, hence, his effectiveness. "If they know you and trust
you, they'll listen to you and they'll tell someone else
you're a good guy, and you reach a point where if you
put a piece of paper in a member's hand, he knows he's
not going to be blind-sided."

Finally, Walker appreciates how members of Congress
"spend most of their time taking care of their constituents' problems with the government—so it becomes difficult to do good legislative work. So to an extent we be-

come an extension of the staff. A member of the House said in the cloakroom the other day that he needed an amendment for part of the energy bill in conference, so we drafted it for him."

Although it is nearly impossible to tell whether a lobbyist is changing the course of legislative events or merely choosing to represent the side with the upper hand, Walker claims he helped persuade Congress to increase the investment tax credit from 7 to 10 percent; saved some Eastern railroads from bankruptcy by persuading a reluctant Nixon administration to pour federal funds into Conrail; won big tax breaks for the nation's five largest airlines and for the Cigar Association of America, and helped lead the business effort to discredit President Carter's plans to introduce major tax law reforms in 1978.

LABOR LOBBYISTS. Pushing Congress from another ideological vantage point is the labor lobby. The linchpin of labor's effort is the AFL-CIO's lobbying arm, for a quarter century headed by the well-known Andrew Biemiller until his retirement in 1978. (He recalls how George Meany told him just three things when he began lobbying: "Don't beg, don't threaten, and don't think you are always 100 percent right.")

In recent years labor has been stymied on many strictly "labor issues," such as the labor law reform bill, common situs picketing, and cargo preference. These losses are variously attributed to a declining union membership (now barely 20 percent of the labor force), the growing sophistication and expenditures of the business lobby, and George Meany. "A picture of George Meany on the front page of an American newspaper," laments William Winpisinger, the outspoken head of the International Association of Machinists, "has the same kind of impact a picture of Jay Gould or J. Pierpont Morgan once had: that of a cigar-smoking, affluent patriarch." Yet in past years the labor lobby has had some striking successes as part of coalitions working on broader social issues. The golden age of labor's social-progress lobbying was in the mid-1960s, when the Leadership Conference on Civil Rights—an alliance of labor, religious, civic, and civil rights groups, which counted labor as its most powerful member—pushed through civil rights legislation and, finally, over longtime AMA opposition, Medicare. The "liberal-labor" coalition in Congress also rose to successfully challenge Nixon Supreme Court nominees Carswell and Haynsworth.

Apart from these successes, labor has continued to pour the bulk of its energies into a few key issues—like the perennial battle to overturn the Taft-Hartley Act—at times to the relative neglect of others which are worker-related, like environmental protection. Some unions have been stampeded into open opposition to environmental protection proposals as a result of industry-invoked fears of job losses, while others have straddled the fence. In March, 1972, the AFL-CIO undermined a coalition of groups backing stronger water pollution controls in the House by remaining on the sidelines, even after the coalition had included an AFL-CIO-initiated measure to protect workers from continued threats of job layoffs. The United Auto Workers (UAW), Steelworkers, Clothing Workers, and Oil, Chemical, and Atomic Workers (OCAW) did stick with the environmental coalition, and though the bulk of the measures lost, succeeded in passing the worker protection amendment. The OCAW and the UAW are among the few unions which would like the labor lobby to exchange its preoccupation with wage issues for broader social goals—which is increasingly happening, as labor's support of many consumer measures indicates.

SINGLE-ISSUE LOBBYISTS. Ideological single-issue groups often lobby on just one subject, are uncompromising, and have long memories. They have been heralded as a new and dangerous political genre, though they have obvious antecedents. From the Anti-Masons of the 1830s to the Prohibitionists a century later and the Vietnam protestors of the 1960s, there is a long history of groups that organize around not a party or a person, but a cause. The key to such lobbies today—e.g., antiabortion, anti-ERA, antigun control, anti-Panama Canal treaty, anti-SALT, anti-busing, right-to-work groups—is *intensity*. They adhere to the political axiom that a group's power is based less on whom it votes for than what it pickets for. The political implications of such intensity are obvious when one listens, for example, to Howard Phillips, the pugnacious national director of the Conservative Caucus: "We organize discontent. We must prove our ability to get revenge on people who go after us." Thus members of Congress understand well how one outraged group can easily overwhelm several mildly pleased ones. The 1978 election defeats of Senators Dick Clark in Iowa and Thomas McIntyre in New Hampshire are widely attributed to their respective positions on abortion and the Panama Canal.

Single-issue groups are achieving some success because they link up their intensity with computerized mailing lists. Richard C. Viguerie is the king of right-wing mailing lists, having spent fourteen years collecting the names of 8 million conservatives. In 1977, for example, he sent out 75 million fundraising letters which generated $30 million for a variety of conservative causes. That year he raised *three times* as much money for conservative candidates as the Republican National Committee raised. "Any special interest group that has a better mailing list than you owns you," says Rep. Charles Rose (D.-N.C.). "It can reach your constituency better than you can." Single-issue groups can be considered new political parties doing what the old parties used to do—reach constituents and generate funds.

THE OIL LOBBY. When fully mobilized, the oil lobby can send into action lawyers from the most highly regarded law firms, public relations consultants, numerous ex-government officials, newsmen who serve as "advisers," company executives, corporate legal departments, admen from advertising agencies, government officials in several of the executive departments, trade association representatives, and—though only a small fraction of the total—men who actually register as lobbyists. Whenever legislation affecting oil is on the docket, the oilers can easily afford to have a corporate vice president or similarly impressive official assigned to persuade every member of every relevant committee. If reinforcements should be needed, the industry can call on a vast reserve of sales agents, filling station operators, and other small businessmen. In other words, they are different from you and me.

Presiding over these far-flung legions are the oil trade associations, with the most powerful being the American Petroleum Institute. The API is generally regarded as the spokesman for the "majors"—including Exxon, Mobil, Gulf, Arco, Texaco, Shell, Standard Oil of Indiana, and Standard Oil of California—although its membership roster runs on to include some 350 other companies. One of the API's subsidiaries, the American Petroleum Industries Committee, has operated in virtually every oil-drenched state capital, augmenting the work of individual oil companies and a formidable array of state and regional trade groups. Organized to the grass-roots level, the industry also has committees with extensions reaching into local and county governments.

API has an annual budget of $30 million, with much of it, according to the API, spent on "research." This goes to support a staff of four hundred, working in Washington, D.C., plus offices in Dallas and New York. API is joined in its efforts by the Independent Natural Gas Association of America, the National Oil Jobbers Council, the National Petroleum Refiners Association, the American Gas Association, the American Public Gas Association, and the Association of Oil Pipe Lines. These reinforcements proved helpful in the 1973–74 period when the energy shortage provoked consumers—who waited hours at gas stations and spent small fortunes to heat their homes—to write members of Congress to let them know the full measure of their anger.

Whatever API and its companion lobbies spend has been, for them, a very worthwhile investment. For the fifteen years of the oil import quota, according to a much downplayed 1970 White House study, a bonus $5 billion annually shifted from the pockets of consumers to the bank accounts of Big Oil. The oil depletion allowance and foreign tax credits—until they were scaled down in 1975 by a Congress finally suspect of the industry's swollen profits—would save oilmen another $5 billion every year. The added profits from the legislated deregulation of natural gas rates in 1978 and oil prices in 1979 are expected to be many times $5 billion.

FORMER CONGRESSMEN AS LOBBYISTS. A more subtle form of compensation to the legislator for his labors on behalf of a corporation or lobby organization is the potential of a high-paying job when he retires from Congress, what has been called the "deferred bribe." Not that congressmen *expect* to be out of office in the near future, but the unhappy possibility can never be entirely out of their minds.

In fact, later employment in the lobbying sector is a popular career path for retired politicians. They charge higher lobbying fees than others, but their clients know they are worth it. Former members of Congress have a number of built-in advantages as lobbyists. They already know dozens of members and staff and they are schooled in the nuances of congressional rules and bargaining. They retain their rights to use the recreational and dining facilities reserved for members of Congress, they retain their former titles of "Senator" or "Chairman," and they have lifetime visiting privileges in the private cloakrooms and on the floor of the chamber in which they served.

Intent on losing no time after his 1974 election defeat, Indiana Republican Roger Zion sent out solicitations to prospective lobbying clients on his congressional stationery before he vacated his office. He explained that he would continue to be active in congressional social activities, and thus would "maintain contact with my good friends who affect legislation." A tasteful Senate custom holds that the former senator turned lobbyist should not appear on the floor when a measure affecting his client comes up—a custom, however, occasionally honored in the breach. But such excesses are really not necessary, for the normal prerogatives and contacts of former members are usually more than adequate to make their views known and to convince clients they are worth their keep.

This role offended former senator Albert Gore. "As a member of the Senate, I felt resentment when a former colleague took advantage of our friendship and association to lobby for some special interest," he said. But obviously many of his former colleagues disagree. Fully 124 former members have registered as lobbyists under the 1946 lobbying act; but given the widespread noncompliance with that law, it is likely that more than 124 former members return to Congress to lobby their earlier colleagues.

Nearly every big lobby has at least one (and often more than one) ex-member of Congress on its staff. The road from the floor of Congress to the lobby is so well worn that only a few of many examples can be given:

- Frank Ikard was a protégé of House Speaker Sam

Rayburn and served with him as representative from Texas from 1952 to 1961. In 1961, Rayburn died, Ikard resigned, and the American Petroleum Institute got a new lobbyist, one who now heads their Washington office. Ikard said that his change of job was "a question of economics."

• Andrew Biemiller, who, as chief lobbyist for the AFL-CIO, had the money and membership of millions behind him, got his training in legislation as a representative from Wisconsin, serving two terms in the late 1940s.

• John W. Byrnes, a twenty-eight-year veteran of the House from Wisconsin, was ranking Republican on the Ways and Means Committee upon his retirement in 1973. He quickly got a job representing Cabot Corporation and Subsidiaries on issues concerning liquefied natural gas.

• Former Senators Thurston Morton and George Murphy lobby for tobacco interests and Taiwan, respectively.

• Wayne Aspinall, representative from Colorado for twenty-four years and chairman of the House Interior and Insular Affairs Committee, made a rapid comeback following his 1972 primary election defeat. On a $1,750-a-month retainer for AMAX, Inc., a large mining firm, lobbyist Aspinall easily buttonholes former colleagues on mining legislation. During House debate on a strip mining bill of key concern to AMAX, Aspinall strolled onto the House floor in apparent violation of House rules which forbid former members to be on the floor during debate in which they have an interest. When asked about this imprudent move, the former chairman complained of "this new rule," though the rule in its basic form was passed in 1880. Apparently trying to avoid any further embarrassments, Aspinall told a reporter, "I'm trying to stay my distance"—although this determination did not prevent Aspinall from then asking a page to tell the House speaker he would like to see him "for a few minutes at his convenience."

• Harold Cooley has dealt with sugar for a long time—for sixteen years as Democratic representative from North Carolina and chairman of the House Agriculture Committee (where he was known as the "sugar king"), and more recently as lobbyist for sugar interests in Liberia and Thailand. Joining him in the sugar contingent is a relative novice in sugar questions, former California senator Thomas Kuchel of California. Despite his inexperience, Kuchel has earned $200 per hour as a lobbyist.

One of the sugar lobbyists—Thomas Hale Boggs, Jr.— illustrates yet another variation on the congressman-as-lobbyist theme. Young Boggs is the son of the late House majority leader Hale Boggs and of successor Lindy Boggs, and the inheritor of his father and mother's network of congressional associations. Understanding this, several private interests have made use of young Boggs's legal services: Texaco, Boeing, Armco Steel, Chrysler, Readers Digest, and the state of Louisiana, among others. Which is not bad for a 38-year-old lawyer.

LOBBYISTS AS STAFF/STAFF AS LOBBYISTS. Sometimes, outside lobbyists can operate as extensions of inside staff —and sometimes, the reverse.

The tradition of lobbyists drafting legislation is a long one, the result of overworked staffs looking for a shortcut and lobbyists looking for impact. So in 1937 a law partner of Senator Millard Tydings, who represented the National Association of Retail Druggists, drafted the Federal Fair Trade Act to allow price-fixing between suppliers and dealers. Never discussed on its merits on the Senate floor, the measure passed as a rider to the District of Columbia appropriations bill. The next year Congress was vigorously debating a new food and drug act, much of which was drafted by a young lawyer in Covington & Burling named H. Thomas Austern. The bill and his language became the 1938 Food and Drug Act. More recently, business lobbyist Peter Nyce used to have such a clear pipeline into the Senate Interior and Insular Affairs Committee that he often sat in on closed meetings, was allowed to question other witnesses at hearings, and reportedly wrote two Senate bills on mineral leasing.

In other circumstances, some business lobbyists seem to assume that if you can't persuade 'em, join 'em. The American Institute of Merchant Shipping, for example, should get a warm reception from Ralph Casey, former chief counsel of the House Committee on Merchant Marine and Fisheries. Casey came to the committee from his previous post as executive vice president and lobbyist for the Institute. Peter Hughes was a congressional staffer for six years before joining the Boeing Company's Washington office in 1976. A year and a half later he left to become a staff assistant to the Investigations subcommittee of the House Armed Services Committee. There he is playing a significant role in the committee's work on the MX intercontinental missile, on which Boeing has three developmental contracts with the Navy.

The exchange can, of course, be reversed. The banking lobby, for example, counted no less than five alumni of the Senate Banking, Housing, and Urban Affairs Committee's staff among its staff during its successful 1970 effort to soften a Senate bill to regulate one-bank holding companies, a device which banks can use to take over other industries. Sometimes, though, this cultural exchange can get politically crass. When two former aides of Senator Abe Ribicoff (D.-Conn.) formed a consulting firm, they circulated a memorandum to prospective tax clients seeking fees of up to $200,000. They explained that they were "in an unusually good position to influence the outcome of the debate" on Senator Ribicoff's proposal on the taxation of Americans abroad because Jeffrey Salzman of the firm "has been the principle [sic] drafter of all variations of that approach. (He was, of course, formerly Legislative Assistant to the Senator.)" Ribicoff says he was "shocked!" by the memorandum—a memorandum unusual for the world of Washington lobbying only in that it became public.

WASHINGTON LAWYERS. When a lobbying assignment calls for the maximum in prestige, legislative strategy, and delicate dealing, as well as inside influence, the men who are often called upon to do the job are Washington lawyers, the aristocrats of powerlaw. Lawyer-lobbyists in Washington are often men of liberal persuasions who came to Washington in high posts with a Democratic administration and then stuck around to make the most of their well-developed contacts in government. Among the best known of the Washington lawyers are such luminaries as Thomas ("Tommy the Cork") Corcoran, former New Deal brain truster who has often been retained by gas and airline clients; Lloyd Cutler, who, as hired lobbyist for General Motors, successfully had the criminal penalties

section deleted from the 1966 Automobile Safety Act;
Abe Fortas, still representing large business interests despite his celebrated exit from the Supreme Court; and,
most notably, Clark Clifford, adviser to presidents from
Harry Truman to Jimmy Carter, who saved Du Pont
hundreds of millions in taxes with a special bill in 1962
dealing with the firm's court-ordered divestiture of General Motors stock. Until he was appointed secretary of
defense in 1968, neither Clifford nor any of the other
members of his firm registered. "We did no lobbying and
never have." What he is doing is simply keeping his corporate clients "informed on policies and attitudes in government."

Michael Pertschuk, a veteran watcher of Washington
lawyers and now chairman of the Federal Trade Commission, does not similarly understate their talents and
impact. As he said in a 1974 article:

> The mischief lies with the lawyer-lobbyist who
> parks his conscience and personal moral accountability
> on Delaware Avenue outside the Old Senate Office
> Building. Far too many lawyers have conveniently lost
> sight of the origin of that peculiar societal role which
> permits the lawyer to suspend his own moral judg-
> ments. It is the *courtroom* not the *legislature* that
> frames the adversary system. When the State seeks to
> deprive a citizen of his liberty, it is proper that the
> lawyer undertake the defense of the accused without
> regard to the lawyer's own judgment or morality. . . .
> But imagine, if you can, a lawsuit which followed this
> bizarre scenario: Instead of a courtroom, the relevant
> events take place in floating forum. To be sure, there
> are several minor scenes played out in a Congressional
> hearing room, which displays the familiar props of
> a court-like tribunal, such as witnesses testifying pub-
> licly upon a record. But the scene, and the forum,
> shifts abruptly:
> —now to the cramped enclave of a beleaguered
>   junior staff counsel;
> —next to the sixth hole at Burning Tree Country
>   Club;
> —back to a spare, obscure Committee room, packed
>   with a curious amalgam of Administration bu-

reaucrats and corporate lawyers and sprinkled
with a handful of sympathetic Congressional
staff;
—next a circuit of quiet, ex parte sessions in Senatorial offices;
—on to Redskin stadium, intermission of the Dallas
game;
—and final argument over the diet special at the
Federal City Club.

If this forum seems elusive, so do the parties. At
least one party may be identified with certainty; a
corporate entity with a heartfelt economic stake in the
status quo. But the adversary party or parties appear
in several guises, including "competition," "labor,"
"the consumer," "the environment," and "the public
interest." These adversaries are as fairly matched as
the New York Yankees and the Bushwick little
league irregulars.

Other key lobbies now at work:
• The military armaments lobby is the instrument of
what President Eisenhower memorably dubbed the "military-industrial complex." Aside from its powerful connec-
tions in Congress, the defense industry relies on ties within
the military itself: between 1971 and 1973, 2,214 retired
military officers of the rank of major or higher were
employed by defense contractors. In 1974, Senator William Proxmire listed forty-one military-oriented organizations, including Army and Navy associations, veterans'
groups, and industry teams, which by protecting their interests "drive the defense budget upward." In 1977–78,
the ten largest defense contractors spent $1.1 million in
congressional races, which was twice as much as they had
spent just two years earlier. When compared to their $11.4
billion in contracts, this spending seems almost modest.
• The tobacco lobby has as its cornerstone the Tobacco Institute, a consortium of the leading companies
which spent $4.5 million in 1977. Though their product is
under criticism from HEW and health specialists for causing 325,000 premature deaths a year, "We have never
lost anything" in Congress, boasts Jack Mills, its top
lobbyist.
• The automobile lobby has mushroomed in the past

several years in Washington to fight tougher auto safety standards and air pollution requirements and to push for favorable tax privileges. Its repeated refrain is that federal safety and environmental controls cost consumers between $500 and $1,000 per car annually. Yet when the National Highway Traffic Safety Administration obtained data from the automobile manufacturers on how much cheaper a car would be if there were no federal standards, the answer was $80 a car.

• The American Medical Association, opponent of Medicare before its passage in the 1960s, is the propagandist for the system which gave U.S. doctors an average annual salary in 1977 of $65,000. In part through the AMA's lobbying efforts, Americans have watched medical costs rise at a rate double that of the cost of living or the Gross National Product, so that by 1978 we were paying more than $165 billion annually for medical services. The AMA represents just under half of the country's practicing physicians, a proportion which is declining due to dissatisfaction in the profession over the AMA's public-be-damned performance. And, as mentioned, the AMA gave more campaign contributions than any other lobby group in the country, over $1.7 million to some 400 candidates. This spending is widely credited for the defeat of President Carter's hospital cost containment bill by one vote in the House Commerce Committee in the 95th Congress.

• The American Bankers Association has a membership of 14,000 banks, 93 percent of all banks in the country. It maintains an extensive network of "contact bankers" in congressional districts. As one of their admiring staff aides observed, "Most of the members don't realize the reason they are hearing from bankers back in their district is that Mr. Lowrey [the head of the office] over on Connecticut Avenue has pressed the computer button."

• A relative newcomer to Washington is the lobby for the nation's cities. With $85 billion a year going from the federal government to states and localities—eight times as much as two decades ago—it is not surprising that state and local lobbyists have sprung up like mushrooms after a rain. The cities are represented by the National League of Cities/U. S. Conference of Mayors, two organizations that merged in 1969.

In addition, at least 30 states and 80 cities have their own representatives. California, if you combine all its jurisdictions, has thirty-five staff in Washington; New York State has seven. And the results are often very worth it. Much credit is given to Liz Robbins, a $22,000-a-year New York City welfare lobbyist, for helping the city keep $650 million in federal welfare payments that it might have had to repay to the government. Bob Horn, of the Michigan governor's office, helped organize Michigan representatives to lobby the administration of (Michiganer) Gerald Ford for federal money for a transit system in Detroit. They got $600 million, says Horn, because the state's representatives worked together. "Without the congressional delegation, we could stand on our heads and spit nickels, we couldn't get a thing done ourselves."

• Another group of lobbies aims at government policies rather than federal money. One of the older and more influential of these is the million-member National Rifle Association, spokesman for the nation's rifle and gun owners. The NRA operates out of an eight-story building in downtown Washington and has a staff of 250 and an annual budget of $8 million. It is supported by gun owners, gun manufacturers, and gun dealers and claims the ability to trigger 500,000 letters on forty-eight hours' notice for its pro-gun causes. After each of the political assassinations of the sixties, it was mainly the NRA that discouraged Congress from passing tough gun control laws. Although twelve national polls in the past twenty years have shown majorities of two-thirds of the public favoring strict gun control laws, and although 9,000 Americans a year die from guns, senators and representatives understand how organized gun interests can electorally retaliate against their perceived enemies. They fear the minority of Americans who are gun enthusiasts and who, speaking through the NRA, will vote for or against a candidate solely on this issue.

• The environmental and public interest lobbies began arriving on the lobbying scene in the late 1960s. Before that time, conservation groups had largely refrained from lobbying in an effort to protect their tax-exempt status and, hence, their ability to raise money easily. Because it lobbied against Grand Canyon dams, for example, the Sierra Club was stripped of its tax-deductible status in

1968. Now, having established affiliate organizations which are allowed to lobby, active environmental/conservation lobby groups include the Sierra Club, Environmental Action, Friends of the Earth, the Environmental Policy Center, League of Conservation Voters, Council for a Livable World, and Wildlife Federation. These groups have applied pressure on environmental issues as well as on a wider range of public problems.

They tallied their biggest victory in 1971, when Congress ended the taxpayers' subsidy for the SST—an aircraft whose saving of a few hours for transoceanic business travelers was far outweighed by its environmental costs. Environmentalists won passage of a strip mining bill in 1977. Though weakened in its final form, it required that most strip-mined land be returned to its appropriate original contour, that certain land be off-limits to strip mining, and that state and local governments would jointly enforce these provisions. But losses have at least equaled successes. The defeat of the environmental coalition's move in March, 1972, to strengthen the industry-gutted House water pollution bill signaled a hardening opposition to the movement for environmental change.

In 1973, Congress authorized construction of the Alaskan pipeline, and prohibited any legal action to stall or bar the pipeline on environmental grounds. Although ecology is fashionable in name and concept, converting it into legislative reality is quite another matter.

Completing this recent list of "public" advocates is an increasing number of young lawyers who strive to counter the private interests' well-connected Washington lawyer-lobbyists. Creating "public interest" law firms, they undertake court litigation and advocacy before the state and federal courts, the federal regulatory agencies, and the Congress. Together, this array of public lobbyists has been instrumental in the passage of several new laws: public financing for presidential general elections, auto safety, job safety, credit reform, increased Federal Trade Commission authority, better meat and poultry inspection, and a national bank to extend credit to consumer cooperatives.

But compared to the silent successes of the business bloc—the declining corporate income tax, procurement cost overruns, regulatory nonfeasance, which endure uninterrupted—the successes of citizens' groups have been indeed modest. One problem is the overwhelming size of the opposition forces. Consumers' Union estimates that all annual consumer lobbying resources equal only .3 percent of business advocacy advertisements ($3 million versus $1 billion). While special interest groups can keep their agents stationed at all the important pressure points in Congress, the public lobbyists are lucky to have among them the equivalent of a single person working full time on any major issue.

Profit-making businesses can deduct their lobbying costs as a business expense—in effect, subsidizing private lobbies. The consortium behind the Alaskan oil pipeline aggressively lobbied Congress, while the public interest lawyers who had earlier brought a successful lawsuit did not lobby for fear of losing their tax exempt status—as the pipeline passed the Senate by a single vote.

The business lobbies have found another way of making the victims bear the cost of their anticonsumer political efforts: they can pass it along in the form of higher prices. So when the lobbies for the economic interests succeed, they are further enriched, enabling them to send a bigger lobby back for an even bigger piece of the pie. The public lobbies receive nothing, even though they may save the taxpayer billions or clean up the poisoned environment or protect the consumer from an unjustified price increase.

To a Congress accustomed to servicing private interest lobbies—who have time, information, and potentially, campaign money—the public lobbies stand at the back of a long waiting line. "There's the 23-year-old consumer lobbyist and the businessman who gives you $5,000," congressional aide Peter Kinzler says. "Whom are you going to listen to?" One environmental lobbyist recalls waiting outside a closed committee session, surrounded by milling lobbyists from numerous industrial interests, known and unknown. Seeking stringent pollution control measures, he was heartened when, during one of the breaks, a congressman walked out and said, "I got one of yours in." His elation was tempered when he realized that the same congressman was delivering what looked like similar good tidings to the other lobbyists clustered in the hall. But the doling out of table scraps can hardly satisfy those motivated by a kind of gnawing hunger when there is a feast under way for others. A former key committee aide in the Senate described the legislating process this way: "It's like there's a bushel basket in the middle of the table. Everyone is trying to throw as many of their things into the barrel as they can." By taking careful aim, the public interest lobbies have begun to hit the basket with increasing frequency. But for the most part, it's still brimming over with a variety of special interest plums.

How Lobbies Work

Beyond the fundamental technique of delivering substantive analyses in face-to-face meetings with legislators, lobbyists can work in very inventive ways. On behalf of a business client, Abe Fortas once got a minister to call a senator to give a pitch—a tack which infuriated the legislator, who hung up. And while Senator William Proxmire was taking his morning jog to his Capitol office, a Pan Am pilot ran alongside, uninvited, and explained to an irritated Proxmire why the government should bail out his floundering corporation. Usually, though, the organized lobbies have developed and refined more conventional techniques. Four of them follow:

WINING AND DINING. "I've never known a lobbyist who wasn't a nice guy" is a familiar refrain. Which should be expected, for savvy lobbies understand Marshall McLuhan and politics: the context is more important than the content, and an amiable delivery can camouflage any bias.

To develop a congenial ambience, lobbyists for large economic interests come equipped with the traditional expense accounts to make life more pleasant for select congressmen. The sweeteners can range from imported perfumes to Christmas gifts "carted in by the cartload" according to one Senate aide. *Washington Post* reporter Ward Sinclair described the atmosphere during a recent Christmas: "It is Christmas season on Capitol Hill, the one time of year when the flow of goodies is reversed. Instead of dishing it out, the legislature scoops it up. Wreaths and flowers, liquor, cheese, pens, datebooks and calendars, small appliances . . . are among the holiday remembrances flooding the hill." GE sends around small deep-fat fryers; 3M, kits of cellophane tape; and Kraft Food, cheese packets. Nor does the giving stop on December 26.

Atlanta Congressman Wyche Fowler, Jr., tells how he three times told Atlanta-based Coca-Cola to stop plying his office with cartons of free Coke—but each time the Coke kept coming. Fowler, a strong-willed and independent representative, bowed to the inevitable. If you visit his office, more likely than not you'll be offered a free guess-what.

Then there are the parties. Come the spring, the large party rooms off the corridors of the Rayburn Building are full of lobby groups, making the end of the day a little more pleasant for hard-working representatives. In June, 1974, the Grocery Manufacturers of America invited all 535 national legislators and their families to a carnival and picnic at a fashionable local country club just before a crucial vote on the consumer protection agency bill, a bill the GMA vigorously opposed. "Certainly senators and congressmen have been entertained on a small scale," the Freight Forwarders' Washington representative Stanley Sommer concedes, "but it's nothing more than a three-hour cruise down the Potomac."

Former senator Paul Douglas has explained the process:

> The enticer does not generally pay money directly to the public representative. He tries instead, by a series of favors, to put the public official under such a feeling of personal obligation that the latter gradually loses his sense of mission to the public and comes to feel that his first loyalties are to his private benefactors and patrons. . . . Throughout this whole process the official will claim—and may, indeed, believe—that there is no casual connection between the favors he has received and the decision which he makes. He will assert that the favors were given or received on the basis of pure friendship.

To nourish this friendship, the good lobbyist prides himself on knowing where and how to find anything the congressman may desire. A Washington lobbyist told correspondent David Sheridan that he makes discreet arrangements for one congressman who enjoys an occasional lady of the night. Good lobbyists don't forget the staffers, either. Many don't have to worry about forgetting their lunch money, as companies stand in line to take them to favorite dining places.

This thoughtfulness eventually makes its point. "You begin to look forward to those three or four lunches a week with the lobbyists at the good restaurants," one committee aide said, "to the $25 bottles of Scotch, the football tickets, the occasional junkets, and if you don't watch out, you get pulled into the lobbyist's frame of reference." Or as Maurice Tobin, who has seen the goodies flow from both directions (as counsel to the House Public Works Committee and, more recently, as legislative consultant to a number of corporations), summed it up, "Everybody likes freebees."

POLITICAL STOCKBROKERING. Even more than freebees, politicians like currency in their campaign chests, as the previous chapter demonstrated. This is where the glad-handing lobbyists can really win gratitude, respect, and occasionally even fear. Not only do the special interest lobbyists exploit the financial credit already built by their groups, but—so there will be no mistake—they often collect and deliver the funds themselves.

There is a long tradition of lobbyists coming to congressional offices to drop off cash in envelopes, ostensibly for "campaign contributions." Rep. Richard Ottinger saw the process happen to him, he said in an interview, and he rejected the offer. (Ottinger concluded, from his experience, that a seat on the House Interstate and Foreign Commerce Committee was worth a substantial amount of money.) Rep. Pete McCloskey said he "was upset to find lobbyists leaving behind envelopes with $100 bills." He is convinced that straight cash from lobbyists in the form of campaign contributions is a subterranean corruption of great significance in terms of its influence on the behavior of recipient congressmen. But at least one such recipient disagrees. This congressman willingly took $250 in cash at a Washington bar from an industrial lobbyist, and then turned to a Washington reporter and indignantly protested, "That son of a bitch thinks he can buy me for $250." But he kept the money.

One freelance lobbyist explained that he serves as a "political consultant" to his clients, advising them where to place their election money for greatest effect. Every two years, for example, he reminds certain construction companies to contribute about $4,000 to a key Southern congressman whose committee approves construction of federal hospitals. A well-known clearing house for oil money used to be lobbyist Peter Nyce, who once explained his method of doing business: "I made oil companies ante up for various candidates." So it was not entirely surprising that when two merchant shipping lines presented nearly $6,000 in illegal campaign contributions to important House and Senate committee members, they chose lobbyists to make the delivery.

William Whyte, a vice president of U.S. Steel, coordinated a secret campaign fund in 1972 which the company collected from its executives. The company then found a good use for Whyte. He sent a telegram to several congressmen on behalf of U.S. Steel, urging them to support the federal water pollution bill "without any amendments." On the other side were twenty-five civic, farm, labor, and environmental groups who thought the bill perforated by loopholes preferential to industrial polluters. But these groups could only confront members with critical citizen letters, not the loss of a significant campaign contribution. No one who observes this or dozens of other lobbying campaigns will be surprised by former Senator Joseph Clark's even-handed assessment that the Republican and Democratic campaign finance committees are "prisoners of the lobbies."

GOING TO THE "GRASS ROOTS." Rather than simply buzzing in the legislator's ear in Washington, the aim of "grass-roots" lobbying is to subject him to mass appeals from people back home, or people who supply his campaign money, or simply any people whom he cares about. According to Hilton Davis of the Chamber of Commerce, "We really put a lot more stock in what people at home can do to influence members of Congress than what we can do by talking to Congressmen. We don't vote in their districts." A House subcommittee in 1978 estimated that business lobbyists spend up to a billion dollars a year generating such grass-roots "support" for their issues.

The oil industry has always excelled at this lobbying tactic, particularly when the large companies pool their efforts. In one carefully orchestrated industry effort on the depletion allowance, for example, an oil company asked its stockholders to write to Congress; another worked at mobilizing its retired employees; another aimed at service station operators; a fourth mailed off brochures to its credit card holders. Intent on preserving an impression of spontaneous revolt emanating from the hinterlands, the Washington coordinators of oil's campaigns have on occasion remained conspicuously silent while the letters and requests to testify flooded in.

To help its members put the pressure where it does the most good, Gulf thoughtfully prepares "complete dossiers of all congressmen from the states in which Gulf has an interest. . . . These dossiers will include not only voting records, but everything that will assist Gulf's people in obtaining a more complete understanding of their elected representatives." Armed with their dossiers, the "grass roots" of the corporate lobby are ready to go into action when the trumpet sounds.

PERSONAL ASSOCIATIONS. One day in 1926, Pennsylvania Senator David Reed—whose father had been a key member of the Gulf Oil controlling syndicate—went to lunch with the president of the Mid-Continent Oil and Gas Association. The Mid-Continent man told Reed of the heavy burden that drilling costs were forcing on the industry. The senator was so moved by this complaint that he rushed to tell his colleagues on the Senate Finance Committee of the oilmen's desperate plight. Out of that discussion was born the oil depletion allowance.

It was, of course, natural that Reed, raised under the roof of Big Oil, would be dining out with another oilman. Men in Congress obviously have social acquaintances and former, if not present, business acquaintances outside of Congress. That simple fact gives the business lobbies one of their most important conduits into the Congress.

The danger arises because the average congressman is not the average American. Allard Lowenstein has commented that "the House in some ways isn't very representative. There's almost never anyone here under 30. . . . And, of course, there are only nine blacks [in 1969, though in 1978 there were sixteen] when proportionately there should be about fifty." This disproportionate representation is even more skewed for women and blue-collar workers. The fact that members of Congress come almost exclusively from professions that serve mostly business clientele or from business itself gives the corporate community a several-step head start over other citizens in making Congress work for them.

The average citizen gets little opportunity to see lobbying operations in action, as they are seldom covered in the news media. One that did make the news occurred in connection with the 1970 lobbying effort of the banking industry on one-bank holding company legislation. The American Bankers Association wrote to the officials of three banks asking them to get in touch immediately with three key members of the relevant House-Senate conference to ask them to oppose stringent controls. The three members happened also to be large stockholders in the respective banks. The banker asked to contact Rep. J. William Stanton of Ohio also happened to have been Stanton's campaign treasurer in the previous election. The Bankers Association letter stressed an important point: "If at all possible, please make your contact in person."

One prominent example of legislators sympathizing with their natural professional constituency involved the August, 1972, battle over federal no-fault automobile insurance in the Senate. The idea of a no-fault system (which pays auto victims regardless of who is at fault) is essentially to eliminate the necessity for a trial, and trial lawyer, in most cases. But a proposal to eliminate business for lawyers predictably dismayed the American Trial Lawyers Association (ATLA), whose members earn a good part of their keep by going to court on auto accident cases. (A Senate Commerce Committee report showed that 16 percent of all lawyers' earnings comes from auto negligence cases.) ATLA alerted its members, and lawyers in Congress were swamped with calls from old law school classmates.

The ATLA lawyers had more going for them than just classroom ties. "Some of these lawyers earn $80,000 a year fighting auto negligence cases," an aide to one senator told United Press International. "They can be counted on for a contribution of $3,000 or $4,000 or $5,000 to a senator running for reelection. A phone call from one or two can be effective." More than one or two called in. In just a few hours before the vote was taken, one senator told Morton Mintz of the *Washington Post* that he got calls from twenty lawyer friends urging him to help shelve the proposal.

Senator Tom Eagleton showed that blood is thicker than politics by his surprise vote in mid-1972 to bury no-fault auto legislation in the Judiciary Committee. He had been lobbied by a group of his trial-lawyer father's colleagues, men whom the senator, by profession and by upbringing, had come to respect. He explained ingenuously that his father had been a trial lawyer and would have "rolled over in his grave" had he voted against the tort system.

Finally, as perhaps the ultimate in intimate association, a third of the American Medical Association's district lobbying representatives happen to be the general practitioners who delivered either the congressmen or their children.

Case Studies of Lobbying Techniques in Action

LABOR LAW REFORM BILL. This 1977 bill was among the most heavily lobbied pieces of legislation in history. Labor and business groups representing millions of members together spent more than $8 million and strained the postal system with 20 million pieces of mail. George Meany called it a "holy war" and one business coalition called the bill "Big Labor's latest assault on the individual human rights of every wage earner in America."

"It's our macho vs. their macho," one lobbyist told the *Washington Post*. Each side, for example, commissioned a poll showing that a majority of Americans agreed with its position. Each side paid for expensive economic impact studies to show congressmen how a victory by the other side would damage the economy. Both labor and business warned that campaign endorsements and contributions for the 1978 elections would hinge primarily on this issue. Why this effort? Because in Washington, where the appearance of power is often as important as the ability to exercise it, both sides believed the outcome would affect their entire legislative program and industrial relations in general.

Easily forgotten was the substance of the legislation,

which aimed to ensure prompt elections among unorganized workers on whether to be represented by a union. It included stronger penalties against business violators (including double back pay for fired union organizers) and required speedier decisions by the National Labor Relations Board on charges of unfair labor practices.

The Right to Work Committee opposing the bill said it sent out about 12 million pieces of mail during the six months preceding the June, 1978, filibuster. They were joined by the more credible National Action Committee for Labor Law Reform, a business coalition led by powerful organizations such as the Chamber of Commerce, the Business Roundtable, the National Association of Manufacturers, and the National Federation of Independent Businessmen. Right to Work mailings were done by mass mail specialist Richard Viguerie. Using his preciously accumulated tapes that list all known supporters of conservative causes in America, Viguerie's mailings aim to propagandize, to solicit funds to cover his costs (usually with a handsome profit), and to ask that attached postcards be mailed to the recipients' senators. At least 4 million of those little yellow cards found their way back to Washington.

Even before the House approved the reforms by a wide margin in October, 1977, the AFL-CIO had raised an $870,000 lobby fund from its affiliated unions by a special tax. George Meany had placed eleven key staff people on a special Task Force on Labor Law Reform to lead the lobby battle in Washington. More than 2,000 local union leaders were brought to Washington for briefings on the bill. They left armed with a twenty-one-page manual to help them resume the lobby battle on the home front. This organization helped the unions send more than 3 million pieces of mail to Capitol Hill and put 1 million signatures on petitions in support of cloture.

This double mass bombardment by mail put many senators under political pressure, and their offices under administrative burdens just processing all the generated letters. Democrat Dale Bumpers of Arkansas was one of twelve uncommitted senators courted relentlessly by both sides during the series of cloture votes that could have ended the filibuster. There were 50,000 Right to Work solicitations sent into his state. Concerned by the business deluge, a labor union official appeared in Bumpers's office carrying shoe boxes filled with 8,700 postcards supporting the reform. He even offered to send more if the 1,000 or so a day Bumpers was receiving were inadequate. "Labor felt senators were impressed by the volume of mail they were getting [from business] and so they felt they had to generate a like volume," Bumpers said afterward.

The protagonists sent in not only mail, but lobbyists. One Senate staffer estimates that he saw 500 people on this one bill. After the Chamber of Commerce sent its predominantly small-business membership a newsletter headlined "Big Labor Versus Small Business," virtually every small business association in Washington joined the corporate giants like Sears and Firestone to aggressively oppose the legislation. The U.S. Chamber of Commerce began paying for delegations of businessmen to come and spend a week lobbying on the Hill to counter the AFL-CIO's local COPE presidents, who had also flown in to do some arm-twisting.

In the end, labor needed only two more senators for cloture, but no one wanted to stick his neck out and be the sixtieth senator. Unable to find two more votes and unwilling to gut the bill in order to get something, labor capitulated. Majority Leader Byrd shelved the bill after nineteen days of filibuster and a record six cloture votes. So while a 60 percent majority vote in the House had been considered a smashing success, nearly the same margin in the Senate was a major defeat. "The biggest thing working against us," said a bitter Howard Paster, the UAW's chief lobbyist, "was an undemocratic system."

CONSUMER PROTECTION AGENCY. What can you say about a bill that passed the House or the Senate five times in seven years, that was endorsed by President Carter, Speaker of the House O'Neill, and 150 consumer, labor, elderly, and citizen groups, that the public supported by a 2 to 1 margin in Harris surveys—and yet was defeated 227–189 in February, 1978?

For eight years consumer groups had pushed the idea of a small, nonregulatory advocacy office which would promote consumer interests before other federal agencies. As the fourteen Democratic and Republican members of the Senate Governmental Affairs Committee unanimously concluded in 1977, "At agency after agency, participation by the regulated industry predominates—often overwhelmingly. . . . For more than half of the proceedings there is no consumer participation whatsoever. In those proceedings where participation by public groups does take place, typically it is a small fraction of the participation by the regulated industry." The purpose of this consumer advocacy office was to make regulation work better by making the adversary process work better.

On one side stood a coalition of citizen groups, who visited every undecided member of the House and who organized a "nickel campaign" that generated the mailing of 40,000 nickels to 83 undecided representatives. (A nickel represented the average cost per citizen for this "costly" new agency.) Arrayed against them were big-business interests—such as the U.S. Chamber of Commerce, the Business Roundtable, the National Association of Manufacturers, Armstrong Cork, Procter and Gamble, and Sears—who made the bill a litmus-test issue of a representative's fidelity to their creed. Speaker O'Neill said that he had "never seen such extensive lobbying" in his quarter century in Congress.

For example, the Business Roundtable* hired Leon Jaworski to lobby against the bill in early 1977, and later hired the North American Precis Syndicate (NAPS) to send canned editorials and cartoons against the consumer agency to 3,800 newspapers and weeklies. These prepared statements—statements that never acknowledged as their source a business lobby opposed to the bill—appeared approximately 2,000 times, according to NAPS. Identical hostile editorials appeared in ten newspapers around the country, newspapers not of the same chain (*Oxnard Press-Courier,* Calif.; *Thomasville Times,* N.C.; *Mount Vernon News,* Ohio; *Middletown Journal,* Ohio; *Ypsilanti Press,* Mich.; *Santa Paula Chronicle,* Calif.; *Greenwood Com-*

---

*A study of the Roundtable released by Congress Watch shortly before the vote documented that 58 percent of the 157 members of this group had in the past five years either admitted to an illegal or improper payment, been named in an antitrust case by the Antitrust Division, or been named in a Federal Trade Commission complaint.

monwealth, Miss.; *Roseburg News-Review*, Ore.; *Kentucky New Era; Murray Ledger and Times*, Ky.).

The U.S. Chamber of Commerce conducted a national poll in 1975, which it cited often over the next three years, concluding that "81 percent of Americans are opposed to a new consumer agency." The Library of Congress, however, discredited this survey as biased and unfair because the key question was phrased as follows (italics added): "Those in favor of setting up an *additional* consumer protection agency on top of *all the other* agencies . . ." This poll led an outraged Senator Charles Percy to denounce it from the floor, saying, "The dissemination of useless poll information does nothing to help the image of American business, which is at an all-time low."

Finally, business opponents were able to parlay their financial resources into success. One California Democrat in a meeting with consumer advocates half-joked that he might vote for the consumer bill if their groups could throw him the "$100,000 fundraiser" he was forfeiting by supporting their position. Two swing House members candidly told labor lobbyists that they had recently and for the first time raised $20,000 to $40,000 from small-business groups, who had been instructed by the Chamber of Commerce to be opposed. One representative was told by his campaign finance chairman that their major contributors were opposed to the bill—at which point, to his credit, the representative fired his finance chairman. One Florida representative told Ralph Nader that he had no objections to the bill, but added, "I'm afraid that the Chamber will run a candidate against me in the primary."

Ultimately, the opposition lobby had the money and machinery to propagandize that the issue was "big government"—not consumer fraud, not consumer health and safety, not one-sided regulatory proceedings. Thus the repeated refrain that the Office of Consumer Representation was just more "OSHA-like" regulation stuck—even though there was no reasonable comparison between the Occupational Safety and Health agency, with its $136 million budget and the power to order business to redesign its workplaces, and a $15 million nonregulatory advocacy office armed only with the power of an advocate.

As the vote neared, many members acknowledged that they supported the bill on its merits, but didn't, as one said, "want to explain 500 times in my district why the consumer office wasn't just more government." One Southern Democrat who swam against the current and voted affirmatively said, with some bitterness, "If we had voted today on a bill to abolish the U.S. Government, it probably would have passed." Despite a fiery floor speech by Speaker O'Neill, the vote tally against the measure hit 227, at which point business lobbyists watching from the House galleries stood up and cheered and applauded. Chairman Jack Brooks of the Government Operations Committee, a major sponsor of the bill, was not pleased. "Those who want it all," he remarked, "will lose it all."

ENERGY BILL. Unlike the labor law reform bill, the battle over President Carter's National Energy Act resembled less a titanic duel than a marathon brawl among hundreds of narrow special interests. The bill, really a combination of five different bills, covered conservation, utility rate reform, natural gas policy, coal conversion, and energy taxes and tax credits. Each of these pieces contained controversial provisions with important impacts on industry, business, and consumers, which individually would have been enough to prod dormant lobbyists into action. Faced with the five initiatives all at once, the Washington lobbying scene exploded.

"We can be sure that all the special interest groups in the country will attack the part of this plan that affects them directly," President Carter warned in April, 1977, when he introduced the bill; ". . . if they succeed with this approach, then the burden on the ordinary citizen, who is not organized into an interest group, would be crushing." Sure enough, the hearing rooms were clogged with dark-suited, briefcased lobbyists monitoring the hearings in order to report back to their client companies.

"Every time I turn around I run into a horde of lobbyists," complained Rep. Marty Russo (D.-Ill.), a member of the House Interstate and Foreign Commerce Committee. The scene on the Senate side of the Capitol was little different, according to Senator Henry Jackson (D.-Wash.), chairman of the Senate Energy Committee:

"You have to wade through the Senate reception room to get past all the lobbyists," he said.

The lineup was diverse. Oil and gas interests, including many of the major multinational oil firms, sought to work quietly in the background rather than risk sparking a political backlash against "big oil." Lobbyists like Andy Vitali of the American Petroleum Institute and Bill Timmons, representing Standard Oil of Indiana, maintained a vigil for the large integrated oil firms. The American Gas Association was particularly alert for an opportunity to decontrol gas prices, which would generate tens of billions of dollars in additional revenues. The American Bus Association sought a $1 billion tax credit on behalf of, it said, "low income people who ride buses."

Consumer and labor groups fought against the deregulation of natural gas rates and for state utility rate reforms. Home heating oil dealers opposed a provision requiring electric utilities to carry out home inspections because that might induce residential homeowners to switch from oil to electricity. The Electric Consumers Resources Council, made up of large industrial firms like General Motors and Union Carbide, was formed specifically to fight the Carter administration's proposal to reform a utility rate structure that rewarded big users with lower rates when they used more electricity. Perhaps the most creative attempt to capitalize on the president's call to bear arms in "the moral equivalent of war" was made by the trucking industry, which sought a tax credit for windscreens on their trailers on the grounds that the decreased wind resistance would save fuel and reduce our reliance on foreign oil.

Like any guerrilla movement, the lobbyists spread their ranks and money and began waging war in the countryside far from the besieged District of Columbia. Congress Watch revealed that nine members of the Finance Committee received more than $547,000 for their 1974 or 1976 election campaigns from oil and gas industry sources or from lawyers representing them. Common Cause found that during the five months between January and May, 1977, industry and trade groups placed energy advocacy ads costing $1.3 million in just five newspapers—more than the oil and gas industries reported spending for all lobbying that same period. Mobil ran advertisements, according to its manager of communication program Donald Stroetzel, "in nearly every Congressional district."

The struggle eventually came down to natural gas deregulation. Despite his initial opposition and despite the estimates of his own experts that the compromise would cost consumers up to $32 billion more over seven years than his original proposal, President Carter had become anxious for a bill—and the energy lobbyists knew it. The president found himself searching for support from industry and members of Congress as the closing days of the 95th Congress neared. The nuclear industry, with the help of Senator James McClure (R.-Ida.), was able to extract a broad commitment to breeder reactor research in return for the senator's support for the compromise. Major steel companies reversed months of opposition to the natural gas bill after being given a special audience with high administration officials responsible for managing the level of foreign steel imports permitted to compete with domestic production. Similar overtures for support were reportedly made to other big industrial users like the textile industry, just as trade ambassador Robert Strauss was preparing to go to Japan to attempt to restrict textile exports to this country. The administration's effort proved just sufficient, as the natural gas provision passed its major hurdle in the House, 207–206.

Ultimately, President Carter's warnings about lobbyists proved painfully accurate. Lobbyists did swarm around the bill, and were so successful that they forced the administration itself to do an about-face on natural gas and lobby for what it had opposed. The result was the National Energy Act of 1978.

Organized special interests engage in their lobbying legerdemain largely free of public scrutiny, for Congress has only the flimsiest of lobbying disclosure laws, laws even more primitive than those in the campaign finance area. In Franklin Roosevelt's day, Rep. George Tinkham (R.-Mass.) once introduced legislation which would have required that lobbyists register and that written certifications be renewed each month. The House debate on the bill went so far as to suggest that lobbyists wear conspicuous clothing or badges to identify themselves. One congressman only half-jokingly proposed that lobbyists be required to wear uniforms designed to reflect their rank, importance, and affiliation.

The current lobby law, instead, has its origin in the Legislative Reorganization Act of 1946, whose language is so ambiguous that courts have interpreted it as applying only to groups and individuals that collect funds for the principal purpose of influencing legislation through direct contact with members. This leaves three gaping loopholes: (1) groups that do not collect funds *specifically* for lobbying purposes are not covered by the law; (2) if the group's *"principal purpose"* is not lobbying, it does not have to file disclosure reports; (3) only *direct* contact with Congress (not mass mailings, phone calls, etc.) is covered by the act.

To ensure that citizens know who is pulling the levers of power in Congress, new lobbying legislation is needed to identify major lobby groups, the issues they work on, the monies they spend. Equally important are the ad hoc techniques for bringing the lobbies out into the open. TV documentaries, increased press coverage, congressional investigations, citizen-sponsored investigations, countervailing lobbies exposing one another—all these need both institutional and informal encouragement.

But whatever is done to air the actions of the organized lobbies, a citizens' lobby must at the same time become a political counterweight, growing in numbers, resources, and sophistication. Public interest advocates can be created within the government itself, as in the recently defeated proposal for a Consumer Protection Agency. Or it can be encouraged by the government via tax credits for contributions to public interest lobby groups, or by at least putting these groups on an equal tax basis (regarding deductions) with private business lobbies. But ultimately, the backbone of any citizen's lobby must be citizens—active, organized, and informed.

3

Who Rules Congress?

*The Committee member who has served twenty
years is not just 5 percent more powerful than
the member who has served nineteen years. If he
is chairman he is 1000 percent more powerful.*
—Rep. Morris Udall

We all recall the neat textbook diagrams in our civics
books outlining "how a bill becomes a law," that very
logical process which is our legislative trademark. A congressman submitted a bill; it went to a committee which
refined it and then reported it to the floor; if it passed,
and if the other chamber had passed a similar measure, it
went to a "conference committee" to iron out any differences; after repassage, the president signed it into law.
Things were so simple.

Unfortunately, life does not imitate art. The diagrams
don't show 535 local heroes and potential presidents joust-
ing among themselves for power and prestige. They don't
at all show who holds the cards, or how those who control the process control the law. They don't explain the
dynamics of power, the shift and flow of forces that make
our laws. To get a more realistic picture, we must look at
the ruling forces of Congress: the committee system,
which gives disproportionate power to forty-odd men;
the seniority tradition which, to an extent, still chooses
the men who will exert the power; the rules of secrecy
and power-brokering, which can seal the system off from
the people. "The parliament of the world's greatest democracy," concluded Rep. Morris Udall several years ago,
"is not a democratic institution."

Committees—"Little Legislatures"

"Congress, in its Committee rooms," Woodrow Wilson observed in his 1885 *Congressional Government,* "is Congress at work." Permanent congressional committees are a necessary outgrowth of the heavy and complex work of Congress. A division of specialized labor became necessary as far back as the early nineteenth century in order to handle proposed legislation. In the Third Congress (1793–95), the House created 350 ad hoc committees, one to handle each bill. This clearly would not do, so by 1825 Congress had trimmed the system to 43 standing (i.e., permanent) committees, each with a designated area of authority.

But, as often happens, neither house could control its creations. Committees began to proliferate, as each member wanted "his" committee to provide him with a platform. By 1913, at the system's grandiose height, there were 61 standing committees in the House and 74 in the Senate. Reforms in 1946 cut the numbers to 19 and 15 respectively, but a new form of committee growth emerged: subcommittees. By 1970, counting standing committees and subcommittees, there were a total of 305 in both houses.

Committees vary in size and importance, and there is a distinct committee caste system. The House Ways and Means Committee and the House Appropriations Committee, with 37 and 55 members respectively, determine our tax structure and federal budget, which touch the pocketbooks of us all. These two, plus the Senate Finance Committee and the Senate Appropriations Committee, are the big four of Capitol Hill, the ones with the most power and, by Washington's perfect logic, the most prestige. When Professor Richard Fenno asked members of Ways and Means and Appropriations why they sought out their committee assignments, the overwhelming majority said they sought "power," "prestige," or "importance." "The Appropriations Committee is the most powerful committee in the House. It's the most powerful committee in the Congress," said one representative. "This is where all the money starts rolling." Another said proudly of his Ways and Means assignment, "It's the top committee in the House of Representatives. The entire revenue system is locked into the committee."

The appointment of freshmen to these committees is a matter for great care. Traditionally—with the notable exception of 1975—they rarely get on the best committees because, said one veteran, "It would be too risky to put on a person whose views and nature the leadership has no opportunity to assess." A careful screening ensures that nonconformists do not slip through. Sam Rayburn and LBJ never let anyone sit on House Ways and Means or Senate Finance without asking what he thought about the oil depletion allowance. When a Maryland representative was being considered for membership on the House Interstate and Foreign Commerce Committee, he was asked by Kentucky's John Watts, "What's your position on tobacco?" The representative replied half-jokingly, "I don't smoke"—and was not appointed to the committee. And when an occasional liberal would find himself on one of the major committees, he would often be from a "swing district," one which made it unlikely he would stay around for decades.

Newcomers still want to get on the "best" committees possible and struggle as intensively as the old pols to get there. For they appreciate, as the *New York Times* once editorialized, that "a good committee assignment can make the difference between a brief and obscure service in the House and the kind of influence that means tenure for decades." (Each party in each chamber has a committee of the committees to place congressmen on committees; the twenty-four-person Democratic Steering Committee, run by the speaker, took over this function from the House Ways and Means Committee in late 1974.) Freshman congressmen begin jockeying for choice posts immediately upon arrival, if not sooner. Don Riegle from Michigan, for example, on the night of his election in 1966, called House Minority Leader Gerald Ford, also from Michigan, to lobby for a seat on the Education and Labor Committee. Representative-elect Herbert Harris of Virginia spoke to about two hundred members in 1974, including most of the Democratic Steering Committee, in his successful bid to be seated on the Post Office and Civil Service and the District of Columbia committees. Another imaginative member, returning to Congress after an absence, desired a seat on a prestigious committee. So he hired an investigator to uncover the vulnerabilities and desires of their speaker Carl Albert. Armed with this information, he made his case to Albert—successfully.

The appointment process is closely followed, if not shaped, by the special interests. Why? Because of the two crucial functions served by committees. First, of course, they are the workshops of lawmaking—the place where legislation is buried or where it matures to be reported to the full chamber. If a bill fails to get out of committee, it is usually dead. If it is reported out unanimously, it nearly always passes. A study of the 84th Congress by Donald Matthews found that if a proposal was supported by 80 percent or more of the committee members, it passed every time (35 of 35); if 60–79 percent of a committee supported a proposal, it would pass 90 percent of the time; but if only 50–60 percent supported it (i.e., almost half the committee opposed it), it would pass only 56 percent of the time. This is not because committees are a representative sample of the whole chamber's views, but because legislators tend to follow the committee's judgment unless there's an unusual reason to doubt it.

"When internally unified and buttressed in parliamentary privilege by special rules," wrote Stephen Bailey, "[the committees] can almost at will dominate the business of the parent chamber." This is especially true after the reforms of the 1970s, according to R. D. Markley, Jr., for twenty years a major auto industry lobbyist. "The way Congress has been restructured, if a measure you don't like gets to full committee, forget it, you've had it. It's down here in the subcommittees where you've really got to do your work."

Aside from processing legislation, the committees have a second important function: holding hearings to obtain information and publicize issues. The success and effect of the hearings, in turn, depend on two things: how carefully prepared and tightly focused the hearings themselves are, and how heavily the press covers them. Neither element alone is usually enough for public impact. When Rep. Kenneth Roberts held a series of revealing hearings on auto safety in 1956, the press ignored them and Congress passed the issue by. Nine years later, Senator Abraham Ribicoff's, and later Senator Warren Magnuson's, auto hearings were front-page news; one of the results was the National Traffic and Motor Vehicle Safety Act of 1966.

Colorful and well-covered hearings helped establish Senators George McGovern (Senate Select Committee on Hunger), Frank Church (subcommittee on Multinational Corporations) and Howard Baker (Watergate committee) as national figures and presidential contenders. "If the sound of congressional voices carried no further than the bare walls of the chambers," former representative Clem Miller wrote, "Congress would disband. . . . To the congressman, publicity is his lifeblood."

The Rules of Congress

The committee system guarantees that *someone* will dominate Congress. An elaborate set of congressional rules determines just who those leaders will be and how they will work their will.

SENIORITY. Congress employs a seniority system to allocate power. Parodying Darwin, the system has simply ensured the survival of the survivors. No other federal legislature in the world selects its leaders by seniority. Yet under the seniority custom—enshrined neither in law nor in written rules—committee chairmanships have been automatically awarded to the members of the majority party with longest continuous service on the committee. While Congress mandates retirement for federal employees at 70, a fifth of all the congressional chairmen are over 70 and three-fourths are over 60. While the average committee chairman a hundred years ago was in his forties, and in 1910 was 50, today he is 63.

The seniority system itself is less antiquated than the chairmen it perpetrates. From 1910, when it took hold, until 1945, seniority determined only three of every four House chairmanships. But between 1945 and 1975, it guaranteed chairmanships to all ranking committee members—except Adam Clayton Powell, whose misfortune it was to be both spendthrift and black, a handful of ornery veterans who crossed party lines, and the four chairmen purged at the start of the rebellious 94th Congress in 1975. In the Senate, where seniority began in the 1840s, only five senior members in 125 years have been refused chairmanships, the last one 50 years ago. And those who become chairmen stay chairmen. Only one member of Congress, Theodore F. Green, chairman of the Senate

Foreign Relations Committee, who stepped down in 1955 at the age of 91, has found the chairmanship of a full committee too wearing. Only after the late senator Karl Mundt of South Dakota had lain in a hospital bed for two years, wholly incapacitated by a stroke, did Senate Republicans in February, 1972, reassign his position as ranking minority member of the Foreign Relations Committee.

Mere antiquity, of course, is certainly no crime. Though occasional relics gain chairs, in what Jack Anderson hyperbolizes as the "Senility System," infirmity is not the chief vice of the seniority system. Its faults are more serious. A legislative branch encumbered by the seniority custom belongs in neither a republic nor a democracy: it bequeaths inherited congressional power to unrepresentative lawmakers in an undemocratic way.

In a country whose population is young, urban, and geographically dispersed, the seniority system has historically turned over most positions of power in Congress to "representatives" who are old, rural, and Southern. As long ago as 1859, a Northern Democrat bewailed the seniority system which gave "senators from slaveholding states the chairmanship of every single committee that controls the public business of this government. There is not one exception." Southerners consistently held more than half of all committee chairs in Democratic congresses from 1921 to 1966. In 1969 they headed ten of the sixteen standing Senate committees. They chaired the five most important in the Senate in 1977: Appropriations, Finance, Foreign Relations, Armed Services, and Judiciary. But then, in an unprecedented development, even the seniority system surrendered to the infirmities of age. Within a year John McClellan (D.-Ark.), chairman of Finance, died; and John Sparkman (D.-Ala.) and James Eastland, chairmen of Foreign Relations and Judiciary respectively, announced their retirements. With only three of sixteen chairmanships at the start of the 96th Congress, Southerners no longer disproportionately controlled the levers of senatorial power.

Seniority is not without its supporters, mostly older congressmen. It assures, they argue, independent leaders who strengthen Congress's position relative to the dominant executive branch. But the price of using seniority as a way of insulating Congress from the president is to insulate certain members from the voters and the rest of Congress. Assertions are also often made that seniority places men of experience in power, thereby assuring competence and continuity. But if age implies talent, why was the average at the Constitutional Convention (even including 81-year-old Ben Franklin) merely 43? Why did cabinet officers under President Nixon average twelve years younger than congressional committee chairmen? President Johnson's seventeen years younger? President Kennedy's nineteen years younger? As the adage goes, thirty years' experience may be no more than one year's experience relived thirty times.

The worst excesses of the seniority system were resolved in recent House and Senate reforms. In a significant shift in 1973 (discussed below), the House Democratic Caucus decided to *elect* chairmen. As a result, in January, 1975, although sixteen panels had their most senior Democratic member as chairman, five did not. The Senate Democratic Caucus also decided to elect committee chairmen in 1974, though out of historical habit every chairman chosen was still his committee's longest serving majority member. Thus, the seniority custom still appears to be the most influential consideration in the selection of chairmen, but it no longer dominates Congress as it once did.

SECRECY. Congressional secrecy, especially secrecy in committees, began at the beginning of Congress. From 1789 to 1795 the Senate met and voted entirely in secret, fearing slanted newspaper coverage. Then it finally decided to open its doors for regular legislative sessions, but still held secret ("executive") sessions to consider all treaties and many nominations.

Committees have traditionally enveloped their activities in secrecy, though recently things have opened up more. In the 1970 Legislative Reorganization Act, committees had to make public their roll-call votes—which some chairmen avoided by simply not taking roll calls. Many committee sessions used to be closed altogether. In 1969, 36 percent of all committee sessions were held in secret; in 1972, it was 40 percent—despite the Legislative Reorganization Act, which tried to encourage open proceedings. Then, in 1973, the House voted to require all committees to meet in public *unless* the majority voted otherwise, and the Senate permitted each committee to set its own policies—as some adopted the 1973 House rule. The next year, as a result, only 25 percent of all Senate committee sessions and 8 percent of House committee sessions were closed to the public.

Beyond usual meetings and hearings, committee "markup" sessions and "conference committees" should also be public. At the markups, the details of a proposed bill are reviewed by its committee; it is here that outside interests can slip in a loophole with the help of a committee staffer. To prevent this, the public should have access to markups, which is increasingly the case.

Conference committees settle any differences between Senate and House versions of a bill. Calling them the "third house of Congress," Senator George Norris lamented in 1934 that "the members of this House are not elected by the people. . . . There is no record kept of the workings of the conference committee. Its work is performed, in the main, in secret. . . . As a practical proposition we have legislation then, not by the members of the House of Representatives, but we have legislation by the voice of five or six members." As he left the Senate in 1970, Tennessee's Albert Gore blasted the conference committees as "secret meetings often not even announced until the last minute [where] a few men can sit down and undo in one hour the most painstaking work of months of effort by several standing committees and the full membership of both Houses." At times the chosen conferees are hostile to the bill being negotiated, or unrepresentative of the views of their chamber. So in 1970, when the House voted $290 million for the SST and the Senate voted to *end* the program, the conference committee (stacked with Senate SST supporters) agreed on a "compromise" $210 million funding.

Secrecy here can twist the results. "You certainly get some different attitudes in a conference than you would anticipate by listening to speeches on the floor," one member told the Brookings Institution's Charles Clapp. "There is one senator, for example, who is known primarily for a particular position on foreign aid. Yet in conference I never saw anyone fight more ardently for a different position." In a memo that got into Jack Anderson's hands, a Ford dealer summarized a discussion an aide had on auto safety with former Senator John Pastore: "The senator . . . told Bob that when a consumer issue is before him and the cameras are on, he is not about to be anything but supportive of the issue." In 1978, even a conference committee as significant as the one handling the comprehensive energy bill often met in rump, secret sessions.

When members have to be publicly accountable for their actions, however, the result can sharply differ from secret lawmaking. Before the advent of recorded "teller voting" in 1970 (previously votes on amendments, which make up the bulk of our laws, were never recorded), SST funding was easily approved, with only 188 members voting. But the first year that members had to go on public record with their SST vote, it was defeated 217–203. During 1977, there were more than 700 recorded teller votes, while fifteen years ago there were about 100. Yet since a member's subcommittee votes can be the most important ones cast in Congress, they should also be recorded and disclosed.

THE HOUSE RULES COMMITTEE. On paper the House Rules Committee makes sense. Before any bill moves to the floor for debate, this committee sets the agenda for its debate, for example, specifying how much time will be allowed and whether members can offer amendments. But in practice the Rules Committee can become a star chamber for bills which do not strike its members' fancy, for they have the power to block a proposal by simply not reporting it to the floor. As Rep. Morris Udall wrote in a newsletter, "The Rules Committee has an almost complete power to determine on important issues *whether the rest of us can vote at all*" (emphasis his).

From the 1930s until the early sixties, the House Rules Committee was dominated by a coalition of Southern Democrats and conservative Republicans who frustrated much progressive legislation. A reform called the twenty-one-day rule was introduced in 1949. This allowed the committee which first considered a bill to force it out of the Rules Committee if it had lingered there for twenty-one days. Two years later, the rule was repealed. Its power restored, the Rules Committee later showed that it could thwart the will of *both* houses. After President Eisenhower's proposal for federal aid for school construction had passed both the House and the Senate, the Rules Committee refused to send it on to a House-Senate conference, thereby killing it.

The new Kennedy administration had similar troubles and decided it could not tolerate this nest of obstructionist conservatives. With the cooperation of Speaker Sam Rayburn, the administration managed to increase the size of the committee from twelve to fifteen, and to stack it with enough liberals to get an 8–7 liberal majority. Subdued, the committee has flaunted its power less since then.

But it still lashes out occasionally. In 1970 it refused to report for floor action bills to create a consumer protection agency and to strengthen the powers of the Equal Employment Opportunity Commission, though both had been approved by their respective House committees. In 1974, under the chairmanship of Ray Madden, the committee voted 13–2 against a bill which would have kept the American Electric Power Company from building a hydroelectric project that would dam the New River in North Carolina and force 3,000 people off their pastures and cropland—a bill favored by the Senate, the EPA, and the Interior Department. This led columnist Colman McCarthy to accuse the committee of acting "like a government within a government, a medieval court of magnificos and viziers that holds terrifying power over people's lives and uses that power without fear of accountability."

The Rules Committee of the 1980s, however, will undoubtedly be different from the committee of the sixties or seventies. The chairmen in the sixties were Howard Smith (D.-Va.) and William Colmer (D.-Miss.), two autocratic men with a plantation ideology who were out of step with the national party. The next decade saw Ray Madden (D.-Ind.) and James Delaney (D.-N.Y.), moderates of modest skill. They have been succeeded by Richard Bolling (D.-Mo.), a highly regarded analyst of the House who is a protege of Sam Rayburn and close to Speaker O'Neill.

THE FILIBUSTER. In 1808, a New York representative, Barent Gardiner, was shot and nearly killed by a Tennessee colleague who had become irate as Gardiner droned on week after week on some matter on the House floor. Probably not as a result, the House has adopted rules limiting debate, since it would be cacophony, not democracy, to allow any of 435 representatives to speak without limit on any issue.

The Senate, however, is a different story. Its tradition of allowing unlimited debate—known and ridiculed as the filibuster—is, like the seniority system, an unofficial custom which has acquired the durability of Divine Law. Senators can talk on the Senate floor until hunger, sleep, illness, nature, or cloture stops them. Cloture, as established by Rule 22 in 1917, is a two-thirds vote to stop debate. Between 1917 and 1975, 100 cloture votes were taken, and only 21 in those fifty-eight years were successful. The record for consecutive talking in the Senate is Strom Thurmond's twenty-four hours and eighteen minutes in August, 1957, against the civil rights bill of that year. In second place, talking for twenty-two hours and twenty-six minutes on the tidelands oil bill of 1953, was the late Wayne Morse, who would pin a rose to his lapel and threaten to hold forth until the petals wilted.

Recently, filibusters have not had to go through the ceremony of droning on and on and . . . Instead, when Majority Leader Robert Byrd, Jr., is apprised that a filibuster will ensue, he arranges for a cloture vote a reasonably short time after debate has begun, since he assumes one will come sooner or later.

To its supporters, the filibuster is the highest example of the right of free speech. "I think it is of greater importance to the public interest, in the long run and in the short run, that every bill on your calendar should fail than that any senator should be cut off from the right of expressing his opinion," said Senator George F. Edmunds, expressing an unusual sense of proportion, in 1881. Governor Adlai Stevenson saw it differently. "Every man has a right to be heard," he said, "but no man has the right to strangle democracy with a single set of vocal chords." To cartoonists and comics, the filibuster is a gold mine, providing scenes of posturing politicians reading selections from the phone book, or favorite recipes.

But the filibuster is more than a caricature of itself; it is an offense to the concept of majority rule, a device which allows a minority to obstruct what it does not like. It has been used in a variety of situations, most commonly and notoriously during civil rights debates in past decades. Proposals to allow cutting off debate by majority or 60

percent vote rather than the two-thirds vote of the old
Rule 22 have been periodically made—without success in
1958 and 1968. But 1975 witnessed the most important
change affecting the filibuster since Rule 22 was established. For the first time, the Senate (voting 51–42) and
its presiding officer, Vice President Nelson Rockefeller,
agreed that the Senate could constitutionally change its
rules at the beginning of each Congress by a simple majority vote despite the two-thirds cloture rule. But as
Senate reformers, led by Senators Mondale and Pearson,
were patting each other on the back about a 60 percent
cutoff, the late and wily Senator James Allen exploited
obscure procedural rules to *filibuster* the reform against
the filibuster. It seems that Senator Pearson's reform motion contained two parts, one of which was not debatable
but one of which *was*. "Jim Allen is a very good practi-
tioner of the rules and he caught a mistake we made,"
sighed a chagrined Walter Mondale.

Several weeks of political stratagems and procedural min-
uets followed, which concluded in a compromise reform:
to cut off a filibuster would require not two-thirds of those
voting but 60 senators no matter *how* many were voting.
Thus, if 100 senators were on the floor, the new rule
made it easier to end a filibuster, but if only 80 senators
were there, the new rule would require a three-quarters
cutoff rather than a two-thirds. It was a step forward—
but how big a step?

One giant loophole in the filibuster reform soon became
apparent—the postcloture filibuster. Once cloture is voted,
debate on all pending amendments is strictly limited to
one hundred hours, or one per senator—*except* that time-
consuming roll-call votes, quorum calls, and other parliamentary procedures do not count against a senator's one
hour. Master parliamentarian James Allen (D.-Ala.) used
these postcloture devices, including forty roll calls, to hold
up a civil rights bill for two weeks in September, 1976.
Senators James Abourezk (D.-S.D.) and Howard Metzenbaum (D.-Ohio) filed 508 amendments to a natural gas
deregulation bill for postcloture resolution in 1977, causing
the first all-night Senate session in thirteen years. Their
effort was snuffed out when an irked Robert C. Byrd got
Vice President Mondale, the presiding officer in the Senate, to agree that Mondale could rule such amendments

dilatory and out-of-order. After the full Senate agreed 79–13, Mondale called on Byrd, who called up one amendment after another, with Mondale ruling each out of order. Abourezk jumped up to appeal Mondale's rulings, screaming about a Senate "steam-roller," but the Vice President refused to recognize him.

Their filibuster had been broken, but in an unpopular fashion. And Byrd's device could only work when the majority leader and Vice President were in full agreement. So early in the 96th Congress Byrd persuaded his colleagues to limit postcloture debate to 100 hours, with any procedural motions or amendments coming out of those 100 hours.

The Rulers of Congress

1. COMMITTEE CHAIRMEN. In the 67th Congress, during the 1920s, Rules Committee Chairman Philip Campbell of Kansas at times refused to report to the House resolutions approved by a majority of his committee. When they protested, he said, "You can go to hell. It makes no difference what a majority of you decide. If it meets with my disapproval, it shall not be done. I am the committee."

Today's autocrats are less blunt than Chairman Campbell, though still very powerful. Congressional reforms in 1946, 1970, and 1973–75 have checked some of the worst excesses: regular meetings are to be held; a majority can force a meeting over a chairman's objection; and a majority of each chamber's Democratic Caucus can eject a committee chairman—an ultimate sanction no chairman can entirely ignore.

Committee chairmen, nevertheless, can exercise their power in an impressive variety of ways. First, with some exceptions, they can set up subcommittees and choose selected cronies to head them. Here seniority is not rigidly observed, as when ex-chairman John McMillan of the House District Committee skipped over senior critics to appoint allies to head up four of his subcommittees. "I don't think any chairman in the Congress who has any sense would appoint subcommittee chairmen who wouldn't back him," he said. Once subcommittee heads are properly picked, a chairman can then refer a bill to whichever subcommittee he thinks will treat it best. Former Ap-

propriations chairman George Mahon once simply transferred environment and consumer matters from one
subcommittee to another dominated by his conservative
allies. More impressive yet was the technique of Senator
Russell Long and Rep. Wilbur Mills in, respectively, the
Senate Finance Committee and House Ways and Means
Committee. By refusing to create any subcommittees (until late 1974), they kept their committees' entire jurisdiction right under their thumbs.

A second tactic is adroit use of committee staff. Chairmen hire and fire committee staff; if the staffers are at
all shrewd, they learn to be loyal to the chairman rather
than to the committee at large. Consequently, the chairman can garner information the others lack, and the rest
of the committee becomes even more dependent on him.

Third, powerful chairmen can offer bargains that regular congressmen can neither match nor resist. To get his
way, the chairman can offer to set up a subcommittee, to
pass a bill with the representative's name on it, to allow
liberal traveling expenses, to sponsor hearings where the
representative can make his name. He can usually decide
when a committee will meet and what it will hold hearings
on. He decides the agenda for meetings, chooses the floor
manager of a bill, and helps the speaker or majority
leader select delegates to the conference committee. With
these and other powers at his disposal, there is little beyond his power—other than acting so openly brazen and
unfair that the Democratic Caucus will remove him, which
is possible though unusual. So it was not entirely hyperbolic when a *New Yorker* cartoon saw one congressman
saying to another on the House steps: "There are days,
Hank, when I don't know who's President, what state I'm
from, or even if I'm a Democrat or a Republican, but
God I still know how to bottle up a piece of legislation
in committee."

Chairmen as a group are quite diverse in terms of personality, intelligence, stature, and drive. But they hold one
thing in common: congressional power. Some who have,
or had, this power follow:

• *Russell Long*—"If you want to know Who Runs Congress, I don't understand why you're talking to me," Senator Jim Abourezk said before he retired in 1979. "You

should go talk to Russell Long. He's the son of a bitch who runs this place." Or as one of Long's staff put it, "Working for Russell Long is like being chained to the baddest gorilla in the jungle; nobody will hurt you, but you sure get bruised."

Long is as comfortable in the Senate as if he grew up there—which he literally did. Both his parents served as senators and at age 60, Long has been in the club half his life. He did not reach the constitutional minimum age to serve until the day after his election in 1948. He ranks fourth in Senate seniority; no Republican has run against him since 1962, when he rolled up 75 percent of the vote.

Unlike his father, Huey, Russell is a corporatist with a cornpone exterior—the Senate's ablest defender of the work ethic and the capitalist system. His views carry weight because of his position as chairman of the powerful Senate Finance Committee since 1966, where he has a stranglehold on most legislative initiatives dealing with taxation, welfare reform, social security, national health insurance, tariffs, and the national debt. He and fellow Democrat Carter quickly became at odds over plugging business tax loopholes ("Entertainment is to the selling business what fertilizer is to the farming business. It increases the yield"), comprehensive welfare reform ("You ought to make work more attractive than welfare"), and energy conservation ("This country must place far more emphasis on the production side").

Long's climb to power was not uninterrupted. In 1965, as a result of skilled floor strategy and advocacy, he became majority whip, the successor to Robert Kerr as "the uncrowned King of the Senate," according to columnist Tom Wicker. His power accumulation continued the next year when he took over the chairmanship of the Senate Finance Committee.

But after the mid-sixties his influence declined. Trying to repeat his success at floor advocacy, he achieved the opposite result in his defense of Senator Thomas Dodd. Oratory became intimidation, and persuasiveness was replaced by stalling tactics, which outraged allies and opponents alike. A widely known though not widely reported drinking problem also damaged his standing in the eyes of colleagues. The Louisiana politician was clearly visible, but the place was the Senate of the United States, not Plaquemines Parish. In 1969, when Ted Kennedy challenged him for the majority whip position, Long went down to a decisive defeat.

Afterward Long solved his drinking problem and began to demonstrate a personal popularity, technical skill with the tax code, oral brilliance, a sense of humor ("Tax reform means, 'Don't tax you, don't tax me, tax that fellow behind the tree' ") and a legendary feel for wheeling and dealing that has made him the undisputed baron of his committee and domain.

"He knows the Senate is full of guys that posture a lot but have something in their closet," one veteran tax lobbyist told *Congressional Quarterly*. "Every one of them has some constituency, some interest he has to deal with. Long knows their interests, he knows their weaknesses, and he exploits them." For example, when he needed votes from Nevada Senator Howard Cannon for another tax "Christmas tree," Long allowed his committee to vote to begin taxing gambling gains as income. As headlines blossomed back home, Cannon had to beg Long's help to defeat the amendment on the Senate floor. The price, as it is so often, was a vote in favor of the amendments Long *really* wanted to keep.

Long has even less subtle means of ensuring loyalty among Finance Committee members, whether liberal or conservative. When liberal Floyd Haskell of Colorado was strapped for cash during a tough reelection campaign in 1978, colleague Long came to the rescue by attending major fundraisers and asking friends to contribute. When Daniel Patrick Moynihan (D.-N.Y.) and Spark Matsunaga (D.-Haw.) joined Finance in 1976, according to a senior Senate Democrat, "Long decided to create two new subcommittees—Moynihan got cities, Matsunaga got a subcommittee on sugar, and Long got their votes for anything he wants." And in the view of political scientist Norman J. Ornstein, "Even people like Gaylord Nelson and Abe Ribicoff love Russell Long. You won't see any revolution coming out of the Finance Committee. He has some personal power over them."

Given all his talent and sensitivity, what has Long accomplished? He and his staff list the public financing of presidential campaigns, the earned-income tax credit for the working poor, blockage of President Nixon's family assistance plan, and Long's amendments that encourage companies to establish worker stock ownership plans. "My father was a *revolutionary*. I'm more of an *evolutionary*," Long explains of his record.

Others are less charitable. Long often loads up tax bills with special measures that benefit particular private interests. In August, 1978, for example, Long was caught holding three amendments to a poppy straw duty bill, each bestowing special benefits on just one entity—Texas International Airlines, E. F. Hutton & Co., and the owner of the New England Patriots. Most members of Finance accept these provisions, since some day they may need the chairman's help on one of their own. But not all senators are sanguine. During consideration of the 1976 "tax reform" bill, Senator Edward Kennedy declared on the Senate floor that "the method by which these special interest provisions make their way into the tax legislation is a scandal and a disgrace." He called them "midnight loopholes tucked in the Finance Committee bill at the end of a long day of executive sessions, with little discussion and virtually no analysis."

President Carter, among many others, privately grumbles about Long's invulnerability and his conflicts of interest. (Long reports a net worth of $2.3 million, nearly half of which consists of royalty interests in oil and gas holdings. Of his favoritism to the oil industry, Long claims that his personal interests overlap with Louisiana's interests—though the state presumably has energy consumers as well as energy producers.) There may be more to Long's sympathy for big oil. Once reporter Patrick Sloyan asked why, given his senatorial power and political invulnerability, he never took on the oil interests. After describing how an oil firm, annoyed over some pro-labor votes, had financed an opponent, Long replied, "You just don't know what they can do to you."

● *Henry (Scoop) Jackson*—As lackluster and unsuccessful as his 1972 and 1976 presidential campaigns were, Senator Jackson (D.-Wash.) has nevertheless excelled at operating the levers of power on Capitol Hill. In the same way that Russell Long plays a pivotal role in all legislation dealing with tax expenditures and receipts, Henry Jackson—in Congress since 1940, in the Senate since

1952—has developed great influence on legislation dealing with natural resources and national defense. Deploying wide contacts, committee chairmanships, and developed expertise, in the Senate he is Mr. Energy, as well as the thorn in the side of détente and SALT.

Jackson chairs a major committee and two subcommittees. As chairman of the Energy and Natural Resources subcommittee, Jackson proved the central figure in the battle to save key elements of President Carter's national energy plan. Jackson worked assiduously for months to fashion a conference committee compromise on phased natural gas deregulation, while the Democratic administration waited in helpless anxiety. As chairman of the Arms Control subcommittee of the Armed Services Committee, he has at times entered into SALT and other strategic arms negotiations with the force of a sovereign third power. As the second-ranking Democrat on Armed Services, he is the heir apparent to chairman John Stennis, who is expected to retire shortly. The senator from Washington is also chairman of the Government Affairs Committee's subcommittee on Permanent Investigations, which he has at times made a personal forum to castigate oil company executives for exploiting the oil crisis and to criticize the conduct of American foreign policy. Many, however, believe these hearings exhibit more political blister and bluster than investigative substance. With some exceptions, overall he has built up a record as a domestic liberal (he was one of the first to oppose Senator Joseph McCarthy) and international hawk (he was a strong proponent of the Vietnam War).

His reputation as a genuine, tough, dawn-to-midnight, and bland politician has followed him since childhood. At his high school commencement he lectured his classmates about the evils of disrespect for the law. As a city prosecutor in 1938 he became known as the persistently moralistic D.A. who ran the gamblers, prostitutes, and bootleggers out of town. With this reputation, "Soda Pop" Jackson, as he was then called, easily won election to a vacant seat in the U.S. House. "He's got strong views he'll fight for, but he retains somehow his small town manner after all these years. Long is the ultimate manipulative game player, but Jackson does not come off at all like that," says Fred Wertheimer, senior vice president of

Common Cause. Yet when Jackson's energy conference committee discussed trade and accommodations on the natural gas issue in Carter's energy package, most of the sessions were closed. One day David Cohen, president of Common Cause, reminded Jackson that he himself was an early advocate of open conferences. Jackson blew up and shouted at Cohen that he didn't need Common Cause or anyone else to lecture him on how to set moral standards in the Congress.

Among his major legislative accomplishments, Jackson counts the National Environmental Policy Act, which created a comprehensive federal policy on environmental protection that required environmental impact statements for the first time, and an amendment to an arms control bill that directs that future agreements with the Soviets not leave the U.S. with inferior numbers of weapons. He is also a diehard supporter of Israel in the Senate and has led a controversial fight to free Soviet Jews. In 1974, he insisted that the U.S.-Soviet trade agreement be amended so that Russia would have to liberalize its emigration laws to obtain U.S. trade concessions.

When it comes to arms control issues, Jackson is even more confident and dominating. According to a Senate staffer on Jackson's Arms Control subcommittee, "while he's very relaxed, open to suggestions, congenial and easygoing on energy. when it comes to SALT he turns into a hardnosed advocate, closed to new ideas, abrasive, defensive, aggressive . . ." Unlike all but a few other senators, he has taken the time to master the technical details of our major weapons systems and strategic balance. But as another high Senate staff aide involved with SALT said, "He is very selective in the facts he chooses to marshal. It's not a balanced judgment that he reaches. One has to be steeped in the lexicon of military jargon to understand just how slanted and selective his explanations are."

• *Edward M. Kennedy*—At first he was merely a dynast, the legatee of a famous name. His 1962 senatorial opponent said he would never even have been in the race were his last name not Kennedy—and surely this was true. But the people of Massachusetts apparently didn't mind, and gave him brother Jack's old seat when he was 30 years old, the constitutional minimum.

In return, he has proved to be more than a nostalgic name. Franklin D. Roosevelt, Jr., after all, probably had a more illustrious birth certificate, yet never managed to parlay it into more than a few undistinguished terms in the House. Yet even as Ted Kennedy began h¡s chairmanship of the Senate Judiciary Committee in 1979—predecessor James Eastland had wielded the gavel since 1957 —he was already the most forceful if not the most influential progressive U.S. senator of the past quarter century.

Several interacting ingredients enabled him to achieve this stature. First, his personal mix of shrewdness, toughness, plodding hard work, and Irish charm bring to mind Justice Oliver Wendell Holmes, Jr.'s comment that the two Roosevelt presidents had been so accomplished less because of their brilliance than their temperament. Second, Kennedy's eloquence in public addresses gives him wide coverage and exposure. In private conversations he talks in fits and spurts, his sentences often jumbled and incomplete. Yet his eulogy to Robert Kennedy, Jr., his address to the Democratic midterm convention in 1978—when he thundered that "sometimes a party must sail against the wind"—are not easily forgotten. Third, a solid political base in Massachusetts frees him—as Louisiana frees Long—to say what he thinks and do what he says. He can favor compulsory school busing for racial reasons and a woman's right to abortion, without fear of being driven from office.

Finally, there is his staff and "inevitability." He gathers together a very aggressive and talented staff, who are highly motivated ("I think every day, 'What is a coming issue we should be working on?' " says one) and with whom he has individual daily contact. So the staff work for Kennedy and not for other staff—which enhances their impact and credibility with the outside world. And of course, there is the unavoidable sense that this senator is a future president. Such perceptions can become self-fulfilling, as colleague Edmund Muskie explains: "He knows that power is constantly enhanced when people perceive that you could be President someday; it gives you the clout to get the things done you really want done in the Senate."

The result of this confluence of skill, pedigree, and lady luck is that, at 47, Senator Ted Kennedy has become, in columnist George Will's phrase, the Democrats' "heavy hitter." Despite the Chappaquiddick incident, which would have ruined most public figures, and despite a liberalism that is supposedly out of step with the times, he is a major voice in the Senate, and beyond.

This notoriety creates a predictable amount of envy and resentment in an institution of ample egos. As one former Senate staff aid put it, "What is amazing is how much he does even though most of them up there hate him." What Kennedy does is to take the lead on an unusually broad range of issues. He has recently been a leading sponsor of national health insurance, airline and trucking deregulation, tax reform, "public participation" funding, congressional representation for the District of Columbia, antimerger legislation, a new federal criminal code, new FBI and CIA charters, a drug reform act, and the rejection of same-state senatorial vetoes on federal judges—not to mention legislation on small claims courts, consumer class actions, and hospital cost containment.

Kennedy's chairmanship of Senate Judiciary should provide him a new bully pulpit from which to advocate his already lengthy agenda. The initial evidence was that he would be a strong chairman. On taking over he replaced Eastland's seventeen-person staff with forty of his own, reduced the subcommittees from ten to five in number, began holding much key legislation at the committee rather than the subcommittee level, and laid claim to an antitrust part of the trucking deregulation issue that infuriated Senate Commerce Chairman Howard Cannon, who successfully claimed the subject should be in his committee.

He also managed to persuade the Democratic leadership to replace three former conservative Democratic senators on Judiciary (Eastland, Allen, McClellan) with three moderates/liberals (Baucus, Heflin, Leahy), thereby giving Kennedy a working majority on his panel. "It was only an 'organization meeting,'" wrote the *Washington Post* of Judiciary's first get-together in 1979, "but a large Senate hearing room was filled with spectators and reporters anxious to watch the first act of what promises to be a popular show this season."

● *Jamie Whitten*—Secretaries of agriculture may come and go, but Jamie Whitten—often called the "permanent secretary of agriculture" and the most senior member of the House—seems to go on forever. First sent to Congress from rural Mississippi in a special election one month before Pearl Harbor, Whitten has been firmly ensconced since 1949 as chairman of the Appropriations subcommittee on Agriculture and Related Agencies, where he exercises line-by-line control over the $18 billion Agriculture budget. He does his homework, knows more about agriculture appropriations than anyone else in Congress, and does not let anything happen that he does not want to happen. An official of the Agriculture Department (USDA) commented:

> Whitten runs the subcommittee the same way he ran the prosecutor's office down home. He conducts hearings by himself, selects the witnesses, asks all of the questions, and generally runs the show . . . The other members don't have the knowledge to go into the depth that he does—but even if they did, they wouldn't have a chance.

On the one hand, Whitten remains a Southern gentleman. One former USDA official who was often called to testify before the committee recalls a particularly harsh interrogation by Chairman Whitten. But on leaving his chair, Whitten moseyed over to the witness and asked him out for a drink.

On the other hand, his velvet glove sheaths an iron fist. As James Risser reported in the *Des Moines Register:*

> Agency officials who come before the rural Mississippian do so in nervousness and fear. Whitten is cordial to agency heads who administer programs he likes. Toward those whose programs he disapproves of, Whitten is altogether different. He badgers the witnesses, insults their programs, and accuses them of working unjustified financial requests.

In the 1960s, for example, Howard Tolley was the head of the Bureau of Agricultural Economics. Engaged in a study on the future of cotton in the South, Tolley decided to include Whitten's northern Mississippi district in the report. The study recommended that cotton produc-

tion be cut back to increase prices and end sharecropping.
The chairman was not pleased. He held up the entire
USDA appropriations bill until Tolley was fired and the
study dropped. Then there was Whitten's run-in with Robert Lewis, the head of Agriculture's Rural Development
Program. In the mid-1960s, Whitten wanted to end the
program to expand industry in and diversify the econo-
mies of rural areas, and Secretary Orville Freeman didn't.
The chairman cut out funds for the program. Freeman
and Lewis then shifted a million dollars from each of
several other agencies with Agriculture to the Rural Development Program. Not to be outflanked, Whitten then
cut the funds of each of these agencies by the amount
they gave Rural Development, and held up the entire
Agriculture appropriation until the program was terminated and Lewis fired.

Over the years Whitten has also become a master of
the House rules, and often resorts to procedural sleight-
of-hand—especially when he does not have the votes to
win on the merits of the issue. One of his favorite tools,
a "line item" added to a lengthy bill or report, allows him
to slash funding for health-safety, environmental, and consumer legislation with the stroke of a pen. In 1978, for
example, the chairman attempted to delete a consumer
program called Public Participation—which would reimburse citizens who lack the resources to participate in
Food and Drug Administration proceedings—by adding to
a 123-page staff report a single line prohibiting the program. When half of the subcommittee members said that
they would vote to remove the line item, Whitten relented.
Whitten also lost when a House-Senate conference agreed
to keep a similar $200,000 USDA appropriation—which
did not stop Whitten from calling another conference
committee meeting, giving the minimum notice of only
one hour, to attempt unsuccessfully to get the conferees to
reconsider their action.

Whitten's power, especially his ability to give or deny
pork for representatives' districts, has largely deterred major challenges to his subcommittee chairmanship. But in
1975, when other senior chairs were being challenged,
some liberal junior members of the Democratic Caucus
moved to depose him. The threat was serious enough
that Appropriations Committee Chairman George Mahon

(D.-Tex.) pressured Whitten to give up his subcommittee's jurisdiction over certain consumer and environmental programs and agencies in order to save his position.

When Mahon retired in 1978, Whitten was the senior member of the Appropriations Committee and therefore the first in line to become chairman. Again he was challenged by liberal critics, such as Rep. Toby Moffett (D.-Conn.), who pointed out that the Mississippian voted more often with the Republicans than with the Democrats. His average support for Democratic programs was 33.4% over ten years, a level of Democratic loyalty worse than all other chairmen save one (Rep. Ray Roberts, of Veterans Affairs). The House Caucus eventually supported him for the pivotal post of Appropriations chairman by a vote of 157–88, but not until Speaker O'Neill had assured critics that Whitten would hear and respect all points of view. One of the last Southern gentlemen-autocrats had taken over one of the major House committees, assuring "Secretary of Agriculture" Whitten a "cabinet" seat that would no doubt survive many presidents.

• *Wilbur Mills*—He is today just a Washington tax lawyer, best known for his cameo appearance in the Tidal Basin with Fanne Fox. But it should not be forgotten that for a decade Wilbur Mills of Arkansas was the most powerful man in the House of Representatives, or perhaps the Congress. While the speaker and the majority leader watched helplessly, Mills used his power as chairman of Ways and Means Committee to control Democratic Committee assignments and the flow of tax and revenue legislation.

As chairman of Ways and Means since 1958, Mills's jurisdiction spanned Medicare, national health insurance, and welfare, as well as taxes, revenue sharing, tariffs, and trade quotas. He used his power over tariff and tax legislation to perform such feats as persuading Japanese textile manufacturers to "voluntarily" restrict their U.S. exports, and unceremoniously quashed President Johnson's proposed tax increase at a closed committee session in 1967. If foreign governments and presidents had good reason to court Mills, so did American businessmen, for he held the key to their special tax breaks.

Mills set himself apart from his House colleagues by his

brilliant understanding of the complicated tax code, sheer endurance, and an innate skill at Machiavellian maneuvering. When he became chairman he abolished all subcommittees and concentrated all the power in his own hands. He kept junior committee members starved for information. They sometimes learned about hearings by reading about them in the morning newspaper. Mills prohibited committee members from bringing their professional staff into secret sessions, although he occasionally let dozens of Treasury Department staff sit in and participate. One legislator was shocked to discover that his congressionally passed amendment to a Social Security bill was not in the law signed by the president; it seems that Mills quietly excised it en route to the White House.

In theory, the rest of the House could repudiate Mills's creations on the floor. But because of the closed rule on any tax matter reported out of Ways and Means, other members could not amend a tax bill on the floor; they could only vote it up or down. And the latter proved hard to do on complex tax issues where Mills had apparent committee unanimity behind him.

When Mills was bitten by the presidential bug in the fall of 1971, many of his House colleagues were puzzled. Rep. Sam Gibbons of Florida asked him, "Wilbur, why do you want to run for president and give up your grip on the country?" Between 1972 and 1974, however, Mills faltered somewhat. His presidential campaign flopped, and worse, it was tarnished by at least $145,000 of illegal contributions from a milk co-op and several major companies. Still, other congressmen and the national press, perhaps out of habit, continued to drape him with superlatives. Mills was widely considered to be powerful, shrewd, invincible, a straight arrow and a tireless worker.

However, after the early morning of October 7, 1974, Wilbur Mills would never enjoy such kudos again. A usually blasé Washington gaped in astonishment as it read how a local 38-year-old stripper, Annabel Battistella—a.k.a. Fanne Fox, the Argentine Firecracker—had been pulled out of the Tidal Basin by police after she jumped from a Lincoln Continental, one belonging to and containing the House Ways and Means Committee chairman, intoxicated and bleeding from the nose.

Following denials issued from seclusion, Mills three days

later admitted his role in the escapade, and vowed to campaign hard for reelection. The Arkansas voters forgave Mills's antic behavior and reelected him in a landslide. Even the House might have eventually forgotten this brouhaha except that shortly afterward, with photographers shooting away, Mills inexplicably cavorted on a Boston stage with his stripper friend. Would this appearance hurt him? Mills was asked. "This won't ruin me," he said; "nothing can ruin me."

This proved to be hubris before the fall. Immediately after the Boston incident, Mills entered the National Naval Medical Center—his admission of alcoholism would come later—and the House Democratic Caucus, coincidentally meeting at this time, agreed that Mills would not be reelected Ways and Means chairman. "He was one of the greatest congressmen of my generation," said a gracious Carl Albert, "but he is a sick man."

These and other chairmen obviously wield substantial power, though not quite so autocratically as they once did, due to events that came to a head in 1974. The reforms erupting at the start of the 94th Congress led even such veteran observers as Eric Sevareid and the *New York Times* to say, respectively, things like "a minor miracle" and "the House will never be the same again." Yet what happened was not a one-month phenomenon following an unprecedented election, but the culmination of more than a decade of a committee reform drive that began with a ripple in the late fifties and ended with near tidal force in the seventies.

Ever since at least the 1920s, the House had been ruled by committee chairmen who, selected by the divine hand of seniority, were accountable only to their longevity. After the Democratic landslide of 1958, leading Democrats were dismayed to discover that they still couldn't implement their program because entrenched and conservative committee chairmen were not responsive to the electorate. This conundrum gave rise to the Democratic Study Group (DSG), composed of reform-minded congressmen, founded by then Representative Eugene McCarthy. Their zeal, however, noticeably abated in 1961. "With a Democrat in the White House, the need for change around here was not as apparent," says Richard Conlon, now the DSG staff director. "This was especially true for LBJ, who could work magic with his old buddies, the southern committee chairmen." Or, the president proposes and Congress disposes.

Yet, President John Kennedy had to team with Speaker Sam Rayburn in 1961 to compel the obstructionist House Rules Committee—a Cerberus at the gate of reform legislation—to add three members to give the administration a favorable majority. The sixties also heard from Rep. Richard Bolling, a cerebral member who exposed the House's ineffective and authoritarian ways in two books, *House Out of Order* and *Power in the House*. "It is here [in the House Caucus] that methods should be adopted," urged the prescient Bolling, "to assure that reform Democrats rather than Tory Southern Democrats control the essential committees."

The concern of Bolling and the DSG founders came into full play with the election of Richard Nixon in 1968. No longer could congressional liberals lean on their president for succor and inspiration. They were on their own . . . and under the thumb of the same old committee chairmen. By 1969, according to a DSG study, one-third of the Democratic committee and subcommittee chairmen were voting against Democratic programs *more* frequently than the average Republican! Alarmed, the DSG began to mobilize. Unable to do anything about the sitting president—impeachment, of course, was merely a historical curiosity in 1969—the DSG turned its attention to its own chamber —and to the largely moribund House Democratic Caucus as a forum to educate the members about seniority and to push ultimately for elective chairmanships. Their strategy was based on an irrefutable fact: though reformers did not have a majority of the House, they did have a majority of the House Democratic Caucus; and if that body could guide committees and committee selection, it could break the grip of the Southern chairmen.

Even this proposal met resistance from traditionalists. "When O'Hara would go around and tell colleagues that the Caucus had to be the instrument of party policy and power," recalls former UAW lobbyist Dick Warden, "people would just stare at him and ask what he was talking about." DSG leaders nevertheless pushed ahead and asked Speaker McCormack to hold monthly caucus meetings.

The kindly Boston octogenarian, perhaps seeing what was to come, initially refused, until then majority leader Carl Albert changed his mind. "It was to become a Greek horse," wrote reporter Mary Russell, "inside the walls of Troy."

The caucus began reforming things, slowly at first. In 1971, it decreed that members could not chair more than one subcommittee, a move that made some congressional elders grumble but opened up influential spots to more members. The caucus also, in a breach of the pure seniority system, permitted a vote on any committee chairman if ten caucus members publicly asked for it.

This was progress, but at best a half-step. House decorum being what it is, few thought it likely that members would publicly announce the need to challenge a particular chairman.

1973 saw the great leap forward as the caucus approved of an automatic vote for each chairman. In fact, Government Operations Chairman Chet Holifield was weakly challenged that year by a group of critics led by Rep. Ben Rosenthal. Still, few focused on the potential of this development, thinking approval of the chairmen would be pro forma.

1974 did not promise to be the year the reformers had long been waiting for. Rep. Richard Bolling had chaired a special committee empaneled by Speaker Albert to study the unwieldy committee structure in the House. Bolling's proposals managed to irritate members of every House constituency; he urged that a too-encompassing Ways and Means Committee give up some of its jurisdiction and expand its membership, which got many conservatives upset; he urged that the Education and Labor Committee be split up, which got many liberals angry; and he proposed a new energy committee to consolidate consideration of energy matters, which environmentalists feared would be stacked with energy industry apologists. The Bolling program was rejected 203–165 in October, 1974, because, said Rep. Joe Waggoner (D.-La.), "it was too drastic; it went too far too quick."

Yet six weeks later a confluence of events launched the House on its most drastic and far-reaching reform in sixty years. The preeminent event was the election of 75 freshman Democrats who would comprise over one-fourth of the 291-member Democratic Caucus. Younger and more liberal than their colleagues, neither wedded nor indebted to the *status quo ante,* largely from swing districts where they had run anti-Watergate reform campaigns, this freshman bloc would become, in the only partly hyperbolic phrase of the *Washington Post,* "the Red Guard of the revolution."

The freshmen provided the DSG reformers with the sine qua non of their strategy: the votes to control the caucus. With the election in December, 1974, of former DSG head Philip Burton as caucus chairman—the canny Burton being the most liberal member of the House leadership within memory—the caucus completed its four-year transfiguration from cub to lion.

Its work would be aided by three developments. First, lobbying groups like the UAW, Americans for Democratic Action, Common Cause, and Public Citizen's Congress Watch had been pressuring Congress to alter its antiquated ways. Indeed, Common Cause, four days before the crucial vote on committee chairmen in mid-January, 1975, sent every member a thirty-one-page "report card" documenting the abuses of several chairmen, a report providing crucial information for undecided members. Second, of course, there were the public antics of the usually staid Wilbur Mills.

Finally, the freshmen developed an unprecedented maneuver. After the House Caucus had voted one morning in December to elect all Appropriations subcommittee chairmen, the freshmen recessed for a luncheon meeting. Suddenly Appropriations Chairman George Mahon appeared and lectured the uneasy though respectful newcomers on how they had made a dreadful mistake in discriminating against Appropriations subcommittee chairmen. Which gave Connecticut Democrat Toby Moffett an idea. "This shows why it's a mistake to listen to chairmen on *their* terms," he told his peers after Mahon had departed. "Let's invoke them on *our* terms." With Floyd Fithian (D.-Ind.) taking the lead in developing the concept, the freshmen began organizing sessions where chairmen would come to them to be questioned. One veteran television newscaster ridiculed their audacity. "You've got to be kidding. They'll never come."

But they did, in a congressional rendition of the mountain coming to Muhammad. On the mornings of January 9, 10, 11, and 13 a total of fifteen chairmen trekked into H-140, the august Appropriations Committee chamber in the Capitol Building, to answer a series of prepared questions. Armed Services Chairman Hébert for example, was asked, "Would you be willing to make public the budget of the CIA?" and "Will you support keeping open all bill-drafting sessions of the Armed Services Committee?" Some of the committee chieftains were contrite, like Banking Chairman Wright Patman, who even brought along, and read in its entirety, a prepared fourteen-page statement lauding reforms and his committee; some inflicted wounds on themselves like Otto Passman, chairman of a Foreign Relations subcommittee of the Appropriations Committee, who was asked why we gave foreign aid money to countries that tortured prisoners, and who replied, "Well, there are troublemakers in every country." Others were more testy, like Chairman Hébert. Yet all were treated civilly and with deference. "We gave each one of them a standing ovation at the end," said Moffett.

With the applause still ringing in the chairmen's ears, the freshmen and the caucus began making their moves on January 15 against the more oppressive and unpopular chairmen:

• The imperial habits of F. Edward Hébert, chairman of the House Armed Services Committee since 1970, finally caught up with him. He had assigned committee members to subcommittees without obtaining their preferences; he would not refer bills to their relevant subcommittees if they were opposed by the Pentagon; he refused to hold hearings on controversial administration policies he supported, like the Cambodian bombing and military aid to South Vietnam. Nor did he impress the freshmen in their meeting. Hébert announced that, rather than withdraw from Vietnam, we should have sent *more* men and weapons in order to win the war. Nor did it help his cause when he referred to the freshman members as boys and girls. He was booted out of his chairmanship 152–133.

• What caught up with Wright Patman was not imperialism but age. By 1975, the Texas populist was 81, had been in the House forty-six years and had been chairman of the House Banking Committee for twelve years.

Apparently, in the minds of a majority of the caucus, this unblinkable fact mattered more than his widely admired record.

Patman's first act as a representative in 1929 was to urge the impeachment of Treasury Secretary Andrew Mellon for conducting outside business while in office. For the next four and a half decades he fought high interest rates and the banks. Patman was instrumental in passage of the 1969 one-bank holding company act and in derailing the proposed Penn-Central bailout loan in 1970. In 1972, he successfully challenged Wilbur Mills's tax giveaways known as "member bills"; and he attempted to issue subpoenas to investigate Watergate *before* the 1972 election, but was overruled by his committee. "Patman was the only man in Congress since Estes Kefauver to stand up to corporate power," James Ridgeway and Alexander Cockburn would write. But critics could acknowledge all that and still argue that he was out-of-touch, sometimes rambling, and incapable of effectively running his committee. Also Henry Reuss—intellectual, articulate, and "only" 63—presented himself as an attractive alternative. Patman went down 152–117.

• Seventy-four-year-old William Poage of Texas marched to a different drummer from most of his Democratic colleagues. *Congressional Quarterly* voting studies showed that between 1968 and 1974, Poage voted with the Republican majority and against the Democratic majority fully 54 percent of the time. His penchant for ultra-conservative candor could also be discouraging. He once intoned, "I am in favor of establishing a university of thugs, mugs, and other hippies in the southwest corner of the walls of Huntsville"—which is the Texas state prison. During a hearing on food stamps, Poage asked an Urban Coalition witness why he was "so concerned in maintaining a bunch of drones. You know what happens in the beehive? They kill those drones. That is what happens in most primitive societies. Maybe we have just gotten too far away from the situation of primitive man." For such wisdom Poage narrowly lost his House Agriculture chairmanship, 144–141, to Rep. Tom Foley (D.-Wash.).

As the headlines reflected in early 1975, it was the House which did the most reforming, perhaps because

it had the most to do. Still, not to be entirely outdone,
the Senate stuck a toe in the Watergate-reform current.
The sixty-one-member Senate Democratic Caucus routinely
approved all chairmen by a voice vote. But the caucus
agreed that whenever 20 percent or more of them, at the
beginning of a Congress, indicated disapproval of a committee chairman by secret ballot, they would get an up
or down vote on him within forty-eight hours. The key
was the secret ballot. Previously any senator could
publicly ask for a secret ballot of any chairman, but
none ever had. "There was a fear of retribution," confided
one senator. This change situated the Senate where the
House was in 1973: there was the potential to vote out
abusive chairmen whenever the Democratic Caucus got
the votes and guts to do so.

Mills. Hébert. Patman. Poage. The Senate rules changes
on electing chairs. Since these developments in late 1974,
no senior member of a major committee in either chamber
has been denied the chairmanship though a handful of
subcommittee chairs have not gone to the longest sitting
member. At the same time, no chairman can easily in-
dulge in old-fashioned arrogance without to some extent
looking over his shoulder.

2. THE LEADERSHIP. The "leadership" usually means
the speaker of the House, the House majority and minority leaders, and the Senate majority and minority
leaders. Yet the "leadership" has not always led. Jack
Anderson wrote of John McCormack's speakership: "Under 'Old Jawn,' the office of speaker, formerly the second
most powerful post in the country, has become Buckingham Palace—honored and respected, but more ceremonial than functional." And under Speaker Carl Albert,
as well as Senate Majority Leader Mike Mansfield, this
trend continued. Leaders became more buffers than
bosses, elevated more because of inoffensiveness and general popularity than because of leadership abilities. (Majority Leader Robert Byrd and Speaker Tip O'Neill are less
passive than their predecessors, though still more likely
to mirror their chamber's consensus than to shape it.)
One representative accurately said of congressional leadership, "They want someone who will do them favors
and speak at their fundraisers and not make too many

demands of them." A House aide added in 1978: "They couldn't stand a Sam Rayburn again but they do want a certain amount of leadership without having bills shoved down their throat."

It was not always so. Henry Clay, a brilliant thinker and powerful orator, entered the House in 1811, at age 34, and was promptly selected speaker. His power and charm were so abundant that soon he and his "War Hawks" had actively seized control of their chamber and were pressuring the hesitant President James Madison into declaring war on the British. One leading student of the speakership, Mary P. Follet, has concluded that Clay was "the most powerful man in the nation from 1811 to 1825."

Clay deposited some of his power and prestige in the office. Few of his successors have equaled his eminence, but others have exploited the job's potential power. James Blaine, chosen in 1869, "Czar" Thomas Reed in 1890 ("The only way to do business inside the rules is to suspend the rules"), and Joe Cannon in 1903 were some of the strongest. Cannon, for example, decided whether a congressman could speak after first finding out what he intended to say. Eventually this was too much for the rest of the House, and rebellious members stripped Cannon of many of his powers in 1910. The main blow was removing the decisive power of appointing committee chairmen. Since then, speakers have had a harder time dominating, but one managed: Sam Rayburn. His central ability was that of forming coalitions by dint of his personal persuasiveness—a talent equaled in modern times only by his Texas protégé, Senate Majority Leader Lyndon Johnson.

In the Senate, strong leaders have been even rarer than in the House. Woodrow Wilson observed in the late 1880s that a senator, "however eminent, is never more than *a* senator. No one is *the* senator. No one may speak for his party as well as for himself; no one exercises the special trust of acknowledged leadership. The Senate is merely a body of individual critics." Even after the Senate created floor leaders in the 1920s, Wilson's observation remained largely true.

A number of key prerogatives have been retained by the top leadership positions in each house. The speaker presides over his chamber and has the right of recognition, decides points of order, refers bills to appropriate committees, appoints half of the Democratic Steering Committee, can create ad hoc committees to handle significant bills, and selects House members of conference committees. When he is not presiding, the Senate majority leader can be recognized by the chair before all other senators, participates in handing out committee assignments, and can help determine which senators will get money (and how much) from the Senate Democratic campaign committees. As chairman of the Democratic Policy Committee and the Democratic Steering Committee, the majority leader is well placed to shape his party's and the Senate's legislative program.

Institutional arrangements, however, often have less to say about the power of these offices than does the personality of the man in the office. Sam Rayburn and John McCormack held the same job, with the same strings to pull and hurdles to overcome. But Rayburn used it as a base for single-minded domination of the House, while McCormack listlessly observed events. A look at the present congressional leaders shows their strengths and weaknesses:

• *Thomas P. ("Tip") O'Neill*—Second in line to the presidency as the speaker of the House, often called "Jimmy Carter's best friend in Washington" for his nearly paternalistic counseling of the novice president, the gregarious and genial Tip O'Neill is more at home playing poker and drinking whiskey in East Boston than he is dropping names and gossip at Georgetown dinner parties. His father was a Cambridge city councilor and later the city superintendent of sewers. So for the young Tip (named after a baseball player who consistently foul-tipped off strikes until he walked), politics was as much inherited as acquired. O'Neill ran a losing campaign for the Cambridge Council in 1932, while still in college. Since then his career has been a remarkably unopposed rise to the top.

The next year he won a seat in the State House and became the youngest speaker in Massachusetts history eight terms later, in 1949. As state speaker he demanded absolute party loyalty. On one occasion he locked the chamber doors to prevent a maverick Democrat from abstaining on a key vote.

His political stock rose further when he succeeded John F. Kennedy as the representative from Massachusetts's Eighth Congressional District. He became a protégé of Majority Leader John W. McCormack of South Boston, who urged O'Neill's appointment to the powerful Rules Committee early during his second term. Though it was unusual for a representative to straddle the leadership ladder so early in his career, O'Neill's position was strengthened when his mentor McCormack ascended to the speakership and his friend Kennedy occupied the White House.

In 1971, O'Neill supported Louisiana's Hale Boggs for majority leader over liberal Morris K. Udall. Boggs rewarded O'Neill with the whip position, and after Boggs disappeared in a plane crash over Alaska in 1972, O'Neill announced his intention to seek the leadership. His only opponent withdrew, saying O'Neill did not have "an enemy in the House."

"I intend to be a strong Speaker," O'Neill declared shortly after his Democratic colleagues promoted him by acclamation to succeed the weak and cautious Carl Albert of Oklahoma, who retired in 1977. Like his predecessors, O'Neill presides over the House, controls the whip system, decides when legislation will be considered, and serves as spokesman for the House and for his party. He largely controls the steering and policy committee, which names new members to committees. And he maintains some leverage by his power to bestow or deny appointments to leadership committees, prestigious special committees and international delegations, or good space assignments in House office buildings.

O'Neill was able to demonstrate the strength of his leadership at the start of the 95th Congress by winning passage of a tough new ethics code and most of President Carter's proposed energy package. "Davey," O'Neill told Rep. David R. Obey (D.-Wis.), chairman of the Commission on Administrative Review that was responsible for shaping the new ethics code in 1976, "if you're going to write one, go all the way. I want a damn good code I can be

proud of. You produce it and I'll back it up." He kept
his word and although even many liberal members
were upset with the provision limiting outside earned income to 15 percent of their salary, the new speaker tied
the income ceiling to a pending congressional pay hike
as if it were a moral issue. (See chapter 6.) To get the
energy package passed he established a special rule governing floor debate that effectively frustrated technical
amendments from crippling the bill. The *Washington Post*
called it a "legislative miracle."

Yet O'Neill's record is marred by some surprising defeats. He supported the scandal-tarred Robert Sikes for
chairmanship of an appropriations subcommittee and
lost by 2 to 1 on the House floor. His efforts on behalf of
legislation for a common situs picketing bill, a consumer
advocacy agency, cargo preference, and public funding
for House races failed to persuade a majority of his
colleagues. In 1978, he watched with rage as Ways and
Means Democrats gutted Carter's tax reform bill.

Whatever the cause—the devolution of the powers of
the speaker, an antipathy to Rayburn-like arm twisting,
the decline of Democratic party funds for candidates,
the noncoattails of President Carter—this lack of party
cohesion in the face of Republican solidarity has con-
sternated Tip O'Neill. "What the hell is going on here?"
he bellowed when he was told that up to 100 Democrats
would be voting against a consumer protection agency
bill. "They're all independent now. Voters aren't as loyal
to the Democratic or Republican ticket anymore. People
are not awed by the president or me either."

Some members, however, are quicker to blame a lack
of "philosophical commitment" and political judgment
in the leadership itself. Rep. Phil Burton, whose narrow
defeat for the majority leadership in 1976 was allegedly
aided by O'Neill, said: "There has been no effective
orchestrating by the leadership to achieve progressive
ends. Sequence and timing are of fundamental importance
in presenting legislation. I don't see Tip as having a sense
for this timing." Other writers complain about what
friends call his sense of loyalty; others, about his bad
judgment of character. He supported Sikes; he demanded
immunity from prosecution for Richard Nixon both before

and after his resignation; and in 1978, he nearly severed diplomatic relations with the White House after his friend, Robert Griffin, was dumped as deputy administrator of the corruption-riddled General Services Administration. The speaker's greatest embarrassment, however, was the disclosure that he attended a birthday party given in his honor by South Korean rice dealer and political operative Tongsun Park. O'Neill insists he barely knew Park and only attended the Georgetown Club extravaganza at the insistence of his colleagues and because the vice president and a number of Nixon cabinet staff members were expected to attend.

For the Congress and the general public, though, O'Neill's most important feature appears to be that he is the one Northerner, the one old-fashioned New Deal liberal who has been in a position of real influence in domestic affairs in recent years. Although he was initially an adamant supporter of America's role in Vietnam, O'Neill broke with his friend Lyndon Johnson on the war issue in 1967, becoming the first congressional leader of either party to do so. He opposed the SST and quietly supports busing. In 1971, he pushed an amendment that forces roll-call votes, not just unrecorded voice votes ("teller votes") on most key amendments; he whisked labor law reform through the House and worked hard to switch the needed votes on the consumer advocacy bill. He looks like an old pol. He *is* an old pol—but one who has not shed a progressive philosophy he has carried with him for forty-five years in public office.

• *James C. Wright, Jr.*—He is a twelve-term incumbent who spent 1978 polling, shaking hands, doing favors, fundraising for colleagues, giving out $300,000 from his own PAC to Democratic candidates for the House, and speechmaking in over 100 districts from coast to coast. No, he's not running for president. Jim Wright of Texas spent his first two years as House majority leader in a precarious position—for instead of standing firmly on the leadership ladder looking up, he had to keep looking over his shoulder. He seemed constantly worried that an opponent like California's Rep. Phillip Burton might have the votes to replace him as leader; or, failing that, to best him for the speakership when O'Neill retires.

If Wright is vulnerable, it's because his victory in the December, 1976, Democratic Caucus elections was so narrow and unexpected. Democratic Caucus Chairman Phillip Burton was the clear front runner (he was lining up commitments for two years before the vote), with liberal elder statesman Richard Bolling of Missouri solidly in second. Yet Wright and a few friends felt that if the liberal vote split enough for him to survive two ballots, he just might exploit the issues of Burton's hard-to-get-along-with reputation and Bolling's age. The strategy worked. After Wright squeezed past Bolling in the second round by two votes, Rep. Richard C. White of Texas emerged from ballot counting in the speaker's lobby holding one finger high. The final count: Wright, 148, Burton, 147.*

Wright is often described as a pragmatic conservative. Yet, while demonstrating a conservatism that floats well in his district, he can adeptly maneuver to port or starboard to ride out a political storm. He began his career as a liberal Texas state legislator in 1948, calling for abolition of the infamous poll tax and supporting an antilynching bill, integration of the University of Texas law school, and a strict law requiring lobbyists to register. Then he lost his seat, turned conservative, then more moderate when he needed labor support for a Senate race, and then finally in 1976 he veered left again. During the 94th Congress he voted with the conservative coalition of Republicans and southern Democrats 59 percent of the time. After he became majority leader, however, he voted with a majority of Democrats against a majority of Republicans 77 percent of the time in 1978.

Wright entered Congress in 1955 and landed immediately on the Public Works Committee. His twenty-two years on the committee have been the cornerstone of his legislative career. From the beginning he championed the

---

*With a one-vote margin, any of 148 could be argued to have made the difference. Much attention, however, focused on the vote of freshman Barbara Mikulski of Maryland, a liberal activist who demonstrated how so often in politics personal relations count more than ideology. "Congressman Wright was very helpful to me last summer in breaking the ice with the Baltimore business community," she said after the vote. ". . . they felt I was a left-wing bomb thrower because of my populist background. And I was there when Wright needed me."

kinds of pork-barrel defense and public works spending
that stimulated his district's economy and pleased labor
and the military suppliers. Besides dams, canals, and highway projects, Wright led the fight for production of the
hotly debated F-111 fighter jet and the B-58 bomber—
both made by General Dynamics, which has a large plant
in his district. Wright was a decorated B-24 pilot during
World War II and a supporter of America's role in Vietnam to the point that he sponsored resolutions of bipartisan endorsement of former president Nixon's war
policies.

In public, Wright reveals a studied eloquence and mel-
lifluence. In person, Wright is warm and folksy, a veritable
caricature of the soothing, arm-around-the-shoulder style
of "let's reason together" Texas politics. He complains
frequently about the "frenetic pace" that allows members
precious little time to ponder the important issues.

Yet Wright appears very approachable in the hallways
and even more relaxed behind his mammoth oaken desk.
The majority leader's inner office is a spacious, airy room
with fifteen-foot ceilings and tall windows (built before
air-conditioning to help let a breeze in and avoid stuffiness
and smoke-filled rooms, he says). There is an elaborate
fireplace crowned with a gilded eight-foot mirror. A picture of every House leader's hero, Mr. Sam Rayburn of
Texas, graces the wall on the leader's right. The crystal
chandeliers, Wright explains with a wink, were sent over
from the White House because Teddy Roosevelt said the
breeze-blown tinkling made him nervous but might keep
the congressional leaders awake.

Wright realizes that he does not speak for his party and
cannot operate independently. "The Speaker ultimately
has to be the leader of the House," he told the *National
Journal* in 1978. "It would be intolerable for the Majority
Leader to work at cross-purposes." Indeed, he and the
speaker's styles appear to complement each other. O'Neill
is principally a legislative strategist and organizer. Wright
often takes the floor just before key votes to hold or sway
wavering Democrats. He does not, however, demand party
loyalty the way the speaker and president are prone to do.

"Party discipline is a two-edged sword. It's easy to say
there should be more, but then you encounter that old

stumbling block called democracy. There aren't any rewards or punishments the leader can use to force grudging colleagues to vote his way. If you can't persuade them by logic and facts then maybe you shouldn't carry the day," Wright says in an interview. Having fewer carrots and sticks than his predecessors, he believes the majority leadership has become "primarily a hunting license to persuade." Arch-rival Phil Burton criticizes him for not doing the aggressive legwork necessary to push through a progressive Democratic program, but Wright is obviously comfortable with this low-key approach. "I never ask a member to violate a promise to his constituents or a deeply held conviction," he said. "However, I do ask them to give the leadership the benefit of the doubt when they aren't committed. This lack of arm twisting pays off in the long run, because when I do come to them on a crucial vote and they know I need it, they're generally good about giving it to me."

• *Robert C. Byrd* of West Virginia has always been an irrepressible climber, a disciplined organization man, and, in his own words, a "workhorse," not a "showhorse." He is also the majority leader of the United States Senate (a title he proudly prints below his autograph) and as such the man who runs the Senate—or at least schedules it.

Byrd's up-by-the-bootstraps rise to preeminence resonates of Horatio Alger. The future majority leader was born in 1917 and abandoned by his father ten months later, after his mother's death. Raised by poor relatives in the hills of West Virginia, he didn't learn his real name until he was 16. He began college at Georgetown University sixteen years after finishing high school; ten years of night school later he received his law degree, in 1963. After laboring for years as a butcher, welder, and grocer, the musical Byrd literally fiddled his way into the state legislature at age 29. He still saws out country music on hectic one-day swings back home and has even released an album. He's a home-state hero and is never challenged electorally, even though he hasn't actually lived in West Virginia for over twenty-five years. After three terms in the House, he advanced to the upper chamber in 1958.

He was now a senator, but Byrd still hadn't "made it"

in his own mind. The fastidious Byrd began driving himself day and night to meet the personal needs of individual senators. A willingness, even eagerness to take care of the detail work disdained by most of his colleagues enabled Byrd to build up a large ledger of political IOUs. He advanced inch by inch, and in 1967 he was chosen secretary to the Democratic conference, until then a largely meaningless position. By 1970, Byrd was the indispensable insider responsible for scheduling votes, lining up supporters, and undertaking small favors. Since he did most of the work, Byrd reasoned, why not get the credit? In a coup that surprised nearly everyone but himself, Byrd called in his IOUs and defeated Ted Kennedy 31–24 for the position of majority whip, in 1971.

When benign majority leader Mike Mansfield let Byrd assume the day-to-day drudgery of legislative leadership —such as scheduling and negotiating unanimous consent agreements with the often hostile minority—Byrd came to the aid of his colleagues in ways large and small. (When the wife and daughter of freshman Senator-elect Joseph R. Biden (D.-Del.) were killed in a car accident just days after his election in 1972, Bob Byrd drove two-and-a-half hours at night in the rain to attend the memorial service. He was the only senator to show up.)

Thus, when Mansfield retired in 1977, Senate Democrats gave Byrd by acclamation the leadership role he had already filled. Some of his colleagues worried about his political past and views. Byrd spent many years living down his youthful apprenticeship in the Ku Klux Klan ("a mistake," he now admits) and his fervent opposition to civil rights legislation. He kept the Senate in session all night when he filibustered the 1964 Civil Rights Act by reciting police cases against black men who attacked white women. He opposed Thurgood Marshall's appointment to the Supreme Court, but fought to save Nixon nominees Haynsworth and Carswell.

After 1970, he took several measured strides leftward into the Democratic mainstream. This moderation of his natural Southern conservatism helped make him palatable to enough Northerners to dump Kennedy for the leadership. He voted for some antiwar amendments; he led unsuccessful battles to block the nomination of Richard

Kleindienst as Nixon's attorney general, in 1972; he mercilessly grilled Nelson Rockefeller about his wealth; his relentless cross-examination of acting FBI Director L. Patrick Gray in 1973 helped flush out some early facts about the Watergate cover-up. Although he still vigorously opposes busing, Byrd voted to extend the Voting Rights Act in 1975—a measure he had opposed twice before. He also supported committee reform, public financing of congressional campaigns, and a stronger ethics code for senators. As Tip O'Neill did in the House, Byrd made the ethics code, in 1977, a test of his leadership strength. By 1978, even Senator Edward Kennedy, commenting on Byrd's scheduling of progressive legislation on the Senate floor, said that his original doubts about him as majority leader are "no longer justified."

Although Byrd insists he is a legislative leader and not merely a technician, he seems more interested in making the Senate run on time than on steering its policies to the right or Southward. "His method is somewhere between Lyndon Johnson's crotch-and-lapel technique and Mike Mansfield's find-your-own-pace viewpoint," one Senate liberal told *Newsweek*.

Byrd personally and institutionally does not exhort his party as much as Speaker O'Neill does. In the 435-member House, the speaker uses his whip system to run down colleagues and relay his question: "Can you give us a vote?" In the Senate, Byrd allows his whip only a token role on most issues and his pitch to colleagues is seldom more than a quiet request for "consideration" on an issue. Furthermore, since Senate rules such as the filibuster are stacked in favor of the minority, Byrd must look to the Republican side to obtain winning margins. When there is no consensus he claims to let the Senate "work its will," a phrase he uses to excuse his lack of advocacy for some key Democratic initiatives, such as Carter's comprehensive energy package.

As the Senate's ambassador to the White House, the majority leader insists that the Senate "is not meant to be a rubber stamp and it isn't going to be a rubber stamp." Only five days after President Carter's inauguration he blasted the new president for not consulting the Congress enough. Later, he advised the president to fire his best

friend, Bert Lance, who was in trouble about financial
dealings. His relations with the White House remain cordial, even if distant. In 1978, Byrd fought hard for labor
law reform and backed Carter's bids for a Panama Canal
treaty, an end to the Turkish arms embargo, and a Middle East plane sale package.

But through it all, Byrd remains more an institutional
party man than a leader on substantive issues. "He doesn't
get involved in the substance of legislation, and if he did it
would do more harm than good," Senator Sam Nunn of
Georgia said in 1977. "The most effective way he can
help the administration is to move the agenda along. The
senator is a creature of the Senate itself."

• *Howard Baker*—Jimmy Carter could claim two major foreign policy victories in the Senate during his first
two years as president and, ironically, he owed both of
them to the Republican leader, who covets Carter's job as
he works at his own.

Howard Baker was born 53 years ago to a very pros-
perous and political family in a small town in eastern
Tennessee. "The place is built around the Bakers," a neigh-
bor said once to a profiler. "It's like a feudal setting, and
Howard was raised very much like the lord of the manor."
After service during World War II, he went on to join his
father's Knoxville law firm and marry Illinois Senator
Everett McKinley Dirksen's daughter Joy. When his father
died near the end of Baker's seventh term in the U.S.
House in 1964, he ignored his family's advice and ran for
the Senate seat vacated by Estes Kefauver. Though he
lost, Baker garnered more votes than any other Republican in the state's history. He became the first Republican
senator ever elected from Tennessee in 1966, and has been
running for higher office ever since.

The courtly Baker first gained national attention alongside former Senator Sam Ervin during the televised Senate Watergate Committee hearings in 1973. Displaying his
flair as a country trial lawyer, vice chairman Baker twirled
his eyeglasses before 70 million viewers and dramatically
asked, "What did the president know and when did he
know it?" Yet Baker was a party man to the last. Watergate majority counsel Samuel Dash accused Baker in 1976

of having been a White House double agent, trying to scuttle the investigation—a charge Baker vehemently denies. "I think he was working hand-in-glove with the Nixon White House at the time," one senior senator told the *Washington Post* in 1978.

Whatever Baker's role during Watergate, he played it with just enough of the virtuoso not only to escape going down with the Republican ship, but to float to the top as the photogenic do-gooder his tarnished party so badly needed.

In 1969 and in 1971, Baker had tried unsuccessfully to succeed his father-in-law as Senate minority leader. He also failed twice to capture the vice presidential nomination under Nixon and Ford. Tiring of embarrassing defeats, Baker made an untypically low-key bid to deprive lackluster Whip Robert Griffin of the leadership in 1977. Griffin was the heavy favorite after serving seven years of drudgery as former minority leader Hugh Scott's whip and picking up the tacit endorsement of his fellow Michigander, Gerald Ford. Griffin believed he had solid commitments from at least twenty or twenty-one of the party's thirty-eight senators and his staff had even chilled a stock of champagne for his victory party. It was never held. Baker unexpectedly won 19–18, with one abstention.

Baker sought the minority leadership less because he has any particular ideology to espouse than because, as leader of the "outs," he would have a national forum from which to criticize the president. A conservative Republican, Baker is an outspoken advocate of big business, fiscal conservatism, and massive defense spending, and is against public works and welfare spending. On civil rights he claims to be moderate to liberal and on environmental affairs a liberal. Overall he sees himself in the very middle of the Republican political spectrum. Baker's greatest skill has been to carve a middle ground from both wings of his party while accumulating concessions from the majority party. "He's the man from the great land of compromise," Baker's press secretary enjoys telling observers mystified at the senator's famed political ambivalence.

While predecessor Hugh Scott worked primarily to sustain presidential vetoes during the eight years Nixon and Ford occupied the White House, Baker aggressively exploits divisions between liberal and conservative Democrats. Although the Republicans are outnumbered nearly 2 to 1, Baker claims he controls the "single largest voting block in the Senate." Indeed, Baker deployed this Republican cohesion and the filibuster to defeat the important labor law reform bill and public financing of congressional campaigns. Near unanimous Republican opposition caused Carter to abandon as hopeless his $50 tax rebate proposal in 1977. But the wily Baker has cast himself in a far more important role than spoiler. In return for his crucial, eleventh-hour support of Carter's Panama Canal treaty and Mideast plane sale package, the president had to swallow the two conservative "Baker amendments": one allowed U.S. military intervention in Panama; the other secured twenty additional fighter planes for Israel and a Saudi assurance that American-made planes would not be flown against Israel.

Despite his boyish good looks and Cheshire cat grin, Baker's greatest enemy seems to be his reputation for deviousness. "He is slick, and I think, cold," one senator said. "People aren't passionately for him or against him . . . and that is his strength." Another senator described the majority leader as "an enigmatic and devious character." Whatever his motivations or future political fortunes, however, Baker remains a force whom the majority leader and president must consult before introducing controversial legislation.

Instead of an open system with people and ideas in a state of creative flux, congressional rules and rulers have historically encouraged secrecy, procrastination, and baronies of power—which in turn entrench the rulers more firmly. In the past half decade, there has been some change: recorded votes on amendments, some younger members appointed to important committees, more open committee and conference meetings, and the election of committee chairmen by the House and Senate Democratic caucuses. Still, the longest serving member of a committee or subcommittee almost invariably becomes chairman, a right to filibuster in the Senate remains, a balkanization of committees and subcommittees stymies efficiency, and committee chairmen are "1,000 percent as powerful" as other committee members.

These impacts are not spread evenly among Republicans and Democrats, liberals and conservatives. For though it may confuse European allies with their strong parties and cabinet governments, the U.S. Congress is governed by the Democratic party only in the most nominal sense. Decisive power has long resided in a Southern Democrat-conservative Republican coalition—partly due to congressional rules that give determined minorities the leverage to block majority action. Also, as House minority leader John Rhodes says, "We are the largest cohesive force on Capitol Hill. When the Republican Policy Committee takes a stand on an issue, an average 86 percent back it." When that bloc is combined with many Southern Democrats and many independent young Democrats beholden to only their contributors and local organizations—"You know, there is nothing the leadership can offer me, really nothing," says second-termer Richard Gephardt (D.-Mo.) —the "opposition party" swells to near majority numbers.

Ironically, several liberals, in the late 1970s, ascended to positions of substantial authority in their houses—Tip O'Neill, of course, as speaker; John Brademas, as majority whip; Phillip Burton, for a time, as House Democratic Caucus Chairman; Senators Kennedy and Church, as chairmen of Senate Judiciary and Foreign Relations—just at a time that a conservative mood has supposedly seized their institutions. At the same time, reforms have dispersed power more evenly among all the members—for example, the 1973 change allowing a secret ballot in the Democratic Caucus to elect committee chairmen. So while traditional House baronies saw their power reduced by some procedural changes, not all of it devolved to the speaker. Much of it filtered down to subcommittee chairmen or was simply scattered among individual members. As Jim Wright observes, "The problems of leadership are greater today than ever before. Sam Rayburn used to get things done with the help of just a dozen men, but things have changed. . . . There are more bases to touch, more people to persuade." Rep. David Obey (D.-Wis.) puts it more bluntly: "Because we have such a decentralized system, any little special interest can worm their way into the process by finding some subcommittee chairman to give them a hearing." The final irony is that as chairmen and the leadership became less tyrannical, the House became

more vulnerable to the outside "permanent government"
—those "special interests" of Woodrow Wilson's opening
quotation, who still guide the Congress and exploit its procedures and players.

4

Congress vs. the Executive:
The Constitutional Ebb and Flow

*Oh, if I could only be President and Congress too
for just ten minutes.*
—Theodore Roosevelt

Throughout the history of the United States, there have
periodically been shifting power alignments between the
executive and the legislative branches of government.
Varying with the era and the character of the president,
sometimes the Congress predominated, more often the
executive. This continuing constitutional tug-of-war is the
result of the Founders' design of a unitary executive
which can respond quickly in the event of an emergency,
balanced by a large, slow-moving deliberative body, the
Congress.

More than a hundred years ago, in the decades leading
to the Civil War, those who remained in Congress—men
like Daniel Webster, Henry Clay, John C. Calhoun—had
more to do with directing the nation's policies than did
presidents like Millard Fillmore or Franklin Pierce. John
Quincy Adams ran for a seat in the House after retiring
from the presidency in 1829; one could hardly imagine a
Lyndon Johnson or Gerald Ford doing the same thing in
the modern era.

This change in the president's relation to Congress—the
transformation of the presidency into the summit of prestige and power—happened so long ago that, until recently,
it was no longer newsworthy. The events which have led
to the greatest growth of presidential power have been
wars. President Abraham Lincoln responded to the exi-

107

gencies of the first few months of the Civil War by declaring martial law, calling up 75,000 troops, suspending *habeas corpus*, and spending $2 million in treasury funds without the consent of Congress. When Congress convened several months into the war, Lincoln dutifully asked it to approve of his actions, explaining that he had not had the time to wait for Congress to gather. Presented with such *faits accomplis*, Congress agreed.

Democrat Andrew Johnson succeeded Lincoln to face a hostile Republican Congress. In part because of policy differences over Reconstruction, but largely for personal and political reasons, Johnson was impeached and tried, but not convicted—an episode that began a shift in power toward the Congress which would not be reversed until the presidency of Teddy Roosevelt. The power and influence of the president have gradually risen since that time—except for dips following the first and second world wars and the laissez-faire presidency of Dwight Eisenhower. Franklin Roosevelt, in his attempts to deal first with the Great Depression and then with the war, expanded the executive powers vastly, and perhaps more lastingly than any other president.

Presidents Lyndon Johnson and Richard Nixon contributed measurably to making Congress a "broken branch" of government. Johnson's ability to manipulate Congress, his prosecution of the war and his secrecy about its costs accorded little more than lip-service to congressional prerogatives. And when the 93rd Congress convened in January, 1973, so great was Richard Nixon's contempt for Congress as a coequal branch of government that he did not even deign to deliver his State of the Union address in person, choosing merely to send it to the Capitol by messenger. The "imperial presidency" was in its heyday. By the end of that Congress in December, 1974, however, it had passed major bills increasing congressional control over war-making and over spending, and had forced the president from office. Within five years—and an unelected president and a federally inexperienced president later—it seemed hard to recall when presidents imperially dictated policy to an acquiescent legislature. Generalizations about the relative power of these contending branches of government seem to be continually in need of revision.

This brief chronology notwithstanding, it is misleading to discuss the legislative and executive branches so as to suggest that an equal struggle is on between two sides, and that whichever side is stronger on an issue will prevail. A battle does go on—and Congress has indeed recently won several important skirmishes—but the field of play exists far from the executive goal line. No matter how hard the Congress may struggle on one issue, it is usually overwhelmed by the vastly greater forces and focus of the presidency.

Perhaps the clearest example of lost legislative initiative is in the proposing of new laws—among the most basic of Congress's jobs. In the years before 1900, the great majority of laws passed each year originated with Congress; senators or representatives drafted them, pushed them, saw them passed. During this century, however, the source of legislative initiation has shifted. The greatest change came at the beginning of the New Deal, when the president was so firmly in control of lawmaking that the speaker of the house could address freshman representatives like a pack of Marine recruits and say, "We *will* put over Mr. Roosevelt's program." Since then, according to political scientist James Robinson, Congress has "yielded to virtually exclusive initiation by the executive." Putting it more plainly, a Republican representative told a witness from President Kennedy's administration, "We're not supposed to draw up the bills—that's your job, then you bring them to us."

In large part, Congress's loss of initiative is the result of a lack of expertise to deal with the myriad issues that confront it. While Congress has substantial committee and personal staff to help it conduct its business, this is no match for the executive, which has the enormous resources of the bureaucracy to draw upon. The result has been that in the last three decades perhaps 80 percent of the major laws passed have started in the executive branch, including nearly all foreign policy bills. This is not to say that whatever proposals a president sends Congress will become law. But most of the laws that *do* pass will be proposed by the executive —a fact true even of Jimmy Carter, the first president since Eisenhower who came to office lacking a congressional background. Despite legislative rebuffs, successful domestic bills such as civil service reform and a windfall profits tax were his creations.

Logrolling and Arm-Twisting

To persuade Congress to pass the laws he sends them, the president can use the time-honored technique of log-rolling. This is a game of trading favors, in which the president gives congressmen bonbons and pastries to make them give away steak and potatoes.

Willing to make innocuous appearances or concessions to obtain a vote for a bill, the president can obtain it at little cost by showing up alongside a representative at a local school dedication, or giving him a pen used at the ceremonial signing of a bill announcing mammoth outlays for his district. It is more than vanity which lets congressmen succumb to these blandishments. For many congressmen, especially those who have moldered away in the House for years, a presidential pat on the back can be a big boost. Even if the congressman is from the other party, the impact is to let the voters know that their man circulates with the prominent man in Washington. If his daily schedule prevents traveling to the state or district, the president can give a congressman the feeling of power even more easily. The president or one of his top associates (Nixon used Henry Kissinger, Carter often turns to Walter Mondale) will telephone the congressman or take him aside and whisper a few words in his ear. The congressman, obscure and ill-informed only seconds before, suddenly becomes an insider. He now understands the president's burdens—which his carping colleagues cannot fathom.

The most common type of presidential patronage is the distribution (or alternatively, the withholding) of government favors. Consider the case of former representative Chet Holifield, a 69-year-old member in 1971. He represented the city of Whittier, an area dear to President Nixon, but he was more important to the White House as chairman of the House Government Operations Committee. In 1971, Nixon revealed a proposal for reforming the government: an executive reorganization plan, announced in a special address, which would have lumped seven existing departments into four giant agencies. To no one's surprise, Congress hated the proposal; since each congressional committee takes as much interest in the executive department it oversees as an Italian prince did in the security of his small domains, Congress naturally resists any change. Holifield leapt to the front of the opposition, denouncing "the whole grandiose plan" as "political grandstanding for the purpose of putting Congress on the defensive for the political use of the president in the 1972 campaign." His opposition mattered, because his committee would consider the plan.

But Holifield had other interests besides the minutiae of executive organization: main among these was nuclear power plants. Like other early boosters of nuclear energy, Holifield hoped that the final stages of the system—breeder-reactors—would be finished before he was. By coincidence, many of Holifield's constituents also worked for one of the main contractors, North American Rockwell.

Inconveniently, the Nixon administration did not share Holifield's passion for breeder-reactors. Not that is, until March 26, 1971, when Nixon invited Holifield to take a ride on the presidential jet *Air Force One*. There is no way to know what was said on the flight, but afterward Nixon pushed the breeder-reactors, and Holifield found new virtues in the reorganization plan. Never a great bargainer, Holifield made another flight five months later in the plane, with similar results, Nixon again pushed breeder-reactors and Holifield supported an administration version of a consumer-protection law.

Government largess not only can help induce congressional action, it can be a useful tool in preventing it—as the late representative Wright Patman found out to his dismay four months after the Watergate break-in and one month before the 1972 presidential election. At that time, as chairman of the House Banking and Currency Committee, Patman decided to hold hearings on the break-in and called his committee together to approve the subpoena power necessary to the hearings. According to Marjorie Boyd, writing in the *Washington Monthly*, the vote to approve failed when several Democrats crossed party lines to vote with committee Republicans. Instrumental in delivering the Democratic votes against Patman was Georgia Democrat Robert Stephens. Stephens maintained that he voted against the subpoena power in the interests of fairness and nonpartisanship, but three days later the Department of Housing and Urban Development suddenly announced its decision to transfer the funds necessary for the construction of a long-delayed $2 million, eleven-story apartment building in the heart of Stephens's district. Any investigation into Watergate was thus postponed until after the election.

Since the many offices on the president's side of government determine when and where much money will be spent, the president can offer other favors. For John Stennis of Mississippi and former senator Margaret Chase Smith of Maine, the president's Defense Department had arranged contracts for local shipyards. Even if the decisions are already made, the president can use them as bargaining tools by making them appear to be the product of a diligent congressman. And so, when President Nixon was fighting for Senate confirmation of his Supreme Court nominee G. Clement Haynsworth, he channeled an announcement of a $3 million urban renewal grant through the office of West Virginia Senator Jennings Randolph (instead of the usual route, through Rep. Ken Hechler, who represented the district). *You scratch my back:* Randolph looked to the voters as if he'd fought for extra money. *I'll scratch yours:* Haynsworth got Randolph's vote.*

But in its eagerness to collect votes, an administration can go very far. In mid-1978 the Carter Administration was very eager to get its hospital cost containment bill reported out of the House Commerce Committee. With the vote expected to be close, Rep. James Florio (D.-N.J.) of the committee made it clear to White House lobbyists that he wanted a $75 million Veterans' hospital built in his district. He got his hospital—"we've had to fight fire with fire," said an Administration source, "because the . . . AMA has been fighting us so hard"—and the bill got one more vote. (It lost anyway, 22–21.)

Though he entered office renouncing the use of deals

---

*Although voting down the Haynsworth and Carswell nominations gave senators a taste of their rights and powers, they should not be taken as signs that the president's appointment power is seriously checked. During Nixon's first year in office, Congress had to approve 72,635 appointments—most of them with only a few seconds' "deliberation."

and logrolling, Jimmy Carter reverted to traditional patterns when his prized Panama Canal treaty went to the Senate. The issue was obviously of major importance—to the nation and to an administration then badly in need of a big legislative win. Consequently, the White House launched a major lobbying effort, from signing up John Wayne and Gerald Ford to exhorting and/or logrolling the undecided senators. Edward Zorinsky (D.-Nebr.) delighted in telling of repeated calls he received from the president, the secretaries of state and defense, and others —one from President Carter as the senator dined at a French restaurant.

The courting of undecided senators such as Zorinsky showed those who had clearly declared their intentions —and received little more than a smile in return—the error of their ways. Senator Herman Talmadge (D.-Ga.) was widely reported to have decided in favor of the treaty following a White House promise to support his $2.3 billion emergency farm bill. Carter made Senator Dennis DeConcini (D.-Ariz.) an offer which he could refuse. The administration promised to buy a $250 million stockpile of copper to put aside for a rainy day— copper being a chief product of Arizona's mines. But DeConcini held out and, near the close of the debate, demanded that in exchange for his vote a "reservation" be added to the treaty to allow the United States to send troops anywhere in Panama to keep the canal open. When the Senate leadership realized that the treaty would not pass without the "DeConcini reservation," a version of it was approved—and so was the canal treaty, with one vote to spare.

The president's role as leader of his political party opens up whole new crates of favors to hand to congressmen. These include promotion of the loyal: in return for unquestioningly defending Ford administration measures in Congress against Democratic attacks, Senator Robert Dole of Kansas became chairman of the Republican National Committee. When dealing with congressmen from the opposite party, the president may also give the political blessing of "benign neglect." On the night of October 15, 1978, President Carter was searching for the votes to sustain his veto of the $10.2 billion public works bill, which he had criticized as being inflationary.

He placed a call to a conservative Ohio Republican, Rep. Sam Devine. Reporter Martin Tolchin described the late-night call:

"Sam, I need your help on this public-works veto that I'm sending up," the President said. "The Democratic leadership is against the veto, and I have to call on my Republican friends."

"Mr. President," Mr. Devine replied, "it's pretty ironic your calling on me, when you're doing everything possible to knock me out of the Congress."

It seemed that the President and Rosalynn had both made trips to his district to help his opponent, and Miss Lillian had also been scheduled to speak there. The following day, he voted with the President, however, and the veto was easily sustained.

Representative Devine was one of 53 House members, many of them Republicans, who received telephone calls from the President on that issue. Some say the President told them, "Go along with me on this vote, and I'll see what I can do for you," and promised that it was a vote he would not forget.

If the carrot and stick technique fails, the executive moves into the massive-retaliation stage of persuasion—a process Charles Goodell could well describe. Long an unexciting representative from upstate New York, Goodell landed in the Senate to fill Robert Kennedy's seat in 1968. In the more invigorating air of the Senate, he expanded and quickly became a major irritant for the Republican administration. After failing administration tests on Haynsworth, Vietnam, missile systems, and other issues, Goodell had to run against both the Republicans and the Democrats in the 1970 election. Although he was running on the Republican ticket, Goodell endured regular haranguings from Vice President Agnew, and knew that the administration backed Conservative party candidate James Buckley, the eventual winner. After the 1970 election, President Nixon foreswore any further fratricidal ventures, but liberal Republicans like Senator Charles Mathias still glanced nervously behind them when they voted against the party line.

The president's stranglehold on recalcitrant congressmen tightens an extra bit when he takes advantage of his enormous propaganda power. As Max Ways wrote in *Fortune* magazine, "The President—any President—is easier to write about than any congressional situation. Journalists minimize the importance of Congress because they are reluctant to explain that 'can of worms.' This neglect, in turn, leads to an actual reduction of the power of Congress, because public expectation clusters around the more readily communicable person of the President. In this society, which is perhaps more democratic than is usually supposed, power tends to go where the people think it is. . . . Journalists who will risk life and limb to find out what the President had for breakfast wouldn't walk around the corner to hear a Congressman deliver a reasoned explanation of his vote."

Congressmen come to resent the slavish attention which television and newspapers give the slightest utterance from the executive oracle. Compared with the difficulty a representative has getting his proposals into any printed page besides the *Congressional Record,* the president has not only free advertising for himself and his program, but also a guaranteed pulpit from which to blast his enemies. When faint-hearts had been making trouble about the way the Vietnamization policy was going, presidential aide H. R. Haldeman appeared on the "Today" show to suggest they were traitors. In the same vein, Henry Kissinger told a group of prisoner-of-war families that the people delaying their sons' and husbands' releases were the doves of Congress. But the networks *refused* an offer by a group of antiwar senators to buy time to explain their position. "I could buy time to sell soap or woman's underwear," complained Senator Harold Hughes, "but not to speak as a U.S. Senator on issues of war and peace." As Majority Leader Byrd said in support of an experiment to televise Senate floor debate:

> Where a struggle exists over spending authority, the President can use television to veto a bill in full view of the American population—he can take what could conceivably be a private act and make it public. The subsequent Senate vote to override or sustain the veto, however, cannot be seen by the general public, only

by the 426 persons accommodated by the public gallery.

Thought Control

Like the private interests which prefer to avoid the bother of lobbying by getting the "right kind of men" elected in the first place, the executive would just as soon pass up all the arm-twisting and character assassination. The way to do this is to make sure the congressmen never get to know anything that would put wrong ideas in their head. The formal name for this is "congressional liaison," but the best metaphor for it is an Oriental court in which the emperor, sealed off from the world by high walls, knows only what his courtiers and mandarins whisper in his ear. In time, he becomes their tool, since his world is bounded by what they choose to tell him.

To a surprising degree, Congress knows little more than what the executive branch tells it. When it gets ready to pass a new law for missiles or highways, it turns to the Defense Department and the Federal Highway Administration. While a stray outside witness—from a public interest group, or a wandering refugee from academia—may turn up at congressional hearings, the bulk of what congressmen find out about new laws comes from the president's departments. Congress itself is largely to blame, since committees can choose their own witness lists.

A major practical explanation for this dependency is its staff capacity vis-à-vis the executive branch. Another important reason is that Congress has not fully figured out that "Information Is Power." Executive departments started to get the message shortly after World War II, and jumped into action. Led by the ever-vigilant Defense Department, they set up the congressional liaison system— which means congressional lobbying by the executive. Starting with one lone assistant secretary of defense for congressional liaison, the network has grown to include at least 531 agents from twelve departments. They have charmed their way into not only the congressional heart but its buildings as well; the alleged space shortage on Capitol Hill does not keep the Army from spreading its offices over a huge suite in the Rayburn Office Building.

The point of stashing these agents within the halls of

Congress is to make sure Congress knows the right facts about each department. In theory, the liaison agents are not supposed to "influence" the congressman, especially by appealing to the public to put pressure on Congress. A 1913 law, the Executive Antilobbying Act, says that "no funds may be used . . . to influence in any manner a member of Congress to favor or oppose, by vote or otherwise, any legislation or appropriation by Congress." The only exception is that executive agents may "communicate with Members of Congress on request, through proper channels"—a clause that has been opened up to let the whole liaison troop roll through. Ready to answer any congressional request with an illustrated brochure about, say, New Steps in Defense or Advances in Securities Regulation, ready even to anticipate requests and shove possibly interesting documents into open hands, the liaison offices assume that politicians, like mountains, can be worn away by light but steady pressure.

Many congressmen are unhappy about the hazards of relying on the executive, but their moans are often muffled as they sink deeper and deeper into the executive lap. One of the most heavily dependent committees has been the House Armed Services Committee. Rep. Ron Dellums, reported the *Washington Post,* once "took excerpts of the committee section [of an authorization measure] on aid to South Vietnam and compared it to the testimony of the Pentagon witness, a major general. The Committee had copied the general's statement nearly word for word."

What's wrong with this cooperation? Not just danger that the departments will deceive—as a former liaison for the Equal Employment Opportunity Commission said, "We don't lie to them. We just tell them what will be the most persuasive, and don't volunteer all the facts." The real issue is that Congress might as well not even bother studying or approving the executive's plans when all it has to go on is the executive's information. As an exasperated Senator Muskie remarked in February, 1973, to Roy Ash, then the director of the Office of Management and Budget, the administration policy was to spoon-feed Congress "the information you decide we ought to have in the way you decide we ought to have it and at the time you decide we ought to have it."

The final problem is that Congress often can't even get

the information it specifically requests. More and more
the real policy decisions are made not by various department heads but by the president's personal staff. These
men don't have to talk unless they want to. One week before the Cambodian invasion of 1970, Secretary of State
William Rogers calmly told a congressional committee that
nothing big was about to happen. Henry Kissinger, as Nixon's personal foreign policy adviser, rarely appeared before Congress. Senator William Fulbright considered it a
great coup when Kissinger deigned to eat lunch with him
in lieu of showing up before the Foreign Relations Committee.

As the presidential staff grows strong from sustenance
gained at the expense of its satellite departments, Congress might well contemplate two further threats to its
power. One is the president's blunt intrusion into the
mechanics of legislating. Despite laws forbidding the Oval
Office to formally lobby, in August, 1972, the Senate
was voting on the president's arms-limitation agreement
with the Russians. As reported in the *Congressional
Record:*

> *Sen. Church:* Some could be misled as a result of
> what is going on right now out in the Vice Presi-
> dent's office. I was taken in there a few minutes ago
> and shown two models. One model is of the [Russian]
> SS-9. It stands . . . fully two feet off the table. It is a
> very menacing looking weapon. One is especially
> struck by the size of the scale model of the SS-9 when
> it is compared with the model, also to scale, of the
> [U.S.] Minuteman missile which sits next to it . . .
> *Sen. Fulbright:* May I ask the senator, since I have
> not been invited into the Vice President's room, wheth-
> er the Vice President is now a substation of the National
> Security Council? Is it used for the purpose of in-
> fluencing the votes of the senators? . . . I thought it
> was a ceremonial hall for the Vice President. How-
> ever, it is now an exhibit hall for the National Security
> Council. Is that what it is now?
> *Sen. Church:* Apparently so.
> *Sen. Fulbright:* Mr. President, this is rather pe-
> culiar in view of the fact, that officials of the National
> Security Council, including Mr. Kissinger, refuse to

come to the Hill for committee hearings. Now instead
of coming to the Hill to testify, they have the exhibits
here and ask senators into the Vice President's room
so they can see these models.

White House lobbyists have even more concrete means
at their disposal in their efforts to determine the outcome
of a vote. To shore up their defenses in a Senate debate in
1973, White House aides sent an Air Force plane to fetch
back Oklahoma Republican Senators Dewey Bartlett and
Henry Bellmon from a quail hunt to vote against cloture
on a campaign financing bill. Often, in the wake of a presidential veto, the lobbyists can be even more helpful. As
Nixon lobbyist William Timmons once observed, in a remark true of other administrations, after a bill is vetoed
"we tell Congress exactly what the President would accept
in a modified bill. We sometimes have a substitute bill
ready for introduction as soon as a bill is vetoed so that
members will know precisely what the alternatives are."
    Unlikely as it sounds, the other danger of increased
presidential power is the *even greater* amount of pander-
ing to private interests it encourages. After a brief look at
Congress's many cozy ties to private lobbies, it may be
hard to imagine that any other part of the government
could be as thoroughly influenced. Recent presidents, however, have not just responded to the secret desires of private industries, but have actually spurred them on. The
clean water bill of 1971 illustrates the story.
    Trying to please both sides, President Nixon had talked
himself into a corner on one bill. Early in 1971, he had
nagged Congress for not passing his environmental bills,
concluding with a rhetorical outburst:

> The fundamental fact is that of choice. We can
> choose to debase the physical environment in which
> we live, and with it the human society that depends on
> that environment, or we can choose to come to terms
> with nature, to make amends for the past, and build
> the basis for a balanced and responsible future.

Congress responded more eagerly than Nixon had expected, and by November the Senate had passed a strict
water-quality bill that meant a high pollution-control out-

lay for many industries. The law's sponsors, notably Edmund Muskie, had packed in a series of tough clauses, including one which let the federal government veto state water standards if they seemed too lenient.

In public, the president's staff opposed the bill because it infringed on "states' rights." But four days before that, in an extraordinary display of concern for the corporations of America, the president's staff had held a pep rally to encourage private interests to fight the bill. "The notion that somehow industry 'got to' the administration and pushed them into [opposing the bill] is really the reverse of what happened," said Douglas Trussel, vice president of the National Association of Manufacturers. "The administration took the initiative, and many executives were ignorant of what was going on." At a November 4 meeting—when seven trade representatives came to the White House to see presidential aides John Whitaker and Richard Fairbanks—Fairbanks made what one trade agent called "an incredible speech":

> His pitch was, "We fought a lonely battle over here on this bill. Where the hell were you guys when we needed you? We could have gotten some of the worst provisions changed if you'd gotten into this in a big way."

This view of the president as promotion man is hardly reassuring to those who dream of a separation of Business and State. But it cannot come as a surprise when so many administration officials are on brief sabbatical from corporate work. It is useful to recall Eisenhower's cabinet of, as the *New Republic*'s TRB dubbed it, "eight businessmen and a plumber." Lyndon Johnson's former aides Clark Clifford and Myer Feldman now work as lawyer-lobbyists in Washington law firms. Nixon's former congressional liaison Bryce Harlow had to leave his job as congressional liaison for Procter and Gamble to come to the White House. When he left the administration, he returned to P&G where he teamed up with Mike Manatos —former special assistant to Lyndon Johnson. Peter Flanigan and John Connally both toiled for business interests in Washington after serving Richard Nixon's interests. The Nixon and Ford administrations' energy advisers, from

William Simon to John Sawhill to Frank Zarb, all came from the Wall Street financial community. All in all, they make the presidential lobby into what Lambert Miller, senior vice president of the National Association of Manufacturers, called in 1971 "the most pervasive, influential, and costly of any such in the whole country."

Power of the Purse

Money may not buy happiness, but it can buy power. If Congress gets ignored, or lied to, or lobbied, or manipulated in passing legislation—why should it care? It still holds the purse strings. Let the president send up missile plans or domestic programs: since Congress determines where the money goes, it should be able to reorder the priorities to suit its taste. Military programs getting costly? Trim down the funds. People starving in the city? Send in a little more aid. President bowling congressmen over? Just use the power of the purse to put him in his place.

In practice, however, Congress has not been able to find salvation through appropriation. Even more miserably than in passing laws, Congress has historically failed to manage the budget. It has retained the right to control the budget, but not the ability to do so. In the few cases where it has not dutifully rubber-stamped the president's programs (usually with a few modifications to salve its conscience), it has found that the president can do what he wants anyway.

Forty years ago, economists figured out that if countries wanted to avoid the boom-and-bust cycles which had led to the Great Depression, then *someone* had to keep track of how much money was coming into the government (through taxes) compared with the amount flowing out. The president was set to take on this job, since the Budget and Accounting Act of 1921 had given him the power to draw up a "national budget" for the whole federal government. Congress might have tried to share the power—and, for a few brave years in the forties, it did prepare a "legislative budget"—but it gave up. This simple abdication reveals why the president appropriates money, not Congress. He who makes the budget sends the money on its way. Those who "approve" the budget are spectators.

The trouble Congress has had dealing with the budget is a much exaggerated version of its troubles passing laws.

By the time the congressional appropriations committees sit down to examine budget requests, the president's staff has already invested more than a year of research and scheming in them. Through rounds of haggling and calculation, the Office of Management and Budget (OMB) and the various executive departments have worked out compromise estimates for the next year's programs. When they send the figures to Congress, they're not in the mood to make many more changes. However much HEW may have protested (in the secret counsel of the executive) when OMB decided to end a special education program or shift funds elsewhere, few bureaucrats want to bring the complaint into the open before Congress.

Perhaps the greatest problem which has hindered Congress's efforts to use the power of the purse effectively has been the lack of information and expertise. When administration representatives testified on their budget requests, Congress had to accept the accuracy of the testimony since the executive was the only source for information. In the 1960s, for example, congressional committees were reduced to speechlessness by Defense Secretary Robert McNamara's virtuoso budget presentations. When Senator William Proxmire once pressed former budget director Robert Mayo, asking questions about items in the Defense request, Mayo loftily replied that "the president's flexibility is better served by not getting into a debate on what is and what is not in the Defense budget."

Another reason Congress traditionally couldn't make a budget—at least until the establishment of the Senate and House Budget committees—was that Congress worked in a fashion so fragmented that no overall planning was possible. There are parts of the legislative process where that doesn't matter: those who authorize agricultural subsidies don't need to know a thing about new weapons systems. But when dividing a set amount of money among many competing needs, there must be one giant funnel through which all the decisions pass. OMB and the White House provide that; Congress has been a funnel turned upside down. As long as there was someone else to take an overview, Congress's anarchy was not disastrous; it simply meant that the president would make the budget and Congress only minor, tinkering repairs.

Finally, the ancient rite of carving up the pork perverts

both the congressional and executive budget process. Even those who complain loudest about federal spending reverse field when *their* state or district is affected. Senator Proxmire of Golden Fleece fame is from the dairy state of Wisconsin and long wondered why the United States lacked a national laboratory devoted to research on dairy forage (what cows eat). As a member of the Senate Agriculture Appropriations subcommittee, he succeeded in getting $1.1 million for the Department of Agriculture to establish a Dairy Forage Research Center, part of which will be constructed at the University of Wisconsin. Another member of this subcommittee is Senator Milton Young, an octogenarian from North Dakota. It is in Grand Rapids, North Dakota (population 41,000) that the Agriculture Department built the nation's largest laboratory devoted exclusively to human nutrition. Thomas J. Clifford, president of the University of North Dakota, told the *Washington Post*'s Thomas O'Toole: "The man responsible for this laboratory is Milton R. Young. He has done much for agriculture, not only for North Dakota, but for the entire nation as well. But," O'Toole adds, "mostly for North Dakota."

In 1974, however, Congress tried to overcome this desultory record and passed a major budget reform bill. The Budget and Impoundment Control Act, in part a reaction to President Nixon's high-handed treatment of the Congress, sought to provide Congress with its own source of budgetary information and to centralize overall congressional budget decisions. The major provisions of the bill, which became fully effective in 1976, include:

• The creation of new House and Senate budget committees to consider each year's budget as a whole, recommend specific levels of spending, revenues, and public debt, fix target budgetary surpluses or deficits, and divide up the total among a number of broad categories of spending, such as defense and education. The various appropriations committees continue to act on individual spending bills, but do so within the committees' budgetary guidelines. Congress has to vote on the committees' target figures in May before taking up the individual appropriations, and again in September, in order to reconcile its budgetary goals with its actual spending outlays.

• The establishment of a congressional Office of the

Budget as a counterbalance to the OMB. Armed with computers and a professional staff of about 250, the office helps the committees draw up the congressional budget and provides the experts and information needed to analyze the presidential budget and the mountains of data that accompany it.

• A requirement for additional information to be submitted with the president's budget in January. The new law requires the OMB to submit a listing of "tax expenditures"—revenues lost to the Treasury through special exemptions or other preferential tax treatment—as well as detailed statistics on long-range projections and advance appropriations.

• A change in the federal fiscal year from July-through-June to October-through-September, which gives Congress an additional three months from the start of each session to complete all of its funding work on time.

In its infant years, the Congressional Budget Office and budget committees have provided competence and confidence to Congress in the budget process. The CBO keeps a running tally of the total costs of legislation passed by both House and Senate, estimating the cost of each program as it is passed and comparing it with the budget target. It supplies five-year projections of the costs of each authorization, and it provides Congress with a comprehensive and systematic analysis of the president's budget. Scrutinizing administration estimates of spending and taxation, CBO has not shied away from disputing OMB's conclusions.

Along with budget analysis, CBO is responsible for policy analysis. It analyzes legislation and possible alternate policies, citing the pros and cons of each. And each April 1 it issues a report on alternative budget options for the Congress. A member of the Commission on the Operation of the Senate, in a typical comment, wrote that "none of the formal reports I have examined are shoddy or biased, most are highly credible and knowledgeable. . . ." As House Budget Committee Chairman Robert Giaimo (D.-Conn.) said, "I can now get information on a specific program [without having] to go down and beg for it from an agency." Still, CBO is not OMB. It does not make policy; rather, it is a tool to help the Budget committees and the Congress make it. And unlike OMB,

CBO is not an advocate; it does not make recommendations, but offers choices. Finally, it does not lobby for proposals, as OMB does before Congress.

It is up to the Budget committees to make the policy. These panels have the power to tell *other* committees to restrain their generosity to their favorite programs. And once "budget target" figures are agreed on in a Budget committee, it becomes very difficult to overturn them on the floor. On the Senate side, there has tended to be a consensus between Democrats and Republicans, due largely to the efforts of Budget Committee Chairman Edmund Muskie (D.-Me.) and ranking Republican Henry Bellmon (R.-Okla.). But bipartisanship has largely been lacking on the House side. House Republicans have tended to view budget decisions as intensely political issues, and have often voted against budget targets. Also, as a House Budget Committee aide notes, "We don't have any clout—we have no pork to give away. Public Works has the Rivers and Harbors Bill and Ways and Means has their annual Christmas tree. Our only influence is through moral suasion."

Part of the difficulty in the House is due to the failure of the process to live up to the expectations of conservative members, most of whom hoped that it would help to put a lid on spending and balance the budget. But liberals too were disappointed when the Budget committees did not shift priorities to social programs. Part of the difficulty is that the budget is not as malleable as many legislators would like. Long-term allocations for weapons systems and public works projects, mandated interest payments on the national debt, the spending for Social Security programs means that roughly 75 percent of the budget is committed even before the OMB and congressional committees get a good look at it. At least, though, a respected body in Congress *is* looking at it, rather than surrendering all authority to an ascendant OMB.

The Executive Shell Game

Even if Congress passes a law on its own initiative and funds it according to its own ideas, the executive can still get its way. In the civics textbooks, there is not a hint that the president can run programs that Congress has outlawed, or delay forever laws the Congress thinks have gone into effect. But a set of innocuous-sounding practices—"impoundment," "reprogramming," "transfers" —have given the president additional control over the government's financial affairs.

"In apportioning any appropriation," says a clause in the 1950 Budget Act, "reserves may be established to provide for contingencies or to effect savings whenever savings are made possible by or through changes in requirements, greater efficiency of operations, or other developments." In other words, the president need not spend all the money Congress gives him so long as the reasons are good. This sounds acceptable in theory. In practice, presidents have repeatedly withheld funds, often for blatantly political reasons. In these cases, Congress might as well never have bothered to propose bills, pass them, and appropriate money. By impounding funds, the president can ignore Congress:

• The Nixon administration asked for $2 billion for the food stamp program in 1972; Congress added $200 million more. Instead of vetoing the bill, the president just told the OMB to set the "allowable spending" level at $2 billion.

• In water pollution control, the Nixon administration spent only $262 million of the $800 million appropriated in 1970 and $475 million of a $1 billion appropriation for 1971. Together with freezes in urban renewal, highway construction, and dozens of other programs, the impoundments totaled $12 billion in 1971. By January, 1973, the figure had climbed to $17.7 billion.

Presidents have always had some discretion over the timing of federal spending, but as political scientist Louis Fisher has pointed out, "An entirely different situation has developed under the Nixon administration, where funds have been withheld from domestic programs because the president considers those programs incompatible with his own set of budget priorities . . . To impound funds in this prospective sense—holding onto money in anticipation that Congress will enact an administration bill—is a new departure. . . . Impoundment is not being used to avoid deficiencies, or to effect savings, or even to fight inflation, but rather to shift the scale of priorities from one administration to the next, prior to congressional action."

By spending money only where he pleases, a president can write his own laws.

Its resentment smoldering, Congress—and the courts—began to challenge the use of impoundment. In 1973, there were over three dozen court decisions on impoundment, nearly all declaring the action illegal and ordering the release of the withheld funds. That same year, both the House and the Senate passed bills limiting impoundment in the future, but the two versions proved irreconcilable in conference. A year later, anti-impoundment restrictions did become law as part of the Budget and Impoundment Control Act. The act repealed the offending clause in the 1950 Budget Act and established two procedures to deal with future cases. In cases of presidential decisions simply to delay the spending of funds, Congress can force their release under the new law if either House passes a resolution calling for their expenditure. If a president decides to terminate a program altogether or to reduce total spending levels, his action will be revoked if either House fails to approve it within forty-five days. Congress has thus set limits on a president's power to impound funds, but within those limits it may have acknowledged a power which he did not—under the Constitution—previously possess. Following the act, the frequency of executive impoundment declined. Still, between 1975 and 1978, Presidents Ford and Carter requested a total of $56.7 billion in impoundments, the bulk of which were not disapproved since they were largely the result of contract delays and other events which eliminated the need for funding in that year.

Impoundment is only half the picture. If the president could *spend* money with the same abandon with which he withholds it, his bypass of Congress would be complete. He's not there yet; but, like impoundment, "reprogramming" and "transfers" have vastly expanded the president's ability to run the country the way he wants.

In an article in the *Washington Monthly,* journalist Timothy Ingram pointed out the full range of devices the executive branch can use to write its own appropriations. His list includes:

• Transfer authority: The secretary of defense is allowed to shift up to $600 million from the program Con-

gress authorized to some other use. He may also send
funds from civilian to military programs if "security"
demands it. A provision of the Foreign Assistance Act
says that 10 percent of the money earmarked to any one
country may be rechanneled to another. President Nixon
took advantage of all these loopholes when financing the
Cambodian invasion of 1970. By the time he asked Congress for $255 million to pay for the project, he had al-
ready spent $100 million of it.

• "Obsolete" excess stocks: At a time when Congress
kept reducing money for aid to Taiwan, the Defense Department kept a flow of military goods running from its
piles to extra weapons.

• Secret funds: Louis Fisher estimates that $15–$20
billion of appropriations, mainly for defense, is never even
explained to Congress. While some congressmen denounce
this—but cannot, of course, find many details to support
their argument—the late senator Allen Ellender took a
milder view. "What can you do?" he asked. "I believe in
having one strong commander in chief. Once war matériel
is ordered, no member of Congress—no one—is supposed
to follow through to see how it's used. It's to be used by
the commander in chief as he sees best."

• The pipeline: Some appropriations have to be used up
during the fiscal year or returned to the Treasury. Others
have "full-funding" clauses, which means that the money
stays in the department's hands if not spent. A variant of
this technique was employed in March, 1975, when, in the
midst of a national debate over whether to send additional
military aid to a besieged Cambodia, the Pentagon con-
veniently "found" $21.5 million in the Cambodian ac-
count. It seems that Cambodia had been "overcharged"
for military aid by that amount in 1974, so it had money
coming back.

• Cost overruns: A Defense Department statute allows
the Pentagon to pay for cost overruns whenever the "national defense" is at stake. Liberally defined, this has
excused many billions of dollars in overpayments. The
Pentagon can go even further to accommodate erring
contractors by changing the terms of the deal along the
way. When, in 1968, the Pentagon discovered that its
C5-A was going to cost roughly $2 billion more than esti-

mated—$5.3 billion instead of $3.4 billion—its accountants obligingly changed the contract from a fixed-price one to "cost-plus," an open ticket for whatever the company wanted to spend.

Congress can now and then rebuke the executive for the worst of these abuses. But, as Timothy Ingram says:

> It can threaten fund cutoffs, mandate the use of funds as directed, and exercise its oversight function. But as the executive detours proliferate, Congress discovers that its problems go beyond relative weakness. Increasingly, Congress is less the underdog and more the old fighter who is no longer even invited into the ring.

The Invisible Czars

When Congress fails in its oversight responsibilities, two outcomes are possible: the agencies and departments may roll along unsupervised, or someone else may pick up the reins Congress has dropped. The second has happened, with the presidential staff in the driver's seat.

To see how the White House has succeeded, we need only review why Congress has failed. To do a good job of oversight, Congress would need, first, a much larger staff of investigators. It would need some system for regular review of the agencies, instead of relying on haphazard coverage. It would need to know when policies or performance changed. Most of all, it would need to know whether what the administrators told it was true.

Rolled together and placed on the White House staff, these reasons describe the Office of Management and Budget. As part of the reorganization which changed its name from the Bureau of the Budget, the OMB was given greater responsibility for reviewing the impact and worth of programs, as well as their budgets. This, of course, is another way of phrasing "oversight." The OMB has gone at its task with a vigor the Congress might well imitate.

Because of its privileged position within the executive, the OMB can exercise both before- and after-the-fact review. Before any programs get under way, OMB analysts have screened budget requests and program proposals. While the projects are running, the OMB parcels out the money, or withholds it. And when agencies propose new rules or decisions, the OMB can often screen them before Congress has its chance.

This has led to a situation in which an appointed agency, entirely shielded from public scrutiny, has more impact on administrative policy than any elected congressman, or group of them. A few illustrations show the danger. While the president should have the right to coordinate the policies of the Labor Department or HEW, he has no place setting the policy or priorities of the independent agencies, which are not part of the executive branch. But in February, 1972, the chairman of the Federal Power Commission, John P. Nassikas, came to Congress to complain that the president was doing just that. Nassikas told a Senate subcommittee that his agency was disappearing into the White House. Because he had to send his budget requests through the OMB—not directly to Congress—his agency was subject to the same policy coordination as the executive departments. This OMB screening, Nassikas said, "results in some control of the policies, programs, and priorities of the independent regulatory agencies." Drawing on Nassikas's testimony, Senator Lee Metcalf proposed a bill which would let the independent agencies send their budgets directly to Congress, avoiding the OMB filter. It did not pass.

The OMB can interfere even more directly in the agencies' policy process. A famous memorandum, issued on October 5, 1971, required *all* federal departments and agencies to send the OMB copies of new regulations "which could be expected to . . . impose significant costs on, or negative benefits to, non-Federal sectors" (that is, private industry) before they are publicly announced in the *Federal Register*. Congress has no such chance for a preview screening of regulations; the public certainly does not. And OMB has even altered the regulations. In 1971, the Environmental Protection Agency drew up a new set of guidelines for state air pollution control boards. They were tough—so tough that OMB diluted them before they were published. Peter Bernstein of Newhouse News Service described the process:

> OMB intervened at the request of Commerce Secretary Maurice Stans, Federal Power Commissioner

John Nassikas, and several other federal officials who share big industry's viewpoint. Government sources say [EPA Administrator William] Ruckelshaus defended the original draft at subsequent meetings, but finally lost out when two key White House aides intervened on the side of big industry. They were presidential assistants John D. Ehrlichman and Peter M. Flanigan.

While exercising tight supervision over executive departments and "independent" agencies, OMB can also interfere with whatever attempts Congress may make to assert its own supervisory power. The most important technique for doing so is OMB's screening of testimony administration witnesses plan to give Congress. Combined with the witnesses' usual ellipses, this means that congressmen are often frustrated when they try to oversee the executive. On July 26, 1972, a Pentagon witness demonstrated an extreme degree of noncooperation. Appearing before a Senate subcommittee investigating "environmental war" (rainmaking) in Vietnam, Benjamin Forman, assistant general counsel at the Defense Department, refused to answer Claiborne Pell's questions:

> *Pell:* Are you under instructions not to discuss weather modifications in Southeast Asia?
> *Forman:* Yes, sir.

In 1974 Congress took a few steps to check the power of the OMB by passing legislation that made its director and deputy director subject to Senate confirmation. But Congress's experience with President Carter's choice for OMB director, Bert Lance, demonstrated that Senate confirmation alone is of dubious value. After a cursory investigation of his background and finances, Lance was confirmed by a near-unanimous vote of the Senate. As part of a new Carter effort to avoid conflicts of interest among members of the administration, Lance promised that within a year of assuming OMB duties he would sell his holdings in the Georgia bank of which he was president. But six months later, the White House asked a Senate committee to release Lance from his pledge. When the administration explained that the planned sale of the stock would cause Lance financial hardship, some members of the press began to investigate the situation. Early revelations that the man most responsible for drawing up the nation's half-trillion-dollar budget was unable to handle his own affairs and was involved in various financial dealings prompted congressional, Justice Department, SEC, and other investigations. Ultimately it became clear that Lance had engaged in unethical, if not illegal banking practices, and Carter—after a long delay—was forced to "accept the resignation" of his close friend and trusted adviser.

War Powers

From Abraham Lincoln to Franklin Roosevelt, warmaking power has increasingly lodged in the president, the commander-in-chief. The most recent demonstration of this tendency was, of course, the conduct of the Indochina War by Presidents Johnson and Nixon. Whenever Congress attempted to reduce our involvement—by repealing the 1964 Gulf of Tonkin resolution, by voting a series of end-the-war amendments in the seventies—it found either that (as Nicholas Katzenbach told a hearing in 1967) the president didn't need the Tonkin resolution in the first place, or that (as Nixon said after an antiwar resolution was passed in 1971) the president could simply ignore antiwar clauses. In 1973, Congress finally managed to cut off Nixon's bombing of Cambodia that year, but only after failing to override his veto of efforts to end the bombing immediately. When Nixon said he would only accept a cutoff if given six more weeks in which to bomb, Congress acquiesced.

But angry over its diminished authority—after all, Article I, Section 8 of the Constitution says that "The Congress shall have power . . . To declare war"—Congress did pass the War Powers Act in 1973, over President Nixon's veto. The act requires greater prior consultation by the president with Congress before committing troops and allows Congress to direct the president to disengage troops if committed without a declaration of war or specific statutory authority. In a way, though, the act takes full advantage of Congress's traditional reluctance to act. Its key provision states that a president must stop hostilities after sixty days unless Congress votes its approval of his actions. But in the end, as Senator Thomas Eagleton has argued in *War and Presidential Power*, Congress may have simply conspired in its own undoing by passing a law which recognizes presidential powers that many feel do not exist under the Constitution in the first place.

A similar evolution has affected what are called "executive agreements." Although these secret arrangements, signed by the president and a foreign country, have the force of treaties, Congress knows little about them. According to former senator Clifford Case, some 4,000 of the agreements were in effect in the mid-1970s. In fact, presidents have increasingly used such agreements for some of their most important decisions with other countries, while treaties have been employed for less important matters. "Every day we vote on treaties that have to do with trivial matters," Senator Frank Church complained in an interview in *Harper's* magazine. "In fact, the more trivial the matter the more inclined the executive is to submit it to the Senate for ratification as a treaty." In 1972, Congress passed a law requiring such agreements to be reported to Congress within sixty days, but did not require that they receive Senate approval.

From Impotence to Overkill—Legislative Veto and Sunset

The framers of the Constitution devised the presidential veto as a principal means of check and balance between the executive and legislative branches—though they never intended it to be employed as frequently as it is today. Like the congressional power to impeach, the framers envisioned the veto as an emergency safeguard to be used to correct outrageous and temporary legislative whims.

But after FDR became a master at using the veto to protect his New Deal programs, his successors continued using the veto as a political tool. Former President Ford vetoed 17 bills in just one year (1975). President Carter has occasionally vetoed legislation passed by a majority of his own party—perhaps to prove that even a Democratic Congress can't push him around and get away with it. Yet if Madison and Hamilton could not envision the routine use of presidential veto power to thwart the will of the people's representatives, they could hardly have foreseen the congressional counter-assault and overreaction known as the "legislative veto."

With the federal bureaucracy about as popular as small-pox, the idea of the "legislative veto" is proving nearly irresistible to members of the House frustrated by in-dependent-minded executive agencies. When made part of a bill, a legislative veto provision gives one or both houses of congress, and in some cases a congressional committee, the authority to overrule specific agency regulations within a specified number of days, usually sixty. For example, legislative veto provisions cover such matters as the commitment of American troops abroad, large international arms sales, Federal Election Commission regulations, some Department of Transportation rules, Office of Education rule-making, and most executive re-organizations.

While the legislative veto is not new, its popularity ac-celerated recently, following Richard Nixon's abuses. First enacted during Herbert Hoover's administration, the legis-lative veto was used sparingly during the many years when both the White House and the Congress were con-trolled by Democrats. Between 1932 and 1968, Congress included them in an average of only three bills a year. Yet twenty-four legislative vetoes were passed by the 93rd Congress alone. The Congressional Research Service found that by 1978, 295 legislative veto provisions had been scattered among 196 pieces of legislation.

The impulse behind the legislative veto movement is understandable, and its rhetoric fetching. Its boosters, led by Rep. Elliott H. Levitas (D.-Ga.), argue that as presi-dents appropriated more and more power from acquies-cent Congresses, and as bureaucrats increasingly allocated billions in benefits and costs, the bureaucracy became a fourth branch of government. As Levitas testified before the House Rules Committee in May, 1978:

> We have seen our legislative efforts frustrated and distorted when the implementing rules and regulations are published. . . . The ratio between bureaucratic rules and regulations and acts of Congress runs about 18 to 1. . . . Are we going to continue to let unelected bureaucrats continue to pass laws without effective Congressional controls? . . . Who makes the

laws in this country—the elected representatives of the people or the unelected bureaucrats?

Understandable and fetching—but also unconstitutional and unworkable. The constitutional objections are substantial. Article I states that to become law a bill must pass both houses of Congress and be signed by the president—or be vetoed by the president and then overridden by two-thirds of each chamber. The legislative veto simply erases the president from this process. It turns the Constitution on its head to have the president write the laws and Congress veto them. Furthermore, the Constitution vests legislative authority in the House and Senate acting together. But one-house veto plans would let either house unmake the laws alone. Thus, whenever the House and Senate disagreed, they could veto each other when the regulations were published. Not only might this reduce the incentives for compromise, but with thousands of rules and regulations to worry about, Congress could easily become even more fragmented, frenzied, and frustrated than it is now.

The burden-of-review argument has won more adherents in the Senate, where far fewer legislators are available to examine the daily truckload of statutes that will flow down Pennsylvania Avenue to the Capitol. (The House in 1978 voted for legislative veto provisions in bills by 2 to 1 majorities—or about the same margin that the Senate rejected them.) Just one agency, the Environmental Protection Agency, issued 249 rules, consuming 762 pages in the *Federal Register* and producing 2.9 million pages of back-up documents in 1976; a Library of Congress study found that in one typical month, February, 1976, nine agencies within the jurisdiction of the House Interstate and Foreign Commerce Committee issued 149 rules or proposed rules. Congress digests 15,000 bills a year and the average member casts 700 votes annually. To load onto this structure the responsibility of reviewing tens of thousands of agency decisions in the name of countering bureaucracy undermines the general policy-making function of Congress and converts Congress into a super-bureaucracy itself.

The widespread use of legislative vetoes would also likely "politicize" the agency process. A political review in the Congress will often be tantamount to a "special interest review." Opponents claim that the legislative veto would turn a chamber of Congress, or a relevant committee, into a kind of political court-of-last-resort. This development, however, would reverse the historical *raison d'être* of agency proceedings—where regulatory and expert judges are supposed to decide complex economic issues according to the merits of the case and not the muscle of the interested industry in off-the-record meetings.

Wealthy and organized special interests would have the resources and self-interest to lobby massively the relevant committee and to reverse an unfavorable ruling; but non-wealthy, unorganized individual citizens affected by that rule could not comparably make a case. With corporate PACs proliferating and tens of millions of dollars at stake over specific rulings—e.g., the FTC decides that optometrists can't prohibit price advertising, HEW promotes the use of generic drugs, OSHA issues brown lung standards—one could expect optometrists, drug manufacturers, and textile companies to pour millions into last-ditch lobbying campaigns. "Rather than increasing Congressional control," says Rep. Bob Eckhardt (D.-Tex.), "this legislation will simply provide more business for the high-priced Washington lobbyist."

Still, legislative veto won't go away until the problem that propels it is solved—how to control the bureaucracy. A majority of the House now sees this device as a way of restoring its wounded institutional pride and assuring the folks at home that the bureaucracy is being checkmated. But there are other ways a frustrated Congress can watch and oversee agency actions.

If Congress doesn't like an agency decision, it can pass a law to reverse it or discipline the agency through the oversight process. So when the Department of Transportation implemented Henry Ford's unpopular suggestion of a buzzer-interlock system in new cars, Congress voted its disapproval; when parts of the Real Estate Settlement Procedures Act proved ineffective, those parts were simply repealed. As Rep. Levitas himself testified: "Greater oversight, stricter standards for the appointment of cabinet members, agency chairmen and commissioners and greater reliance on the authorization and appropriations process are additional tools available to Congress to control the executive and independent agencies in general."

Going further, Congress has the authority to abolish an agency it thinks is performing poorly or to deregulate in whole or in part (as it began doing to the Civil Aeronautics Board in 1978). It can refuse to confirm nominees whose views clash with those of Congress. It can pass legislation providing for "public participation funding," which would encourage citizens' groups to appear in agency proceedings when they have a contribution to make but lack the funds needed to appear. As House Government Operations Committee Chairman Jack Brooks has said, "Congress is not a pitiful, helpless giant in its dealings with the bureaucracy."

Like the legislative veto, the idea of "sunset" legislation shows how an insecure Congress can overreact to its historic weakness *vis-à-vis* the executive. The idea behind sunset is simple. Because Congress inadequately oversees the executive branch (see "Congress's 'Oversight' " below), an action-forcing mechanism is needed to terminate periodically all federal programs unless a program can justify its continued existence to Congress.

Undoubtedly, the task of reapproval is massive, but no one knows just how massive. The number of programs to be reviewed depends on who is defining the term "program." While a Governmental Affairs Committee "table of federal programs" lists 1,250 units, the Senate Rules Committee estimated there could be 50,000 programs. Even taking the lower figure, Congress would have to review more than 200 programs per year under the proposed S. 2, or better than one program each day that Congress is in session. Colorado's sunset process, involving just thirteen regulatory agencies a year, is one thing; one program per day is quite another. As Senator Thomas F. Eagleton observed, "I hear my colleagues mutter about how we senators are becoming captive creatures of our burgeoning office and committee staffs; with sunset, 'burgeoning' may well become 'bloated.' "

The workload problem cannot be easily dismissed, especially for a proposal that would guillotine agencies if Congress did *not* act. Given this burden and the fact that the Congress, like many college students, does most of its work at the end of the term, the likely result would be a perfunctory thumbs-up or thumbs-down on many programs. Yet such a cursory review is the very evil to which sunset is addressed.

Worse is sunset's inherent bias against "people" programs—those protecting consumer health and safety, safeguarding civil rights, aiding the needy. While it is not difficult to tally up the costs to business of health and safety legislation, such as the Auto Safety Act or the Occupational Safety and Health Act (OSHA), it is difficult and at times impossible to quantify the benefits to society. How do you put a price tag on the avoidance of cancer in future generations because the government prevented an employer from using a toxic substance? Or the benefit of a six-year-old not being disfigured by flammable pajamas?

Human welfare programs usually have diffuse and unorganized constituents: welfare mothers, consumers who may buy a dangerous car or drug, workers who may lose an eye. Corporate welfare programs usually have politically powerful constituents, such as major contractors for weapons systems or the merchant marine for the Maritime Administration. In the struggle to keep Congress from failing to renew their programs, the latter are far better equipped to play power politics. For example, the most prominent federal agency terminated has been the Office of Economic Opportunity (a benefit program for poor people), not the Department of Commerce (a benefit program for big corporations). Congress abolished the Renegotiation Board, an agency which benefits taxpayers generally but is strongly opposed by military contractors seeking the highest benefits possible.

Due to powerful corporate opposition, health/safety programs often require a catastrophe to come into existence. Tough food and drug laws were passed in the wake of the 1938 and 1962 drug scandals; a report on 30,000 annual deaths from product hazards led to the creation of the Consumer Product Safety Commission. Their extinction should not depend on a successful filibuster or a presidential veto. Opponents of these social programs—needing only 145 House votes or 34 Senate votes to sustain the veto of a Ford-like president—would have undue leverage over the content of fundamental programs. As Sierra Club official Carl Pope has written, "By the end of Gerald Ford's unelected term in office, under some sunset proposals, we would have lost the Clean Air Act, the Clean Water Act, OSHA and possibly NEPA (National Environmental Policy Act). Each of these would have been up for review, and none would have been signed by the President in an effective form."

To say that the sunset solution is defective is not to say that the problems of inadequate congressional oversight and executive agency misregulation are not real. Yes, Congress must exercise ultimate control over federal programs. So why not require instead congressional committees (i.e., an "action forcing" mechanism) to undertake periodically a "zero-based" review of the cost, performance, need for, and alternatives to all federal programs and tax expenditures? A program or authorization would then be eliminated only if Congress affirmatively passed legislation, which was then signed by the president, but not if it did nothing.

This shift in burden would help protect against extinguishing agencies, in the words of a Senate Finance staff report, "through scheduling inadvertencies or from being held hostage by a President or by a determined minority interest against the will of the majority of Congress." For Congress to insist that elimination result from nonaction betrays a lack of confidence in its own ability to act where necessary, and, like the legislative veto, may be a cure worse than the disease.

Congress's "Oversight"

Congress is, or ought to be, the watchdog of the public purse. Even if it no longer initiates legislation, even if the president can play a shell game with the funds Congress has appropriated, Congress should vigorously and constantly yap at the executive's heels to make sure that funds are not squandered, that incompetent administrators don't fritter taxpayers dollars away on worthless or marginal projects, that the executive is obeying the laws and enforcing the laws. Congress is the only representative of the people—whose money, after all, is being spent—that has the power to see that the executive is doing its work.

With felicity rare for congressional jargon, this area is called "legislative *oversight*." The double meaning is a perfect guide to the topic. For just as Congress tries to oversee its laws once they are passed, much of its weakness here is due to oversights. The reason for oversight—or "review"—is that laws don't always live up to their ambitions. Everyday experience provides examples of legislation that has not accomplished its purpose. In 1967, for example, after a series of nauseating articles about packinghouses, Congress passed the Wholesome Meat Act. By 1969, all state slaughterhouses were supposed to meet federal standards or be taken over by the U.S. (except for a special one-year grace period in some cases). The deadline came and went, and federal inspectors moved into only one state. The others were approved—not, in most cases, because they had improved their standards, but because the federal standards had dipped to meet them.

In addition, Congress is responsible for the "quasi-legislative" agencies. These regulatory bodies, such as the Interstate Commerce Commission and the Federal Trade Commission, officially function with powers delegated by Congress. Because Congress cannot deal with each railroad rate claim or advertiser's complaint, it passes the powers to regulatory agencies. Congress is still responsible to see that the powers it has delegated to the agencies are used well.

The procedures for congressional oversight range from special hearings, or investigations of an agency, to informal queries, or questions at appropriations time. The important fact about all of them is that they have proved increasingly inadequate. As Jerry Cohen and Morton Mintz wrote in *America, Inc.*:

> In theory the deficiencies of the independent regulatory agencies and of units of the executive branch with regulatory powers would be alleviated and on occasion maybe even corrected if Congress reliably and seriously exercised its responsibility to oversee their performance. The unhappy truth is that reliable, serious, and sustained oversight is the exception rather than the rule on Capitol Hill. Not even in remote degree have the oversight mechanisms of Congress kept pace with the enormous growth of the executive.

The reasons behind the failures of oversight are displayed clearly in the few *successful* instances of oversight. Rep. John Moss (D.-Calif.) retired from Congress in 1978 after thirteen terms, but not before he had earned a reputation as "the father of oversight." As chairman of the House Oversight and Investigations subcommittee, in the 95th Congress alone, he tackled and issued major reports on HEW birth control policy, unnecessary surgery, the cost of drugs, pesticide regulations, Firestone tires, and the world uranium cartel, among others. He threatened to hold HEW Secretary Joseph Califano in contempt for failure to turn over documents pursuant to a subpoena—until Califano finally complied.

There are occasional other instances of effective congressional oversight. Senator Proxmire's solo scrutiny of the Defense budget has often embarrassed the Pentagon into response. Former chairman William Fulbright of the Foreign Relations Committee went so far as to have that committee hire its own investigators to make on-the-spot studies in Laos, Greece, and elsewhere. Also, the chairman of the Administrative Practices and Procedures subcommittee, Senator Edward Kennedy, creatively sent out "protective subpoenas" to FDA medical officials—which enabled them to publicly testify, without fear of agency reprisal, about the way the FDA harasses staff who raise too many safety questions about pending drugs.

But far more common is the congressional committee which perfunctorily reviews executive activity—one member once complaining that "you wait two hours so you can get a shot at the secretary of defense, and then it lasts only five minutes. The only thing you know is that you're getting bullshit from him, and there's nothing you can do about it." And more common yet are no oversight hearings at all by the responsible committees.

Why? To an extent, bills sponsored and projects obtained can be used in the constant quest for reelection, but oversight usually wins little public attention. More importantly, congressional staff—whose mission it is to undertake executive oversight—simply lack the numbers and information to perform adequately. Congress's other potential ally is the General Accounting Office, the legislature's staff of investigators. The GAO is a relatively bright spot in Congress's general prospect, and any reassertion of congressional investigative power will probably begin there.

The GAO is an arm of Congress; its job is to help congressmen study the government. Before 1950, it spent most of its time doing purely accounting work. After the Korean War, however, Comptroller General Joseph Campbell led GAO into more adventuresome areas. Campbell began a series of studies of war industries and produced, during the fifties, reports on profiteering and wasteful construction. Campbell, who had been treasurer of Columbia University before coming to the GAO in 1954, favored a candid style rare in government reports. His audits were studded with such phrases as "excessive cost" and "congressional intent as to cost limitations circumvented," shockers in a society accustomed to squishy government prose.

Campbell soon ran afoul of the Defense Department and the defense contractors; by 1965, they had conveyed their unhappiness to Chet Holifield. In his response to the Pentagon complaints, Holifield illustrated one of the most potent executive tactics for controlling the legislature: by setting up one congressman with favors and patronage, the executive can count on him to beat down other critics. The Committee on Government Operations held hearings on the GAO in 1965, which then chairman Holifield began by mentioning "the great concern that has been shown in industry circles, and, recently, in the Department of Defense over the difficult and sometimes awkward situations created by the GAO audit reports." By the end of the hearings, the GAO had been tamed. It agreed to a list of conditions, including an agreement to stop using company names in the reports and an effort to be more "constructive."

With that behind it, and with cautious bureaucrat Elmer Staats now as comptroller general, the GAO walks a fine line between toadyism and giving offense, but it still is the most important investigative tool Congress has. It showed its split personality well in a recent study of, once again, defense contractors. While the audit itself was factual and critical—revealing that seventy-seven weapons systems would cost $28.7 billion more than estimated and that the average profit rate was a fantastic 56 percent—the GAO sent the report to the industry before publishing it, and then incorporated many industry alibis into the text and toned down its own charges.

Despite its occasional disappointments, the GAO offers congressmen their main defense against the analysts of the White House and the OMB. Whenever members ask, the GAO will make studies of specific problems. Rep. Elizabeth Holtzman (D.-N.Y.), for example, was dissatisfied in 1976 with the Department of Labor's answers to her questions about its CETA jobs program. She requested a GAO study which uncovered many abuses in the program. Unfortunately, few members of Congress take advantage of the service. In 1978, for example, fewer than 500 reports were made to members of Congress and congressional committees. In fact, only 25 percent of GAO's studies are done at the request of representatives and senators—the remainder are the result of the GAO's own initiative.

If, indeed, information is the key to the executive's power, Congress will have to do more than ask for an occasional GAO study. What is needed is a major overhaul of Congress's information sources so that it can better monitor the executive. As Joseph Califano, former special assistant to President Johnson and now HEW secretary, once wrote between his stints in government:

> The Congress is presently the separate but unequal branch of the federal government. . . . The basic reason for the decline in congressional effectiveness and status, however, lies not with the executive branch or some federal bureaucrats. . . . Responsibility for its separate but unequal status rests largely with the Congress itself.
>
> The Congress is dependent upon the executive branch for most of its information, with an occasional and too often superficial assist from outside experts.
>
> Congress has ignored the revolution in analytical technology. . . . The Congress has only three or four computers, and those computers operate in large measure on payrolls and housekeeping matters. Contrast the executive branch, which now has some 4,000 computers working almost entirely on substantive policy issues.
>
> The stark fact is that neither Congress nor any of

its committees has the consistent capability—without almost total reliance on the informational and analytical resources of the executive branch—of developing coherent, large-scale federal programs.

Belatedly, press revelations have shaken Congress awake to the need for effective oversight and information about executive branch activity. After Seymour Hersh reported in the *New York Times* that the Central Intelligence Agency, contrary to its charter, had conducted domestic spying operations, and after the *Washington Post* disclosed that the FBI had been collecting derogatory information on the members themselves, Congress erupted with expressions of indignation and outrage. As members and committees began vying to investigate the charges, the Senate and House each gravely announced the creation of special select committees, similar to the Watergate committee, to investigate not only the FBI and the CIA, but the intelligence units of the Army, Navy, and Air Force, the Secret Service, and the Justice and State departments, not to mention a host of less well-known agencies pocketed throughout the bureaucracy.

The alacrity with which Congress responded to these disclosures hardly spoke well of the oversight that had apparently not previously existed. Neither the FBI nor the CIA had been subjected to anything but the most cursory examinations in the past, even though the CIA was the specific responsibility of no less than four subcommittees in the House and Senate. Before these subcommittees finally came in from the cold, however, their collective failure was probably best summed up in an exchange between Alan Cranston of California and former senator Allen Ellender—then the chairman of one of the subcommittees —in a 1971 debate on CIA operations in Laos:

> *Cranston:* The Chairman stated that he never would have thought of even asking about CIA funds being used to conduct the war in Laos. I would like to ask the Senator if, since then, he has inquired and now knows whether that is being done?
> *Ellender:* I have not inquired.
> *Cranston:* You do not know, in fact?
> *Ellender:* No.

Cranston: As you are one of the five men privy to this information, in fact you are the number one man of the five men who would know, then who would know what happened to this money? The fact is, not even the five men know the facts in this situation.
Ellender: Probably not.

Even after Watergate had unearthed a substantial amount of evidence of questionable CIA activity, the subcommittees took no action. Fully a year before the *New York Times* disclosures, CIA Director William Colby had briefed the chairmen about the domestic spying operations, yet they still could not bring themselves to take any kind of action. In 1974, one of the committees managed to meet six times, another met five times, one met twice, and one had no records of any meetings. It took the promise of national publicity, the forced resignation of several CIA officials, and the beginning of a presidential investigation to force Congress to face an issue—and by 1979 it has still not been resolved.

The CIA and FBI investigations are surely spectacular, but the most momentous test of Congress's oversight capabilities came in the vice presidential confirmation hearings of Gerald Ford and Nelson Rockefeller. The power that the resignations of Spiro Agnew and Richard Nixon placed in the hands of Congress was unprecedented: for the first time the country had a president and vice president who had not been elected by the voters but judged only by the Congress.

The Senate Rules and House Judiciary committees began their hearings into Ford's nomination with the increasing possibility that Nixon's days in office were numbered; the Judiciary Committee in fact was scheduled to begin an impeachment inquiry as soon as it had completed its hearings on Ford. Although his personal background had been well documented in a 1,400-page FBI report and in an examination of his income tax returns, the committees paid far less attention to his public record—even many who opposed his political philosophy felt it should not enter into their discussion of his qualifications for this office. After the scandal and corruption that had brought down Agnew and was beginning to topple Nixon, most members were both relieved and gratified by the lack of evidence against Ford's personal integrity. As Alan Cranston remarked during the Senate debate on the nominations, "I doubt if there has ever been a time when integrity had so surpassed ideology in the judgement of a man for so high an office in the land." Within a relatively brief six weeks from the start of the hearings, Ford was sworn in as vice president after overwhelming votes in favor of his selection in both houses.

Nelson Rockefeller's hearings before the same committees lasted two and a half months longer and were more acrimonious, but in the end the differences were more superficial than real. While Senate Rules Committee members spent hours asking the nominee detailed questions concerning his gifts to friends and his indirect financing of a book derogatory to gubernatorial opponent Arthur Goldberg, they devoted practically no time to delving into his philosophical and policy views. As Richard Reeves wrote, ". . . with all the preoccupation with questions of integrity in the wake of Watergate, there was precious little questioning about Mr. Rockefeller's view of detente, defense, inflation, recession, energy, pollution, and hunger. . . . in the end, [he] sailed through the hearings a grinning, winking, unbending winner, just as he sailed through four gubernatorial campaigns in New York."

The House Judiciary Committee's treatment of the nomination was even more slipshod. House Speaker Carl Albert, at the time next in line to the presidency, had let the committee know that they were to come up with a vice president in a hurry, and the members, only recently recovered from the strain of impeachment and the November elections, were in no mood to argue. Also, committee Chairman Peter Rodino was reportedly reluctant to have it appear that the committee was rejecting Rockefeller simply because he was wealthy. Relying heavily on the information provided by the Rules Committee, the Judiciary Committee subpoenaed no bank records, took no sworn depositions, and failed to call a number of key witnesses who might have answered questions about what the recipients of Rockefeller's gifts did with the money he gave them and whether or not there had been any undue influence gained by the gifts. The staff was ill-equipped in both time and expertise to examine carefully the limited financial reports on Rockefeller they were provided.

The committee's questioning of the nominee was for the most part ill-informed and hasty. Allotted a mere five minutes apiece, members had little time for follow-up questions. The Judiciary Committee voted to confirm Governor Rockefeller (26–12). By the time the issue came to the floor of the House, the Senate was already putting the finishing touches on preparations for Rockefeller's swearing-in that same afternoon.

Perhaps the most obvious example of ceremonial congressional oversight was the House Judiciary Committee's meeting with President Ford on his decision to pardon Richard Nixon. The pardon had produced a storm of public controversy and had prompted in Congress the use of an obscure means of obtaining information called a "resolution of inquiry." Rep. Bella Abzug had first revived the practice in an unsuccessful effort to obtain information on the Indochina War. After the pardon, both she and Rep. John Conyers introduced such resolutions, which asked fourteen questions about the circumstances under which Ford had made his decision.

After two weeks of letters and telephone calls from Judiciary Committee member William Hungate, Ford volunteered to appear in person before Hungate's subcommittee on Criminal Justice rather than supply written answers to the questions. His unprecedented decision to testify overwhelmed most of the Congress with amazement and gratitude, but there were, nevertheless, a few cynics. Rep. George Danielson, for one, was worried that the president might be so "open, frank, and congenial" that the subcommittee might surrender "like the farmer's daughter . . . beware of Presidents who come with a broad smile."

As it turned out, a smile was about the only direct response the subcommittee members got out of Ford's televised testimony, a result for which they had only themselves to blame. Most of the members seemed so enraptured by the president's mere presence in the committee room that they appeared to forget that he was there for any particular purpose. They praised him politely for coming, he thanked them for letting him come, and everyone talked about how historic the whole affair was.

With the exception of Rep. Holtzman, most of the subcommittee members seemed to do little more than feed

Ford cues as he proceeded to tell them for the most part what they already knew. Holtzman, however, attempted to treat the president as a witness at a hearing rather than as a guest star on a TV talk show. After pointing out the general weaknesses of the hearing's format—the lack of time for questions, the absence of the necessary witnesses and documents—she proceeded to ask Ford a number of specific questions aimed at discovering what the hearing was supposedly all about: the reasons behind Ford's decision. All she received in return, however, was a general monologue from the president and a reprimand from Rep. Lawrence ·Hogan, who professed himself to be "amazed" at the "gentlelady's accusatory speech."

Watergate and Impeachment

The most spectacular recent example of congressional oversight was also the most significant confrontation of the past century between the president and Congress—Watergate, that "third-rate burglary" that grew into a constellation of crimes that eventually toppled a president. Looking back, it appears an obvious morality play—Richard Nixon's arrogance and excesses versus the decency and righteousness of John Sirica, Peter Rodino, and Sam Ervin. Congress slays the dragon. Yet if it were not for a vigilant, contentious press and the president's own self-wounding ways, Nixon might never have had to take a helicopter off the White House lawn on August 9, 1974. "Nixon essentially impeached himself," said Rep. John Conyers, a member of the House Judiciary Committee. "Most of the Members had a clear distaste for impeachment. Where the evidence was so overwhelming as to be unavoidable, they had no choice—Nixon had done everything possible to show them how guilty he was. We were just lucky, that's all." And far from an easy-flowing stream of revelations, the proceedings hesitated and tripped along the way toward their conclusion. Or as an aide to one Judiciary Committee member noted:

> It's important to understand that the process ·wasn't as inevitable as it's beginning to look now that it's all over. Congress wanted a way out of this decision and an appearance of irresponsibility on the part of the committee would have given them the excuse they

needed. It could easily have gone the other way if too many false steps had been made in the beginning.

The congressional beginning was of course the Senate Watergate hearings, a major spectacle unfolding amid the chandeliers and high marble pillars of room 318 of the Old Senate Office Building. People whose TV fare encompassed only daytime soap operas now turned to the Watergate hearings like a junkie to a fix. They learned more about their president and their Congress than they had ever known before, or perhaps wanted to know. But lavish media attention, while heightening the committee's impact and importance, did not obscure its weaknesses. Follow-up questions on important points often went unasked, while witnesses who showed the proper signs of contrition were sometimes dismissed with an oratorical slap on the wrist.

Once the process shifted to the House Judiciary Committee, Chairman Peter Rodino, a 64-year-old representative from Newark, New Jersey, became the focus of attention. An undistinguished and obscure back-bencher who had been chairman less than a year, with a scratchy voice more "Joisey" than Churchillian, Rodino was an unlikely individual to weld the bipartisan majority essential to preserving the credibility of the inquiry. But Rodino's meticulous efforts to mold the committee into at least a semblance of nonpartisan unity and sober judgment went far to make the idea of impeachment less frightening to Congress and the public. It also helped to undermine the White House tactic of dismissing the committee as a "partisan lynch mob" intent on harassing a beleaguered president.

On one side of the inquiry were seven insistent impeachment advocates, ranging from Father Robert F. Drinan (D.-Mass.) to wily Texas millionaire Jack Brooks. The Texas Democrat found it achingly difficult to act in the impartial, judicial manner that he thought was expected, as he showed in an interview with James Naughton of the *New York Times:* "It's gonna be a fun year, I'm gonna watch all those Republicans and Southern Democrats sit down to a bullet breakfast . . . In a matter of dealing with Nixon, whom I opposed in '52, whom I've never been close to, who doesn't represent my point

of view—we're just not compatible, that mother——."
Rodino had to struggle to prevent these members from
alienating the unconvinced.

On the other side were nine conservative Republicans
who made it clear from the start that they would go down
the line for the President's defense. They ranged from
Charles Wiggins (Cal.), whose lawyerly bearing cloaked
partisanship with objectivity, to Michigan's Edward
Hutchinson, ranking minority member of the committee,
who stated at the beginning of the inquiry that Nixon
should not be removed from office "for every little impeachable offense." The chairman sought to give the undecided members—such as Flowers, Thorton, Railsback,
Mann, McClory, Cohen, Butler, Froehlich, Hogan, and
Fish—room to move and time to decide. Most of them had
to wrestle with their consciences—and with their constituencies as well. Each of them would face reelection in just
over a year, and it was clear that this was the issue on
which they would be judged.

Rodino recognized that history was looking over his
shoulder and would want to know not only what the
committee concluded about Nixon, but also whether it
had acted fairly. The members were not only judging
Richard Nixon, but were establishing standards by which
to judge all future presidents. Part of this legacy for the
future was a report entitled "Constitutional Grounds for
Presidential Impeachment," which rejected the Nixon
White House notion that a president could only be impeached for committing an indictable crime. The report
pointed out that "some of the most grievous offenses
against our constitutional form of government may not
entail violation of the criminal law," and that "it would be
anomalous if the founders, having barred criminal sanctions from the impeachment remedy . . . intended to restrict the grounds for impeachment to conduct that was
criminal."

This report was supplemented by the staff's presentation,
in closed session, of the evidence against President Nixon.
The members received thirty-six looseleaf notebooks which
contained over 7,200 pages of evidence and 650 findings
of fact. Most of the material focused on the Watergate
break-in and cover-up, allegations of bribery in the ITT
and milk price support cases, domestic surveillance, abuse

of the IRS, and the activities of the special prosecutor. Several of the original subjects of the inquiry, such as the secret bombing of Cambodia and the impoundment of funds appropriated by Congress, were given less attention, or ignored altogether. "Ironically, the allegations that received the least attention from the staff, and, ultimately, from the Committee," recalled one staff member, "were the ones most directly related to the relative roles of Congress and the executive branch and the balance of power between the two."

The staff report and presentation, however, was quickly rejected by the conservative Republicans, who looked instead for absolute proof that Nixon had committed an impeachable offense. The search for a "smoking gun" was enhanced by the White House's self-destructive ability to shock Congress and the nation at frequent intervals. The catch phrases for the building body of evidence against the President—Saturday Night Massacre, 18½-minute gap—were constantly on the lips of the committee members and the nation.

Finally, in July, 1974, committee counsel John Doar began to summarize the case against Richard Nixon, telling the members that "reasonable men acting reasonably would find the President guilty." Doar's presentation was of great importance to many of the undecided members. "It's one thing to have four great big volumes of evidence that tell you the facts about Watergate," said Railsback. "It's another thing to have an advocate's brief that boils down the relevant facts and gives you legal theories. You get a much better picture of the case."

Armed with Doar's summation, and the knowledge that a decision could not be put off much longer, the members of the so-called swing group gradually made up their individual and collective minds to vote to impeach the president of the United States. Walter Flowers described the agony of how he made his decision:

> The more I thought about it, and tried to think about doing something else, I realized I couldn't. Then the undecided people got together and we started talking among ourselves. Most of us probably started out looking for a way to support the President. My whole background and upbringing would make me that way.

Who I am and where I come from. But when you got all of the evidence before us so-called "persuadables" and we all came down on the same side, that really struck us. . . . I tried to look at it from the side of what happens if we fail to impeach. It's worse.

Beginning on July 24, before a national television audience, the articles of impeachment were considered. Three were passed. One, which passed 27–11, charged the president with pursuing "a course of conduct or plan" to cover up the Watergate break-in. The other two involved his failures to "faithfully execute" his office and to respond to congressional subpoenas for 147 taped conversations. Three more articles charging misuse of government moneys, tax fraud, and the secret bombings of Cambodia failed to pass.

A week after the committee filed its charges, the White House bowed to a unanimous Supreme Court and released the transcript of a tape of three conversations between Nixon and Haldeman that proved Nixon had ordered the beginning of the cover-up six days after the Watergate break-in. The tape proved to be the so-called "smoking gun" neither the president nor Congress could ignore. Within hours of the transcripts' release, the remaining eleven Republican members of the Judiciary Committee had announced their support for the first article of impeachment.

What did the committee's proceedings on impeachment have to say to future presidents? Probably that impeachment may be easier to contemplate and more difficult to pursue. Rep. Elizabeth Holtzman (D.-N.Y.) commented that "when the subject of impeachment was first brought up, everyone was saying that the country wouldn't tolerate it, that people wouldn't understand the constitutional and political questions involved. We've shown that they can and we've also made it clear that in future questions of impeachment, a president will be held responsible directly and through his aides."

To John Conyers, however, author of the aborted Cambodia resolution, there was a slightly different lesson. "I think the advice we've left for the next president interested in subverting the constitution is quite simple—don't tape yourself. I think we've set impossibly high standards for any future impeachment inquiry . . . In the areas where there were no tapes and smoking guns, the issues that involved interference with the Congress, we either acted in a very confused manner or we didn't act at all."

Congress vs. Carter—A New Balance?

For decades Congress was a broken branch of government. When confronted with national problems or overreaching presidents, it receded and acquiesced. Its ability to initiate legislation, shape the budget, participate in war or foreign policy, and oversee the executive bureaucracy went slack and atrophied. "The Congress does not like to take responsibility," wrote Elizabeth Drew in 1974. "It would prefer not to have to end a war, delay development of a weapon, raise taxes, or take on a President—except when it appears safe to do so. And after it has taken an important action, it usually wants to take a rest."

Finally, in the mid-1970s, members of Congress responded to their institutional erosion because, as Governor Adlai Stevenson once said in another context, they could "see the handwriting on the wall only when their backs [were] to it." Nixon and Watergate put their backs to the wall. The passage over Nixon's veto of the War Powers Act was the first shot in the power realignment. It was followed by the congressional refusal to approve a supplemental appropriation to "wind down" the Indochina War and the near-unanimous passage of the Budget and Impoundment Control Act of 1974. Finally, the Watergate and impeachment hearings dramatically demonstrated the ultimate power of Congress over the president when executive abuses reach a critical mass.

By the time Jimmy Carter came to the White House, Congress had been in a fighting mood for several years. According to Rep. Morris Udall, "Anybody who took the oath on that January day in 1977 was going to face this giant, which had awakened after slumbering for many years . . . You could have resurrected Lincoln, Washington and Franklin Roosevelt, had a synthesis of them all, and I'm sure [President Carter] would still have trouble." The adversarial habit, provoked and unleashed by Nixon, now seemed hard to stop, which upset Rep. John Anderson. "There is a confluence of historical forces that have brought an erosion in executive power. It was necessary for a while but there has been an overreaction that has caused the pendulum to swing too far." To Senator Alan Cranston, however, the recent congressional assertiveness is not something to fret over. "Congress has reawakened to its Constitutional role," he said in an interview. "Executive-legislative relations were *too* perfect under Johnson. . . . There are supposed to be tensions and differences between the two branches." And Carter, being the first "non-congressional" president since Eisenhower, seemed to pay for his lack of prior allies in the Congress. President Kennedy, for example, won 83 percent of his congressional votes; President Johnson, 90 percent; and President Nixon, with the opposite party controlling Congress, 76 percent. President Carter won 77 percent during his first two years in office. When he was then asked by Bill Moyers what had been the most unpleasant surprises of his presidency, he answered that "one was the inertia of Congress, the length of time it takes to get a complicated piece of legislation through Congress."

But the presidency in modern times is unaccustomed to prolonged periods of subordination to Congress. At worst, Jimmy Carter was a novice, a novice who received an education. "I think I went through a year or more where I was not sure about what the authority of the President was or the influence," he said mid-term. "Now I am beginning to see that there is a proper, stronger role for the President to play than I had thought maybe six months ago." Now "cabinet government" was out, and increased consultation with Congress was in. The President boldly utilized his ability to determine foreign policy (his Camp David negotiations and normalization of relations with the People's Republic of China being two examples), and to mobilize public opinion (prior to a major water projects vote, the White House sent background kits to 1,750 newspapers, 500 radio and TV stations, and 200 columnists). "The Administration became more sophisticated in its dealings with Congress," said Rep. James Florio (D.-N.J.), expressing a widely shared view. "The President learned how the system worked."

The 1970s, then, saw a Congress lurching to and fro between what Arthur Schlesinger, Jr., called "the imperial presidency" and what Daniel Patrick Moynihan called "the imperial Congress." This swing was simply a more compressed version of a historical and constitutional ebb and flow between these two branches of government. Occasionally Congress seems strong—largely due to weak and/or inexperienced presidents. But according even to Senator Edmund Muskie, himself a candidate for the presidency and architect of the Budget Act, "No matter how assertive [Congress] is, or how creative and qualified for leadership individual members are, maybe the institution is not really equipped to act as a strong leader."

There is no such doubt about the powers of the president overall. With few exceptions, the executive branch remains ascendant, due to its sway over national media, the budget process, appointments, foreign policy, projects and contracts, the intelligence and law enforcement apparatus, and the expertise of the bureaucracy. Presidents will predictably complain about their institutional inadequacies—as the chapter's epigraph by Theodore Roosevelt reveals—but they are still the cockpit of power in Washington.

5

Lawmakers as Lawbreakers

It could probably be shown by facts and figures that there is no distinctly American criminal class except Congress.

—Mark Twain

When national leaders cried out for "law and order" in the late sixties and early seventies, no one thought to apply their words to themselves. Now we know better. If nothing else, Watergate—which has become more a cliché than a lesson—should have instructed us that it is folly to assume that people of prominence and power will invariably be law-abiding. A good place to apply this wisdom is the American Congress. The most obvious reason is symbolic: if chosen people have the power to make the law, then they should respect the law. If they do not, they can scarcely expect that others will.

Corruption involving criminal conduct has shaken Congress at least since 1873, when the House censured two members for their roles in the Crédit Mobilier stock scandal. While Congress and the country have passed through fundamental metamorphoses since then, one constant theme has been the public's suspicion of the people it sends to Washington. This was not the constitutional mistrust that had plagued the Founding Fathers—the gnawing fear that men in power would become tyrants. Instead, it was the suspicion of personal venality, that the men in government were somehow turning a profit.

In 1965, Gallup pollsters found that four times as many people thought that "political favoritism and corruption in Washington" were rising as thought them falling. Two years later, as Congress washed its hands of Adam Clay-

156

ton Powell, Gallup asked whether the revelations about Powell had surprised the public. Sixty percent thought that Powell's offenses—which the questionnaire called "misuse of government funds"—were fairly common. (Twenty-one percent disagreed.) Powell had protested, in victimized anguish, that he was only one public scapegoat among many quiet offenders. "There is no one here," he said to his accusers, "who does not have a skeleton in his closet."

The skeletons vary in size. The smallest are the personal peccadilloes—which are the stuff of public amusement, scorn, and regular exposure by Washington columnists. Outweighing these in importance are the systematic violations of Congress's own rules and laws, offenses which are not quite crimes, but which are not quite cricket, either. Conflicts of interest are the next biggest skeletons in congressional closets. Finally, there is the *summum malum* of congressional crime, instances of bribery, perjury, and influence-peddling. Taken together, the pervasiveness of lawbreaking amounts to a grim commentary on those who govern us.

Not Quite a Crime: Peccadilloes, Rules, and Laws

Congressmen are people, and subject to the same temptations and flaws as other people. At times, their visibility makes them suffer more for their failings than they otherwise would. An omission or mistake which would pass unnoticed in a plumber may become big news when attached to a politically important name. This does not excuse congressional misconduct. Just as the public expects higher standards of personal morality from those who instruct its children than from those who fix its drains and pipes, so it expects high standards from those who make its laws.

In order to assure them freedom to exercise their duties free from harassment, congressmen are granted immunity from arrest for statements made, or actions taken, in Congress or while coming from or going to Congress. This desirable privilege, however, has frequently been abused by congressmen caught in unsavory escapades. In his prepresidential days, for example, Senator Warren Harding was surprised by two New York policemen while visiting friend Nan Britton in a hotel room. As the police prepared to arrest him on charges of fornication, carnal knowledge, and drunken driving, Harding successfully argued that as a senator he could not be arrested. It was hardly what the Constitution intended for congressional immunity, but it worked well in that situation.

Several years ago, Texas Rep. Joe Pool rammed his car into the back of another car stopped at a red light. Pool refused to accept a traffic ticket from a policeman and, later, from his sergeant. Instead, he repeated over and over, "I am a congressman and I cannot be arrested." Unimpressed, the police held him for six hours before releasing him. "He kept saying he was a congressman," said the policeman, "but he didn't look like one or sound like one." Later, Pool confided to a friend, "I thought they couldn't arrest a congressman unless he'd committed a felony. But it turns out they *can* unless he's en route to or returning from a session of Congress."

They *can*, but they *don't*. On the way to a party in the summer of 1972, Mississippi Rep. Jamie Whitten—who normally conducts himself with decorum—ran a stop sign in Georgetown and struck a car, an iron fence, two trees, a brick wall, and another car on the other side of the wall. Whitten said his accelerator stuck, but an investigating officer said at the scene, "The guy's been drinking; there's alcohol on his breath. I don't think he's drunk. But he's shook up." No arrest was made and no charges were filed. "The first thing [Whitten] did," said the owner of the wall, "was to get out of the car and begin shaking everyone's hand."

In fact, there are numerous instances of congressmen driving amuck. In August, 1972, House Speaker Carl Albert drove his car into two cars shortly before midnight, as several witnesses reported that he "was obviously drunk"—a characterization Albert denied. In addition, he reportedly told a police officer on the scene, "You can't arrest me, I got you your raise." Of course, there was also the "Tidal Basin incident"—where, among other bizarre happenings, Wilbur Mills's car was speeding with its lights off. All these incidents have two things in common: a congressman was involved and his name never appeared on a police blotter.

Immunity for such indiscretions, however, is not absolute. Rep. Frank Horton (R.-N.Y.) became something of a folk hero in his Rochester district after enthusiastically pleading guilty to a drunk driving and speeding charge and serving a week in jail. Florida Rep. J. Herbert Burke was arrested for (and pled guilty to) disorderly conduct outside a bar featuring nude go-go dancers in 1977. He at first said he was spying on a narcotics deal in progress; voters gave him the boot next year. And Rep. Michael Myers (D.-Pa.) pled no contest to a charge of disorderly conduct in a fight in a Virginia bar in 1979.

Annoying as these cases might be, they are small potatoes. They involve single, unplanned romps, not deliberate self-enrichment or serious affairs of state. If this were the extent of congressional lawlessness, we could require a special driver's education course as a condition of entering Congress or the Oval Office and all sleep a little easier at night.

But it's not. Worse is the hypocrisy of congressmen abusing their own rules. Consider, for example, junketing.

Congressmen who legislate about foreign affairs or military bases may do a better job if they've seen some of the areas for themselves. That's the theory, and it's valid for some. In practice, however, many trips are personal vacations with family rather than public fact-finding. In 1971, then senator William Saxbe had a dismal 45 percent roll-call record because of his many excursions. "I took every free trip I could get," admitted the candid Saxbe. "I like to travel." In the same year, 51 percent of Congress—53 senators and 221 representatives—took foreign trips at public expense; the total cost to taxpayers was $1,114,386. Hong Kong and the Caribbean turned out to be favorite destinations for those supposedly seeking self-education. By 1977, 255 representatives or senators (47 percent) took a total of 415 trips costing $1,532,326. "Scratch hard in December," one congressman has joked, "and you'll come up with a quorum in Hong Kong." There may even be motives beyond the chance of a vacation. "Those who do get away," Jerry Landauer has written in the *Wall Street Journal*, "will enjoy little-known opportunities [double-billings, for example] for lining their own pockets—opportunities that some have exploited in the past."

Congress is aware that American taxpayers do not appreciate such jaunts. But instead of limiting them, the Senate and House—presumably acting on the wisdom that what you don't know can't hurt you—passed a law in 1973 ending the requirement that foreign travel expenditures be published in the *Congressional Record*. Former representative Wayne Hays, who backed this move, explained to a reporter that "we decided we weren't going to spend $8,000 or $9,000 [in *Record* printing costs] to let you guys do your stories on congressional travel." Post-Watergate and post-Hays, Congress restored this reporting requirement in 1976, and one year later prohibited taxpayer-funded trips for lame-duck members.

A second hoary example of bending the rules for private benefit is abuse of the franking privilege—the congressman's right to free postage. Every time you receive mail with his signature where the stamp usually goes, you are receiving franked mail. In theory, the frank can only be used for official business and never for political mail. The line is fine, and the effort it would take to inspect the hundreds of bins full of mail which roll down congressional office corridors every day would hardly be worthwhile.

The cost of abuse can still be serious. In 1968, Senator Everett Dirksen was found to have given some of his franked envelopes to an overtly political organization—a Republican voter registration group. There was no estimate of the cost involved, but there was in an earlier case involving Senator Robert Griffin. After looking through some of the newsletters Griffin had sent out during the 1966 campaign, the Post Office decided that some were political campaign material. In a typical, doomed display of strength, the Post Office demanded $25,000 from Griffin to pay for the postage. Griffin, astonished, said that his mail was no more political than anyone else's. This gives scant consolation to the Post Office or the taxpayers, but it removed the heat from Griffin. The Post Office conceded the struggle with the droll statement that use of the frank is "a matter strictly between the member of Congress and his conscience."

Large-scale juggling of committee rules (as discussed in chapter 3) and committee staff is also widespread. It is almost impossible, for example, to separate men who work for chairman Al Ullman from those who are supposed to serve the House Ways and Means Committee. This sort of thing springs less from any special avarice in chairmen's souls than from the committee and seniority systems. The fond references that a chairman will make to "my" committee show how deep the confusion runs. When a chairman lifts a researcher from "his" committee and puts him to work on some other task, more than the committee suffers. The system of fortresslike power bases, built around the mighty chairmen, grows stronger as well. Before his downfall, Senator Tom Dodd reportedly had thirteen of the twenty-one staff members of the Juvenile Delinquency subcommittee working for Dodd's office. Occasionally, voices rise in complaint. In early 1975, a seven-part series in the *Washington Post* documented the exploitation of committee staff and field hearings in painstaking detail—naming names for those who cared.

Congressmen suffer equally mild twinges of conscience about using their own staff members for political campaigns. The element of abuse is clear: staff people are paid by the government, not by the senator or representative; they are paid to serve the office, not to help the man who happens to be in office to stay there. In 1968, the two Senators Kennedy admitted that twenty of their staffers were working on Robert Kennedy's presidential campaign.

But it *is* illegal: Public Law 89–90 says an assistant can't be paid "if such does not perform the services for which he receives such compensation, in the offices of such Member . . ." Because the law is so widely violated, violation becomes custom, and custom replaces law. There are many instances of this phenomenon. Nearly all congressmen violated the archaic 1925 Federal Corrupt Practices Act (replaced in 1972), which aimed to limit campaign funding and to require some disclosure of campaign finances; yet no one has ever been prosecuted for it. An 1872 law directs House and Senate officials to deduct from a member's salary a day's pay for each day's absence, except for illness; in the last hundred years this has been done exactly twice, although there are unjustified absentees daily.

Nor is Congress always attentive even to international or constitutional law. Former representative John Rooney, for example, for years managed to obstruct American funding of the International Labor Organization because he disliked its allegedly leftist leanings. In so doing, he violated our UN obligation to help support the ILO. And an enterprising *Fort Worth Star-Telegram* reporter in 1974 discovered that at least twenty senators and representatives had odd requirements for staff positions, like "only a white girl, prefer Floridians" (Rep. James Haley, D.-Fla.), "white only" (Senator William Scott, D.-Va.), "attractive, smart, young, and no Catholics . . ." (Rep. Albert Johnson, R.-Pa.). Indeed, in August, 1974, the Congressional Office of Placement and Office Management had to delete discriminatory job requirements from some 80 percent of the job orders from 140 congressional offices. Senator John Glenn (D.-Ohio) calls Capitol Hill "the last plantation."

Violation of equal opportunity standards is only one of several laws members of Congress might violate—*if* they permitted the law to apply to them. But since they are the lawmakers, they have decided that they are above the following laws that private employers and citizens have to observe:

• Conflicts of interest. Federal law prohibits executive branch employees from participating in federal transactions involving companies in which they have a financial interest. Members of Congress have no such restriction.

• State and municipal taxes. Members are exempt from paying local income taxes in Maryland, Virginia, and Washington, D.C.

• Equal Pay Act. This law guarantees women the same pay that men receive everywhere, except on Capitol Hill.

• Age Discrimination in Employment Act. Workers between the ages of 40 and 65 are protected from discrimination by this law, except in Congress.

• The National Labor Relations Act. Congress is exempt from this law, which requires employers to recognize unions, and protects employees from unfair labor practices.

• Fair Labor Standards Act. This law, which set minimum wage, overtime pay, and child labor standards, affects all institutions except Congress.

• Freedom of Information Act. Congress ordered the executive branch to open its files to the public, under this law, but decided to keep its own records closed to the people who pay the congressmen's salaries.

• Privacy Act. Congress ordered the executive branch to

tightly guard the personal records of individual citizens, but exempted itself from the law.

• Occupational Safety and Health Act. This law requires all employers, except in Congress, to maintain federal health and safety standards in the workplace.

In feudal societies, man and job were identical. The king and the shepherd lived their roles every hour of the day. When 5:30 p.m. rolled around, they did not put down their work and retire to identical houses in the suburbs. The king had his courtiers and courtesans to remind him of his rank; the shepherd slept with his sheep. Though things have changed since Louis XIV said, "L'état, c'est moi," the pull of old ways is strong—especially to those on top. Like their feudal predecessors, the men who make our laws begin to see themselves as part of the law itself. They are only temporary potentates, brief occupiers of office—but in their few moments of power they feel themselves as durable and as permanent as law. They know that they will decide the rules that the rest of us must live by. If they can shape and manipulate the laws that are to come, can they not manipulate the laws which already exist?

"Men tinged with sovereignty," Senator Paul Douglas once said, "can easily feel that the king can do no wrong." The privileges of the office—the staff, the prestige—inevitably start to seem like natural rights. In most cases, congressmen do not think they are doing wrong. For such small stakes—avoiding a traffic ticket, junketing to Hong Kong—few would consciously hazard the glories of office. If money were their only goal, they could follow George Smathers's route from the Senate to the wealthier fields of Washington lobbying. The lawlessness we see is simply the result of guidelines gone rotten from neglect.

Conflicts of Interest

Congress correctly demands a high standard of impartiality from those it confirms for executive and judicial appointments. In 1969, when President Nixon tried and failed to get Judge Clement Haynsworth onto the Supreme Court, the most compelling reason against the nomination was that Haynsworth had tried cases involving businesses in which he held small bits of stock. When industrialist

David Packard was nominated as assistant secretary of defense, Congress required that he put $300 million of his personal fortune in a "blind trust," one which manages the money entirely out of Packard's sight. The ex-president of GM, Charles Wilson, and the ex-president of Ford, Robert McNamara, had to unload $2.7 million and $7.1 million respectively of their companies' stock before being confirmed as secretary of defense. The rationale behind these requirements is biblical and clear: since no man can serve two masters, Congress insists that federal officials put their private interests aside before assuming public duties.

Unfortunately, this diligence stops when it comes to the congressmen themselves. No one insists that members sell sensitive shares of stock. The only group with the power to screen the members—their voting constituency—is usually too ill-informed to make any serious judgment. And such conflicts are not considered a crime. In many states they violate the law, but not in Congress, simply because Congress, which writes the laws, chooses not to call what it does illegal.

With so few barriers against it, potential conflict of interest becomes commonplace in Congress. "If everyone abstained on grounds of personal interest," former senator Robert Kerr claimed, "I doubt if you could get a quorum in the United States Senate on any subject." Kerr's own position neatly illustrated the problem. As a millionaire oilman from Oklahoma, Kerr stood to lose or gain huge sums, depending on the government's tax rules for oil. As a powerful member of the Senate Finance Committee, Kerr was one of the men who decided what the tax laws would be. It does not take long to see the conflict. "Hell," Kerr bragged, "I'm in everything."

In 1976, 81 House members reported an interest in or income from banks, savings and loan associations, or bank holding companies—including two on the Banking Committee and eight on Ways and Means.

Indeed, favors from banks to congressmen are frequent. In 1962, the first new national bank to receive a District of Columbia charter since 1931 let Senator John Sparkman—then heir-apparent to the chairmanship of the Senate Banking Committee—buy $10,500 of its shares at preferred terms. Rep. Seymour Halpern got even more personal attention. While struggling to pay off loans outstanding, Halpern in 1969 managed to get another $100,000 from banks in unsecured loans. His committee was considering banking legislation at the time. The First National City Bank of New York, for example, loaned $40,000 to Halpern while its lobbyists were pushing for a mild version of the bill Halpern was considering.

The same pattern extends to other business holdings. From evidence turned up in 1976 financial disclosure forms, *Congressional Quarterly* reported that 44 representatives had holdings in one of the top 100 defense contractors, 48 had real-estate interests, 41 held oil or gas stock, and 20 were in pharmaceuticals. That year, 12 representatives and nine senators had direct or family interests in commercial radio or television stations.

In the late 1960s, Clarence Brown of Ohio, for example, held the majority stock in a broadcasting station—and sat on the House subcommittee regulating broadcasting. Brown might have been wise enough to keep his personal affairs out of public decisions. But whenever he took a stand—such as his opposition to public television—his financial stake in the outcome gave at least the appearance of impropriety. (In rebuttal, Brown claims that technical FCC rules prohibited him from selling his stock for three years. Accepting this, why then continue to sit on a broadcasting subcommittee?) Rep. Robert Sikes (D.-Fla.) sat on the House Appropriations Committee that approves the Pentagon budget; at the same time he was a director and shareholder in an insurance firm that sold more than $300 million of life insurance to servicemen on and around military bases—despite the fact that, according to investigator Philip Stern, 145 companies offered cheaper rates.

One of the few congressmen who have bothered to defend such self-serving behavior openly is millionaire Senator Russell Long of Louisiana. Like Kerr, Long is an oilman. In the five years before 1969, his income from oil was $1,196,915. Of that, $329,151 was tax-free, thanks to the curious oil depletion allowance. Long is also chairman of the Senate Finance Committee, which recommends tax plans, including oil depletion clauses, to the Senate. A conflict of interest? Not to Long. "If you have financial interests completely parallel to [those of] your state," he explained, "then you have no problem."

What Long is saying is that each senator is the sufficient judge of his own propriety. Once he convinces himself that his companies are really in the best interest of his folks back home, "then you have no problem." It must ease Long's conscience to know that he is helping others when he helps himself.

Occasionally there are men for whom even these lush fringe benefits of political office are not enough. They count the moments wasted which they must spend on the tedium of bills and votes. Such a man was George Smathers. Even while serving as a Florida senator, Smathers was melancholy. "A person with my background can make more money in thirty days [as a lobbyist]," he said, "than he can in fifteen years as a senator."

In preparation for the easy days ahead, Smathers spent the closing days of his Senate career collecting IOUs from private interests. According to *Newsday*, Smathers led a posse of Florida congressmen in a secret attempt to salvage a floundering Florida company, Aerodex. Because of what the Air Force called "poor quality work which was endangering the Air Force pilots and aircraft," the Defense Department wanted to cancel a multimillion-dollar contract with Aerodex. After Smathers's effort, the contract stood.

In 1969, when Smathers retired, he claimed some benefits. He became a director of Aerodex and got an attractive deal on stock: $435,000 worth of it for $20,000. The company also put Smathers's Washington law firm on a $25,000-a-year retainer. Smathers is now comfortably installed as a lobbyist, fulfilling his earlier exuberant prediction that "I'm going to be a Clark Clifford. That's the life for me."

The second important type of conflict of interest comes from congressmen who maintain legal practices. The moral problem here is subtler than that of the oilmen or bankers. A lawyer's business, like a doctor's or writer's, is built on reputation and skill. But when a lawyer also holds government office, his clients might conclude that he can do more for them than another person of similar talent. A widely circulated, widely respected study by the New York City Bar Association strongly condemns the lawyering congressmen. They are the fiduciaries of the public—administrators of public functions, the 1969 bar study says. Accordingly, they must administer this public trust for the public's benefit, not their own. Instead, "law practices have played a disproportionate role in the history of congressional scandals."

More than a century ago, New Hampshire's Daniel Webster kept in practice for his Senate orations by appearing as a private lawyer for the Bank of the United States. He argued the private bank's case some forty-one times before the Supreme Court. There was no Committee on Ethics then, and Webster did not have to conceal the relation. When, in his senatorial role, he was considering legislation to extend the bank's charter, he wrote his clients to remind them that "my retainer has not been received and refreshed as usual." While the standards change, certain practices do not. The irrepressible Thomas Dodd, writing to his Hartford law firm for more money, stated the problem candidly: "I'm sure you know that there's a considerable amount of business that goes into the office because of me. Many men in public life receive a steady income from their law practices because of the value of their association [and] my name and association is a realistic fact which definitely has value."

Dodd is gone, but in 1976 there were still 66 members who reported at least $1,000 in income from outside law practice. During the debate over the ethics bill in 1977, some member-lawyers warned about the impact outside earnings limits would have on their practices. "There are four guys here who have admitted to me they earn more than $130,000 from outside law practice," said Rep. David Obey (D.-Wis.), head of a major House inquiry into its ethical practices, in an interview. "One of them told me, 'I don't spend any time practicing law. As my seniority and committee influence increases, these groups keep throwing more business to my firm and I get my cut.' "

If a congressman can endure the Bar Association's frowns, there is little to stop him from keeping up a law practice. There is a point, however, when the law imposes a limit. An 1863 statute forbids congressmen-lawyers from representing clients who have claims before the federal government. To avoid embarrassing problems while keeping the business thriving, congressmen have therefore devised an ingenious "two-door" system. On the front door of the law firm is the congressman's name; through this

door come the many clients who value his help. Another
door is just the same, except the congressman's name is
missing. Here enter those proscribed clients with claims
before the government. The ruse is within the letter of the
law, but it still irritates purists. Journalist Robert Sherrill,
for example, wrote that former representative Emanuel
Celler's double doors were "one of the longest-standing
and most notorious embarrassments to Congress." To this,
Celler had a standard reply: "Your constituents are the
final arbiter of any conflicts, and I'm always reelected."

In 1972, after fifty years in the House, Emanuel Celler
lost in his Brooklyn Democratic primary to Elizabeth
Holtzman.

Crime and Punishment

It takes no special knowledge of franking laws or staff
rules to understand the overt crimes, the calculated offenses against law and morality, committed by congressmen. Motives are easy to find: when the potential payoff is
millions of dollars, risks for some people become worthwhile. Between 1941 and 1971, according to journalist
William Grieder, there were fifteen criminal prosecutions
against members, or one every two years. Between 1972 and
1978, there were twenty-one prosecutions, or three per
year—a fivefold increase. Overall in the 1970s, twenty-nine
members of Congress and nine staff were either convicted
of crimes, under indictment by 1979 or being investigated
for serious charges by an Ethics committee: "The arrest
rate for members of the 95th Congress," wrote journalist
Jack Newfield, challenging two stereotypes simultaneously,
"was higher than the arrest rate among unemployed black
males in Detroit."

What follows is a "Roll Call of Congressional Illegality"
in the 1970s, and profiles of some of the most prominent
members who lost their ethical compass.

ROLL CALL OF CONGRESSIONAL ILLEGALITY

NAME	CHARGE	DISPOSITION (June 1, 1979)
1. Members of 95th Congress		
Sen. Edward Brooke (R.-Mass.)	Failure to disclose finances accurately to Senate	Senate Ethics Committee in 1979 concluded that he gave "false testimony under oath" and that "violations within the jurisdiction of the committee had occurred"; since violations were "minor," no sanctions were recommended. Previously defeated for reelection 1978.
Rep. J. Herbert Burke (R.-Fla.)	Disorderly intoxication, resisting an officer—in connection with incident in bar	Pleaded guilty. Fined $150 and sentenced to 3 months probation. Lost reelection bid, 1978.
Rep. Charles Diggs, Jr. (D.-Mich.)	Federal mail fraud and salary kickbacks	Convicted on 29 counts, 1978. Sentenced to 3 years. Appeal pending. Reelected overwhelmingly after his conviction. Currently under investigation by House Ethics Committee.
Rep. Joshua Eilberg (D.-Pa.)	Conflict of interest	Pleaded guilty Feb, 1979, to illegally accepting money for aiding the procurement of a federal grant. Sentenced to 5 years probation, $10,000 fine. Defeated for reelection, 1978.
Rep. Daniel Flood (D.-Pa.)	Bribery, conspiracy, and perjury	Indicted, 1978. Hung jury, 1979. Reelected to 96th Congress but lost Appropriations subcommittee chair. Retrial scheduled for mid-1979.

NAME	CHARGE	DISPOSITION
Rep. George Hansen (R.-Ida.)	Campaign financing violation	Pleaded guilty in federal court, Feb., 1975, to charges of failing to file one campaign financing report and lying in another. Sentenced to 2 months in jail, reduced to $2,000 fine.
Rep. James Jones (D.-Okla.)	Campaign financing violation	Pleaded guilty, Jan., 1976, to a misdemeanor charge of failing to report receipt of a cash contribution from the Gulf Oil Corp., in 1972. Fined $200.
Rep. John McFall (D.-Calif.)	Violation of ethics rules for failing to report campaign contribution of South Korean businessman Tongsun Park	Reprimanded by House, 1978. Defeated for reelection, 1978.
Rep. Edward Roybal (D.-Calif.)	Same	Reprimanded by House, 1978.
Rep. Robert Sikes (D.-Fla.)	Conflict of interest	Reprimanded for unethical conduct by House in 1976; deposed from Appropriations subcommittee chair.
Sen. Herman Talmadge (D.-Ga.)	Incomplete and inaccurate campaign expense reports; using campaign gifts for personal activities	Currently under investigation by Senate Ethics Committee.
Rep. Charles H. Wilson (D.-Calif.)	Lying to the House Ethics Committee about money he took from Tongsun Park	Reprimanded by House, 1978.
2. Former Members (1970s)		
Rep. Frank Brasco (D.-N.Y.) (1967–75)	Conspiring to accept bribes	Indicted, Oct., 1973. Convicted and sentenced to 3 months in jail and fined $10,000.

NAME	CHARGE	DISPOSITION
Rep. Frank Clark (D.-Pa.) (1955–74)	Mail fraud, perjury, income tax evasion	Indicted, 1978. Pleaded guilty to one count of mail fraud, one count of income tax evasion in Feb., 1979.
Rep. John Dowdy (D.-Tex.) (1953–73)	Perjury	Indicted, Mar., 1971. Convicted and sentenced to 6 months and fined $3,000.
Rep. Nick Galifianakis (D.-N.C.) (1967–73)	Lied to House about taking $10,000 from Tongson Park	Indicted, May, 1979.
Rep. Cornelius Gallagher (D.-N.J.) (1959–73)	Income tax evasion	Indicted, 1972. Convicted and served 6 months and fined $10,000.
Rep. Richard Hanna (D.-Calif.) (1963–74)	Conspiracy to defraud government	Pleaded guilty. Sentenced to 6–30 months in prison.
Rep. James Hastings (R.-N.Y.) (1969–76)	Mail fraud, salary kickbacks	Indicted, 1976. Convicted on 28 counts, 1977. Sentenced to 20 months–5 years. Paroled, 1978, after serving 14 months.
Rep. Wayne Hays (D.-Ohio) (1949–76)	Misuse of office account	Resigned from Congress, 1976, after disclosure that he kept mistress on congressional payroll in return for sexual favors.
Rep. Henry Helstoski (D.-N.J.) (1965–77)	Bribery	Indicted, 1976. Case still pending.
Rep. Andrew Hinshaw (R.-Calif.) (1973–77)	Bribery	Indicted, 1975. Convicted, 1976, and sentenced to 1–14 years. Served 7 months.
Rep. Martin McKneally (R.-N.Y.) (1969–71)	Failure to file income tax report	Indicted, 1970. Pleaded guilty, 1971; placed on probation, fined $5,000.

NAME	CHARGE	DISPOSITION
Rep. Bertram Podell (D.-N.Y.) (1968–75)	Bribery, conspiracy, conflict of interest	Pleaded guilty to conspiracy and conflict of interest, 1974. Sentenced to 6 months in prison, fined $5,000.
Rep. Richard Tonry (D.-La.) (1977)	Violation of federal election laws	Pleaded guilty, July, 1977. Served 6 months in prison.
Rep. J. Irving Whalley (R.-Pa.) (1960–73)	Mail fraud, obstruction of justice	Indicted and convicted, 1973; 3 years probation, fined $11,000.
Rep. Wendell Wyatt (R.-Ore.) (1964–75)	Failure to report expenditures of campaign funds	Fined $750, 1975.
3. Recent Congressional Staff		
Robert T. Carson (Sen. Fong)	Perjury, conspiracy to accept and offer bribes	Indicted, 1971. Convicted and sentenced to 18 months in prison and fined $5,000.
Albert De Falco (Rep. Helstoski)	Extortion	Indicted, 1975. Convicted and sentenced to 6 years.
Stephen B. Elko (Rep. Flood)	Bribery	Indicted, 1977. Sentenced to 3 years in prison. Received immunity for testimony against Rep. Flood.
Pauline Girvin (Speaker Albert)	Mail fraud	Pleaded guilty, 1975, to misdemeanor extortion charge. Sentenced to 1 year in jail. Reduced to 60 days plus 2 years probation.
George A. Haag (Rep. Collins)	Mail fraud, obstruction of justice	Convicted, 1972. Sentenced to 6 months–3 years.

NAME	CHARGE	DISPOSITION
Michael McPherson (Rep. Clay)	Mail fraud	Pleaded guilty, 1976. Sentenced to 6 months in prison, eventually served 3½ months.
Alfred Porro (Rep. Helstoski)	Obstruction of justice	Indicted, 1976. Case still pending.
Martin Sweig (Speaker McCormack)	Perjury	Convicted, 1970. Sentenced to 30 months and fined $2,000.
Vincent Verdiramo (Rep. Helstoski)	Conspiracy to obstruct justice	Indicted, 1976. Convicted Sept. 21, 1977. Sentenced to 2 months in jail and paid $2,500 fine.

BOBBY BAKER. In 1942, with sixty dollars in his back pocket, 14-year-old Bobby Baker left Pickens, South Carolina, and never looked back. Like a lamprey searching for a host, he made his way to Washington, found the Senate, and attached himself for a twenty-year ride. First as page, then as clerk, he moved up the ladder. His break came when he made a friend, Lyndon Johnson. His friend became majority leader of the Senate and did not forget the small people he had met along the way. From 1955 until 1963, even after Johnson had left the post, Baker was secretary to the majority leader. "You're like a son to me," Johnson purred as he helped Bobby up. To Baker, Johnson was, if not a father, at least "my best friend around the capital." By 1960, Baker was being introduced to freshman page boys as "a powerful demonstrator of just how far intelligence combined with a gracious personality can take a man."

The tragedy of 1963 was a bad omen for Bobby. His old friend had become president—but had risen too high to keep in touch with Bobby. Critics began to grow suspicious about Baker's wealth. From a net worth of $11,000 in 1955, he had become a multimillionaire—an annual rate of increase of $200,000–$300,000—all while earning a salary of $19,600 per year. One explanation for the gap came when a civil lawsuit claimed that Baker had used his influence to help a firm win a government contract. With that, the Senate Rules and Administration Committee took a closer look at him. By 1965, the Democratic majority had issued a report citing "many gross improprieties" in his behavior—but no legal violations. To many senators, both Republicans and Democrats, this looked like a crude whitewash. Over the next few months, Senator John Williams of Delaware earned himself the title "conscience of the Senate" by hounding Baker and his apologists.

The legal ax fell in 1966, when Baker was finally indicted for fraud, larceny, and tax evasion. The major charge was that he had collected $100,000 from a group of California savings and loans executives for campaign contributions, and then kept $80,000 of it himself. Even as he protested his innocence, Baker realized that his exposure was straining some of his former cronies. "My friends in Congress," he said with slight bitterness, "have had no choice but to think of me as a bad dream or something."

No one had less choice about the matter than Baker's best friend, the president of the United States. He retained public composure, even indifference, over the matter—which did not entirely surprise Baker, who had seen friendships bloom and die in the seasons of convenience. He knew that "the American people would have destroyed and defeated President Johnson had he attempted in any way to do anything on my behalf."

Baker went to trial, was convicted, and was sentenced to one to three years. By 1971, when he was released, the bad memories may have lingered, but the punishment was over and he was still rich. And unremorseful. His 1978 best-seller, appropriately titled *Wheeling and Dealing*, tried to excuse Baker's crimes by portraying him as a "child of the Senate":

> Like my bosses and sponsors in the Senate, I was ambitious and eager to feather my personal nest. . . . As they presumed their high station to entitle them to accept gratuities or hospitalities from patrons who had an axe to grind, so did I. As they took advantage of privileged information to get in on the ground floor of attractive investments, so did I. As they used their powerful positions to gain loans or credit that otherwise might not have been granted, so did I.

ADAM CLAYTON POWELL. It was not his romances that drove the white folks mad—his colleagues had tolerated that in others—nor was it his laziness, nor his endless vacation trips. It was not even the way he turned every power of his office toward his boundless hedonism. Congress had seen it all before, and had forgiven. Adam Clayton Powell's sin was flagrance—his refusal to hide what he was doing. Others might filch dollars from the cash box at night: Powell skimmed off his profit in full public view. While Congress was in session and the committee he chaired slogged away at its work, Powell posed for photographers with Miss Ohio at his island haven in the Caribbean.

For a while, Powell tapped a special mood of the times. The same panache which enraged other congressmen made Powell a hero to his Harlem constituents: he was winning at the white man's game. In the two decades of his prime

—at the time when he was being ridiculed in the House cloakroom as "the congressman from Bimini" or "the Harlem Globetrotter"—Powell sailed through elections as if anointed. He won his first term in 1944. By 1961, enough other congressmen had died or lost so that Powell became chairman of the Education and Labor Committee —the second black chairman in congressional history.

Toward the mid-1960s, after an earlier vigor and productivity, Powell began to spend large chunks of the terms vacationing—sometimes using false names, usually with lady friends, always at government expense. He kept up his family ties by putting his wife on his office payroll at $20,000 per year, a gracious gesture to a woman then living in Puerto Rico. A first brush with the law left Powell unscarred: in 1958, he was indicted for income tax evasion, but escaped the charge after paying $28,000 in back taxes and penalties. If he had stopped then, curbing the excesses and cutting down on the publicity, Powell might have spent another ten terms as pleasantly as the first ten.

He could not, or did not, stop, and in the late sixties Congress caught up with him. Already he had become an exile in his own district. After being convicted of libel—for calling a black woman the "bag lady" for a graft operation —Powell could not return to the district he represented for fear of being arrested. In 1966, the disgruntled members of his committee began to hack away at his powers. Other congressmen sharpened their knives, too.

Their grievance was that Powell was bringing them all down. When one congressman is a clown, how seriously could the rest take themselves? Their own self-respect was only part of it. The constituents were also angry. "Nobody blames me for Howard Smith or H. R. Gross," one congressman said, mentioning two of the chamber's troglodytes, "but whites all over America blame their congressman for Adam." Morris Udall produced a letter from a constituent, addressed "in care of Adam Clayton Powell's Playboy Club (formerly U.S. House of Representatives), Stinksville Station (formerly House Post Office), Washington, D.C."

In 1967, the Democratic Caucus voted to remove him as chairman. By a thumping 365–65 vote, the full House then voted to deny him his seat pending further investigations. Soon afterward the Justice Department compiled a fifty-page draft indictment telling of falsified expense vouchers worth $20,000 and of Powell's secret destruction of incriminating papers from his committee; but the department never sought an indictment. Finally, the House declared his seat vacant and ordered a special election for April.

Powell won the election, and then won a more important victory when the Supreme Court ruled that his exclusion had been unconstitutional. The only formal losses were his seniority and a $20,000 fine for penance. Powell had survived, but in the process something had gone sour between him and his district. In 1970, he lost in the primary to Charles Rangel. Two years later, unrepentant, he died, at age 63.

In a Congress of untainted men, the harassment Powell underwent might have been understandable. But as Richard Harwood put it in the *Washington Post:*

> Like former Representative James Roosevelt of California, he has acquired three wives and a reputation for his romantic goings-on. Like Rep. Wayne Hays of Ohio, he has journeyed first-class to Europe at public expense accompanied by female assistants. . . . Like Rep. Joe Pool of Texas, he has ostentatiously defied the orders of an American court. Like Rep. Richard Bolling of Missouri and others, he has placed a wife on the congressional payroll. . . . Like the late Speaker Sam Rayburn of Texas, he dispenses whiskey in his Capitol office.

"You are looking at the first black man who was ever lynched by Congress," Powell had said.

THOMAS DODD. "I believe in God and Senator Dodd and keepin' ol' Castro down," Phil Ochs sang. And Dodd fit the billing. When the young Tom Dodd faced one of life's forking paths, he grappled with the question of whether he should become a priest. Instead, he plowed his energies into politics. If he was not combating sin in the individual soul, he could attack its manifestations in the national spirit; perversion, pornography, Communism—all must be defeated.

Although Dodd's targets were the classic ones, his attacks in the Senate won him few friends. In a body which is almost as tradition-conscious as the Church, the Connecticut senator stepped roughly on others' dignity. He overlooked the minor niceties; he called names; he impugned motives.

Thomas Dodd would not be a household word today if impoliteness had been his only error. Dodd's talent—his malign genius—was invested in another cause, his financial frauds. His staff were the first to notice. They had gathered evidence of a stunning range of dishonesty. Dodd had pocketed, for private use, at least $160,083 raised at campaign dinners, supposedly for campaign expenses; he had double-billed the government and other groups for other expenses, keeping the surplus; he had taken repeated private vacations and charged the government; he had used his office to promote the career of a retired major general who was a propagandist for German right-wingers; he had taken money from private firms, and then pressured government agencies for special treatment.

Doubts and difficulties afflicted the staffers. "To whom do you go to get a U.S. senator investigated?" asked James Boyd, Dodd's closest aide for the previous twelve years. The Senate Ethics Committee was likely to forgive an erring brother; the Justice Department was part of Johnson's administration, and Johnson was one of Dodd's friends; even the FBI was suspect, since Dodd had once been an agent. Their minds set, Boyd and Carpenter eventually took seven thousand documents from Dodd's files and gave them to the trustees of frustrated exposés, Drew Pearson and Jack Anderson.

Pearson and Anderson unloaded the charges in twenty-three columns, but for a while Dodd felt safe in ignoring them. Senators closed ranks against their threatened fellow; Birch Bayh wrote, "We're all with you on this yellow attack by Pearson," while Russell Long said, "I'll support you all the way on this, Tom, even if you're guilty." Dodd had his own explanation for the trouble: "The Communists have always regarded me as a prime enemy."

But Dodd made a crucial mistake. He demanded a Senate inquiry. It was a dramatic ploy, but one which proved his undoing. "Never ask for an investigation," one of his cohorts had said. "You might get one." The Senate Ethics Committee thus began its first investigation. Its report was less than Boyd might have hoped, but did unanimously recommend that Dodd be censured on two counts: for diverting the campaign money, and for the double-billing. On June 23, 1967, Dodd was officially censured by the Senate for the first count. His defense was an inspired peroration on the Senate floor, which concluded, "I am telling you the truth and I am concealing nothing. May the vengeance of God strike me if I am doing otherwise!" The plea moved many but convinced very few. By a vote of 92–5 (Dodd, Ribicoff, Tower, Thurmond, and Long against), the Senate censured Dodd for his personal use of the campaign funds. Having done this much, the Senate pulled back and refused, by a 51–45 vote, to censure Dodd for double-billing.

Dodd's formal punishment was light. He served three more years in the Senate, then gamely but unsuccessfully ran as an independent for reelection in 1970. But the scandal left Dodd broken. He died of a heart attack in 1971, a bundle of contradictions. Exhorting law and order, he placed himself above the law; demanding staff loyalty, he was loyal to none but himself. In the mid-sixties, after Bobby Baker's fall but before his own, Dodd had angled to get the great glass chandelier that hung in Baker's office. He never got it, and shared with Baker only his acquisitive ways.

DANIEL BREWSTER. He loved the races, whether the contestants were horses or politicians. In 1945, Daniel Brewster returned from the war to Baltimore County, Maryland, a hero with seven wounds and a bronze star. A millionaire's son, he turned first to horse racing, and became a moderately successful steeplechase rider on the East Coast Hunt racing circuit. But he was also interested in politics, and got elected to the Maryland house of delegates in 1950. Although money was no problem, Brewster shortly thereafter joined a law firm. Success followed success. He was elected to the House of Representatives in 1958 and 1960, and, when a Senate seat became vacant in 1962, he ran and won it.

For Brewster, success became ruin by late 1968. He lost his reelection bid that November, in a three-way race. While in June, 1968, he had been a trim, youthful, and vigorous campaigner, seven months later, after defeat by

Charles Mathias, he was noticeably heavier, with red-lined cheeks and a slow step. He turned up in Annapolis in early 1969 to ask Governor Marvin Mandel for a Democratic party job, but he left empty-handed. Then on December 1, 1969, Brewster, whose fortune was more than $2.4 million, was indicted for allegedly accepting $24,500 in bribes from a mail-order house to influence his votes on postal rate laws.

The trial was delayed several times because of Brewster's ill health. "Former Senator Daniel Brewster of Maryland . . . suffered a severe mental lapse and is not competent to stand trial," said an Associated Press dispatch of February 24, 1970. "The report said that the chronic effect of alcohol was a contributing cause." He recuperated at his wife's Ireland estate. Brewster did appear at a hearing in May of that year—in rumpled suit, his hands trembling slightly, a stubble of white whiskers on his face—to plead innocent. District Court Judge George Hart, Jr., dismissed all charges under the theory that congressional immunity encompassed any alleged bribery connected with a senator's vote. But the Supreme Court disagreed and ordered a new trial. One was held, and Brewster was found guilty of accepting an "illegal gratuity" in 1967. But in August, 1974, a U.S. Court of Appeals overturned the verdict because Judge Hart—this was not the judge's best case—gave the jury faulty instructions. Eventually, Brewster pled "no contest" to "accepting an unlawful gratuity" and was fined the maximum amount under the statute, $10,000.

WAYNE HAYS. Sometimes a congressman abuses his public position with such skill and arrogance that only an incidental scandal can finally force his colleagues to investigate his conduct. A classic case is former representative Wayne Hays (D.-Ohio), a behind-the-scenes House potentate who manipulated three committee chairmanships to control everything from the price of haircuts in the Capitol barbershops to staff salaries and the dispersal of Democratic campaign contributions. "I got where I am because people feared me," he once told reporter Myra McPherson.

One person who did not seem to fear Hays was his

tattletale ex-mistress, Elizabeth Ray. In 1974, Hays made Ray a clerk in, appropriately enough, his Oversight Committee and paid her $14,000 a year in public funds. "I can't type, I can't file, I can't even answer the phone," Ray admitted, adding that her main responsibility was to pander to the personal needs of Chairman Hays. Following a press and public uproar, the House leadership pressured Hays to resign from Congress.

Hays's power to intimidate derived from his ability to single-handedly control the flow of perquisites representatives have grown dependent upon. As chairman of the House Administration Committee, Hays had the power to increase, without a House vote, the size and salaries of House staff and allowances available to members. He also took responsibility for writing the campaign finance laws and no doubt earned some IOUs by slipping in an amendment to the federal election law of 1974 that reduced the statute of limitations on illegal campaign contributions from five years to three. Hays also waged a rearguard action designed to weaken the Campaign Finance Act of 1972.

As chief housekeeper, Hays treated service employees like personal staff and appeared to relish his tyrannical control over them. Following an altercation with two elevator boys under the jurisdiction of the House Judiciary Committee, Hays threatened to hold up appropriations for the then pending Nixon impeachment inquiry; the elevator boys, after meeting with an anxious Chairman Peter Rodino, quickly apologized. As chairman of the Democratic Congressional Campaign Committee, Hays decided which candidates got how much money and when. From his International Relations subcommittee chair he pulled the strings on precious foreign travel junkets and was himself dubbed "Marco Polo" for spending $6,589 of tax money overseas in just one year.

All this may mean no more than a few bucks to Peoria, but it put high in the House saddle one of the most hostile and acerbic of congressmen. "Getting into a debate with him is like wrestling with a skunk," said a representative. "The skunk doesn't care; he likes the smell." But whether he obtained his status despite his arbitrariness or because of it, he had, as the *Washington Post* noted, "carved out a

position of power in the daily operation of the House un-
matched by any member except [then] Speaker Carl
Albert."

Hays's power base, though, was being challenged well
before the sex scandal gave Democratic leaders an excuse
to purge him. Democrats uncomfortable under Hays's arbi-
trary bureaucratic discretion to dispense patronage and
services tried to dethrone him as Administration Committee chairman in 1975. Hays not only survived, but he
retaliated by creating new bureaucratic structures to rein-
force his influence. He created new subcommittees on
packing and paper conservation, as well as ad hoc committees to manage House restaurant operations and the
computer system. Finally, he created the infamous Oversight Committee—to keep an accurate check on what all
the other committees and subcommittees were doing.

However influential, his style of intimidation fore-
doomed his dreams of becoming majority leader. And
before the scandal broke, one Hill observer prophesied his
demise to author Marshall Frady: "One of these days ole
Wayne's going to violate one amenity too many and find
he's run out of grace all of a sudden. Then they'll converge
on him, and when they're done, all he'll have left of his
empire is the stub of his gavel."

CHARLES C. DIGGS. Stylish and apparently wealthy, the
first black congressman elected from the state of Michigan,
the son of the first black state senator elected in Michigan,
Charlie Diggs was for years a relatively popular and powerful spokesman for black interests in the House. His
Detroit constituents liked the idea that their representative
was the most senior black in Congress and was called "Mr.
Africa" due to his self-made expertise on that continent.
His people believed in him so completely that they overwhelmingly reelected him to a thirteenth term in November, 1978—despite his October, 1978, conviction on
twenty-nine counts of federal mail fraud and taking salary
kickbacks from his congressional staff.

Diggs entered politics while still studying law, in 1951.
He replaced his father in the Michigan state senate after
the elder Diggs was refused his seat because he had been
sent to prison for taking graft from a lobbyist. In 1971, he
helped found and became the first chairman of the con-

gressional Black Caucus, a group originally established as a "shadow cabinet" to monitor federal enforcement of civil rights laws. Two years later he became chairman of the House District Committee and he soon pushed through a compromise home rule bill giving the predominantly black district government more autonomy and power. He also served until 1979 as chairman of the House Foreign Affairs subcommittee on Africa, a post he used to make frequent and controversial tours of Africa at public expense.

Diggs's corruption and fall from power began about twenty years ago when, reluctant to live less elegantly than his better situated peers, he began borrowing and refusing to repay. On top of this overextension were his family obligations. Married three times, divorced twice, with six children and his mother to support, Diggs faced alimony payments and private tuition bills in addition to gambling losses and extravagant tastes in clothes and furnishings. When the family funeral business went bankrupt, Diggs saw approaching financial and political doom as creditors closed in and began taking him to court.

By 1973, his personal predicament was so taxing he decided to solve it the only way he saw available—by appropriating a slice of the public funds he was trusted to manage. His indictment alleged that between 1973 and 1977, Diggs "did devise and intend to devise a scheme and artifice to defraud the United States of America [of more than $101,000] in the form of salary kickbacks from certain House of Representatives employees and payments to others on the House of Representatives payroll who performed no work for the House. . . ." Diggs supplemented his income by giving three of his aides big salary increases, then pressuring them to kick back as much as two-thirds of their salary to pay his personal debts. He also paid the family lawyer, accountant, and a funeral home employee with federal funds, though they did not work for the government. Diggs was convicted and sentenced to three years in prison in October just before the 1978 elections and he agreed to stay away during the remaining three days of the 95th Congress. The next month he was easily reelected.

But the issue of his role in Congress remained. Realizing how demeaning it is to the rest of Congress for a convicted lawbreaker to remain a full participant in the drafting, passage, and execution of our laws, the Democratic majority in the new Congress had to face the issue of what powers Diggs should exercise while his appeals remain pending. Republicans and several young Democrats called for Diggs to resign his committee chairmanship, refrain from voting, and consider resigning from Congress.

Intense pressure by the Democratic leadership did cause Diggs reluctantly to resign his two committee posts, but he insisted he had the right to remain a voting member of Congress. Diggs's defenders argue that to deprive him of his right to work in committees or vote on legislation would mean unconstitutionally disenfranchising his district. His lawyers also charged that since taking public funds for personal use was "relatively common" in the House, Diggs should not be singled out for punishment.

Majority Leader Jim Wright argued that the caucus can withhold chairmanships, since establishing committees at all is an administrative prerogative of the members; but preventing an elected member from serving his constituents is a different matter. "I don't think he should be expelled from the House," Wright said. "Membership in the House is not ours to bestow. We can't give that to anybody. The constituents are entitled to have the representatives of their choice." Wright argued that expulsion is such an extreme sanction that only three members have ever gotten the boot—all in 1861, for supporting the Confederacy in the Civil War. He also noted that the House did not expel Andrew J. Hinshaw (R.-Calif.) who was convicted of bribery in 1976, or J. Parnell Thomas (D.-N.J.), who was convicted in the late 1940s for offenses similar to Diggs's.

The oust-Diggs group, led by the Republican leadership and Rep. Peter Kostmayer (D.-Pa.), argue that Wright and the keep-Diggs contingent are trying to obscure the difference between expelling and excluding a member. When the 90th Congress tried to exclude former representative Adam Clayton Powell, the Supreme Court held that in deciding whether a member is fit to be seated, "Congress is limited to judging members in terms of the qualifications [age, citizenship, and residency] prescribed by the Constitution." However, Justice Douglas's concurring opinion in that case noted that the Congress does have the constitutional prerogative to expel any of its members, once sworn in, by a vote of two-thirds or more. The Constitution reads: "Each house may . . . punish its members for disorderly behavior, and, with the concurrence of two-thirds, expel a member." To many congressmen, it is inconceivable that systematically embezzling tax money, an offense for which a president could be impeached, does not qualify as conduct unbecoming a congressman.

DANIEL FLOOD. During his more than thirty years representing the impoverished anthracite coal region of northeastern Pennsylvania, Rep. Daniel J. Flood (D.-Pa.) has been a hero to his blue-collar constituents back home in Wilkes-Barre—and it was not merely due to the waxed moustache, cape, and cane he acquired during his youthful days as a Shakespearean actor.

Because Flood had been a member of the "College of Cardinals"—the nickname given Congress's thirteen powerful Appropriations subcommittee chairmen—he was able to go far beyond the usual individualized constituent services his colleagues thrive on. As chairman of the Appropriations subcommittee for Labor and Health, Education, and Welfare, Flood had a virtual stranglehold on many agency budgets within those departments. Thus, aggressive pork-barreling and federal largess have made it possible for Flood's constituents to be born at the Daniel J. Flood Rural Health Center, educated at the Daniel J. Flood Elementary School, employed in the Daniel J. Flood Industrial Park, and retired to the Daniel J. Flood Elderly Center.

He was also a ranking member of the Defense Appropriations subcommittee, a position he used in 1960 to persuade the Army to convert its 8,000 coke-burning barracks furnaces in West Germany to use Pennsylvania anthracite. Army efforts to reconvert the furnaces to oil, which would save more than $20 million annually, have all died in the House Appropriations subcommittee. "Hell yes, I stopped it," he said with typical flair. "I did it by twisting arms and hammering heads." And when Hurricane Agnes and the raging Susquehanna River devastated most of his district in 1972, Flood obtained needed supplies and equipment from the Pentagon and rushed home aboard Secretary of Defense Melvin Laird's personal helicopter, declaring, "This is going to be one Flood against another."

Despite his renown as an effective and hard-working ambassador from Wilkes-Barre, Flood developed a tendency over the years to use his legislative skills to feather his personal nest as well as his district. Most of the charges against Flood originated with his administrative assistant Stephen Elko, who was sentenced to three years in prison after admitting, in 1977, that he took $25,000 in bribes from former Washington lobbyist Deryl Fleming. In exchange for immunity from further prosecution and a reduced sentence, Elko told how his former boss received some $100,000 in cash and bank stock from various organizations in return for legislative favors. Or as Flood reportedly told him, "Get all you can while you can get it."

Among the subsequent tangle of other illicit deals for which Flood is being either prosecuted or investigated:

• While sitting amidst the wreckage of Hurricane Agnes in his relief "command post," Flood took $5,000 in a cash bribe from a businessman trying to sell disaster relief housing to the federal government, according to testimony by the businessman at Flood's trial in January, 1979.

• In 1972, a chain of California trade schools were about to lose their accreditation, and millions of federal aid dollars as a result. But after Elko and Flood each allegedly received a series of payoffs—a total of $50,000 by company accounts—former education commissioner Sidney P. Marland, Jr., bowed to persistent pressure from the Appropriations chairman who oversees his agency and gave the unqualified school temporary accreditation.

• In return for Flood's drafting helpful legislation and pressuring the Labor Department to grant millions of dollars in federal subsidies to a small religious school in Brooklyn, Rabbi Lieb Pinter testified that he gave Flood at least five $1,000 bribes. The money was covered up as an honorarium for Flood's appearance at a 1975 dinner in New York. Although the school used some of the subsidies to provide a free lunch program and training for Jewish immigrants from the Soviet Union, the judge gave Pinter a two-year jail sentence because the people had a right to believe that there was not "a price tag on their representatives."

• A Pennsylvania home-builder testified that he personally handed $2,000 in cash to Flood in return for his help in obtaining federal financing for a housing project.

• Banker Joel Harpel testified that his bank transferred $4,000 worth of bank stock to Flood's account in return for his influencing the Treasury Department to approve the merger of two banks.

• Elko also described how he served between 1971 and 1973 as the delivery boy for regular cash payments from the Arlie Foundation to both Flood and former representative Otto E. Passman (D.-La.). The foundation president, Dr. Murdock Head, allegedly passed as much as $42,000 to the two representatives in return for their help in increasing AID's family planning funds in 1972. Elko also testified that Head was so anxious about election surveillance and fingerprints that he would only meet Elko in places like Arlie's soundproof screening room, would write with marker on a flip-chart instead of speaking, and would only handle the cash-stuffed envelopes with facial tissue.

To a man with enough nerve to wear red, white, and blue sneakers to a formal dinner at the White House, however, defeat does not come easily. Despite the federal prosecution of Flood on eleven counts of bribery, perjury, and conspiracy to defraud the U.S. government, his home town named him Man of the Year in 1978 and his home district reelected him in November. And in January, 1979, a mistrial was declared when the jury could not agree on a verdict. Later, the lone holdout against conviction on several counts acknowledged that although he thought the 75-year-old Flood was guilty, he "would never vote guilty because Mr. Flood was too old" to go to jail.

ROBERT SIKES. Voting unnecessary projects for constituents just to get a bigger slice of the appropriation pie than the next congressman is just a few steps away from voting questionable projects for yourself or for generous friends. Conflicts of interest abound. A classic case of communal greed turned personal is former representative Robert L. F. Sikes (D.-Fla.), veteran of nineteen terms and former chairman of the House Appropriations subcommittee on military construction.

Sikes represented and gained the adoration of the people in northwest Florida from 1941 to 1979. His constituents called his seniority and his control over military construction appropriations the Florida Panhandle's greatest asset. When Sikes first left for Washington, the only sign of military spending in his district was the Pensacola Naval Air Station. After serving on the Foreign Affairs and Armed Services committees, Sikes in 1949 maneuvered his way to a coveted seat on the Appropriations Committee, and then onto its subcommittee on military construction.

Sikes became a defense hardliner and supported almost every request by the military-industrial complex for more money to purchase "national security." And the Pentagon suddenly began seeing northwest Florida as an increasingly hospitable area to build bases, station troops, and spend a disproportionate share of the defense budget. Sikes, a reserve officer who served only three months of active duty on an inspection tour, found that Appropriations Committee membership brought indulgences from the Pentagon. In 1950, he was promoted to colonel; in 1960, he was made brigadier general. Meanwhile, fourteen new military installations had opened their doors in his district by the mid-1960s. According to the Bay County Chamber of Commerce, the Pentagon pours $600 million into the area's economy each year and employs nearly a third of its labor force.

Whatever their value to the Panhandle, apparently his efforts also had value to himself. For on May 12, 1976, the House Ethics Committee chose self-made millionaire Sikes as the target of its first formal conflict of interest investigation.

The charges against Sikes were serious: in 1974, he voted for a defense appropriations bill awarding a $73 million contract to Fairchild Industries—a hometown airplane manufacturing company in which Sikes owned 1,000 unreported shares of stock. He urged state and federal officials to establish the First Navy Bank at the Pensacola Naval Air Station, then bought 2,500 shares of stock in it. And, in what the Ethics Committee called an "obvious and significant conflict of interest," Sikes sponsored legisla-

tion in 1961 and 1962 to remove commercial development restrictions from land his company owned off the
coast of Florida, greatly increasing the land's value.
He disclosed none of these holdings on his financial
statement, although he was required to do so by House
rules.

When a member has such a direct pecuniary interest in
pending legislation, even the old House Code of Ethics demanded they make his conflict clear and abstain from
voting. Sikes's defenders said that the Code of Ethics he
violated was valid only for the session of Congress that
adopted it in 1958. Unfortunately for Sikes, only three
of his colleagues agreed; a total of 381 others concurred
with the Ethics Committee's charge of conflict of interest
and voted to reprimand Sikes, during the summer of
1976.

The slap had no immediate political impact on Sikes.
"These allegations were not news to the First District,"
a Republican candidate for commissioner told correspondent Judith Miller. "Everybody's known about these ru-
mors for a long time, but most people seem to feel
that since all of us have money from the military's presence here in the Panhandle, there's no reason for Sikes
to have abstained." As a Democratic Sikes supporter bluntly
put it: "People here didn't care, just as long as he kept
his share of the take down to around 10 percent." Though
challenged in the 1976 Democratic primary for the first
time in many years, he still faced no Republican in the
general election and rolled up a majority of better than
70 percent.

Less senior representatives pushing for a tough new
ethics code did not react quite so generously when Sikes
reappeared unscathed in the 95th Congress. Despite the
opposition of party leaders O'Neill and Wright, the House
Democratic Caucus voted 189–93 to relieve Sikes of his
Appropriations subcommittee chairmanship.

Sikes's reaction to all the fuss was like that of a man
who sincerely believes he did no wrong. After thirty-
eight years of unchallenged influence at home and thirty
years tenure at the helm of a powerful appropriations subcommittee in Washington, it is easy to begin believing
"Le district c'est moi." "I was even contemplating not
seeking reelection this year," Sikes said after his victory

at the polls in 1976. "I wanted to come home to Florida and enjoy life for a change—go hunting and relax. But I wasn't going to let the liberal Eastern establishment press run me out of office. A man, you know, has to preserve his integrity." Rep. Sikes did not run for reelection in 1978.

HERMAN TALMADGE. The son of late Georgia Governor Eugene Talmadge, Herman Talmadge was thrust (briefly) into the governorship at the age of 33. In 1946, the state legislature selected him to succeed his father, who had died just after his reelection to a fourth term. Unfortunately for young Talmadge, the state supreme court agreed with the duly elected lieutenant governor that *he* should rightfully succeed. So after a term of sixty-seven days, Talmadge was forced to step down—but not for long. Two years later he ran and won in his own right, and was reelected in 1950.

In 1956, Herman Talmadge entered the Senate, defeating twenty-five-year veteran Walter George—then Chairman of the Foreign Relations Committee. Reelected with little opposition ever since, Talmadge rose to the chairmanship of the Agriculture Committee, and is next in seniority behind Chairman Russell Long on the Finance Committee. Yet his rich history was overtaken in the late 1970s by some tawdry facts.

The unraveling began in the course of a property settlement following an acrimonious divorce in 1977 when a *Washington Star* reporter discovered a curious item. From 1970 to 1976 the millionaire senator had written only one check to "cash." At first Talmadge said that he did not know where he got his spending money. But the Senate Ethics Committee began to examine his finances after *Star* reporter Edward Pound disclosed—and Talmadge acknowledged—receipts of "small gifts of cash . . . to cover his expenses" from the Georgian's friends and supporters. "They come up and say they know I have a lot of expenses back in Washington and they want to help me," Talmadge said. The help came in the form of cash, free meals, lodging, and clothing as well as special "birthday dinners" sponsored at $25 a plate—none of it reported as income (for tax purposes) or as campaign receipts.

By December, 1978, the Ethics Committee completed a

preliminary investigation and listed five areas of possible violations. The most serious was the charge that Talmadge maintained a secret bank account in which he deposited illegal campaign contributions. The committee's special counsel said: "Although [Talmadge] has continuously claimed that his source of cash was small gifts made by friends and supporters, the evidence will disclose that he had cash on hand in fairly substantial amounts, and that it came in whole or in part from [a secret campaign account] . . . or from other campaign contributions."

Talmadge denies all wrongdoing and calls his former top aide and chief accuser, Daniel Minchew, "a proven liar, cheat, and embezzler." Minchew testified that he had opened the account at a local Washington bank in Talmadge's name and on his orders. The *Star* reported: "Nearly $39,000 in mostly unreported campaign contributions and illegally claimed senate reimbursements were funneled through the account and converted to cash." (Talmadge finally repaid $37,000 for the expense account overpayments, claiming they were due to oversights by members of his staff.) The ethics panel also charged that Talmadge had received about $24,000 in payments from the Senate for vouchers submitted by the senator for "official expenses" which he had not incurred. Another $11,000 was for items actually spent but not considered legitimate official expenditures by the Senate.

If the Ethics Committee finds Talmadge guilty of these charges, it could recommend a censure, loss of seniority, or expulsion from the Senate. Such sanctions are almost unprecedented; indeed, the Ethics Committee has only sanctioned one member in its history—Tom Dodd in 1967. But as the evidence and pressure mounted against Herman Talmadge—who was hospitalized in early 1979 for alcoholism and exhaustion—the prospect increased that he might again have to step down from public office if his mid-1979 hearing went badly. Unlike his departure of a quarter century before, however, this one would not be based on a technicality and might not be overturned by an approving electorate in the next election.

"KOREAGATE." Far broader than any individual wrongdoing was the episode tagged Koreagate, which seemed crafted after an espionage thriller, with secret foreign

agents, code words, black market deals, squealing defec-
tors, and handsome political payoffs delivered in plain,
unmarked envelopes. The *Washington Post* called the
charges in late 1976 "the most sweeping allegations of
congressional corruption ever investigated by the federal
government." Others dismissed it as "third-rate bribery,"
an ironic example of reciprocal foreign aid. However
broad and deep the corruption, it is clear that Koreagate
cost Congress a great deal of time and integrity, and
proved how difficult it is for a legislature to investigate
itself.

The plot began in 1968 when former representative
Richard T. Hanna (D.-Calif.) and Tongsun Park met in
Seoul with then-Korean CIA Director Kim Hyung
Wook and agreed to have Park appointed the Korean
government's exclusive agent for purchasing rice in the
U.S. In return, according to the KCIA chief's testimony,
Hanna and Park agreed to use a portion of the $9 million
they received in rice commissions between 1970 and 1976
to organize a campaign to influence the American Congress on Korea's behalf. Hanna, for example, initiated
"goodwill trips" to Korea for congressional officials, who
were showered with expensive gifts (brought back duty-
free), honorary degrees, and envelopes full of "expense"
cash to cover the cost of bringing their wives.

From the Korean perspective, Park's "Operation Ice
Mountain" seemed quite reasonable. Park Chung Hee's
prosperous little regime lives in constant fear of its Communist half-brother to the north. With Seoul's skyline
nearly within artillery range of a hostile border, the
South Koreans felt justified in using almost any means to
keep getting plenty of U.S. military and economic aid.
And, after all, they were using methods learned from
their trainers, the American CIA. Korea wanted to buy
off what they considered to be "leftist" and "pro-Com-
munist" forces in the U.S. Congress—including legislators
like Speaker Tip O'Neill, Majority Whip John Brademas,
and former whip John J. McFall.

One important suspect in the whole scheme was Korean
ambassador Kim Dong Jo. His official spokesman at
the embassy testified before the House Ethics Committee
that he saw the diplomat stuffing two dozen unmarked
envelopes full of $100 bills. When asked where he was

taking the bulging briefcase of money, Kim looked at his aide as though the question was naive and replied, "To the Capitol." A secretary to Rep. Larry Winn, Jr. (R.-Kans.) testified at the same hearings that Kim gave her boss an unmarked envelope that Winn returned when it was found to contain what she described as "more money than I'd ever seen in my life."

If Leon Jaworski, the symbol of rectitude recruited by Speaker O'Neill to take over the stalled investigation in late 1977, could have acquired the testimony of Ambassador Kim, many congressmen might have found themselves behind bars. Jaworski himself said he had "not the slightest doubt that he [Tongsun Park] was serving as a foreign agent," but he couldn't prove it. While congressmen who took cash from Park could always say (and they did) that they were unaware he represented the KCIA, no congressman accepting an envelope from an ambassador could claim he did not know he was violating Article II of the U.S. Constitution, which forbids accepting remuneration of any kind from a foreign government. But Korea kept Kim under close wraps.

"This whole thing was run right out of the Korean embassy," Jaworski said, and he accused Congress and the State Department of impeding his efforts to force Kim's testimony despite Korean claims of diplomatic immunity. He finally quit the investigation, like his predecesssor Phillip A. Lacovara, bitter at Ethics Chairman John J. Flynt, Jr. (D.-Ga.) who Republican leaders accused of "foot-dragging" to protect Democratic members.

By 1979, when the inquiry ended, evidence indicated that Korean rice dealer Tongsun Park had handed out more than $850,000 in "gifts" to thirty-one House members between 1970 and 1976—and that at least ninety current and former members of Congress accepted gifts and favors from the South Korean government and its agents. While fifteen members were mentioned in the Justice Department's 1977 indictment as recipients of cash, it took the House Committee on Official Standards of Conduct (more commonly known as the Ethics Committee) eighteen months to finally release a report that wrist-slapped four current members, and cleared nine others with a suggestion that they be more careful about whom they take money from.

The four accused of breaking rules were former majority whip John J. McFall, who admitted back in 1976 that he did not report $4,000 in cash received from Park in 1972 and 1976, but instead placed it in a secret office account; and Edward Roybal, Charles Wilson, and Edward J. Patten, all California Democrats, who failed to report and then lied to the committee about $1,000 contributions they received in cash from Park between 1974 and 1976. The committee referred perjury charges against former representatives John R. Rarick (D.-La.) and Nick Galifianakis (D.-N.C.) for lying in sworn depositions about cash they took from Park in 1974 and 1972, respectively. The Democratic Caucus showed how seriously they take the Ethics Committee by blocking, just months after disciplinary action was urged against the four, an attempt to deprive Roybal and Wilson of their subcommittee chairmanships. (Meanwhile, the Senate Ethics Committee concluded that three senators may have violated senate rules or public law: two deceased senators, Hubert Humphrey [D.-Minn.] and John McClellan [D.-Ark.] allegedly received campaign contributions from Park and failed to report them; it also said that Birch Bayh accepted a contribution from Park in the Capitol—it is a crime to receive a political contribution in a federal building—though Bayh denies the charge.)

When he discussed the House's handling of the Koreagate probe before the American Bar Association convention in late 1978, Jaworski said the investigation was hampered by public skepticism about the ability of Congress to investigate itself, by the rules of the House, by "camaraderie" among the members who seem determined to protect each other, and by the inability of committee members to sit and listen to witnesses, ask hard questions, and devote the time necessary for a proper investigation. Jaworski argued forcefully that any future investigations of wrongdoing by members of Congress or the executive branch must be handled by an outside commission appointed by the president.

These cases portray some of the ways Capitol Hillers can run afoul of the law. And they illuminate how they are caught, how they explain their behavior, and how they are sanctioned.

Most congressional corruption is discovered and publicized either by staff whistle blowers or by outside muckrakers, like Jack Anderson. Tom Dodd's staff ultimately decided their highest loyalty was to the public, not their employer. Boyd then went to Pearson and Anderson, whose revelations have discomfited many officials. One can be quite certain that many politicians in Washington immediately scan the Anderson column in the *Washington Post* to check whether that bribe/lady-from-Duluth/slush-fund has been publicly exposed. When they are—as James Boyd describes the scene—

> The Senator's strength drains out in a puddle. He slumps in a flaccid heap and stares glassily at the accusing phone; the knowing place in the pit of the stomach sinks into infinity. . . . It is the moment of maximum hazard to a political career; a too-defiant denial, a telltale dodge, an injudicious admission can . . . undo 30 years of patient conniving. The Senator's glazed eyes conjure up newspaper headlines, the dock, the recall of Congressional credit cards, the cell door clanking shut.

This moment of "maximum hazard" can be met in various ways whether the accused is culpable or not (false but spectacular charges are an occupational risk for politicians). Some of the following categories were developed in the *Washington Monthly* by Boyd himself, not unfamiliar with what he calls "the ritual of wiggle."

• Ignore it—Some disconnect their phones, leave for a trip, or simply say "no comment." The idea is that the thing will blow over. It can work if the accused or the event is inconsequential enough (a condition Abe Fortas did not appreciate) or if the reply is sufficiently disparaging (e.g., Dirksen said he could not "make heads or tails" of charges over abuse of his congressional frank, and the issue disappeared).

• Blame invisible enemies—This is especially handy for crusaders, who can always blame their problems on their historic targets. Of course, such targets may never have been prosecutors or accusers, but when one seeks scapegoats this does not matter. Thus we had Dodd's "Communists" and Diggs' "racists" (though he was convicted by an all-black jury).

• Deny the obvious—If repeated often and honestly enough, it can sometimes work. After Rep. Seymour Halpern, already in debt, got his $100,000 in unsecured loans while ruminating over banking legislation, he announced that there wasn't any conflict of interest. He suffered some bad publicity but was easily reelected. Robert Carson, former aide to Senator Hiram Fong, claimed that his $100,000 offer to Richard Kleindienst to help out an indicted friend was just a campaign contribution. The jury, however, called it a bribe and gave him eighteen months in jail.

• Say you'd do it for anyone—In 1971, lobbyist Nathan Voloshen and Martin Sweig, a close associate and aide, respectively, of Speaker McCormack, were convicted of influence-peddling and perjury; specifically, they defrauded government agencies by using the speaker's office and prestige on behalf of private clients. At their trial, Rep. Robert Leggett testified that it was not odd to give a lobbyist the run of one's office. He considered the whole country as his constituency and would certainly be willing to allow anyone to use his office for commercial clients. This performance led one juror to say that "after hearing him, it is my opinion they should investigate *all* the members of Congress."

• Announce for reelection—This because the best defense is a good offense. Dodd declared for his third term the day he was censured. McCormack did so on the day he held a press conference to deny participation in Voloshen's and Sweig's schemes.

• Plead for mercy on national television—The Nixon–Checkers and Kennedy–Chappaquiddick speeches are too well known to belabor, but their successes have not been forgotten.

• Say you'll give it back—In the early sixties, Rep. John Byrnes, then a ranking member of the House Ways and Means Committee, helped get a favorable tax ruling for the Mortgage Guaranty Insurance Corporation from the IRS. He then purchased $2,300 of their stock on terms not generally available, and within two years it was worth $25,000. In an emotional, lachrymose floor speech denying any wrongdoing, Byrnes announced that he would give any profits made to a scholarship fund for needy youth. His colleagues cheered. Seymour Halpern, when his bank loans were questioned, said he would pay them back, if necessary, by selling off his prize collection of famous signatures, which he had spent a lifetime collecting. It was, to many, a touching and convincing gesture.

• Threaten suit—This hardly ever works, but it makes good copy. The difficulty is that it is nearly impossible to prove libel under existing law when the person at issue is a "public figure." Dodd actually filed a $5 million libel suit against Pearson and Anderson, losing every count.

• Get a senatorial OK—Although all that may be involved is some classic backscratching, it is helpful to get exonerated by An Important Person. Former senator George Murphy began to worry shortly before his 1970 race about his arrangement with Pat Frawley of Technicolor. Frawley gave the senator $20,000 annually, gave him free use of a credit card, and paid half of his $520 monthly rent. Murphy first asked Dirksen if the arrangement was unseemly, and Dirksen gave his blessing—as he had given it to himself many times. Then Stennis, chairman of the Senate Ethics Committee, performed the laying on of hands. Senator Edward Long also got Senator Stennis to whitewash Long's "referral fees" from teamster lawyer M. A. Shenker, with hardly a glance at what really went on. But the voters sent both Murphy and Long looking for a new line of work.

• Claim immunity—Failing other ploys, many take refuge in procedural defenses. Congressional immunity is one way to finesse a tense situation, at least temporarily. Former representative Thomas Johnson was convicted in 1963 of pocketing $17,500 in exchange for helping a savings and loan office escape federal prosecution. But the Supreme Court reversed the conviction because part of his offense involved a floor speech for which, the Court said, he was immune. (He was reconvicted in 1968 and went to jail for six months in 1970.) Daniel Brewster also was able to convince a lower federal court that congressional immunity somehow exonerated an alleged bribery, although the Supreme Court later reversed this decision.

What, finally, were the sanctions meted out to the thirty-six members and staff listed in the Roll Call of Congressional Illegality? Sixteen were convicted of felonies and sentenced to jail, including nine representatives (Diggs,

Brasco, Dowdy, Gallagher, Hanna, Hastings, Hinshaw, Podell, Tonry). Nine others were convicted of various crimes, but never spent time in prison; four representatives were reprimanded by the House; five members or staff are currently under investigation or awaiting trial for illegal or unethical conduct by either the Justice Department or one of the ethics committees. And of eleven incumbents involved in or charged with illegal conduct who ran for reelection, four were defeated (Brooke, Burke, Eilberg, and McFall) and seven reelected (Diggs, Flood, Hansen, Jones, Roybal, Sikes, Wilson). It is obvious that scandal does not always override a district's habit of returning an incumbent to the office he has been guilty of abusing. The attitude often seems to be "he may be a thief, but he is *our* thief." Indeed, Jim Curley in the forties, Tom Lane in the fifties, and Adam Clayton Powell in the sixties all initially won reelection despite the fact that the first two were actually in jail and the last had been forbidden to participate in House activities.

"The problem is that we used to rely on the people's sense of smell to police this place," Rep. Barber Conable, Jr. (R.-N.Y.), told the *New Yorker's* Elizabeth Drew in 1977. "In other words, we put our faith in democracy. But that only works when the choice is viable. Now the people's sense isn't enough. The power of incumbency is so great that a Wilbur Mills can get reelected after the Tidal Basin incident, a Wayne Hays can get renominated after the Elizabeth Ray affair, and Bob Leggett can get reelected after he's admitted he's living with his secretary and forged his wife's name on a deed and had an affair with Suzi Park Thomson." So it is well to realize that Congress at times resembles Gambetta's description of the French Chamber of Deputies—"a broken mirror in which the nation cannot recognize its own image."

The Congressional Response

Timeless customs, inherited from the night-long vigils of tribal societies, bind members of a group together. The doctors' unwritten code discourages one from testifying against another. Opposing lawyers are forbidden to criticize each other in court. Congress, too, watches out for its own. For nearly two centuries after its founding, Congress traditionally adopted a laissez-faire policy on ethics, assuming that each individual member wanted to police his own conduct. Congress, for example, has never attempted to define for its members and the public what constitutes a "conflict of interest." Senate rules have never barred a member from voting when he has a personal stake and, across the rotunda, House rules vaguely advise representatives not to vote when they have "a direct or pecuniary interest." Only the increasing numbers of indicted legislators and the Watergate and Koreagate scandals provided the necessary shove for each chamber to take more formal steps toward self-regulation. In both houses, the immediate response was a two-part system: the establishment of ethics committees and the requirement of financial disclosure.

If the name "Ethics Committee" is encouraging, its creation was not. The Senate Select Committee on Ethics had an almost accidental conception. Its parent was the special Senate investigating committee which dug into Bobby Baker's past. The committee's chairman, Senator Everett Jordan, made it clear to his colleagues that the group might be questioning senators' employees, but was "not investigating senators." That satisfying setup might have lasted indefinitely, save for the Senate's absent-mindedness. At a routine session in 1964, a motion came up to establish a committee to investigate senators themselves. An aide to Clifford Case recalls what happened:

> John Sherman Cooper offered the motion to set up the select committee and, to his and everybody else's amazement, it passed. I remember because I was on the floor talking with Senator Case. . . . As he talked with me he was listening to the tally and suddenly he broke off and said, "It's going to pass," and he went over to congratulate Cooper, and Cooper was looking stunned. Mansfield, who was nonplussed and didn't know what to do next, said "We'll have to consult the lawyers," and they recessed. It was one of the funniest things I've ever seen.

The Senate took to its new offspring with all the glee of a father who has found an illegitimate child dumped on his doorstep. For two years, no senators were assigned to seats on the committee. Few were eager to judge their peers. Even reformer Paul Douglas (D.-Ill.) turned down an offer, his aide said, because "he didn't have the stomach for it." John Stennis of Mississippi finally stood where others had faltered; with Stennis as its first chairman, the Ethics Committee was ready for action in 1966. Its nominal powers were impressive: it was to take complaints, investigate alleged misconduct, and recommend disciplinary action.

Tom Dodd's case was the first to come before the committee, which, to the surprise of many, took the difficult step of recommending that Dodd be censured. Even while doing so, however, the committee shied away from some of the most serious complaints against Dodd. "How will Americans ever learn about patterns of privilege and conflict of interest," complained one of those who had exposed Dodd, "if only 10 percent of his unethical activities —and those the least important—are made public?"

Fears that the Ethics Committee might act aggressively as a partisan tool of the majority proved groundless, not because the Republicans and Democrats each were given six seats, but because the committee did relatively little. By 1975 the Senate committee had only two staff employees and a paltry budget of $54,000—almost all going to the staff. To date, though the committee has conducted a few formal and informal investigations—recently, into Edward Brooke and Herman Talmadge—it has not taken any disciplinary action against a senator since 1967.

The House Ethics Committee (officially called the Committee on Standards of Official Conduct) was established in 1967 after a 400–0 vote ("Who can vote against ethics?" a California representative asked). In its first three years of operation, it conducted just two preliminary investigations—one of Rep. Cornelius Gallagher and another of "ghost voting" (the trick by which members had their votes recorded at times when they are actually away from the Capitol). "If my acknowledging only two preliminary investigations makes it sound like we don't do any work," said a member of the committee's staff at that time, "then it will just have to sound that way." Indeed, in its first nine years of operation, the committee never *formally* investigated a representative. It didn't until Common Cause literally shamed it into investigating Rep. Sikes's conflicts of interest.

The first major investigation the House Ethics Com-

mittee felt worth its time and money was a futile attempt
to discover who leaked a secret committee report on the
CIA to CBS correspondent Daniel Schorr. When it came
to scandals involving possibly illegal conduct by legislators,
however, the two ethics committees seemed less eager.
Congress's institutional reluctance to investigate itself appears hypocritical, coming so soon after investigations by
two congressional committees forced a president to resign
from office. The same Congress that investigated conflicts
of interest among Nixon's staff still allowed its banking
committee members to own bank stock. John Gardner,
chairman of Common Cause, called the ethics committee
in the House "the worst kind of sham, giving the appearance of serving as policeman while extending a marvelous
protective shield over members of Congress."

Instead, the House and Senate committees have been
turned into supermarkets for ethical dispensations. Sen.
Adlai E. Stevenson III (D.-Ill.), chairman of the Senate
Ethics Committee, said that his staff has been overwhelmed by inquiries from members about what conduct
does or does not satisfy the new ethics code. Some offices
check the acceptance of nearly every gift and contribution
with the ethics panel as an insurance policy against future
reprisals. "Members frequently ask us about their activities," said John Flynt, Jr. (D.-Ga.), outgoing chairman of
the House panel in 1978. "We research federal laws, our
own House rules and our House precedents to find the
answer for them. They aren't looking for what you'd call
'blue cover'—trying to justify what already was done.
They are seeking guidance."

It is not hard to understand the political and personal
reasons why elected officials would prefer to give guidance
than to investigate wrongdoing. "It's not much fun sitting
in judgment on your colleagues," said Richardson Preyer,
former head of the House Ethics Committee. At the start
of the 96th Congress, not one Democrat volunteered to
serve on either of the two ethics committees. And it was
perhaps predictable that ethics committees would only respond to public pressure rather than initiate inquiries. The
Senate investigated Dodd after the press thoroughly did;
and the House began probes into Diggs and Flood months
after their misdeeds had been publicly documented. "A

member should be in flagrant abuse of his office for the House to act," Rep. Flynt said. "This committee of ours never was set up to be our brother's keeper."

But then no one ever forced a citizen to be paid $57,500 a year to serve the public in Congress. It should not be impossible to expect that the Senate and House would both avoid conducting witch-hunts *and* avoid drawing their wagons in circles around accused colleagues. An impulse toward the latter clearly predominates. At the start of the 96th Congress, the House Democratic Caucus in secret session voted against two reform proposals: one would have barred any member convicted or indicted of a felony from serving as chairman of a committee or subcommittee; the other would have required the House to vote on the question of expelling any member convicted of a felony. One irate citizen subsequently wrote the *Washington Star* that "an important principle was at issue in the Democratic Caucus. In a civilized country, are certified felons to be allowed to make the laws? A congressional group will probably never be confronted with a simpler, more clear-cut ethical question, and its members did not have the ethical sense to see it, or the political courage to act on it."

While the ethics committees gave guidance and little else, the public became increasingly outraged by what seemed to be a continuing stream of revelations about congressional corruption. A Harris poll conducted in 1977 for the House Ethics Committee indicated that of eleven institutions, the public ranked Congress ninth in integrity, slightly better than large corporations and labor unions. As a result, the House in 1976 established a special Commission on Administrative Review to look into possible ethics, committee and administrative reforms. The commission, chaired by Rep. David R. Obey (D.-Wis.), proposed a new more stringent code of ethics for the House, highlighted by broad financial disclosure rules, an end to office slush funds, an $8,625 ceiling on annual outside earned income by members, and limitations on the franking privilege and foreign travel.

The reform proposals seemed to excite greater passions in the House than any military or civil rights legislation which would affect only the lives of innocent millions. At stake, after all, were formulas for congressional salaries and criminal liabilities. Passions also ran high because Speaker O'Neill strongly supported ethics reform, both to improve public confidence in his besmirched institution and to justify the $13,000 annual pay increase members sought.

The cornerstone of these recommendations is the sweeping requirement of disclosure. The financial disclosure provisions for the House, and a similar version for the Senate, require that congressmen report the source and amount of all income and gifts over $100; any gifts of transportation, food, entertainment, or reimbursement totaling more than $250; the approximate value of any financial holding having a fair market value of at least $1,000; and the identity of any debt of more than $2,500, unless it is a mortgage. Most controversial by far, though, was the proposed limitation on outside earned income to 15 percent of salary. Earned income includes money generated by work that requires a substantial investment of time and effort (law practice, speechmaking), but does not include dividends, capital gains, and family business income. This standard presumes that members of congress should be full-time public officials.

But as memories of Watergate began to fade and the so-called Koreagate scandal began to bore even the guilty, the push for ethics and reform on Capitol Hill rapidly lost momentum in the 95th Congress. Its members were already taking for granted a pay raise nearly equal to the medium family income in America and was regretting all the outside income they had sacrificed to what many saw as a temporary hysteria for ethics.

A backlash spread. Suddenly, by 1978, "ethics" and "reform" became dirty words in the halls of Congress. A package of reforms developed by the Obey Commission, to improve administration of the House and establish a grievance procedure for Capitol employees, was defeated. The House voted against the public financing of congressional elections. Congress did pass an ethics bill dealing largely with the executive and judicial branches—only after House leaders quelled an attempt to repeal the 15 percent limitation on outside earned income.

Even Rep. Obey, author of several frustrated reforms, observed that Congress "just got so damn fed up seeing the House broadbrushed by every damn demagogue in the country and nobody back home is being told how much we've reformed. . . . If you've got a bum the people to blame are the people who elected him, not the people who have to work with him." According to Illinois Democrat Morgan Murphy, "The whole atmosphere here—with all these investigations—is that a majority of the members of Congress are crooks or have something to hide. There's a suspicion every time you call someone in the bureaucracy on behalf of a constituent that you're doing someone a favor because you owe him something. The pendulum has swung too far since Watergate."

Obey and Murphy each have a piece of the truth. The House has adopted several important reforms; and, of course, most members of Congress aren't crooks. Indeed, many are models of probity, independent of the existence or extent of any ethics code. Former senators Wayne Morse and Paul Douglas began publicly disclosing their financial holdings years ago. Senator Charles Percy put his $6 million fortune in the hands of a blind trust in the 1960s. His predecessor, Paul Douglas, also refused all contributions for personal expenses or from people with a financial interest in matters before the Senate. Former representative Ken Hechler (D.-W.Va.) gave up his commission as an Army reserve colonel—one year short of a guaranteed $220 per month pension—when the House considered a military pay bill which would have boosted his pension about 10 percent. Senator Henry Jackson (D.-Wash.) routinely and quietly gives to charity all income from speeches and honoraria that he earns over and above his Senate salary.

But such exemplars are measures of how far their colleagues have to go. It is difficult to ignore that the 1970s saw the greatest documentation of congressional corruption in this century. True, the people of a district may elect a "bum," but this individual influences policies that affect 434 other districts and 49 other states. If the scandals of the past decade were not enough to motivate Congress to prohibit convicted members from serving as chairmen, prohibit members with substantial commercial interests from chairing committees with jurisdiction over such interests, require the public funding of campaigns, insist that its ethics committees investigate charges of corruption and censure rather than wrist-slap those guilty of corruption, then one wonders what will be necessary to spur Congress to complete its clean-up.

Few, if any, people run for public office with the secret intent to profit by illegal means. Rather, there is something in the congressional environment which raises this temptation and then lowers resistance—a something that may well inhere in the legislative process itself. Laws can seriously affect important people; politicians need money to stay in office; important people can give money to politicians in order to influence them. Thus, there are two sides to the coin of the congressional power: there is the potential to improve the lot of all Americans and there is the potential of corruption.

It would be polite to end a discussion of congressional lawlessness by intoning that, while there are a few rotten apples, the overwhelming majority of congressmen are honest. This may be true, but how would we know? Existing public financial disclosures do not tell us enough, nor are the ethics committees vigilant enough to make us sanguine. By failing to police itself adequately, Congress— especially given the cynicism inspired by Watergate and other scandals—has failed to elevate itself above suspicion. A critical observer can hardly take heart at the number of congressmen and staff who have been caught. There are no cops regularly patrolling Capitol Hill corridors, and law enforcement agencies do not devote resources to congressional crime. The luckless few are exposed more by fluke than by investigation, which predictably leads friends and cynics alike to wonder not so much what congressmen do as how many of them get away with it.

6

Games Congressmen Play:
The Capitol Culture

This damn place is a plenary of Rotarians. The
House acts, thinks, and reacts in terms of some
stodgy old Philadelphia club.

—A representative

Every small town has its Elks Club or Kiwanis. But only
Washington has a club which runs the country. Compared
to any Masonic lodge, Congress is not unusually quaint;
compared to the hierarchies of the film industry, or back-
door intrigue at the Vatican, its rituals of power are not
particularly occult. In most of its ways, Congress is, as one
senator put it, "just like living in a small town." Just as
their executive relations and the committee system say something about the way they govern the country, so do the
congressmen's customs and folkways.

The Politics of Deference

When the Constitutional Convention was hammering
out new provisions in 1787, its members did not have to
worry that their comments would be flashed back to local
voters on the evening news. With a candor that modern
publicity makes hardly possible, Pennsylvania's Gouverneur
Morris said at the convention that he hoped the Senate
"will show us the might of aristocracy." Poorly as this
seems to fit normal ideas of representation and democracy,
it comes closer to catching the Senate's spirit than many
other definitions. Spectators watching from the Senate galleries understand Morris's meaning; while members of the
House scurry in and out like harried businessmen or tired

206

farmers, the senators emerge from the cloakroom doors
and glide onto the floor with the weighty tread of men
who know they are being recognized. House members
make fun of the Senate for this difference; but both houses
pay extraordinary attention to rituals designed to boost
prestige.

On first glance, the most noticeable feature of congressional proceedings is the antique language and min-
uettish courtesies which encase them. Before beginning
an attack on another congressman's proposal, a member
will hang garlands of "my distinguished friend" around
his neck. Former House speaker John McCormack, for
example, warmed up for an attack on a Gerald Ford
position by noting that "we are all very happy in the justified and deserved recognition that our distinguished
friend, the gentleman from Michigan [Ford], received
yesterday . . . when the city of Grand Rapids set aside a
special day in recognition of such an outstanding legislator
and in recognition of such a great American." To make
sure that no one missed the point, McCormack's sidekick,
then majority leader Carl Albert, chimed in, "I wish to join
our distinguished and beloved speaker in the tribute paid
to our distinguished minority leader." Then, like boxers
who had completed the ritual glove touching, they dug in.

After sitting through one too many of these syrupy pref-
aces several years ago, Massachusetts Senator Edward
Brooke suggested that if the word "distinguished" were
eliminated from the proceedings, the legislators could save
10 percent of their time. To which Majority Leader Mike
Mansfield replied, "I appreciate the remarks of the distinguished senator from Massachusetts for his views."

The model for this behavior is, of course, the world of
diplomacy—what presidential candidate Adlai Stevenson
once called, in words also evocative of Congress, a place
of "protocol, alcohol, and Geritol." There, each delegate
represents a nation, and a little ceremony is in order.
Congressmen emulate other parts of the diplomatic procedure as well. While the pope or the English queen might
get away with saying "We" instead of "I," congressmen
prefer third-person references to themselves. When he was
majority leader, Lyndon Johnson couched one opinion
in the following cumbersome prose: "The senator from
Texas does not have any objection and the senator from

Texas wishes the senator from California to know that the senator from Texas knew the senator from California did not criticize him." In the haste of quick-moving debate, congressmen may even forget "the senator" and refer to themselves as states.

To keep the rituals up, congressmen have developed a number of unwritten social rules. One, according to Majority Leader Jim Wright, is "that old 11th Commandment that was drilled into each of us as we entered in the 1950s and 1960s. 'Thou shalt not demagogue with thy colleagues.' Some members wear out their welcome here by trying to appear universal authorities on all subjects or making speeches aimed at their home constituencies." Another is "Thou shalt not attack thy brethren." In private, congressmen may call each other (as they did in some of our interviews) "screaming idiots" or "jackasses." In public, this would provoke outrage. There are strains involved—"It's hard not to call a man a liar when you know that he is one," said one senator—but most keep themselves under control. If their resolve slips, they can remember the case of Rep. John Hunter—who in 1867 was formally censured by the House for saying of a colleague's comment, "So far as I am concerned, it is a base lie."

At times the elaborate courtesy and deference that mark Senate proceedings surrenders to playful jibes. During the hectic last day of the 95th Congress, Senator James Abourezk, conducting a one-man filibuster on an energy bill, noticed that the chamber's clerk looked tired. "Mr. President, may the clerk be seated while he is reading?" he asked. "I object," snapped a weary Russell Long. "May the clerk remain standing?" Abourezk shot back. "I object," Long said again. Senator Wendell Ford, the presiding officer, then announced that "the clerk will stand on his head and read." Later that day, when Senator Proxmire wanted to continue the filibuster by demanding a quorum call, he was ruled out of order because there was no pending business. OK, he said, announcing that "I ask unanimous consent that the Republican Party be abolished." "I object," Senator Robert Dole (R.-Kan.) quick-wittedly replied, fortunately for the party of Lincoln.

Yet verbal banter or lack of political etiquette can go

further—into the realm of physical violence. Just as a prim Victorian England encouraged a very racy pornographic subculture, so the constant constraint of deference can at times lead to its opposite. During heated debate over the Compromise of 1850, Senator Henry S. ("Hangman") Foote brandished a pistol at Thomas Hart Benton; before Foote could fire, other senators subdued him. Six years later, during the Kansas debates, a South Carolina representative bludgeoned Senator Charles Sumner so severely that he could not return to the Senate for three years.

Today's violence is not nearly so serious, but it still occurs at times. Ex-members Bert Podell and James Delaney of New York City got into a shoving match at a luncheon in the early 1970s after Delaney dressed Podell down for defeating him for a seat on their party's steering committee. And Senator Strom Thurmond, a physical culturist, engaged in a lengthy wrestling match in the Senate Office Building with former senator Ralph Yarborough when Yarborough tried to dragoon Thurmond into attending a committee hearing.

Since freshman congressmen are inexperienced in proper political deference when they arrive, careful instruction is necessary. In the first few weeks, freshmen from both parties put aside political differences to attend briefings. There they learn, according to a *New Yorker* profile of Allard Lowenstein, "the special political etiquette of favors that members expect from each other and should be prepared to repay." In addition, they learn the wisdom of Sam Rayburn's famous maxim, "To get along, you've got to go along."

The freshmen must also learn their special role in this hierarchy of deference. The more florid levels of posturing are reserved for their seniors. When they do make a sound—in their maiden speeches—they are urged to be concise, modest, and well prepared. In this they follow the advice George Washington gave in 1787 to a nephew who was about to enter the Virginia house of delegates: "Should the new legislator wish to be heard, the way to command the attention of the House is to speak seldom, but to important subjects . . . make yourself perfectly master of the subject. Never exceed a decent warmth, and submit your sentiments with diffidence."

Slow learners get reminders. In the 1950s, a freshman senator found himself sitting next to Walter George, who as longest surviving senator had earned the title of "Dean." Wishing perhaps to show George that he was eager to learn, the youngster leaned over and asked how the Senate had changed during George's countless years as a member. George paused, then icily responded, "Freshmen didn't used to talk so much." And the late Carl Hayden used to recall his first speech in the House in 1913. He had kept quiet for many months until a matter unimportant to the House but very important to his native Arizona came up. Hayden spoke to the chamber for only a minute, and returned to his seat next to a more senior member, who turned to him and angrily said, "Just had to talk, didn't you?"

This system is tolerated only because its victims know that someday they will be on the other end of the sneer. It is perpetuated with a powerful system of informal sanctions. "They can give you the silent treatment," said one representative, "and the real whip is delayed action. You may think you are not going to be punished for your failure to stay in line because there is no immediate penalty. Months later, however, something happens which makes you realize they were just waiting for the proper moment to strike. There is no doubt about it," he ruefully concluded, "if you are going to be independent around here, you are going to pay a steep price for it."

Contrary to form was the 1974 class of feisty freshmen, who voted several senior chairmen out of their positions and spoke out on numerous issues. One of its leaders was Andrew Maguire (D.-N.J.), who said two terms later that "if you trim your sails, if you genuflect to the leadership, if you bow to the committee chairmen, you don't make a difference." Younger members, contrary to tradition, are now far more likely to give passionate floor speeches or introduce major amendments on the House floor, as Reps. Elliott Levitas (D.-Ga.) and Dan Glickman (D.-Kans.) have done. But though such members are far more independent of the leadership than their seniors were, personal civility is still the norm, especially for freshmen. As one of the most independent and outspoken of young congressmen, Toby Moffett (D.-

Conn.) concluded toward the end of his second term, "All the pressures are to be a member of the club."

As in so much else, the senior members of Congress can take liberties no freshman would wisely dare. Senator Bob Kerr of Oklahoma could call Senator Homer Capehart "a rancid tub of ignorance" over a decade ago precisely because he was Bob Kerr, one of the most powerful men in the Senate. In 1972, Senate Minority Leader Hugh Scott knew he would not suffer for saying that the investigating of ITT's connection with the Republican National Committee was Democratic "jackassery."

But there is a line which the nonpowerful cross with hesitation: charges that impugn a congressman by name. Senator Daniel Patrick Moynihan (D.-N.Y.), who has been known to use words as hammers, once called an amendment by Senator Malcolm Wallop (R.-Wyo.) "inane, devoid of intellectual competence or even rhetorical merit . . . Are we to reduce the United States Senate to a playground, a playpen of juvenilia, to the fantasies of prepubescent youth?" The next day, he apologized.

In 1974, then House majority leader Tip O'Neill called a parliamentary maneuver by freshman Republican Rep. Robert Bauman "a cheap, sneaky, sly way to operate." Bauman quickly protested to Speaker Carl Albert that this characterization violated the House rule that one member may not impugn the motives of another. And Speaker Albert upheld Bauman over the majority leader, striking the offending words from the record. Perhaps unfazed, O'Neill, as Speaker, a few years later attacked freshman Rep. Bruce Caputo in an interview because "from what I've been told he has two employees on his payroll who check the sex life of his colleagues . . . It's a rare occasion when a man the type of Caputo comes to the Congress of the United States, and I don't think he's good for Congress." Again, O'Neill had to apologize, this time on the House floor in an unusual one-minute speech. "I guess what it comes down to is this," he concluded, "that as Speaker, a constitutional officer of this House, I must be more charitable and responsible toward my colleagues than they sometimes are toward me."

Indiscretions like these of course occasionally occur, but if they should become chronic—or if they are not followed by repentance, they eventually push their authors into a special class within the congressional society. The newspaper-reading public may think of these congressmen as colorful or frank; but within Congress, they are pariahs. If they please their constituents enough to stay in office and gain seniority, they may eventually get some power in Congress. But such exiles can forget about the many stepping stones open to those who follow the rules.

*Rep. Ronald Dellums, w*ho as a black "radical" was already suspect in the eyes of many colleagues, earned the opprobrium of the House when he told a reporter that most senators and representatives "are mediocre prima donnas who pass legislation that has nothing to do with the reality of misery in this country. The level of mediocrity of the leaders in the country scares the hell out of me." For this comment, Dellums was challenged by Rep. Wayne Hays on the floor:

> *Hays:* Did the gentleman make that statement?
> *Dellums:* Yes. Do you want me to explain it?
> *Hays:* No, I do not need you to explain it. I just wonder if you then want a bunch of mediocre prima donnas to pay more serious attention to your amendment?
> *Dellums:* If I don't, then my statement has double merit. I would simply say that [congressmen] go around strutting from their offices to the floor of the Congress and do not deal with the human misery in this country.
> *Hays:* You may strut around from *your* office to the floor and to God knows where . . . but do not measure, as my father used to say, everybody's corn in your own half-bushel.

But Dellums was apparently unperturbed by criticism from people like Wayne Hays. A person accustomed to saying what he thinks, he denounced the "white, male, chauvinist, racist press" during a House debate on ethics in 1978.

Former representative Bella Abzug probably could have guessed that her reception in Congress would be cool, despite her hats. She followed few of the codes of etiquette, tongue-lashing the House ("I'm tired of listening to a bunch of old men who are long beyond the draft age standing here and talking about sending our young men over to be killed in an illegal and immoral war") and tongue-lashing Speaker Carl Albert ("Now you listen to me, Carl. I'm sick and tired, because it's about time this Democratic caucus went on record against the war. . . . What's the matter with you?").

On September 30, 1971, she especially came to understand the form of congressional retaliation. Shortly before noon, she began walking to the House floor, ready to present a resolution to force the State Department to reveal how deeply the United States was involved in South Vietnam's presidential elections. Although the House formally convenes at noon, routine trivia usually postpone the serious business till 12:30 or later. But on this day, at 12:01, Albert cracked his gavel and quickly called on Rep. Tom Morgan. Fighting hard to suppress guffaws, the House listened to Morgan say, "Mr. Speaker, I intended to yield to the gentlewoman from New York for ten minutes for debate only, but I do not see the gentlewoman on the floor." Within seconds, Albert and the House agreed to table the motion. It was all over by the time Bella strolled in at 12:03.

Such slights became less frequent. Most members became inured to her extravagant and abrasive style and she won their respect by her legislative skill, as when her resolution of inquiry provoked an unprecedented visit by President Gerald Ford to explain his pardoning of Richard Nixon to a House committee hearing. Her relentlessness became a trademark. As Tip O'Neill once told a freshman member, smiling, "You can't say no to Bella."

Former senator James Abourezk (D.-S.D.), who served from 1973 to 1979, had "a marvelous unwashed style and a howitzer laugh that he used constantly to shoot down Senatorial pomposities," wrote Robert Sherrill. His candor was refreshing in an institution that leans toward obfuscation. In late 1973, Abourezk wrote Senator Jackson, supposedly tough on the oil industry, urging that his committee subpoena industry records to see what its oil reserves were; the South Dakotan never received an answer. Once Abourezk complained long and hard on the chamber floor that the Senate was backing away from requiring President Nixon to end the bombing of Cambodia by August 15, 1973. Liberal colleagues urged him to compromise. "How the hell do you compromise when you're bombing people," said the freshman senator. "I was going to talk all night until I found there wouldn't be enough guys to help me." His tenacity forced Minority Leader Hugh Scott, well-schooled in Senate etiquette, to remonstrate, "The Junior Senator from South Dakota hasn't been here long enough to know the ways of operating in the Senate."

Five years later he still hadn't. Believing that the deregulation of natural gas rates was a fundamental bilk of consumers, he began a two-week postcloture filibuster (described previously) that had his colleagues bitter and frazzled. "Flaky," "quixotic," he was called. He called them things in return: "Politicians up here are encouraged to run forever because of the seniority system and the benefits. So they will avoid anything that will defeat them. They figure controversy is what will prevent their reelection." Intensely controversial, he chose not to run for reelection, and left with the same bluntness that characterized his term there. "I can't wait to get out of this chicken-shit outfit," he said at the close of the 1978 session.

As *Senator Mike Gravel* thought more deeply about the horror of the Asian war, and compared it to the daily pleasantries on the Senate floor, he began to doubt that the "antiwar" senators were doing as much as they could. The cracking point came in 1971, with the appearance of the Pentagon Papers. While his colleagues were torn between consternation at what the papers showed, and irritation at the improper and possibly illegal publication of them, Gravel devoted himself to making the information public. He first tried to read then-unpublished portions into the *Congressional Record*. Blocked because there was no quorum, he then called a hasty meeting of the Senate Public Works Committee, of which he is a member. For three and a half hours he read, tears pouring down his face. With passion rare for its sincerity, he concluded, "The greatest representative democracy the world has known, the nation of Jefferson and Lincoln, has let its nose be rubbed in the swamp by petty warlords, jealous Vietnamese generals, blackmarketeers, and grand-scale dope pushers."

Like banqueters who see a starving child staring in through a window, the Senate turned away, angry at the intrusion. What mattered about Gravel's performance was not that the material was true, but that he had broken the rules in releasing it. Republicans Scott and Dole mumbled something about sanctions; Majority Leader Mansfield instead had a "friendly talk" with his erring ward. Managing a measure of contrition, Gravel later said, "Perhaps I did not approach the matter with the same degree of delicacy another would employ. What I did, I felt and continue to feel, will bring credit to the United States Senate, not embarrassment. I would never be party to any act that would not bring credit to this august body." To other senators, this last sentence was ludicrous: by bringing the starving child into the hall, Gravel had humiliated them all.

For those who can adapt to the folkways of the congressional society, there is a reward far different from the exile endured by Gravel and Dellums. This is membership in the "club"—the informal roster of those who meet the Senate's and House's standards. Though the faces may occasionally change, and even some of the rules, the Senate's dignity and pomp—some would say pomposity— endures. To columnist Meg Greenfield, "Even in their stocking feet, senators in the chamber are always 'on,' always looking as if they were aware of their importance, always engaged among themselves in a kind of forced touchy-feely bonhomie—a back pat here, a handclasp there, a playful minishove, an earnest clutch of the other fellow's lapel. . . . The Club: it lives. Senators of every style, age and political persuasion love to tell you about how various forces and individuals outside the Senate make a terrible mistake by offending that august body or inconveniencing it in some fashion."

To enter The Club's portals, some degree of personal submission is required. Ambitious John and Robert Kennedy never learned this lesson, and were never popular among senators. Other traits can offend as well: Wayne Morse was too belligerent and waspish, Eugene McCarthy too detached and cerebral, Jacob Javits too . . . well, too

New York. Those who best qualify have power (Lyndon Johnson and Russell Long), dignity (Richard Russell and Paul Douglas), homespun friendliness (Warren Magnuson, Gaylord Nelson) or seniority (those remaining Southern patriarchs).

Although club perquisites come more naturally to older members and to conservatives than to young liberals, there is no ironclad age or ideological test for those who seek entrance. No clearer proof can be given than the case of Allard Lowenstein, one-term representative from New York. Before his election in 1968, his career as a political organizer and architect of the "Dump Johnson" movement placed him well to the left of most congressional liberals. But on his arrival, Lowenstein managed to play by House rules. Other congressmen "found that he is not the wild-eyed maverick most people thought him to be," said one colleague. "He's quietly doing his homework, and as a result he's gaining much respect in the House." When first introduced to Mendel Rivers—grand promoter of the defense industries Lowenstein fought—Lowenstein said, "Mr. Chairman, I have relatives who are constituents of yours"—adding that their name was Rivers. "Well," rumbled Rivers, "there's been a lot of intermarriage down there." After that, the two would call each other "cousin." He also managed to charm Carl Albert, who told Lowenstein, "You're not a long-hair-and-beard type at all." After he had served a few weeks in the House, Lowenstein won the unusual privilege for a freshman of presiding over the floor for a few minutes in Albert's absence.

Another freshman who managed to win over the clubmen's hearts—and who has a better chance than Lowenstein of staying to reap the rewards—was Republican Senator Charles Mathias of Maryland. In his first term, Mathias established himself to such an extent that one colleague said, "On those quickie votes on amendments, you waltz on the floor and the first things you ask are 'What is it?' and 'Whose is it?' If it is Mathias, that's worth about ten votes."

Called Mac (a boyhood name) by all factions, Mathias has struck the right mixture of dignity and affability. "He's always got that cherubic smile and sort of twinkle in his eye," says one senator. Another adds, "He doesn't take himself so serious as to be ponderous." Mathias deftly displayed a due courtesy toward the Senate's demigods in response to questions about his future goals. He replied that the ideal senator was someone like Robert Taft, Sr., of Ohio, "whose word and position were respected in the areas in which he was a leader."

Congressional Cliques

Richard Nixon has Bebe Rebozo, Harvard has the Porcellian Club, Yale has Skull and Bones—and the American Congress has, among others, the Chowder and Marching Society, the Prayer Breakfast Group, the Sundowners, the Monday Morning Meeting, the Tuesday Morning Breakfast Club, the Wednesday Group, the Blue-Collar Caucus, and the Suburban Caucus.

As in any tradition-ridden society, these clubs play a crucial part in the social structure of Congress. Any implication of frivolity or lightness is usually deserved. Like basketball players on the court, or collegians coming home after heavy dates, congressmen "don't just speak to one another," then representative Donald Riegle once wrote. "They punch each other on the arm, slap each other on the knee, grab each other's jackets and—occasionally—give each other the goose." The main difference between the congressional club system and university fraternities, both of whose members give allegiance to the rules and habits of the group, is that in Congress the fraternity atmosphere makes a difference in the way the rest of us live. In trying to understand some of the inexplicable outcomes of our legislative process, it is important to note the roles of three kinds of social clubs.

The first category is made of the purely good-times groups. Congressmen, like the rest of us, want to relax when the day is over. For some, the best way to do this is with their colleagues. Current social clubs include the Doormen's Society, which meets each year for a "Knight's Night." In 1971, Rep. Gerald Ford was finally made a member; not really joking, he said, "It took me 16 years to become minority leader, but it's taken me 23½ years to become a Doorman, which I take as a measure of its prestige." Older members meet in the Sundowners Club, while former members make up the Former Members of

Congress. This is one of the largest groups—its ranks boosted after each election—and has some four hundred members.

When these recreational activities are loaded with political overtones, they lead to the second category of congressional clubs. In these, business is pleasure; votes are traded over card games and glasses of gin; good joke-telling or expert arm-wrestling may make the difference between success and failure for an education or defense bill. They descend from the nineteenth-century School of Philosophy Club, where it was hard to separate the poker from the politics. An equally misnamed group, Sam Rayburn's "Board of Education," used to meet in the late afternoons in Mr. Sam's hideaway office in the Capitol to sip whiskey and play politics. Today the Chowder and Marching Society (founded in 1949 by, among others, Richard Nixon) gives its fifteen members the chance to talk intimately with a Treasury or Defense secretary. On his admission to the club, Rep. Thomas Railsback said, "It was the best thing that has happened to me from a political standpoint." Another Republican group, SOS (allegedly for "Save Our Souls"), includes all the upper stories of the GOP power structure. "The groups do groom people for leadership," says a Chowder man, "perhaps not by a conscious effort but as a result of the close relationships the members form."

A variant of this type of group is the Prayer Breakfast Club. About thirty to forty-five members meet weekly for prayer and fellowship, creating bonds which appear later in legislative cooperation. Since 1955, a room has been set aside in the Capitol for their prayer and meditation. "Normally used sparingly at the beginning of a session," writes Charles Clapp in *The Congressman: His Work as He Sees It*, "the room is much frequented when critical complex issues are before the House."

The third type of group fits more closely the textbook model of what congressmen do with their spare time. These clubs—like the Democratic Study Group or the Black Caucus—are purely political alliances, the structural manifestations of congressional allegiances and blocs. The first one began in 1959, when eighty House liberals settled on the bland title of "Democratic Study Group" (DSG) in order to discourage the press from referring to them as insurgents. In its early days, the group remained intentionally loose and informal; to do more, Rep. Eugene McCarthy said then, "might be construed as a direct challenge to [House Speaker] Rayburn's leadership." In the last decade the DSG has become more active, providing much-needed information on bills to members, and lining up votes with its own "whip" system. It also produces fact books for the public, such as ones on the defense budget and tax reform, and it has spearheaded the reform drive in the House for making committee chairmen more accountable (partly successful) and for implementing the public financing of congressional elections (not yet successful). Its 1978 membership of 245 is the highest the DSG has ever had.

Another ideological group is the Black Caucus. The seventeen black congresspeople who make up the caucus use the group, with its $260,000 annual budget, as an organizing center for congressional action on issues of importance to black Americans. By holding unofficial hearings, issuing press releases, and developing legislation, the group puts pressure on resistant and vulnerable points in Congress. Because it represents a national constituency, and because its members are usually from safe districts, the caucus can afford to be less reverent toward other congressmen. "There are many congressmen whose constituencies are 35 to 40 percent black who consistently vote against the interests of their black constituents," says Rep. William Clay of the caucus. "We are going to expose the records of those congressmen." Such direct affronts to other members' security are rare elsewhere.

A Little Bit of Pomp

Buckingham Palace would probably run without its guards; the United States Supreme Court would probably not suffer if it had no clerks to yell "Oyez, oyez, oyez . . . God save the United States of America and this honorable court." Congress, too, would survive, shabbier but no less efficient, if its quaint customs and rituals were streamlined away. But Congress would be poorer for the loss—as would forests without their beautiful hummingbirds or envelopes without colored stamps.

Congress has a Capitol architect, who has only rarely been an architect; it declares a national emergency after each summer vacation to comply with a moldy statute permitting autumn meetings only at time of crisis. The most obvious tradition in daily performance is the emphasis on parliamentary decorum. There are tales from prewar Germany of Jewish families who dined in controlled calm as storm troopers burst through the front door. Congress, too, gives that impression of order in the face of adversity. In 1932, a department store clerk leaned from the House galleries waving a gun and demanding a chance to speak. Panic broke out below, and representatives fled for cover. But as Rep. Thomas S. McMillan, then in the presiding officer's chair, decided that his life, too, was worth saving, House parliamentarian Lewis Deschler told him solemnly, "You can't leave. You're presiding." Deschler, who only recently retired as the parliamentarian, was proud of the resolve displayed several years later by Rep. Joe Martin. As four Puerto Rican nationalists began to rain shots down at representatives from the gallery, Martin managed to blurt, "The House stands recessed," before running for his life.

Beneath this crust of decorum, some customs have a more important effect on how well Congress gets its work done. One ritual is the quorum call, a parliamentary device of making sure there are enough members on the floor to conduct business. In practice, it is a stalling technique. When congressmen want to check the arrangements for an upcoming bill, look over the draft of a speech they're making, filibuster, or head off an upcoming vote, they say, "Mr. Chairman, I suggest the absence of a quorum." Then the whole machinery of government grinds to a halt, and buzzers ring throughout the Capitol buildings. Members drop what they are doing—holding committee hearings, listening to constituents—not because there's anything important on the floor, but because they want to have a good attendance record. Most members know precisely how long it takes from the ring of the first buzzer until their name is called, and they time their arrival so they can stride onto the floor, register their presence with an electronic device, and head back without breaking stride. "Two minutes after its conclusion," says writer Larry King, "one couldn't find a quorum with bloodhounds."

Congressmen also spend inordinate time naming days

after local groups. During 1968 and 1969, more than five hundred special days or weeks were proposed—including Service Station Operation Day, Date Week, Break-No-Law-Today Day, National Jewish Hospital Save Your Breath Month, and standard items like Mother's Day and Flag Day. Political maneuvering can be as sharp here as in weightier matters. When Wilbur Mills asked Lyndon Johnson's White House to proclaim National Duck Day on behalf of a duck-calling contest in Arkansas, LBJ proclaimed Migratory Waterfowl Day to emphasize protecting ducks, rather than shooting them.

Few of these charades would be possible or worthwhile without the help of the *Congressional Record*—which is, in its way, the greatest charade of them all. In purely technical terms, the *Record* is an impressive operation: each day, within thirteen hours of the close of debate, the congressional presses have turned out 49,000 copies of another thick edition of the *Record*. The cost is $16 million a year, with 800 workers toiling over 100 Linotype machines. As congressmen arrive for their morning's work, they find tall stacks of the *Record*, still glistening with printer's ink, waiting outside their door by 7:00 A.M.

But while the production of the *Record* may be impressive, its content often is not. The *Record* is a subsidiary xeroxing service for congressmen, producing by the thousands whatever item they choose, coming to rival the Sears, Roebuck catalog or the *People's Almanac* for arcana. The back section of the *Record*—often half or two-thirds of its bulk—is made of various insertions: articles from *Reader's Digest*, speeches boosting some favored constituent, clever items from the home-town paper which have caught the member's eye. One day, shrewd doctors and dentists will learn to stock their waiting rooms with copies of the *Record*, knowing that their anxious patients may relax with items like the following:

> *Rep. Thomas Ashley:* Mr. Speaker, it is with great pride that I take this opportunity to congratulate the Whitmer High School debate team of Toledo, Ohio, for winning its second consecutive national debate championship in the National Forensic League tournament held at Wake Forest University in Winston-Salem, N.C., from June 19 to June 22.

Even the parts of the *Record* which appear to be chronicles of the day's debate are far from accurate. Under a ritual known as Privilege to Revise and Extend, members are able to edit their remarks into coherence— or delete them—before they are committed to print. Without this review, said one congressman, the *Record* "would be really sad reading the next day—the best comic book you ever saw." Realizing that only the handful of people in the galleries know what they really said, members are content to make a garbled statement so long as they later make the *Record* precise. "After you fix your senator's mistakes," says one aide, "you may have to call the staff or the other senator and say, 'How about changing your guy to saying something else so my guy will make sense?' You're not supposed to change the contents of the *Record*, but we do." The benefit of revision can lead to sloppy habits. One congressman complained that something he had said in an interview with the Nader Congress Project was used (accurately) in his profile; "I'm used to amending my remarks," he lamented. But even worse, changes in content can mean changes in the law, since courts trying to determine "legislative intent" may turn to the congressional debate to see what Congress had in mind.,

Until 1978, congressmen could insert "speeches" into the record that were not delivered. The presiding officer would call on the missing representative, pause, and then say "The time of the gentleman has expired." Into the gap went the written speech, looking exactly as if it had been spoken. Then occurred a small concession to truth. Beginning late in the 95th Congress, a small dot, •, would appear at the beginning and end of material not actually spoken—though if only one sentence of a whole speech was uttered, no dots would appear.

However deceptive the *Record* may be, pornographic it is not. In October, 1921, the House censured Thomas Blanton, a Democratic representative from Texas, 293–0, for inserting profane language into the *Record*. He had included an angry letter from a government employee who wrote the following to someone who had fired him, according to the way the *Congressional Record* now reports the proceedings of October 22, 1921: "You are a G-d d-mn liar, you low-down son of a b----."

The *Record* cannot be accused of sensationalism either. When Puerto Rican Nationalists shot five representatives from the galleries on March 1, 1954, the *Record* for that day dryly notes that "at approximately 2 o'clock and 30 minutes P.M. a demonstration and the discharge of firearms from the southwest House Gallery (No. 11) interrupted the counting of the vote; the Speaker, pursuant to the inherent power lodged in the Presiding Officer in the case of grave emergency, after ascertaining that certain Members had been wounded and to facilitate their care, at 2 o'clock and 32 minutes P.M. declared the House in recess, subject to call of the Chair."

To put the appropriate close on these congressional customs, we should note the tradition of prayer. Strict rules govern the prayer which begins each morning's session: the House chaplain emphasizes the bipartisan tone of his calling by sitting first on the Democratic side, then with the Republicans, after his speech; he cannot favor any denomination over another; he can give no spiritual guidance on upcoming votes.

At times visiting ministers are permitted to deliver the prayer. The member who represents the minister's district invariably rises afterward to congratulate the guest speaker, which naturally pleases him and, the member hopes, his flock. One visiting prayer became a classic when the minister decided to incorporate parliamentary jargon into his talk:

> O Supreme Legislator . . . Make seniority in Your love ever germane to their conduct. Make them consistently vote yea in the cloakroom of conscience that at the expiration of life's term they may feel no need to revise and extend. . . .
>
> When the Congress of life is adjourned and they answer the final quorum call, may the eternal committee report out a clean bill on their lives.

Perquisites: Nice Work If You Can Get It

Congress has rarely had a problem recruiting members to fill its seats. But—as part of the sad irony that loads most benefits on jobs that would be satisfying anyway and gives least reward to tasks of dull drudgery—the side benefits (called "perquisites") of being a congressman have steadily risen. Some are small but meaningful: cheap, tax-free meals in House and Senate restaurants; two-dollar haircuts; free plants from the botanical garden; free photography service; free ice; thirty-three free trips home per year; free travel abroad if an official reason can be found. In 1973 the Associated Press calculated that the minimum cash value of these fringe benefits was $8,500 a year.

Other privileges are invisible on the record books, but can take the breath away when seen at first hand. Policemen spread their arms to part the traffic on nearby streets when congressmen pass. Special elevators marked "Senators Only" whisk their occupants away while the masses stand waiting for the unrestricted cars. Congressmen park their automobiles (with their prestigious license plates) at special, nearby garages. Clerks at Washington's National Airport delay planes for tardy congressmen and bump paying passengers to make way for senators. The phone company puts "Honorable" before their directory listing.

Then there is the pav—$57.500. not counting the value of perks—which is a sensitive issue for congressmen, who fear voter resentment over its scale. When Congress voted in 1816 to raise its salary to $1,500 per year, there was a voter backlash which defeated many members. The newly elected Congress promptly repealed the increase. A century and a half later, shortly before voting to approve its present salary, a member admitted, "My lips say No, No, but my heart says Yes! Yes!"

In 1977 Congress said yes to a jump from $44,600 to $57,500—or an *increase* which alone was twice the average annual income for a family of four at the poverty level. (In the Senate, 64 aides earn over $50,000 and 331 over $40,000.) In return, both chambers agreed to limit outside earned income to 15 percent of salary, or $8,625.*

---

*But in what Senator Gary Hart (D.-Colo.) called "a breach of contract with the American people," the Senate, but not the House, in 1979 delayed the $8,625 limit until 1983—first by a voice vote and then 55–44. (The honorarium limit then rose to a $25,000 maximum, which was contained in a campaign reform act.) Of 26 senators who earned about the $25,000 maximum, only one—Donald Riegle of Michigan—voted against the delay. The initial and sudden nonroll-call vote had been engineered by Senator Ted Stevens and Daniel Patrick Moynihan, who argued that senators had been hard hit by the cost of living and needed the money. So do we all.

This move was bitterly protested by members such as James Quillen (R.-Tenn.), who has several thriving real estate and insurance companies on the side, and Rep. Morgan Murphy (D.-Ill.), who earned more than $120,000 in legal fees *while he was in Congress*. But, among others, the *New York Times* couldn't sympathize with their plight. "There seems to us to be a clear distinction between the potential influence of regular returns from coupon-clipping and of receiving a fat check today from a group interested in a vote tomorrow."

For both the taxpayers and the congressmen, the most financially important congressional resource, of course, is the office and staff allowance. For a government that runs on paper, the congressman has ample free allowances at the government stationery store; there is an adequate budget for office equipment. Senators are allowed between $708,000 to $1.2 million, depending on the size of their states, to hire secretaries and professional staff; representatives get $353,516.

Beyond even the perquisites, salary, and expenses are the pensions. After thirty years service a member gets $42,560 a year. Indeed, thirty-three members of the 95th Congress receive yearly pensions of up to $12,000 due to former military service—from Senator John Glenn, who says he earned it and should keep it, to Rep. Charles Bennett, who returns his monthly VA check for $1,109 because "I'm drawing such a big income from the government that I don't want to be greedy."

For the first time ever, members made general net worth statements in early 1978. The Senate had at least nineteen millionaires, led by two freshmen Republicans worth $7–$17 million each, John Danforth of Missouri and John Heinz. The average senator had a net worth of $444,000, and the average chairman a net worth of over $1 million —which suggests that over time all the perquisites and salaries can add up.

Members and their staffs work out of official offices, which themselves become a next level of perquisites; or, as it is said, where a man stands depends on where he sits. Like so much else, allocation of office suites depends on seniority. In order to get a three-room suite in the new and spacious Rayburn Office Building, one has to be at least a five-term representative. (You can also get three rooms in the older Longworth Building, but "the third room may be down the hall or upstairs," said ex-House building superintendent A. E. Ridgell.) As suites open up, the most senior members get first pick. Former governors like Dale Bumpers and Mark Hatfield, accustomed to a state mansion, chauffeured car, and #1 license plate, have the most difficult time adjusting to their lowly freshman status.

Only the most senior can get a crack at one of the seventy-five secret hideaways within the Capitol Building itself. These provide quiet retreats from the bustle outside, and have been used for pastimes ranging from office dictation to parties to Sam Rayburn's "Board of Education." Lyndon Johnson, before moving to 1600 Pennsylvania Avenue, had seven of these rooms, together known as "LBJ Ranch East." To distribute the other rooms, Johnson "put together rooms like a subdivided building or tract," said a senator's aide. "When you wound up in one of those windowless basements where the walls sweated all day, you got a pretty good idea of where you stood with LBJ." More recently, the most splendid secret room belonged to the late Allen Ellender. It had two huge chandeliers, a built-in stove, and a freezer stocked with oysters and Louisiana shrimp. Today the fifty-five most senior senators have such second offices, though the allocation is kept secret by the Senate Rules and Administration Committee. "Everyone is scared because every Senator is on the take" from the Committee, says one Senate aide, "and desperately needs what he gets from the committee and does not want to rock the boat."

To house these offices, stately and lowly, and to give a final perquisite, Congress has sponsored a building boom inspired by the judgment and tasteful restraint of Albert Speer and Ramses II. As recently as 1900, congressmen had no formal "offices." If they couldn't do their work at their desk on the floor, they took it back to their boardinghouse room. As business expanded, and as the committee system added a new bureaucratic order to congressional operations, both houses decided in the early years of the century to outfit themselves with adequate offices. In 1903, the first House building was completed, and a year later the Senate moved into its office building, now called the Russell Building.

The need for working space was certainly acute, but there is reason to doubt that the enormous piles of marble on Capitol Hill are the appropriate remedy. The recent buildings include the Dirksen Building (1958), the extension of the east front of the Capitol (1960), and the Rayburn Office Building (1965).

The Senate is currently completing a third office building, estimated to cost $47.9 million in 1972 and $135 million by 1978. It ran into an unexpected snag, however, with Proposition 13 and a taxpayer backlash against wasteful government spending. And with a planned rooftop dining room, a third Senate gymnasium, 16-foot ceilings, tennis and basketball courts, and use of expensive marble and bronze, the ironically named Hart Building— Philip Hart was one of the least ostentatious of senators— seemed a symbol of wasteful big government. So six years, and $88 million later, a surprisingly stingy House voted (momentarily) against future appropriations for the building. Senator William Proxmire gave it one of his Golden Fleece awards and several representatives suggested it be converted into a parking garage. Despite the snags and teasing, this edifice is supposed to be completed in the early 1980s.

There is also the controversial plan to extend the west front of the Capitol by 88 feet—one of many campaigns overseen by Capitol "architect" George Stewart, who died in 1971. The current western façade is shaky and needs work; but, as the *New York Times* editorialized, "According to the Capitol architect, the only way to prop up the crumbling west front is with two restaurants, two cafeterias, two private dining rooms, conference, committee, and document rooms, offices, a barber shop, a visitors' center—at a cost of $45 million. . . . This is not exactly a bargain. It is, in fact, an outrage."

For precedent, critics of the west front plan need only glance across the Capitol lawns to the glistening edifice known as the Rayburn Office Building. As the construction costs rose from the early estimates of $40–$65 million to the eventual record-setting $122 million, so did the grandiose dreams of its designers. In a design that has been called "Mussolini Modern" and "Texas Penitentiary," its 720 feet of frontage and 450-foot depth contains

50 acres of office space, 25 elevators, 23 escalators, garage space for 1,600 cars, a swimming pool, a gymnasium, and several overnight rooms. In sum, in the words of architectural critic Ada Louise Huxtable, it is "a national disaster. Its defects range from profligate mishandling of 50 acres of space to elephantine esthetic brutality at record costs. . . . It is quite possible that this is the worst building for the most money in the history of the construction art. It stuns by sheer mass and boring bulk."

But it makes congressmen feel important, the way pyramids made pharaohs feel godlike. When the buildings and the offices and the staffs combine with the less ostensible emoluments of citizen deference to the member's station, what one observer has called the "elevator phenomenon" sets in. A new congressman may arrive with humility intact, but when he gets instant elevator service while others are kept waiting, he begins to realize that he is, well, different. For the perquisites and their general status can create a gigantic congressional ego, a state of self-reflection which has a serious influence on how the members relate among themselves and to outsiders. "On the hustings they are all good Joes," said a Senate staffer, "but when they are here [in Washington] a good many of them try to play God." Rep. Otis Pike (R.-N.Y.), upon announcing his retirement in 1978, said that "Congressmen are treated, in Washington at least, like little tin Jesuses. Seven employees are there to fetch me a cup of coffee, get me a hamburger, look things up, take dictation, pamper me, flatter me . . . and generally ease my way through life."

Love and Marriage

In an oft-quoted observation, Mrs. Oliver Wendell Holmes once told Teddy Roosevelt that Washington is "a place full of famous men and the women they married when they were young." One result, especially recently, has been the breakups of politicians' marriages. Nearly all congressmen arrive married; the 94th Congress included only fourteen bachelors. But the tensions of political life apply strains that some marriages cannot endure. Mrs. William Proxmire, who separated from her husband recently and then rejoined him, bemoaned the difficulties of "living in a fishbowl and the long separations." "Everyone else has first claim on the senator," says Mrs. George Aiken (who should know, since she was Aiken's staff aide for years). Consequently, marriage and family life often take a second seat to the fulfillment of the spouse's political career. When Mrs. Albert Quie called her husband to say that her baby was about to arrive, Rep. Quie replied, "Well, I've got to make a speech against Secretary Freeman first." He did, and was still in time to get to the hospital.

Another burden on marriages is the sexual temptations public officeholders face. Using power as a love potion, mixing with the glamorous, some congressmen put aside marital loyalties as carelessly as they shed other duties. There is not much discussion of this in print, since it is unfair to single out a congressman or congressmen as a group for something not unique to Washington. But at the same time it would be naïve to assume that only fidelity flourishes on Capitol Hill.

There can be the old-fashioned, direct proposition. *Washington Post* reporter Sally Quinn describes how "one senator offered me a ride home from a party and it was raining and so I accepted. On the way he mentioned his wife was out of town, and put his hand on my head, then on my neck, and pulled me close. I pulled away from him. 'I thought you were offering me a ride home,' I said. He looked at me and said, 'What do you think I'm running, a taxi service?' "

Or there can be something seamier. Rep. Thomas Steed, annoyed with the Senate's stance against free junk-mailing privileges for House members, threatened a sexual exposé unless the Senate changed its mind. After Senator Everett Dirksen ridiculed Steed as "the white charger from Oklahoma," Steed retaliated with his "exposé": "I personally know of a senator who keeps two call girls on his payroll." Steed eventually apologized for making the charges, but did not retract them.

How accurate or frequent are incidents such as those reported by Steed? Arthur Marshall, state's attorney for a county near Washington, D.C., has said there have not been many prosecutions for prostitution in his area since they arrested a call girl "who had a substantial index file containing the names of many important men, including members of Congress." Agreeing with this view was veteran reporter Eileen Shanahan, who described on CBS's *60 Minutes* "the situation—which I believe to exist— where lobbyists procure call girls for members of Congress and their staffs."

Wives react differently to all the marital strains. The largest number simply "fulfill" themselves through their famous husbands. Others contribute directly to their husbands' work: Eleanor McGovern and the late Marvella Bayh have been political confidants as well as spouses. A few wives chart their own lives: Jane Hart, wife of the late Philip Hart, had been a peace activist, with several proud arrests on her record. Senator Bill Bradley's wife, Ernestine Schlant, was and is a teacher and author.

But some marriages cannot withstand the tension of wives tending the households, alone, while their husbands politick. In the last few years, William Proxmire and Pete McCloskey have separated from their wives; Robert Dole and Donald Riegle have gotten divorced. Edward Brooke and Herman Talmadge have gone through anguishing divorce proceedings that splashed embarrassing financial secrets onto front pages everywhere. Indeed, formal divorces —as opposed to dead but unburied marriages, of which there are many—have become more frequent in recent years, as national taboos have relaxed and as politicians like Nelson Rockefeller showed that a broken marriage need not end a political career.

Relatively few congressmen seem to have considered one other alternative: sacrificing their political hopes. When Rep. Gary Myers announced he would not seek reelection in 1978, choosing instead to return to his old job as foreman in a Butler, Pennsylvania, steel plant, he offered this explanation: "The amount of time it takes to do this job is just not compatible with how much time I want to spend with my family . . . I just wanted to know my kids before it was too late."

At Play

Mike Mansfield would relax in his garden, Rep. James Symington thought karate "a great conditioner," and 71-year-old Senator Strom Thurmond jogs, lifts weights, and performs calisthenics. All is not intrigue in cloakrooms or debate over issues of national moment. Congressmen, too, know how to relax.

Even before Richard Nixon became *de facto* coach for the Washington Redskins, sports were popular on Capitol Hill. Senators Javits and Percy are adept tennis players, rising at daybreak to get in a few swings before starting work. Senator Alan Cranston, 60, is a serious sprinter, the former holder of the world record for 55-year-olds in the 100-yard dash (12.6 seconds). An admitted "track nut," Cranston wakes up at 6:00 most mornings to work out. And nearly every year since 1961, Republican and Democratic House members have squared off in the congressional baseball game. Speaker Joe Cannon had banned the games near the turn of the century because he considered them beneath the dignity of the House. Speaker Sam Rayburn at one time banned them as too dangerous. But they endure because the members simply enjoy them too much. (When the Republicans won 4–3 in 1978 for their thirteenth win in seventeen outings, Rep. Mendel Davis [D.-S.C.] had enough. "I tell you, they're always pulling something shady," he said with a smile. "No wonder Nixon got kicked out of office.")

Many members of the House work out in the Rayburn pool and gym, two places forbidden to visitors. Members of Congress regularly swim in the 20-by-60-foot pool. Perhaps the most popular Capitol Hill sport is paddleball, a cross between squash and tennis. It is rumored that some members will ask for quorum calls so they can sneak down to get a choice court when the paddleball players scatter for the floor. Rep. Guy Vander Jagt was a recent president of the paddleball players and winner of the annual Bullshot of the Year award. While nominally awarded to the congressman who cheats and argues most during a game, it is actually a reflection of peer esteem. (The only responsibility it carries is to preside over the gym's annual dinner, which invariably ends with congressmen dipping their napkins into water pitchers and hurling wetballs at each other in athletic romp.)

A different "sport" practiced by some congressmen is drinking. Given that there are 10 million alcoholics in America, and many millions more who drink heavily, it is understandable in as pressured and fast-paced a world as Washington that not all congressmen are teetotalers. The extent of real alcoholism on Capitol Hill is hard to measure, though Washington correspondent Martin Arnold has written that "there's hardly a reporter in Washington who could not reel off a long list of alcoholic and philandering Representatives [and] Senators . . ." But in a custom of ancient origin, what is known is little discussed— at least not until recent years. Recently, however, Wilbur Mills and Senators Long, Williams, and Talmadge have all acknowledged they were, though no longer are, alcoholics.

There is a rule that liquor cannot be brought onto the floor of either chamber. This was reportedly established in March, 1865, after Vice President Andrew Johnson reeled into the Senate to take his oath of office and triggered a scandal. Nevertheless, many members' offices contain well-stocked liquor cabinets which swing open at the end of a long day. "There has never been one night session of the Senate in all my experience," complained the late Wayne Morse of this practice, "that hasn't witnessed at least one Senator making a fool of himself and disgracing the Senate." As for the impact of all this imbibing, Rep. Richard Bolling revealed in an interview that, as part of the strategy for passing the 1961 plan to expand the House Rules Committee, it was necessary to get one key representative drunk before the voting.

A more open way that congressmen play is to party. Washington has come a long way since a French envoy said upon his arrival there in 1803, "My God! What have I done to be condemned to reside in this city?" If anything, there is a surfeit of partying. There are some hundred embassies which each throw two parties a year. Lobbying groups almost nightly throw lavish get-togethers for interested members in House and Senate meeting rooms. There are many hundreds of national associations, 50 state delegations, and of course 535 senators and representatives, many of whom also throw bashes.

Night life does, at least, enable you to know colleagues and their spouses in a way the House and Senate do not facilitate. When Birch and Marvella Bayh first came to Washington from the Midwest in the early 1960s, they were invited to a typical party. "I wondered how I'd fit

in," Mrs. Bayh admitted. "But everybody was so nice and
so helpful and I realized that almost everybody in Washington had the same experience. . . . I remember one night
sitting next to Senator Estes Kefauver of Tennessee and
he turned and asked me if he could finish my dinner if I
wasn't going to eat it and I thought then how these are just
people like us."

7

Work Congressmen Do

*My father served in Congress from 1909 to 1919
from the state of Texas. . . . A representative got
about fifteen letters a week. Only at rare intervals
would a constituent come to see him. He had no
pressure groups to contend with. Because Congress enacted only a few bills each session, legislation got the deliberative attention it deserved.
. . . A good debater had no trouble getting a
large audience in the chamber. Most of the
member's time was spent on legislation. There
was little else for him to do.*

—Rep. Martin Dies, 1954

As the new congressman heads off in glory to Washington, he knows that power, duty, and a role in the nation's future lie ahead. But he may be puzzled by the same
question that John Kennedy asked himself as he settled
behind the Oval Office desk after his inauguration: Just
what am I supposed to *do* all day?

In the early years of the Republic, the answer would
have been "Not much." A member of the First Congress,
Senator William Maclay, recorded the events of April 3,
1790, in his diary: "We went to the Hall. The Minutes
were read. A message was received from the President of
the United States. A report was handed to the chair. We
looked and laughed at each other today for half an hour,
then adjourned."

Today it's a different story. Joseph L. Fisher, elected
in November, 1974, said he had perhaps "a day off" before being swamped with "about a hundred letters a day"
from lobbyists, special interest groups, and local clubs

234

and well-wishers. After a congressman has been in office a few weeks, the pace picks up. Starting early and sometimes working into the night, a member of Congress goes to committee meetings and listens to hearings; answers mail and woos constituents; fields phone calls and courts government agencies; gives speeches and prepares legislation; seeks out campaign monies and rushes to roll calls; returns to the district and speaks wherever two or more are gathered. "I'm absolutely swamped with work," Clark MacGregor said during his days in Congress. "After the long day, I must do an additional two to four hours of research at home." Across the range of ideologies, from conservatives like Robert Bauman (R.-Md.) to liberals like Elizabeth Holtzman (D.-N.Y.), fourteen-hour days are common. Congress used to convene on March 4 and adjourn by July 4. Now it convenes the first week in January and doesn't go home until sometime in the late fall, if not December.

Although most congressmen work long and hard, it is still impossible for them to accomplish more than a small fraction of what is expected of them. Which is why every member has a staff. As used in Washington, "the staff" refers to one of the great cryptic institutions of government, the secretaries, administrative assistants, and legislative aides who make up a congressman's alter ego. Ranging in number from 10 to 18 per member (depending on whether one is a representative or a senator, from a small or large state), staff assistants can be as important as the members they work for. As Nicholas I once lamented, "Not I, but ten thousand clerks rule Russia."

The staff person's duties are identical to the textbook listing of a congressman's duties. In each stage of the legislative process—from opening the mail to drafting a bill—the staff does most of the legwork. This is a curious institution—in which talented people pour their efforts anonymously into another person's performance and prestige. But it has also become a necessary one as Congress's workload has grown. Someone must answer the four thousand letters Senator Jacob Javits receives each week. And someone must assist Javits, since he serves on four committees and twelve subcommittees and since he may be scheduled for half a dozen hearings in any one morning. Because the number of senators has not expanded to keep pace with the Senate's volume of business ("Our most precious commodity," a staff man has generously said, "is senators"), Javits could not hope to keep up with the work without the help of his staff, which numbers about fifty in Washington. (During one week in 1977, Congress's 54 committees and 269 subcommittees held 249 hearings. A House study that year showed that 38 percent of the time, members are supposed to be in two committee hearings at the same time.)

Less grandly, congressional assistants must gauge what to feed their employer, and when. Too much information is as bad as too little. One aide to the late senator Philip Hart said, "You can walk down the hall with Hart or [the late] Senator Hubert Humphrey and say, 'These are the six things you have to remember—tick, tick, tick, tick, tick, tick.' And they'll remember every detail. But it wouldn't have done a damn bit of good to give them information a week ahead." And they must do what their boss would rather avoid. "You need them for protection," said former senator Eugene McCarthy, "to go to lunch for you."

The ideal staff must be like the ideal hairpiece: effective but unobtrusive. One person runs their show, and at no time should they entertain loyalties to anyone besides "the senator" or "the representative." What lures them to perform this uncelebrated work? Partly it is money; a good senior administrative assistant can earn $47,500 after a few years in Washington. A prominent staff position can provide a platform for a try at elective office itself. Some staff become representatives (like Washington's Norman Dicks) or even senators (like Kansas's Nancy Landon Kassebaum); in all, thirty-eight current members were once staff.

But for most, the goal is not in public prominence. "To be a politician you have to go out and shake a lot of hands," says Ken McLean, staff director of Senate Banking, Housing, and Urban Affairs. "It's a lot more fun to be a staffer." There is the sense of power that comes from intimacy with the mighty—the chance to put one's hand, however lightly, on the nation's legislative tiller. Although the senator's name is attached to a speech or bill, the staff man who wrote it can always think of it as his. But whatever the benefit to the staff assistant, the benefit to the representative or senator is obvious. "A good administrative assistant can make or break his boss," said one staff person. "If he's good he can make an ordinary guy look great. In all the years I worked there, the only times I ever heard of a congressman or senator getting into real trouble came from one or two reasons. His administrative assistant let him down, or there was hanky-panky in his office." Staff overreaching is not unknown. In one blatant example, an aide to a Senate appropriations subcommittee published in a committee hearing volume an entire dialogue between witnesses and senators—for a hearing that never took place. He made up plausible dialogue to show how busy the subcommittee was . . . and was fired.

With such obvious influence, there is the danger, said an aide, that "you begin to think you're brighter than your boss. Some people start acting as if they're really the senator or congressman." There are inevitable references to "surrogate senators," and Senator Robert Morgan (D.-N.C.) matter-of-factly acknowledges that "they give us advice on how to vote and then we vote on their recommendations." All important congressional staff assistants carefully and ritualistically minimize their prominence, crediting all to their legislative employers; so Richard J. Sullivan, 58-year-old veteran chief counsel of the House Public Works Committee, dismisses as "nonsense" suggestions that he really runs that committee, saying that "the job of the staff is to be in the background and carry out what the committee decides." But as Rep. Norman Dicks, who was a staff aide for eight years to Senator Warren Magnuson, says in jest, "People asked me how I felt being elected to Congress, and I told them I never thought I'd give up that much power voluntarily."

Names like Richard Wegman, Peter Murphy, Ari Weiss, and Richard Perle are not publicly known—except by those aware of how Congress really operates. Wegman is the chief counsel of Chairman Ribicoff's Senate Governmental Affairs Committee. Since this committee has the habit of voting not on amendments but general propositions, Wegman and his staff go off and write statutory language in effect *after* the legislation has been approved. Peter Murphy, with a House Appropriations subcommittee involved with military spending, was largely responsible for deleting millions in funding for the development of the E3A airborne warning system. His work demonstrates how staff can have immense subvisible power on seemingly small parts of larger issues, here a $120 billion military budget.

Ari Weiss, who is and barely looks his 25 years, is Speaker O'Neill's eyes and ears around the House. Due to his mentor, he is often courted like some senior chairman, and he is reported to be the author of the idea to have an ad hoc energy committee in 1977. Richard Perle, 36, is a leader of the anti-SALT group in the Senate. Formally he is simply on the professional staff of one senator, but his power lies in (1) his father-son relationship to Senator Henry Jackson and (2) his technical knowledge in a field few senators understand. Some think Perle too influential. Senator John Culver and some other senators blamed Perle and his staff for "a torrent of leaks" about vital national security information prior to the SALT debate.

Even with such superstaff, as well as the others—there were less than 2,000 staff in 1955, and 6,900 by 1979— there are perennial complaints that staff support is inadequate. Former senator Walter Mondale, for example, complained that a 1973 hearing was a case of "myself and one college kid versus the U.S. Navy and everybody who wanted to build a carrier. . . . We foolishly handicap ourselves by failing to properly staff ourselves." This problem has been exacerbating over time. There were only four fewer members fifty years ago, but the population was only half as large and the problems of society far less complex. Workload has recently been increasing: in just the area of legislation, while there were 7,845 measures introduced in the 78th Congress (1943–45), the current 96th Congress will probably process 30,000 proposed bills. Consequently, congressmen and their staffs must carefully choose where to invest their time and energy.

Servicing Constituents

Greenhorn congressmen may imagine that they will spend all day innovating great ideas into laws, which is hardly the way it works. "I thought I was going to be Daniel Webster," said one disillusioned representative, "and I found that most of my work consisted of personalized work for constituents." A 1965 study by John Saloma

III found that fully 41 percent of all staff time and 28 percent of a member's time was devoted to servicing constituents. This included handling correspondence, receiving visitors, answering requests for information, and doing casework.

The reason congressmen invest such effort in constituent services is evident; said one, "My experience is that people don't care how I vote on foreign aid, federal aid to education, and all those big issues, but they are very much interested in whether I answer their letters." The politics of personal favors is not new. King Solomon regularly assisted his subjects with their personal problems—as the story of the two women who quarreled over an infant shows—in a manner not unlike the way congressmen help their constituents understand Social Security laws or veterans' benefits.

"During the last year and a half," said one senator, "I have done favors for about three thousand persons. When you consider the word-of-mouth spread, this amounts to a substantial number of constituents." One representative, of whom B. F. Skinner would be proud, was even more specific. "A survey indicated I had three thousand farmers in my district who had to go over half a mile for mail, so I started a campaign [for mailbox extensions]. By the last election I had gotten thirteen hundred extensions. They think of me every time they go get that mail."

Answering mail is the mainstay of constituent services. Mail is delivered five times a day on Capitol Hill, and representatives and senators get from 5,000 to 500,000 letters a year. Offices are at times swamped by waves of letters. The replies that go out are usually form letters which state the member's views on something and thank the writers for their opinions—a genre which, if done well enough, can make most people believe their member has penned a personal response himself. Some of the requests are for information—a Department of Agriculture booklet entitled "How to Fix Potatoes in Popular Ways," a civil service form from the Justice Department for employment —which congressmen readily forward to the relevant agency. Most agencies try to answer congressmen promptly. The day he was confirmed, former OEO chief Philip Sanchez wrote all his staff that "response to congressional mail takes precedence over every other item of agency business." In 1970, the Pentagon got 200,000 congressional letters, and HEW received 85,000.

In addition, there are the eccentric requests by those who consider their congressman a glorified valet, and there are the crank letters. One woman requested help with replacing her broken china; another asked a representative in the early 1970s to get President Nixon to purchase a wooden spoon for her while he was in Europe; someone wanted a gold brick from Fort Knox; and one citizen asked that travel arrangements be made for his trip abroad with his wife. The crank letters aim more to irritate than inquire. In a classic response to one of this genre, Rep. John Steven McGroarity of California wrote in 1934, "One of the countless drawbacks of being in Congress is that I am compelled to receive impertinent letters from a jackass like you in which you say I promised to have the Sierra Madre mountains reforested and I have been in Congress two months and haven't done it. Will you please take two running jumps and go to hell." Former senator Stephen Young was long envied by his more cautious colleagues for his biting ripostes to crackpot critics. When one correspondent requested that his horse be transported at public expense since the First Lady's horse had been, the irascible Young replied, "Dear Sir: Am wondering why you need a horse when there is already one jackass at your address."

While there are often complaints about the level of incoming mail, many members seem eager to increase outgoing mail. Most offices have staff who pore over local newspapers for notices of weddings, births, deaths, or for Girl-Scout-of-the-Month, Million-in-Sales winners, or college queen contestants. A note of congratulations is immediately shipped out.* Even though the congressman himself may never participate in this process, it shows that he cares. It seeks good will in the short run and some votes in the long run. But it can occasionally backfire. One man in east Texas who shotgunned his wife to death and said he was glad he did it received a condolence card while

---

*Senator Robert Byrd goes even further. He keeps a file of 2,500 cards of key people in his small state of West Virginia. Periodically, Byrd will personally call them up to find out how they are, how the kids are doing, what's on their mind.

in prison from then representative John Dowdy. Due in part to such frivolous enterprises, the volume of franked mail sent by members of Congress has increased from 24 million pieces in 1938 to 65 million in 1958, 178 million pieces in 1968, and *321* million pieces in 1974. (By 1978, the Congress and Post Office had lost count.)

A more serious form of outgoing mail is the congressional newsletter. Ninety percent of the members send them, usually averaging four a year. They tell constituents about important current events, tell them what their congressman is doing, and tell them what a terrific guy he is. Though often merely a form of vanity press, they also include Rep. Henry Waxman's useful tips on how to make the health bureaucracy work for you and Rep. Morris Udall's literate and informative monthly newsletters (his staff swears he writes them himself). Some congressmen include questionnaires in their newsletters. These are supposed to take the pulse of local views while flattering the voter by showing that someone is interested in him. Rep. Charles Vanik, for one, refuses to use them because he considers them statistically invalid. But others don't want to miss out on a good thing. "Polling your people with questionnaires is a greater gimmick than mailing out free flower seed," said one.

Mail is only one component of servicing constituents. Voters often visit Washington and "drop in on their congressmen." It has become a growing burden for many, as noted by an assistant to former senator Eugene McCarthy. "In 1948, we got letters. In 1954, we started getting wires. By 1959, it was telephone calls. And around 1964, people started showing up. Now you get here in the morning and you find people waiting." To avoid wasting work time, some members enter their office through special doors to avoid person-to-person encounters. But others see it as an important part of their job, even giving visitors a tour of the Capitol, complete with a picture taken on the spot.

Personal casework is probably the most demanding component of constituent-induced work. "Casework takes a lot of time," said one representative. "When you go home you cannot go to church in safety. Every time I go, there are thirty or forty people hiding behind automobiles just waiting to bump into me, always quite by accident. Each thinks his individual problem is the most important in the world." In his study of the Senate, Donald R. Matthews observed that senators received pleas from "mental cases, unwed mothers, sufferers from venereal diseases—all kinds of lost and bewildered people who do not know where else to turn." Most of the actual casework involves claims against federal or state agencies which have been ignored or delayed.

Many congressmen and staffs view their role as red-tape cutters as a critical one—to the extent that they hold office hours in their districts to hear such cases. Rep. Charles A. Vanik has two offices in his Ohio district. According to Vanik, they get 125 calls a day. Charles Wolff, a special assistant in Senator Adlai Stevenson III's fourteen-person casework office in Chicago, spends more than 60 hours a week, for example, obtaining instant passports for confused travelers and securing immigration papers for families trying to reunite. Such staff function as local social workers, and often refuse promotion to legislative and political work in Washington, D.C.

Congressmen like to return to their districts just to let the people know they care. Members are allowed up to 33 free trips a year, but some must go far more frequently. As incentive, they recall the case of Senator Robert La Follette, Jr., who stayed in Washington in 1946 to manage the La Follette-Monroney Legislative Reorganization Act in Congress instead of going to campaign in his Wisconsin primary. Result: the La Follette-Monroney Act passed, but La Follette was defeated by Joseph R. McCarthy.

While most representatives and senators realize the political dividends of constituent services, and act accordingly, most also dislike its menial tasks. "I came here to write laws and what do I do?" protested a congressman in Jim Wright's book *You and Your Congressman*. "I send out baby books to young mothers, listen to every maladjusted kid who wants out of the service . . . and give tours of the Capitol to visitors who are just as worn out as I am." When Representatives Otis Pike and Michael Harrington announced their retirements in 1978, they cited, respectively, "wasting time on drivel" and the "errand boy" function of members. When Rep. Robert Leggett (D.-Calif.) also hung up his spikes that year, he too complained that congressmen engage in "busywork where you're very busy working fourteen or fifteen hours a day handling a stack of mail that came in yesterday. . . . You're kind of a godfather to literally hundreds of thousands of people."

There is some worry about the ethical questions raised. What if a local union, a local bank, and a local radio station all financially support a congressman's campaign, and then (1) the union wants pressure applied to the Tariff Commission for higher tariffs, (2) the bank wants a friendly word passed on to the comptroller about its pending merger, and (3) the station wants help at the FCC to enable it to stay on the air more hours? None of these are legislative matters; all are purely administrative problems. There is clearly the risk of preferential treatment if a congressman pressures a downtown agency or even if he inquires about the status of a matter. Of such constituent favors, former senator Joseph Clark noted, "There is a certain amount of wear and tear on the conscience involved in all of them."

The frequency of constituent complaints suggests that citizens should be protected against the pettiness and inefficiency of the federal bureaucracy. But is Congress—with its 535 separate agents, all concerned about individual cases—the best candidate for the job? Such servicing takes away from the legislative process, which is what the Constitutional Convention really had in mind when it formulated Congress in 1787. Congress neglects key legislation and conducts inadequate oversight over independent agencies, as chapter 4 argued, in large part because so many resources are devoted to ministerial tasks for constituents.

This informal, case-by-case pleading by so many members can also hamper efficient administration in the agencies. Two congressmen have proposed different approaches. House Banking and Currency Chairman Henry Reuss suggests the ombudsman, based on a system begun 165 years ago in Sweden. Teams of people trained in draining the administrative swamps would process the casework now bogging down Capitol Hill. Rep. Les Aspin would create an ombudsman for each local district. Trained by a federal center in Washington, the ombudsmen would have similar skills and parallel solutions to problems. Reuss and Aspin's ombudsmen could also call on the back-up authority of congressional committees or members, if necessary, as a way of persuading obstructionist bureaucrats that their requests are to be treated seriously. Still, neither proposal has received a serious hearing. For no matter how much they may complain or hide in their offices to avoid visitors, congressmen are unwilling to sacrifice their brand of Personal Service Democracy. As Rep. Richard Bolling wrote in his book *Power in the House,* "Constituent service can help a member be reelected, and that is the main reason it will not be handed to someone else."

Morris Fiorina, a political scientist, appreciated the irony, if not hypocrisy, of congressional casework in his 1977 book *Congress: Keystone of the Washington Establishment:*

> Congressmen earn electoral credits by establishing various Federal programs. The legislation is drafted in very general terms, so some agency must translate a vague policy mandate into a functioning program, a process that necessitates the general promulgation of rules and regulations and, incidentally, the trampling of numerous toes. At the next stage hopeful constituents petition their congressmen to intervene in the complex process of the bureaucracy. The cycle closes when the congressman lends a sympathetic ear, piously denounces the evils of bureaucracy . . . and rides a grateful electorate to ever more impressive electoral showings. Congressmen take the credit coming and going.

Debating and Investigating

Of the five senators the Senate has selected as its most esteemed—Webster, Clay, Calhoun, La Follette, and Taft —the first three were famed as orators. Schoolboys remember from their history books the Webster-Hayne debates, the 1830 struggle over states' rights versus constitutional sovereignty, which ended with Webster's injunction of "Liberty *and* Union, now and forever, one and inseparable!" Upon hearing Webster speak, a listener said, "I was never so excited by public speaking before in my life. Three or four times I thought my temple would burst with the rush of blood. . . . I was beside myself and I am still so."

Like home canning and minor-league baseball, such
debate has been a casualty of modern times. Congressmen
spend large chunks of time on the floor (26 percent of the
average congressman's working time) and talk a lot there,
but the amount of high-class debate is small. "The Senate
—the so-called greatest deliberative body in the world—
hasn't had even a third-class debate in years," said William
Proxmire in the mid-seventies, "and even if we had it no
one would be on the floor to hear it, except the two or
three senators doing the talking."

Not until March, 1970, did the House get around to
first debating a proposal to end the Vietnam War—the
Nedzi-Whalen amendment. Even then, most speakers were
allowed only one minute to make their points. In another
"debate" over the war, Richard Bolling—who has written
books about Congress's responsibility to asserts its prerogatives—refused to yield the floor to Rep. Robert Drinan because, as he later told Drinan, he was afraid Drinan would
ask him questions he couldn't answer. Instead of debate,
the bulk of congressional proceedings consists of small
inserts for the folks back home—items which only those
from the district could not consider trivial.

Incisive debate is so rare that the late senator Carter
Glass of Virginia, after spending more than thirty years in
both houses of Congress, said that he had never seen a single mind changed by congressional debate. Senator Patrick
Leahy (D.-Vt.) told how the great Panama Canal debate
"resembles the plot line of a television soap opera. You
could listen to the debate for several days, leave for a
week or two, and come back to it having missed very little. All the arguments are being forwarded again and
again." The problem is not merely one of repetition or
boredom, but of content as well. It is not surprising that
members are not eager to engage in floor colloquy with
someone like the hyperbolic Orrin Hatch (R.-Ut.), who
said that the Panama Canal treaty "is the culmination of
that pattern of surrender and appeasement that has cost us
so much all over the world. . . . Is America really going
the way of Rome?"

Not surprisingly, few congressmen take floor activity
seriously. "There is a theory around here . . . that to attend a debate on the floor is a waste of time," observed
Bella Abzug. "If you're seen hanging around the floor

listening to others, you're considered over-earnest. . . . To stay on the floor is to be unsuave and unsophisticated." One reason for this view is appallingly apparent to anyone watching a chamber in session for the first time. Writer Larry King, who spent ten years as a congressman's assistant, described the scene in the House: "Members lounge while signing mail, reading newspapers, or eyeing the visitors' galleries for familiar faces or pretty ones. Some sit with their knees propped against seats in front of them chatting or laughing; others lean on the rail at the rear of the chamber to smoke or swap jokes. Congressmen wander in and out aimlessly."

There are occasional breaks in this tranquil front. In 1954, the late William H. "Wild Bill" Langer, a frontier-type representative from North Dakota, broke the top of his desk by pounding on it during a debate on the Eisenhower farm program. In an unusually blunt 1968 speech, Senator George McGovern rebuked his colleagues:

> Every senator in this chamber is partly responsible for sending 50,000 young Americans to an early grave. *This chamber reeks of blood.* Every senator here is partly responsible for that human wreckage at Walter Reed and Bethesda Naval and all across our land— young boys without legs, or arms, or genitals, or faces, or hopes. . . . Don't talk to them about bugging out, or national honor, or courage. It doesn't take any courage at all for a congressman, or senator, or a president to wrap himself in the flag and say we're staying in Vietnam. Because it isn't our blood that is being shed (emphasis added).

But mostly it is considered bad form to get too strident or argumentative. The demise of debate is most obvious as House floor activity drones on toward dinner. If a bill is pending, impatient members begin to chant "Vote, vote," and woe to the representative who then delays the proceedings.

The other faded glory of Congress is the congressional investigation. In earlier days, this was a sure route to headlines and reputation. The 1913 Pujo Commission investigated the concentration of wealth on the "money trust." The Nye Commission, probing the munitions industry in 1936, popularized the phrase "merchants of death," and Gerald Nye was talked up as a potential Republican nominee for president or vice president. Harry Truman won national prominence as chairman of the World War II Committee to Investigate the National Defense Program. Senator Estes Kefauver became a presidential contender (and vice-presidential nominee) after widely viewed televised hearings into organized crime. Throughout the fifties, other committees investigated topics from the Communist Menace (the Hiss-Chambers and Army-McCarthy hearings) to corruption in business, labor unions, and government (rigged TV shows, disk jockey payola, teamster illegalities, and Bernard Goldfine's vicuña coat).

Some of those investigations may have contributed to the current decline. After watching Joe McCarthy and the House Un-American Activities Committee smear reputations, both Congress and the public appreciated the danger of hearings held for their own spectacle, and not for any legislative purpose. The few senators who have made names in recent investigations have run them less as witch-hunts than as seminars—for example, Philip Hart's Antitrust subcommittee hearings on economic concentration; former senator Fulbright's Foreign Relations Committee hearings on the war: or Senator Edward Kennedy's hearings on the Food and Drug Administration.

On the other hand, the Senate Watergate hearings of 1973 and the Senate and House hearings on the CIA and FBI are spectacular exceptions to the recent lapse of congressional inquiries. Indeed, there is always the possibility they could herald a revival of this declining form.

Legislating and Voting

Debating and investigating lay the foundation for the work most people associate with a member of congress —legislating and voting. Legislation occurs largely within the framework of the committee system. Although this was discussed in chapter 3, it is important to stress again how small a role legislating plays in the life of an average congressman. Representatives farm out their serious legislative research to the Library of Congress; their serious bill drafting to the Office of Legislative Counsel, to the executive branch, or even to private lobbyists; and their serious thinking to committee chairmen and staff. For there is always the problem of the pressure of time. Given all they are expected to do, it is no wonder that their eyes dart around, their fingers drum, and their attention spans go perhaps one minute. As a Louis Harris poll on the allocation of a representative's time concludes, "Rarely do Members have sufficient blocks of time when they are free from the frantic pace of the Washington 'treadmill' to think about the implications of various public policies."

Even for those who try extra hard, there are barriers. It is almost impossible for a representative or senator to have his or her piece of legislation considered unless he sits on the committee that would handle it. "Sometimes you get the idea that everything is managed at the top and that the decisions are none of your business," complained one member. "If I still felt I could change things by myself I would stay. But nobody can," said Senator James Abourezk on retiring in 1978. "Nobody ever lets you get through here with a total victory. . . . All one person can do is harass the establishment and try to prevent the total rape of the consumer and the citizen."

For those outside the ruling circles, getting important bills passed is rare. One member told author Charles Clapp that "people shouldn't have any great expectations that their congressman will be the author of important legislation, especially early in his career. In my six years here I have had two bills passed, both when I was a freshman and my party was in control. One set up an advisory committee on education in HEW—they never bothered to implement it after we got the bill through—and the other provided free dental care to Spanish American War veterans, a bill which I don't suppose my constituents sent me here to push." Some unfortunate congressmen have even worse prospects. When Rep. Abner Mikva proposed a bill to outlaw the manufacture of pistols, it got nowhere. But, says Mikva, "colleagues thanked me for introducing it—so they could denounce it."

The final claim on a congressman's time is voting— the expression of the congressman's will and, theoretically, that of his constituents. With hundreds of bills to vote on, how does the member of Congress make his choice?

A standard reply is that he or she is merely a delegate of his constituents and should mirror their views. As Abraham Lincoln put it during his campaign for the Illinois legislature in 1836, "While acting as a representative, I shall be governed by [my constituents'] will on all subjects." This sounds nice in theory, but how does one know what his constituents want? There are general indicators, like election results, polls, the mail.* But as Senator John Kennedy admitted in his 1956 book *Profiles in Courage,* "In Washington I frequently find myself believing that forty or fifty letters, six visits from professional politicians and lobbyists, and three editorials in Massachusetts newspapers constitute public opinion on a given issue. Yet in truth I rarely know how the great majority of the voters feel, or even how much they know of the issues that seem so burning in Washington."

Such doubts led then senator Kennedy to propound the trustee theory, that a member of Congress is a free agent who should follow his own convictions. Kennedy argued that "the voters selected us, in short, because they had confidence in our judgment and our ability to exercise that judgment from a position where we could determine what were their best interests, as a part of the nation's interests." Edmund Burke's 1774 speech to the English Parliament is considered a classic explanation of this viewpoint. "Your representative owes you not his industry, but his judgment," he said, "and he betrays, instead of serving you, if he sacrifices it to your opinion . . . You choose a member indeed; but when you have chosen him, he is not a member of Bristol, but he is a member of Parliament." (Burke, incidentally, was not reelected.) When members do contradict the perceived opinion of their constituents or of powerful in-

---

*Although it is important evidence of citizen sentiment, the mail is far from a perfect barometer. Often it reflects the view of *aroused* citizens, not all citizens. When FDR proposed repealing a provision of the Neutrality Act in 1939, tons of mail were sent to Congress which ran 5 to 1 against repeal. Yet a poll showed the public for repeal 56 to 44 percent; Congress approved it. In 1940, 90 percent of the Senate mail opposed a selective service system. At the same time, a poll showed the public 70 percent for it; Congress approved the draft.

terest groups, they become, according to Kennedy, "profiles in courage." This does not happen very often, but some members do take risks. Former representative Ken Hechler of West Virginia would fight his state's coal mining interests; Rep. Morris Udall, from hawkish Arizona, was vigorously antiwar; Senator Paul Hatfield (D.-Mont.), in office just a few months following the death of Lee Metcalf, cast the deciding vote in favor of the Panama Canal treaty, which 80 percent of his state opposed according to one poll. He lost his Democratic primary 3 to 1 two months later.

But as one watches representatives and senators enter their chambers for a floor vote, such philosophical approaches give way to more political criteria. Of course some votes are decided back at the office, because of the merits of one position, or staff advocacy, or regional demands, or the exhortations of a major contributor that "we really need this one." But many members go to the floor not knowing how they are going to vote, nor exactly what they're voting on—which is perhaps predictable when there are 700 recorded votes a year in the House of Representatives.

The floor scene itself resembles a cross between a commodities future exchange and Portobello Road. Members are milling and chatting, haranguing and lounging—a great hubbub of noise out of which votes are cast and public policy made. At the most primitive political level, representatives of the Democratic and Republican leadership stand at the doors of the House chamber with their thumbs up or down. There also are the major sponsors and opponents of the bill repeating code phrases about the measure—"oppose more federal spending," "vote for jobs." Hurried members, says Majority Leader Jim Wright, "react instinctively to one or the other of the slogans. It's dangerous. It does not provide the kind of deliberation the public is entitled to."

Simultaneously, our hypothetically undecided representative may seek out a bellwether-colleague he trusts in the area under consideration—perhaps Rep. Fernand St. Germain (D.-R.I.) on banking, or Rep. Barber Conable, Jr. (R.-N.Y.), on taxes. Or he may simply seek out a colleague he socializes with or works out at the gym with, or whose wife is friendly with his wife. One con-

gressman told how many members come over from the
gym with their tennis shoes on. "Someone won't really
understand what the vote is on and will vote the wrong
way. Everybody will then yell at him: Hey, Joe, what're
you doing. You voted the wrong way. He'll then change
his vote."*

Perhaps the member will go along with a colleague on
an item of no great interest to him or his district, so
that he can garner his colleague's vote when the situation is reversed—such horsetrading has long been de-
cried but is as much a part of the ongoing legislative
process as are quorum calls. Perhaps the member will
realize that he recently voted against a major interest
behind the bill—say labor or business—so he now feels
he "owes them one," a balancing act that keeps members
off political "enemies lists." If it's a major issue, Speaker
O'Neill or Minority Leader Rhodes may be on the floor
pleading for party loyalty, though less strenuously than
in the days of Sam Rayburn.

Two final variables enter into consideration. "The largest
factor in members' voting is momentum," said Rep. Toby
Moffett (D.-Conn.). Many representatives hold off voting early, watch the drift of voting, and then coura-
geously join the winning side. And then, of course, there
is the ultimate electoral calculation—who will remember this vote on election day, who will forget it, who
as a result will contribute or not contribute campaign
money, and how much. All these swirling considerations
affect the member, who filters them, weighs them, and
then puts his plastic I.D. card in one console or the
other. It is not a neat process, but it is the way it
works. Or as some wag once said, anyone who likes sausage
or legislation should not watch how either is made.†

---

*The problem of the frenzied last-second vote has only worsened
with the advent in February, 1973, of an electronic voting system
in the House. Instead of the House clerk taking thirty-five minutes
to read through the roster of 435 names, giving the tardy time to
appear, representatives now have just fifteen minutes to tally their
votes by inserting a plastic card in an electronic console.

†Even after a vote, members hover around to possibly reconsider
their action. Representatives may switch their vote if it doesn't
affect the final outcome and will help them back home, or if it
does affect the final outcome and a leader or friend twists their
arm. "Bills are won and lost in the well [of the chamber]," according

For only one of thousands of examples of the results of this hectic process, consider the late senator Lee Metcalf. He walked out of his office on the afternoon of August 2, 1971, fully determined to vote against the Lockheed bail-out bill. No big-business slush funds, the Montana populist said to his staff and himself. But as he approached the floor he was cornered by his friend Alan Cranston of California, home of potentially unemployed Lockheed workers. Senator Cranston beseeched his Democratic colleague not to supposedly throw 30,000 people out of work. Metcalf, weakened, finally chose employment over ideology and voted for the Lockheed loan, which slipped by the Senate 49–48.

But every bill does not possess the drama of such a close vote on such an important issue. Of 30,000 bills introduced each Congress, perhaps 600 bills will become law. In 1978, one floor measure proclaimed National Lupus Week; the Senate approved of the naming of the Roman L. Hruska Meat Animal Research Center and, just before "Sun Day" in May, passed S. J. Res. 128, "Free Enterprise Day," which required a presidential proclamation and called upon "the people of the United States and interested groups and organizations to observe such day with appropriate ceremonies and activities." (The possibilities suggested seem endless; for example, perhaps an "Excess Profit Day" or an "Oil Spill Week.")

A Congressional Composite

Congressmen can easily become homogenized once they adapt to their institution's demands and folkways. But there are still enough differences among the 535 lawmakers to keep journalists busy. Nowhere is this clearer than in their working habits. From the range of potential activities—legislating, handshaking, debating, investigating—each congressman focuses on a few, since there is not enough time for all. As a result, there is a rough division of labor among the members. Some, feeling the pull of national prominence, speak up on every major issue. Others, forever intent on the next election,

---

to Rep. Phillip Burton, wise in the political nuances of the House. "If you see a guy who has voted for you in the well, he is going to switch."

think that the only major issues are those that affect their district. Some legislators seize the reins of power with confidence and talent; others remind one of former senator William Saxbe's remark that "the first six months in the Senate you wonder how you got there. The next six months you wonder how the rest of them got there." When studying members of Congress past and present, certain categories of work styles emerge:

The Overachievers—To them Congress is not a sine-cure but an opportunity to produce reports, release exposés, let fly speeches, and in general stay in the news. "As if increase of appetite had grown by what it fed on," their hunger for work is never sated.

Senator Jacob Javits (R.-N.Y.) is one—his staff invariably impressed at the armful of work he lugs home most nights and his colleagues usually amazed by how he feels the compulsion to speak (knowledgeably) on almost any subject then on the Senate floor. Senator Henry Jackson is another.

But the kingfish overachiever has to be Senator William Proxmire. His high school classmates at Pottstown, Pennsylvania, voted him the class's "biggest grind," and he's been pushing himself ever since. Through Yale, the Harvard Business School, military counterintelligence, newspaper reporting, and three unsuccessful campaigns for governor of Wisconsin, he exercised spartan self-discipline and finally won a special election for the seat vacated by the death of Joseph McCarthy in 1957.

But success never spoiled Bill Proxmire. He jogs five miles to his Senate office every day, rain or shine, after doing one hundred pushups, and then jogs back after work. One can almost see the adrenalin pumping through his taut, hyperactive body. The *Wall Street Journal* called him "one of the Senate's busiest members."

Proxmire used to be saddled with a different reputation, one that any overachiever risks: that of an aggressive maverick. Early in his career, his overbearing ways irritated many of his colleagues. During his freshman term he rebuked Majority Leader Lyndon Johnson on the floor for efforts to "dominate" the Senate. Sixteen years later his outspokenness on a wide range of issues still could not be contained: when the head of the Joint Chiefs of

Staff made some anti-Jewish remarks, within hours Proxmire publicly demanded he resign; when the *New York Times* exposed domestic surveillance by the CIA under Richard Helms, within hours Proxmire demanded that he resign as ambassador to Iran. Such quick-trigger judgments on subjects not covered by his committees make more traditional senators both marvel and mutter. Staff members of his committee told a profiler in 1977 that Proxmire's grandstanding, vanity, and unwillingness to compromise often destroy his effectiveness. This leaves him playing the politics of negativism, they moan—stop a bill here, save a million there—instead of building overall solutions to problems through legislation. And although his Golden Fleece awards generate enormous publicity over absurd spending—$97,000 for a study on "The Peruvian Brothel, A Sexual Dispensary and Social Arena" —many scholars regard his efforts as antiintellectual demagoguery.

But, with a few successes and some seniority, Proxmire has more impact than the "maverick" label would imply. In his specialty, defense spending, he has made "cost overruns" common parlance. He led successful efforts to kill two of the biggest defense "cost overruns" in history—the SST program and the B-1 bomber. He also exposed C-5A overruns, causing Congress to roll back the number of planes produced from 120 to 81—saving some $2.5 billion. In less well-known efforts, Proxmire has pushed ethics reform, opposed the Capitol west front extension, put the Import-Export Bank back under the government budget, authored the Truth in Lending Act, defended A. Ernie Fitzgerald's whistle-blowing activities, and vociferously fought red-lining in the inner cities. He also is close to fulfilling his dream of seeing the Senate ratify the Genocide Convention—the full Senate having heard his advocacy on behalf of the treaty for eleven years.

In 1977, Proxmire welcomed Jimmy Carter to Washington with a barrage of opposition to the appointment of Carter's Georgia banking buddy Bert Lance as director of the Office of Management and Budget and to White House plans to bail out New York City with federal aid. Although he let New York survive in the end, he continued to oppose Lance's confirmation. He grilled him in committee, made a harsh speech opposing his confirmation on the Senate floor, and eventually cast a lone nay vote. "He was simply unqualified. He had no background at all in handling a government budget."

Whatever the gambit or position, however, Proxmire never seems to rest. When the Senate is on vacation, Proxmire is on the job holding hearings. In August, 1971, he suddenly reassembled his Joint Economic Committee to take on President Nixon's sudden Phase I price and wage freeze. As if this frenetic pace on the issues weren't enough, Proxmire has not missed a Senate roll-call vote since 1966 and he returns home to Wisconsin nearly every weekend. The result: he spent all of $100 to win reelection with 73 percent of the vote in 1976.

The Underachievers—To say that they are not household words puts it mildly. Their seats, usually from safe districts, are a form of Social Security to them—steady income for little or no work. Others may do the legislating; these men are content to stay out of sight. There are more of them than of the overachievers.

Former representatives Philip Philbin and Robert Nix exemplified this species of congressman.

Philbin (D.-Mass.), who served fourteen terms ending in 1971, was uncontroversial, uninterested, and inactive in all House affairs. His indifference extended even to the Armed Services Committee, where he became vice chairman through circumstances beyond his control (he had thirty years' seniority). The *Wall Street Journal* wrote that "the 72-year-old Democrat regularly arrives on the House floor for the day's debate, affably greets his cronies, takes a seat up front near the speaker's rostrum—and then almost always falls asleep." But Philbin was a kind and friendly fellow who won affection from other representatives and his district despite his lethargy. He left office long after he had retired from it.

Nix, after sixteen years in Congress, was the second most senior black representative in the 95th Congress (1977–79), as well as the first black representative ever elected in Pennsylvania. Other men might have used this as a platform for legitimate publicity. Nix modestly remained an entire unknown, both in his district and in the Capitol. The Philadelphia political machine, rubbing

salt in the wounds of democratic theory, ensured his reelection (until his defeat in 1978). But once in Congress,
Nix did little but take up space. In the 1970 campaign,
Nix's opponent kept referring to him as "the phantom
congressman." He did gain some notoriety of a sort in
1964 when the NAACP opposed his reelection, saying
that Nix was anti-Negro since he had failed to exert any
leadership to protect civil rights protesters.

The local Philadelphia newspapers rarely covered him,
for there was not much to cover. But in early 1971, a
Philadelphia Tribune columnist managed to interview him
at length one night. After the article had been written, the
columnist discovered that Nix's exact words that evening
on Martin Luther King, the UN, Israel, education, and
income tax had come directly from his October, 1970,
newsletter (he sent out one a year). Nevertheless, Nix got
a fellow Philadelphia representative to insert the article in
the *Congressional Record*. And in December, 1971, an un-
abashed Nix reproduced copies of the *Record* pages containing the article and then sent them out as his *1971*
newsletter.

*Districters—These congressmen worry little about af-
fairs of state. They see themselves as tribunes of the
people, and their highest calling is to serve their constituents' immediate problems. And that usually means in
person, not by mail.*

The exemplar of the congressional tribune was William
Barrett, a fourteen-term representative from southwest
Philadelphia. He flew back to his district *every night*
from Washington to hold office hours from 9:00 P.M.
to 1:00 A.M. At the corner of 24th and Wharton Streets
in south Philadelphia, in the shabby office of a building
he owned, Barrett sometimes saw as many as 750 people
a week, "on marital matters, child welfare, foreclosures,
evictions—everything that affects the human person," he
said. For this, his constituents called him "the Reverend"
and the night sessions "the confessional." Stephen Isaacs
wrote in the *Washington Post:* "Folks line up to tell
Bill Barrett their problems. He sits behind his desk, listening, his fingertips poised—barely touching—in front of
his chin. And, as he has been doing for forty years—
the last twenty-six as a congressman—he does something

about their problems. He gets them taken care of." He cared little about his legislative duties (although he was the second ranking Democrat on the House Banking and Currency Committee), to the extent that one Hill staff observed that "his knowledge of legislation only goes as far as how many patronage jobs it will produce for him in Philadelphia."

Territorialists—Given the vast range of possible subjects to master, some congressmen retreat into specialties. To know one subject well is to gain a certain prominence in an institution of prominent people.

Rep. Paul Rogers (D.-Fla.), 53, from West Palm Beach, knew that there are always two bitter sides to such issues as civil rights, war, or poverty. But health was a motherhood issue, and an important one. So in 1971, forty of sixty-one floor remarks and twenty-one of twenty-eight articles he inserted into the *Record* dealt with health. Eight of fifteen bills he introduced in the first four months of 1972 concerned health. Rogers was chairman of the subcommittee on Public Health and Environment, and nearly all health proposals had to run through his committee's filter. He diligently prepared for all committee hearings, and further, made proposals of his own, such as a federal department of health. All of this led R. John Zapp, HEW deputy assistant secretary for health legislation, to assert that "Rogers is the most knowledgeable man on the Hill on health issues."

The Orators—Following in the tradition of Cicero and Webster, a few congressmen try to make the chamber ring. Although a small band, they occasionally provide bright moments on the chamber floor.

At 5'4" and 150 pounds, former Rhode Island senator John Pastore attracted attention by the discrepancy between the size of himself and the size of his voice. A snappy dresser with a trim moustache, he would jump, prance, jerk, and, with stentorian voice, boom his way through a speech or debate. One Senate worker claims he heard Pastore while sitting at his desk one story above the floor, across a corridor, and behind two closed doors. Pastore's golden moment of oratory was when 65 million Americans heard his typically energetic keynote speech to the 1964 Democratic Convention. "Look, maybe this doesn't read too well," he said about the speech, "but it sounds good. Maybe no one would give me the Pulitzer Prize for this, but I'm not lookin' for the Pulitzer Prize. I'm lookin' for the audience."

Now there is Frank Church, former star of the Stanford debating team and a powerful Senate speaker. As a freshman in 1958, he was chosen by LBJ to deliver Washington's Farewell Address, an honor usually reserved for senior members. His electric delivery inspired applause from the gallery, a rare occurrence. Such efforts led the press gallery to call him "boy orator" in 1958 and led to the choice of him to be the keynoter at the 1960 Democratic Convention.

Church fits the classic orator mold more closely than Pastore. He speaks from a carefully prepared text, but he does so with great emphasis and verve. After Church's speech denouncing President Johnson's Vietnam policy, the visitors' gallery, again, burst into applause. The late senator Ernest Gruening then said, "I believe it ranks with the classics, with the addresses of Daniel Webster and other distinguished orators of the past." Church's speech had deftly combined epigrams, metaphors, repetition, poetic license, and personification of the abstract. "I'd worked very hard over that speech," he commented afterward. "To speak well, and think, you have to be the author of the text yourself. We're beyond the age of great oratory today, but the truly great orators of the past were men who wouldn't be caught dead using someone else's words."

The Outspoken—While both depend on a verbal ability, the outspoken differ from the orators in that they speak more briefly, more ideologically, more bluntly, and with fewer Latin or French words.

Although the supply of orators has dwindled, the outspoken are increasing in number. In the mid-sixties, Senators Wayne Morse and Ernest Gruening were famous examples. More recently there have been members like Abourezk, Gravel, Abzug, Waldie, Dellums.

One of the most prominent is Rep. Robert Drinan of Massachusetts. In character, background, and temperament he has set himself apart from most of his colleagues.

A Jesuit priest, author, former law school dean and professor, Drinan is so frank in his approach that some members say that without his clerical collar he could not get away with it. In person he is gruff, aggressive, and intense, yet religiously honest and adamant in his refusals to compromise on ethical positions for lesser reasons.

Vigorously antiwar, he supported George McGovern early in the 1972 presidential campaign while the rest of the New England congressional delegation were backing Ed Muskie of Maine. When told he should endorse Muskie as a good New Englander, Drinan replied, "What the hell does that mean?" Toward the end of the Vietnam War, Drinan took the unusual tack of denouncing the House Democratic leadership in a *New York Times* op-ed piece for its reluctance to push for a Vietnam pullout date. "I try not to be ashamed to be a member of Congress," he wrote. "I must confront the fact, however, that history will conclude that the House of Representatives in the 92nd Congress acquiesced in the most brutal war in all of history. . . . My mind cannot yet look forward to the hope which may come with the 93rd Congress. I am still stunned, numbed, and dismayed."

He joined the House Internal Security Committee in a successful effort to abolish it, announcing that the House "has been brought into disrepute by the antics of this committee." And, as a House Judiciary member during its 1974 impeachment proceedings against Richard Nixon, Drinan could always be counted on to provide a sharply worded few seconds of commentary to appreciative newspeople. In 1977, he revealed a secret oral agreement between Attorney General Griffin Bell and the former chairman of the Senate Judiciary Committee (J. O. Eastland) that he said violated a clear campaign promise by President Carter to institute merit selection of federal prosecutors. Traditionally the senior senator of the president's party from each state is allowed to fill the powerful prosecuting position as a type of patronage reward. Yet Drinan felt unrestrained by political niceties: "It is just this kind of deception, in which behind-closed-doors agreements nullify campaign promises, that makes so many Americans cynical about the basic honesty and trustworthiness of their government."

*Organization Men—Some men are born great, some
have greatness thrust upon them—and others edge their
way up the greasy pole, almost unnoticed. In big cities, it's
the wardheelers, who take care of the details for their
bosses. In the Senate, it's the people who aid the leadership in their daily chores. It may not be the most glamorous way to power, but it's one way.*

Alan Cranston of California was the obvious choice for
Senate Democratic whip in 1977. His liberal orientation
provided a useful balance to the more conservative Robert C. Byrd. And his accurate, dog-eared tally sheets
made him the resident oracle for head counts on pending
legislation.

A quintessential club member, Cranston never lets
transient concerns like national issues disturb the pleasant
relations he has cultivated among his colleagues since his
election in 1968. He is a classic organization man who
loves the intricacies of the legislative process, doesn't up-
stage his seniors, and usually avoids the limelight sur-
rounding controversial issues and fights. "He is very effective in dealing with—in working with—certain
senators, especially on the Republican side of the aisle.
And he is dedicated in his support for me. He works with
me closely and I have every confidence in his dedication
toward his responsibilities as assistant Democratic leader,"
Byrd has told the *National Journal.*

Cranston, warm and grandfatherly in person, confirms
that he and the leader work together smoothly. "We have
an agreement where if one of us agrees and the other
doesn't [he cited an early difference on the Panama Canal
treaties issue], the one who disagrees will step aside and the
other will lead; except under extraordinary circumstances
the one who steps aside will not lead the opposition."

Byrd obviously understands and appreciates Cranston's
role, since he became majority leader also by working
tirelessly on boring routine floor matters and doing endless favors for fellow senators. Yet he is not going to let
his whip duplicate the assertive and powerful role Byrd
carved out as Mike Mansfield's assistant majority leader.
"Byrd is so excessively jealous of his own power that he
won't give Cranston any role except on a few specific
issues," a former Cranston aide has said. "Everybody knew
it would be a nothing job under Byrd. He got it because

he had been a dutiful, super-head counter for the leadership. It's a time consuming, thankless job with no glory."

Parliamentarians—If you're not keen on policymaking, you should learn the rules of procedure. If you are perennially in the minority, you must learn the rules of procedure. For you can often win procedurally what you could never achieve substantively on the merits. It is a lesson Southern senators and representatives have memorized and taken to heart.

Senator James B. Allen of Alabama was the best recent example. Elected in 1968 at the age of 56, Allen had served in the Alabama state legislature for eight years and as lieutenant governor for two terms. When he came to the Senate, he understood the importance and content of parliamentary politics better than most freshmen. Allen publicized the fact that he won the Senate Messengers Golden Gavel Award three times for spending the greatest number of hours presiding over the Senate. In a newsletter home, he proudly described his role as "keeping watch in the Senate to see that our position is not prejudiced by adverse parliamentary maneuvers."

In August, 1972, Allen showed the value of picayune rules when the Senate considered the House's antibusing bill. Usually bills are read twice and referred to committee. Allen drew on an obscure precedent to prevent the second reading and keep it from going to the liberal Labor and Public Welfare Committee. Instead, it remained on the calendar of the full Senate, where senators intimidated by public opposition to busing were more likely to support Allen's cause.

But Allen's acknowledged forte was the filibuster, which he wielded, in his words, to check "the abuses of an unbridled majority." His filibustering defeated a major tax reform proposal of Senator Edward Kennedy in 1973, and delayed Senate passage of the 18-year-old vote change and campaign financing reform. In late 1974, Allen led a Senate filibuster against a proposed Consumer Protection Agency ("he was a one-man wrecking crew," said one observer of these events), a filibuster that a near record four cloture votes couldn't stop. His crowning performance in the 1975 battle to reform the filibuster has already been recounted. (After Allen died in June, 1978, his wife was appointed to his unexpired term. When Senator William Hathaway of Maine, a prominent liberal, saw her reading the Senate rulebook at her desk, he raced over and pulled it from her hands, jokingly announcing, "My God, we can't let *you* read *that*.")

Absentees and Attenders—Some children play hooky, while others never miss a day of school. And some members of Congress avoid floor activity, while others relish the chance to attend everything.

As already noted, running to and from roll calls and sitting through floor proceedings can be a bore. "It would be a delightful thing," wrote George F. Hoar in 1897, "to attend Unitarian conventions if there were not Unitarians there; so too it would be a delightful thing to be a United States senator if you did not have to attend the sessions of the Senate." Perhaps anticipating this advice, only eight of twenty-two senators showed up at the opening of the first session of Congress on March 4, 1789.

Adam Clayton Powell was, of course, the prince of the absentees. In explanation, he wrote in 1963, "I refuse to answer quorum calls. Most of them are instigated mischievously and very few of them serve any importance whatsoever. . . . To answer or not to answer a quorum call has nothing whatsoever to do with voting. It is, of course, very obvious that it is the vote which counts." By 1966, Powell wasn't even voting, but his distinction between answering quorum calls and voting calls has merit. Some, like Powell, fail to attend because they consider attendance on the floor unimportant, others are just lazy, while yet others have competing commitments. John Kennedy came only 39 percent of the time in 1960, Eugene McCarthy a paltry 5 percent in 1968, and George McGovern 51 percent in 1972. One representative in the early 1960s made only 17 percent of all roll calls; controlling his local party machinery and coming from a "safe" district, he felt no pressure to attend and impress the people back home.

The absentees make the attenders mad. Until her hip operation in 1968, ex-senator Margaret Chase Smith had made 2,941 consecutive roll calls, then an all-time Senate record. (Even Lou Gehrig only played in 2,130 consecutive games.) On December 21, 1971, she attacked her colleagues who failed to show up for work. "The Senate is a club of prima donnas intensely self-oriented," she said, "ninety-nine kings and one queen dedicated to their own personal accommodation." Majority Leader Mansfield, who had to attend regularly because of his job, became testy about the problem. On February 8, 1972, he lectured his colleagues that "none of us was drafted for this job. Every single member of this body sought this position, and with the position goes a duty . . . to attendance on the floor of the Senate. The record of this body over the past month is, to put it mildly, abominable." On September 9, 1974, it seemed that not much had improved. For on that day the Senate voted unanimously for a bill creating an agency to police the commodities exchanges—by a 5–0 vote.

What drives the attenders? To some it is the quintessential way to fulfill one's legislative obligations. Then too, a good attendance record is an easy way to impress voters. Unlike most things a member does, his attendance is quantifiable. If it's good, he can profitably display this record at home. Rep. William Natcher, for example, has made 2,705 roll calls in a row since entering Congress in 1954, and Rep. Charles E. Bennett made every single vote between 1951 and 1974, 3,807 votes in all.

Compelling attendance on the floor is a difficult, and perhaps unwise, task. During a debate over the Lower California River Project in 1927, a no-nonsense presiding officer issued "warrants of arrest" and legally dragged the necessary number of senators onto the floor. Senator Smith recommended expulsion of any member who missed more than 40 percent of roll calls. But these steps surely go too far. A member has many responsibilities, of which being on the floor is only one. A 100 percent or even 80 percent attendance record is no guarantee of congressional efficiency or productivity; a 50 percent attendance record may or may not be an indication of negligence. Short of the draconian solution of arrest or expulsion—and as long as the Senate ignores an 1872 statute that orders deduction of a day's pay for every unexcused, absent day—the contest between the absentees and attenders will no doubt continue, with the only effective judge being the voters.

While being a senator or representative looks glamorous from the outside, it has its drawbacks and disappoint-

ments. Congress devotes itself to what it was not essentially designed to do—running small favors for complaining
constituents. What Congress *is* supposed to do—legislate—it does not do well. It is the executive that now
initiates most legislation, and it is the Supreme Court that
has made many of the important human-rights breakthroughs in the past twenty-five years—equal education for
blacks, reapportionment, rights for criminal defendants,
near abolition of the death penalty, the right to an abortion. To get major legislation passed often requires a major
national trauma: the 1937 and 1962 drug amendments
followed the Elixir and thalidomide scandals; President
Kennedy's death gave impetus to his successor's civil rights
and Medicare achievements.

Legislation-by-trauma, however, can fail for two reasons. First, the crisis still cannot overcome a determined
vested interest (so, after a decade of assassinations by
shooting, there was still no adequate gun control law);
and second, the structure of both houses ensures that a
good piece of legislation can founder on one of many
shoals, with only an occasional one sailing surprisingly
out of the harbor. A new congressman once marveled at
working conditions in the Capitol: "We work in a political
environment, surrounded by lobbyists, constituents, the
leadership, and jangling telephones and we virtually have
no time alone to think and reflect upon the problems before us. The big miracle is that somehow all of this works.
On paper, looking at the situation, you'd say it couldn't
possibly work and yet the fact is that it does." So the
miracle of Congress, as Sam Johnson said of a dog that
could walk on his hind legs, may not be that it does its
task well, but that it does it at all.

But how well it works is another question. Some, frustrated by the formal ways of the Senate and House,
creatively plot out new approaches to solving problems;
Senator Gaylord Nelson sponsored Earth Day, which
helped initiate the entire environmental movement; former
representative (and now Senator) David Pryor worked
secretly as an orderly in a nursing home and later set up
a headquarters in a trailer near Capitol Hill to aid the
elderly, all in an effort to focus attention on the problems
of old age; Rep. Henry Reuss rediscovered the unused
1899 Refuse Act, sent out a kit of instructions on its use,

and thereby encouraged a process whereby water polluters could be hauled into court; after generations of members had genuflected to Pentagon budget estimates and expertise, Senator William Proxmire and Rep. Les Aspin simply developed an expertise and expert staffs of their own to conduct the first congressional counteroffensive against military budget waste.

Such breakthroughs are the exception. Unless they are committee chairmen or chamber leaders, most members readily admit their powerlessness. They come to Washington in the flush of victory and with a sense of self-importance, but are then odds-on favorites to sink into oblivion. "Usually only scandal, longevity, or death distinguishes a member from the pack," writes columnist Mary McGrory. Rep. Dante Fascell metaphorically complained that "being in the House is sometimes like trying to push a wheelbarrow up a hill with ropes as handles."

So why do they do it? Why make less money than they could in another field, and why go to all those weenie roasts in the district every weekend? Power and prestige. They sense that fame can be more fun than money, and that an ounce of history in Washington is worth a pound of success back home. So for most, simply *being there* is reward enough. It justifies (especially for the representatives, with their trying two-year terms) always running for office instead of performing in it, being more content to service specific constituents on personal problems than to represent them all on the larger issues.

8

Staying Elected

All members of Congress have a primary interest in being reelected. Some members have no other interest.

—Former representative Frank E. Smith

It was early in the campaign, and the challenger, Bill McKay, was having trouble developing a strong attack against incumbent Crocker Jarmin in the California senate race. As he went to make a speech, news came that a forest fire had broken out in Malibu. Canceling his engagement, McKay raced to the scene to denounce the disregard for watersheds that led to such fires. As the television cameras and newspapermen crowded around the young candidate, however, a helicopter flew to the scene and Senator Crocker Jarmin jumped out. McKay stood helplessly by while the incumbent announced that he had received the president's personal assurance that federal disaster aid would be forthcoming; in addition, he would introduce a bill on the Senate floor to protect watersheds and to insure the property for those whose property was damaged by mismanaged watersheds.

The Advantages of Incumbency

The scene is from the 1972 movie *The Candidate,* but the script is familiar. He who holds office also holds the powers of office and can use them to promote his own reelection. The only deviation from the script is that in *The Candidate* incumbent Jarmin eventually lost the election. It is not usually so. Since World War II, 93 percent of all representatives who ran for reelection won; in the

266

six most recent elections, of those who ran over 95 percent of House incumbents and over 80 percent of Senate incumbents were returned to office.* Indeed, 61 members faced no major party opponent in the 1978 general election. This overall success rate contrasts sharply with public opinion polls showing that only 20 percent of the electorate give Congress high marks institutionally and only 39 percent approve of their representatives' performance.

According to *Congressional Quarterly's Guide to the Congress of the United States,* in the 1870s more than half the representatives sent to the House every two years were freshmen, and the mean length of service was just over two terms. By 1900, only 30 percent of each new crop of representatives arrived in Washington for the first time; in 1970, the figure was about 12 percent, though by the 1978 elections, newcomers accounted for 18 percent of the House membership. Meanwhile, the Senate has displayed an upward trend in the average length of service for senators, from 4½ years (less than a full term) in 1829 to 11 years in 1975. In both houses, the most striking increase occurred in the years between the Civil War and the turn of the century, as party control of politics hardened.† Nowadays far more members of Congress die or retire—fifty-nine retired at the end of the 95th Congress—than lose.

The reason is incumbency. By comparing a member of Congress's winning margin in his first successful race to his margin in his second, we can get a rough idea of how many votes incumbency is worth. Figures compiled by the writers show that a representative gets 5 percent more of the vote the second time around than he did on his first, an increase which can frequently prove decisive. In recent Senate contests, incumbents gained three percentage points in the vote total over their first run for the roses. While the gain from incumbency is smaller in

---

*In 1978, only 24 of 382 House incumbents running for reelection lost. The Senate saw 8 of 25 incumbents lose, as more new Senators entered that chamber—20—than at any time since 1946.

†A small portion of the increase in length of service must be attributed to longer life expectancies; as fewer senators and representatives die in office, more live to complete their full terms, and to be reelected, than they did a century ago.

the Senate than in the House, it is equally significant, as senatorial elections tend to be closer fought than House elections.

According to Kenneth Harding, who heads the House Democratic Campaign Committee, "There's no reason a House member should ever lose, after a term or two, if he's using the tools of office properly." Or as Fred Wertheimer has put it, "For Congress today we have neither a Democratic nor a Republican Party. Rather we have an incumbency party which operates a monopoly."

The origins of this invulnerability—and of why Congress is unpopular generally though its inhabitants routinely get sent back—are not difficult to find. One reason is simply that the best vote-getters tend to win, and, because they are good vote-getters, to win again and again. But aside from the survival of the fittest, there are powerful special privileges available to incumbents that cannot be enjoyed by their challengers. The most familiar advantage is the one we saw in the scene from *The Candidate*: incumbents, unlike their opponents, are already in office and can service constituents, introduce bills, take credit for bills they have merely cosponsored* and for federal spending in their district or state, or preempt their opponents' ideas by putting them into effect themselves.

Another key advantage that accrues to the incumbent is financial. Even before the November election, the incumbent is much less likely to have to conduct an expensive, hard-fought primary campaign than his opponent. Many have no opposition at all. In 1978, two-thirds of those seeking reelection in the House waltzed through the primaries unopposed. Counting those who had no primary challenger, over two-thirds of the incumbents won their primaries with a vote margin of more than 30 percent.

Challengers can expect a tougher battle. Also, their vote margins are considerably smaller. The ability to avoid a tough primary campaign is especially valuable in one-party states or districts—still common in the South and in ma-

---

*Former representative Frank Clark (D.-Pa.), for example, claimed in three of his newsletters to constituents in 1974 that he "sponsored" or "introduced" more than twenty pieces of legislation. In fact, Clark wrote only one of the bills—he cosponsored nineteen of the others and five were identical to bills already written and introduced.

chine-dominated cities in the North, and by no means rare elsewhere. In these areas, the primary election is often more crucial than the general election. In 1963, a representative from a "safe" district told a Brookings Institution study: "I spend about $1,200 [in the general election] and my opponent even less. In my state the primary is far more important than the election. When I first ran there were eight of us in the primary and I spent about $25,000."

Of course, some incumbents do lose in the primaries, but surprisingly these casualties do not necessarily come from the fierce primaries in one-party districts. Instead, the losers are almost invariably either old men beaten by younger, more vigorous challengers (six defeats in 1972) or incumbents redistricted into another incumbent's district (seven defeats in 1972). Thus the risk of a hard primary battle is not a threat to the vast majority of incumbents—those who have served a few terms—but only to congressional elders who have reaped the blessings of seniority (e.g., Paul Douglas, Clifford Case, Emanuel Celler) or to members unlucky or unpopular with their reapportioning state legislatures.

Despite these automatic advantages, most incumbent members of the House also outspend their rivals. According to the Common Cause Campaign Monitoring Project, which conducted an extensive study of 1972 and 1974 campaign spending, incumbent senators and representatives outspend their challengers almost 2 to 1.

If veterans can double the tenderfoot dollar for dollar, or better, it is because they have easier access to outside sources of campaign funds. Many of the sources of this money have been spelled out in chapter 1, but it is worthwhile to mention several points here. The first financial advantage incumbents have is that they already have been assigned to committees. A corporation or labor union knows whether a given congressman is likely to serve on a committee with jurisdiction over subjects important to it. For example, if a representative has been assigned to the House Agriculture Committee, it is a good bet that he will continue to serve there if reelected—which means that a farm conglomerate will be more likely to give money to him than to his opponent, who might well be assigned to the Public Works Committee. Conversely, trucking executives will sooner support a Public Works committeeman than his opponent, who may end up on Agriculture. It is not impossible that a sly senator or representative might request a committee assignment precisely because a corporation or a union gave him a sizable campaign contribution, with promises of more.

A second financial advantage is that incumbents are "viable candidates." They have won at least once, and they can be expected to win again. No reasonably self-interested campaign contributor wants to throw good money into a losing cause; he wants his man to win. The phenomenon applies to all aspects of campaigning, from collecting endorsements from party celebrities and campaign appearances by them to getting press coverage to getting money. The presidential campaign of George McGovern was like a typical senatorial campaign in these respects. Before he won the Wisconsin primary, party notables were notable for their absence; the media was lackadaisical in its coverage; and the money was coming in in nickels and dimes from small contributors, not from the big ones. Within a week after the Wisconsin victory, the coffers were brimming; as McGovern's momentum built up, the money built up, too. When, after the convention and *l'affaire* Eagleton, McGovern's campaign was in trouble again, the money again dried up, and McGovern went back to the nickel-and-dimers who had served him so well before.

A third asset in fundraising is that incumbent members of Congress are worth more to contributors than freshmen, because they have stored up seniority and the power and influence that came with it. The advantages of seniority are recognized not only by the special private interests who give more to ranking members, but also by the House and Senate congressional campaign committees which distribute party money.

Seniority and committee assignments help incumbents at the polls as well as financially. Democratic Rep. Mendel Davis, who won a special election to fill the seat vacated by the death of his patron, Mendel Rivers, in late 1970, ran his 1972 campaign on the slogan "Building Seniority for You." In his successful 1974 reelection campaign, one of Senator Jacob Javits's advertising themes against challenger Ramsey Clark was "Senior is better than Junior."

(There can even be the advantages of ethnic seniority. One surrogate speaker for Javits would remind synagogue audiences: "Never has a Jew risen so high on the Senate Foreign Relations Committee; we can't afford to lose him.")

Most members are not quite so blatant, but they do trade on seniority as a reason for reelection. If they want to be more subtle, they may suggest to the voters that they cast their choice for the "most experienced" candidate. Of course, experience and seniority ought to make their positions on the substantive issues more responsible. It has been said of one representative, "He does terrible things. What makes him worse is that he does them *effectively!*" Most voters, apparently, don't catch on.

Committee assignments open the much-discussed pork barrel, and the scent of pork brings in votes. Members of Congress can be instrumental in getting a host of federal projects and grants for their constituents: post offices, dams, roads, airports, bridges, harbors, federal buildings, military installations, irrigation projects, shipyards, mass transit systems, sewage plants, veterans' hospitals, and grants for an infinite variety of medical, educational, social welfare, military, environmental, and other projects. These make news back home. Former senator Joseph Clark of Pennsylvania once complained that his major speeches went unheralded by the press in his state, but his routine announcements of new post offices got banner headlines. Congressmen make sure to call attention to, and take credit for, every federal project that lands in their territory. A survey of congressional press releases by the Nader Congress Project researchers disclosed that about one-fifth of all representatives' press releases were devoted to announcing projects.

Attempts to oppose pet projects for reelection purposes meet with about as much success as Sisyphus had with his rock. In 1973, when the Senate Public Works Committee was drafting the Water Resources Development bill, Senator James Buckley of New York suggested that several projects proposed in the legislation be dropped "not because of their cost, but because they appeared to be special interest projects offering localized benefits without reference to any national policy," or "pork" as Buckley clarified his remarks. Not only did Buckley feel that special interests were in the back of the minds of his fellow senators, but he felt that those colleagues with more seniority were getting more projects. When Buckley carried his arguments to the Senate floor, Chairman Jennings Randolph of the Public Works Committee played dumb to the whole issue of pork: "If political pressures were the source of public works projects in the past, it is certainly not true today and has not been during my tenure in the Senate." One wonders which Senate Mr. Randolph has been a part of. Buckley's proposal, of course, failed.

The pressure to vote for pork projects can be heavy-handed and persuasive. Rep. Les Aspin (D.-Wis.) cites the case of Rockwell International, a large aerospace firm and prime contractor of the B-1 bomber, which costs $70 million apiece though many experts believe it is unnecessary. When Rockwell representatives met with Aspin's staff to urge congressional support for the B-1, only brief mention was made of the merits of the plane. The nuts and bolts of the discussion were purely economic: contracts let, number of states involved, jobs created, beneficial effects on the national economy. For Rep. John Seiberling (D.-Ohio), Rockwell even converted its statistics to illustrate the benefits to his Akron congressional district. As long as members of Congress know that elections are won and lost on the basis of pork in their districts, and Rockwell knows that the members know this, then Rockwell will continue to be welcomed on Capitol Hill.

How much is the pork barrel really worth in terms of votes? No one knows exactly, but it appears that it's worth relatively more to freshman congressmen than to veterans. Congress Project researchers took a sample of first-term representatives and grouped them according to the amount of federal spending that went to their districts. Those with the least federal spending added 4.6 percent to their original victory margins when they sought reelection. The next group, with more federal spending, received a 6 percent hike in the victory margin. The lucky ones who procured the most local public works added a whopping 8.9 percent to their share of the vote. After the first term in office, however, the increase in victory margin does not fluctuate with the amount of federal spending. This suggests that a first-termer who wants to be reelected should go all out to bring home the federal bacon, but that he can relax a bit thereafter.

Not all is cushy for incumbents, it should be noted, especially when being a part of "big government" has such an odious connotation. One representative thought he had done his people a big favor by voting for a dam in the district, only to discover that it would cause dozens of farms to be flooded out. The farmers helped send him into early retirement. Further, constituents may have unreal expectations of what their senator or representative can do, and may blame him for things beyond his control. Congressmen also complain that they are hampered precisely because they have a record; this, they say, allows challengers to attack or distort what they have done, without having to endure similar attacks. For example, a member who voted against a major bill to fund the Vietnam War that also contained a small provision for aid to Israel could be labeled—as George McGovern discovered—"anti-Israel" by an opponent. Answering such charges is difficult, because issues can quickly become complicated beyond the attention span of an often uninterested electorate, especially when the charge and the defense are condensed by newspapers and broadcasters.

Despite these and a few other disadvantages, incumbents have far more strength than their opponents. One of the biggest advantages—though many representatives say it's their biggest headache as well—is that an incumbent representative is running all the time he is in office. His reelection campaign begins the moment he takes his oath of office, a fact that led one representative to say, "You should say 'perennial' election rather than 'biennial.' It is with us every day."

Members of the House have complained about the two-year term—the real cause of the perennial campaign—for decades. Since Congress first met, some 120 resolutions have been introduced to lengthen the term to three or four years. (The Constitutional Convention considered a three-year term, but quickly rejected it.) Only two of them ever got out of committee, and only one ever came to a vote—and lost. Even if it somehow managed to carry in the House, such a proposal would die a certain death in the Senate. One of the advantages an incumbent senator enjoys is that the two-year House term makes it impossible for a representative to challenge him without sacrificing his House seat, since no one may run for more than one office at a time. Yet the short tenure of representatives is clearly anachronistic. As Clem Long has written:

> It was instituted at a time when the average congressman represented only a few thousand, instead of hundreds of thousands of constituents; when Congress met a month or two instead of nearly all year; and when the federal government confined its activities to national defense, the excise tax, and a few internal improvements, instead of pervading every aspect of personal and business life and spending a quarter to a third of all the income of the economy.

The many prerogatives of office—the staff allowances, the free trips home, the cut-rate stationery, the allowances for office equipment and for setting up a district office, and, of course, the franking privilege—all help in the perennial campaign. The cost of a member's salary, his or her staff's salaries, Washington and local district office space, furnishings, stationery, and telephone service are worth $567,191 to the average incumbent, according to a 1977 study by Americans for Democratic Action. Other miscellaneous favors from the government, such as subscriptions to the *Congressional Record, Congressional Directories,* wall calendars, and pamphlets (many of which become gifts to constituents), account for $7,611.

Offices in an incumbent's home state or district, subsidized by the federal government, can be a political gold mine. Albert Kimball, for example, who runs Rep. Lester L. Wolff's (D.-N.Y.) district office in suburban Long Island, "attends all the Eagle Scout meetings, the presentations of flags to veterans groups, the awards to kids who compete in Americanism contests and the meetings of civic groups concerned about blockbusting." Why does Kimball attend these meetings? Because, he acknowledges, newspaper people are there, the bankers are there, the storeowners are there, the police are there, and above all else—"They all know we're here. And the important thing is that we're the only politician represented here."

The slavish servicing of constituent demands, described in the previous chapter, is an invaluable reelection tool.

According to John White, chairman of the Democratic National Committee, "What counts in the election of a congressman or senator is how the candidates have met constituents' demands for getting social security checks delivered faster, or helping smooth out a dispute between Washington and the local school district." And in a rare instance of concurrence, his GOP counterpart, Bill Brock, said "I couldn't agree more." For example, at a seminar for newly elected Democrats immediately following the 1974 election, newcomers were told repeatedly by incumbents to "keep in close touch with your district and serve your constituents." Former representative Andrew Young (D.-Ga.) elected in 1972 as the first black member from the Deep South in many years, explained that the 60 percent of his constituents who are white middle-of-the-roaders tolerated his more liberal voting record because of outstanding constituent service. Though this seminar provided many helpful tips to the uninitiated, many of the newcomers could come away from such sessions with the impression that getting reelected was the *only* purpose of their tenure in office.

Doing favors for the home folk and making use of his congressional allowances lets a congressman get a jump on his future competitor: he can campaign even before his competitor is chosen, and campaign before the voters think he is campaigning. As one representative said, "You can slip up on the blind side of people during an off-year and get in much more effective campaigning than you can when you are in the actual campaign." Some representatives find casework personally satisfying, especially during their early years in office, when, lacking seniority, they aren't able to contribute much to more exalted activities of the House. One such representative is Wisconsin's David Obey, who helped out a soldier who received orders that would have sent him to Vietnam two days before his long-scheduled wedding. Obey got his departure delayed a week. He feels good about it—and, as he told a *Wall Street Journal* reporter, he knows that the story of his good deed is being told over and over by the friends and families of the bride and groom.

Media Control

There is one more edge: domination of all the media of electioneering—the mails, the newspapers, radio, and television. Aside from the postage allowance, the basis of incumbent domination of the mails is, of course, the franking privilege.

One new representative was told by his father (a former representative), "Son, I have three pieces of advice for you if you want to stay in Congress. One, use the frank. Two, use the frank. Three, use the frank." Franked mail is marked with a bold, florid signature that supposedly says, "This mail is my official business," but that all too often means, "I want to be reelected." The volume of franked mail goes up as elections come closer, as one might expect. Common Cause has estimated that an incumbent can derive $50,000 in postage-free mailings through use of the frank during an election year. A recent law does forbid the use of the frank by an incumbent within sixty days of an election, a law which is at best mere gesture: no public record is kept of when franked mail is sent and no enforcement machinery exists to encourage compliance; and if an incumbent senator sends out hundreds of thousands of free mailings two days before the cut-offs, as Jacob Javits did in New York State in 1974, a challenger can't do anything about it.

Although the frank is supposed to be used only for "official business," not to aid a member's reelection, it is a rule often observed in the breach. Senator Javits had his Small Business Committee hire a direct mail specialist for his political campaign, a specialist who, in his words, devised a "master plan" to use franked mail for "the kind of identification that can be translated into a vote at the polls . . . ." Another direct mail specialist, Derry Daly, proposed a plan to a senator to mail *6,058,900* newsletters and flyers targeted to particular interest groups in the state. Such developments give credence to the remark of writer Alan Baron that we are in a new era of machine politics, where the machine is a computer.

Congress has defined the franking privilege's "official business" very broadly. The widest of the many loopholes in the law permits any excerpt from the *Congressional Record* to be mailed as official business at taxpayers' expense. When this rule is combined with the custom that permits any member of Congress to stick anything he wants into the *Record,* the opportunity for abuse becomes clear. Rep. Alvin O'Konski prepared for his 1972 reelection campaign by sending a flood of material into the *Record* in December, 1971 (long enough before the election that it would not become a campaign issue)—including the "Biography of Alvin E. O'Konski" and an impressive list of his successes in supping from the pork barrel. (Redistricted into Rep. David Obey's district, the well-advertised O'Konski lost.)

Usually the use and abuse of the frank is done with more circumspection as congressmen ply their voters with newsletters, questionnaires, reprints of speeches on issues of interest, and the like. The newsletters, numbering over 148.5 million a year, help keep the public informed, and also assist the incumbent's reelection. First, they increase the representative's visibility. Second, the content of the newsletters, if not frankly political, often leans that way. In 1966, William C. Love analyzed the materials sent to constituents by congressmen. In the House, Love found that 38 percent of the representatives could be classified as "self-promoters," 22 percent as "persuaders," and 17 percent as combination promoter-persuaders; much smaller percentages were found to be "reticent" or "educators." The Senate was worse: 44 percent were promoters, 28 percent persuaders, and 10 percent a combination of the two. What is more significant is that freshman senators and representatives were much more likely to be self-promoters than the secure veterans, who tended toward the "reticent" end of the spectrum.

Challengers, forced to rely on stamps instead of signatures, cannot hope to compete. To send one mailing to each of the 150,000 households in a typical House district would, at 15 cents apiece, set a challenger back $22,500 just for postage—not counting the printing (which the member, but not the challenger, can obtain at cost).

Domination of the press is another media advantage enjoyed and gleefully exploited by incumbent members of Congress. One 1965 study found that about a third of the members of the House said that newspapers in their districts printed their news releases verbatim, and another third wrote their own columns for the local press—a de-

pendency probably due to the fact that three-fourths of
the 1,760 daily newspapers in the U.S. do not have their
own, or a shared, correspondent in Washington. This press
control traces to the glory and trappings of office, which
shroud the congressman until he doffs his statesman's
gown and reenters the political fray at election time.
Typical congressmen pour out well over a hundred press
releases each year; atypical congressmen, those from not-
so-safe seats, pour out many more.

This formidable press barrage naturally does more
good for congressmen from rural areas than those from
big cities. The small-town editor, anxious to fill his columns, and having no Washington bureau to prepare stories
for him, relies on the newsmaker more than, say, a reporter from the *New York Times*. In Rep. David Obey's rural Wisconsin district, all the daily newspapers and half
the weeklies publish his newspaper column, which appears
every week. Obey and his peers are able to obtain reams
of free publicity that are simply not available to anyone
hoping to challenge them, and at the same time the
columns act as the filter through which news reaches the
constituents.

When Murray Watson challenged nineteen-term Rep.
W. R. Poage in an east Texas Democratic primary, local
newspapers totally ignored Watson's candidacy. "Watson's
name never appeared in the paper except in ads," said
Roger Wilson, his aide. The papers refused to print Poage's
votes on environmental and consumer issues. "We finally
ended up running them as ads," said Wilson.

Domination of the broadcast media, radio and television, follows a similar pattern. More than half of all representatives have their own regular radio or television
broadcasts, which are eagerly aired by stations that must
demonstrate their willingness to air public-service program-
ming if they wish to keep their FCC licenses. The shows
are taped very inexpensively in the Senate and House recording studios, which have a mock congressional office,
with an elegant desk and a window giving a glorious view
of the Capitol dome in the background. The House and
Senate recording studios charge members of Congress only
the cost of materials when they use the studios. The Nader
Congress Project found that an incumbent pays $2,500 to
make a year's worth of weekly reports, though equivalent

production costs for a challenger would cost about
$60,000. The facilities are supposed to provide an inex-
pensive means for a member of Congress to inform his or
her constituents about their congressman's professional
duties and issues of interest.

That's the idea, but it's not always the case. The late
senator Everett Dirksen used the studios to record his
smash-hit single, "Gallant Men," and thus got a leg up on
other recording stars. The Capitol Hill News Service investigated whether the recording studios were producing campaign advertisements. "We don't concern ourselves with
the content of the members' spots," said one House studio
staff member initially. But when asked how frequently the
recording studios were producing budget tapes and films
for incumbents' campaign use, the reply was simply, "Oh,
heavy." Since House floor speeches have been televised,
members now can send tapes of their orations to local TV
stations. Speaker O'Neill admitted in mid-1979 that floor
deliberations were being slowed up by members speaking
to be taped for home consumption.

Another hotbed of incumbency advantage lies with the
House majority and minority printers. They fill print orders
from representatives for just about anything requested—
including campaign literature, posters, and bumper stickers.
Taking an attitude of "If-they-want-it-we-print-it," the
printers (and some members) do not seem to consider that
tax dollars are paying much of the cost of the printing
operation, and therefore, using the facilities for campaign
purposes may not be legal.

Many members also employ a press secretary as a staff
assistant to help keep themselves in the news. It is estimated that senators spend $2.5 million annually in tax
dollars to pay their press secretaries. Though it is understandable that former newspaper and broadcast media
people are often hired as press people for members of
Congress, Rep. Joseph McDade (R.-Pa.) has gone one
step further—he has hired a currently employed reporter
for the *Scranton Tribune* to work part-time as his "public
relations assistant." The managing editor of the *Tribune* sees
no conflict of interest for the reporter. Ex-representative
Otto Passman (D.-La.), in the past, hired Louisiana
newsmen on a part-time basis—including a reporter for
the only television station located in his district. If this

doesn't give the representative adequate control of the media in his district, it would appear that nothing will.

All these self-benefiting rules, techniques, and minor exploitations, along with the fact of their official status, have the desired result: senators and representatives are media celebrities back home. They are sought out whenever the media wants them to comment on the news, which is often. In 1965, members of the House told researchers that they averaged four TV and eight radio appearances a month while Congress was in session. Members of the Senate, who are pursued by the networks for national coverage more often than House members, have it even better. And in an election year, challengers are hard pressed to approach the media impact obtained by experienced and well-connected incumbents.

The result of all this attention in the mails and the press and on television and radio is a much higher degree of voter recognition for the incumbent than a challenger can hope to obtain except by extraordinarily high spending. Though only half the voters know the name of their congressman at any given time, far fewer have ever heard of his or her opponent.

What do they know about the incumbent, besides having heard of him? Voters asked this question will usually answer "He's a good guy," or "He does a pretty good job." Only rarely do they know what he thinks or how he votes. One remarkable survey taken by the American Business Committee on National Priorities found that "in almost every instance, between 80 percent and 100 percent" of the voters were unaware of how their representatives had voted on key issues that had drawn national attention. The Business Committee polled ten House districts represented by important legislators; in all of them, a majority of voters expressed opposition to continued funding of the SST. But eight out of ten representatives voted for the SST, and apparently could get away with it, since 85 percent of the voters didn't know how they had voted and the 15 percent who thought they knew were wrong as often as they were right.

What this seems to mean is that voters are more likely to vote for the image of a man than for his legislative record, and are more likely to vote for the image of a man than for his party. Only this can explain some of the surprising representation sent to Congress. Michigan, for example, would regularly return Philip Hart, a very liberal Democrat, and Robert Griffin, a very conservative Republican, to the Senate. Senators from Hawaii, North Dakota, Iowa, Idaho, and Utah have been similarly contrasting—one liberal, the other conservative.

With the power to supervise the laws governing his own reelection, with the power to make news, with the power to cater to special interests, incumbents have enormous opportunities for corruption, for unfairness, for deceit and manipulation of the public. Members of Congress have from time to time indulged in these opportunities, and stories of votes bought and sold, smear campaigns, and malicious distortion of the facts crop up in every political campaign. But there are far more important conclusions to be drawn from the advantages of incumbency than the predictable one that many congressmen and their challengers don't fight fairly. One of them is that every single member of Congress is a walking, talking embodiment of conflict of interest. On the one hand, he has an interest in staying in office, in being reelected; on the other, he has, or ought to have, an interest in serving his constituents and the nation honorably, conscientiously, and well. The congressman who lambastes the high amount of federal spending will nonetheless accept a public works project in his district, and it's difficult to see how even the most scrupulous member of Congress could refuse what may be a boon for his people, even if it's a boondoggle for the nation.

Clearly, too, the men who framed the Constitution expected that representatives would not get reelected as regularly as they now are; that is the whole argument behind the two-year term for members of the House of Representatives. The Senate would represent continuity, the House change. The Senate (before the Constitution was modified to provide for direct election of senators by the people) would represent the states, the House the people. Ironically, in a mass society, where each member of the House has about half a million constituents, the two-year term has come to accomplish exactly the opposite of its purpose. It was supposed to give the *people* a chance to hold their representatives accountable every two years. As George Washington wrote in a letter, in 1787, power "is intrusted for certain defined purposes, and for a certain limited period . . . and, whenever, it is executed contrary to [the public's] interest, or not agreeable to their wishes, their servants can and undoubtedly will be recalled."

Now, however, the two-year term has given *special interests* a chance to hold their representatives accountable every two years. It would seem to the uninitiated that the need to seek frequent reelection would make representatives listen more closely to the opinions of their constituents. Instead, because the costs of campaigning are so high, the perennial campaign makes representatives listen more closely to their campaign contributors. As the influence of political parties, House leadership, and presidential leadership wanes, the role of big givers in reelection campaigns becomes even more decisive. Unlike many of the voters, the contributors know the candidate's name and how he voted.

The representative or senator who must finance election campaigns is faced with a real and difficult ethical dilemma, which well can be illustrated by the case of former Illinois senator Paul Douglas, one of the most conscientious, honest, and distinguished members of the upper chamber. Douglas had no reservoir of personal wealth to dip into when he ran for reelection. Nor did he use his office to increase his wealth. He had no outside business interests that might have posed conflicts. Every year, he made public his net worth and income. But he did have to run for reelection every six years, and he needed money to win in populous, volatile Illinois. He got a large portion of it from organized labor. And in the Senate, he voted the labor line. While Douglas generally agreed with labor anyway, the fact remains that he could not, politically, afford to offend it.

If even the most scrupulous members face this temptation, it is no wonder that those of less conscience joyfully embrace it. As former senator Albert Gore said, "Any person who is willing to sell his soul can have handsome financing for his campaigns." The congressional Dr. Faustus who sells his soul becomes accountable to the special-interest Mephistopheles who buys it, and who may be looking down upon him from the gallery.

The quest for reelection not only leads members of Congress into special interest dependency, but into a perversion of priorities as well. Congressmen distort the criteria by which they are to be judged, trivializing the work of legislation—except for lists showing how many bills they have introduced—and emphasizing the work of constituent service. There's nothing inherently wrong with servicing constituents; it is useful that aggrieved citizens feel that there is somewhere they can turn. But dwelling on service to the significant exclusion of more substantive legislative work not only misleads voters but encourages congressmen, for instance, to pay less attention to whether more defense spending is needed than to whether the spending is going to their districts. It demeans both the issues presented to the voters and the work done by the members.

But one can't quarrel with the results: the number of "marginal seats" has dramatically declined. According to Professor Morris Fiorina of the California Institute of Technology, in the mid-nineteenth century, 40 to 50 percent of congressional seats changed with each election. Today a third in both chambers have been there more than twelve years. In 1948 four of ten congressional victors won with under 55 percent of the vote; today it is one in ten. This shift, wrote Michael Herwitz in the *Washington Monthly,* "has a direct bearing on the political accountability of congressional incumbents. If congressional seats only change parties because of retirements or sex scandals, the public's control over Congress is seriously endangered."

Such entrenchment can further discourage voter participation, which further weakens the public's control over Congress. "I really don't think there's much you can do about anything," Gladys Grand told the *New York Times* after the 1978 elections. "It's getting to be frustrating. I'm just a little person who doesn't have much pull. But that's the way of the world, I guess." Grand was among nearly 100 million Americans 18 and over who did not vote. Since 1962, the percentage of eligible adults voting has declined steadily in four off-year elections. In 1978, about 38 percent voted, the lowest since 1942. (In Canada 75 percent vote, in West Germany 91 percent.) "Apathy is too mild a word," said Curtis Gans, codirector of the Committee for the Study of the American Electorate. "There are substantial numbers of Americans who are disenchanted with the political process, disgusted with their leaders and disillusioned by the failure of government and of both political parties to meet their needs."

To some extent, citizens are to blame as much as their representatives. People do not make the effort to hold Congress accountable, do not check voting records and campaign financing information, allow themselves to be lulled into a lazy, hazy acceptance of their congressman as he is, not as he ought to be.

But citizens can make a difference. They can lobby their congressmen. They can vote them out of office. They can hold them accountable. But until they do so, the proud lords of legislation can travel luxuriously on taxpayers' money, frolic in the gym, sleep quietly at their desks, vote themselves pork barrel legislation, accept the money of special interests, abuse the franking privilege, obstruct important legislation, and be reassured by the knowledge that it is extremely unlikely that these pleasures and powers will be taken away by the voters.

Epilogue

Taking on Congress: A Primer for Citizen Action

Liberty means responsibility. That is why most men dread it.

—George Bernard Shaw

Some citizens, peering into the chasm between congressional potential and congressional failure, may understandably shrug their shoulders in indifference. But mixed among all the cases of sloth, political hackery, insensitivity to injustice, and business lobbying are remarkable instances of citizen power. Congress has been moved by men and women with no special wealth or influence, little or no political experience, and no uncommon genius, but with the modest combination of commitment to a cause and the facts to make a case. Not often, but enough to show the way, citizen advocates have taken on industrial giants, bureaucratic inertia, public indifference, antipathy to "troublemakers"—and they have won, or at least made a difference.

Abe Bergman, a young pediatrician at Seattle's Children's Orthopedic Hospital, was one of them. In his hospital Abe Bergman saw burned, scarred, and mutilated children —three a week, or even a day—victims of flammable fabrics, lawnmowers, and poisons alluringly packaged. Instead of shrugging off what he saw, he decided to do something about it. He learned how laws governing unsafe products are made—who makes them and what influences their decisions. He learned that one of his senators, Warren Magnuson, as chairman of the Commerce Committee, was in a unique position to change the law. In Magnuson,

285

he found a sympathetic response to the painful accounts of the human tragedies that daily seared his mind. Dr. Bergman became a constant and valued source of information, encouraging Senator Magnuson and the Senate Commerce Committee's staff.

His energetic and informed prodding was among the factors leading Senator Magnuson to introduce amendments to strengthen the Flammable Fabrics Act. In haughty response, the chairman of the board of one of the largest textile firms in the nation, speaking for the textile manufacturers' trade association, vowed that "blood would run in the halls of Congress" before this "unneeded" and "punitive" legislation would pass. Nevertheless, in some measure due to Bergman's testimony and Magnuson's support, the Flammable Fabrics Act Amendments did become law in 1967.

It proved to be an empty victory. For the Department of Commerce, which was to establish standards under the act, postponed their development by deferring in every imaginable way to the textile manufacturers' delays and obstructions. It was not the first time a congressional act had disappeared into a bureaucratic quicksand, and Dr. Bergman, unwilling to be satisfied with a "no-law" law, determined to rescue it from Commerce. To convey the intimate terror of a burn injury, he persuaded a local Seattle television station to run a half-hour film he had produced. The powerful documentary climaxed with gentle nurses and doctors changing the bandages of a scarred and frightened and suffering little girl. This film brought three thousand letters from the Seattle area to the secretary of commerce, insisting that he not delay or weaken the standard on children's sleepwear. At Senator Magnuson's request, the film was flown to Washington, D.C., where the secretary of commerce and his close associates saw it for themselves. Within two weeks, the secretary announced that a strict standard would take effect immediately and that proceedings would commence to raise the age limits of children protected from flammable sleepwear.

Two other citizen activitists also parlayed their peculiar asset—musical, not medical—into legislative result.

Folksinger Harry Chapin, shocked by the mass starvation that followed the drought in sub-Saharan Africa, founded a nonprofit educational group called World Hunger Year, supported by his concert earnings. Through the group (and his lyrics), Chapin has proselytized on behalf of the need for major action to solve world hunger. But he wanted to do more than just inform. After his wife suggested a presidential commission to study hunger, Chapin began an intensive lobbying effort on Capitol Hill to pass a resolution calling for such a commission.

Chapin shed his jeans and work shirt for a proper suit and tie to lobby Rep. Richard Nolan (D.-Minn.), Senator Patrick Leahy (D.-Vt.), and others. Building a core of committed congressional supporters ranging from liberal Senator George McGovern (D.-S.D.) to conservative Senator Bob Dole (R.-Kans.), Chapin's resolution won unanimous support in the Senate and a 368–34 victory in the House. He then sold President Carter on the proposal with an energetic five-minute rush of words in the White House, after which Carter told him, "If this is the kind of energy that was brought to this resolution, I can see why it's reached my desk." Carter signed the bill in 1978 and appointed Chapin to the commission.

Since then Chapin has founded the Food Policy Center (FPC) to lobby on food issues. Working out of a Capitol Hill office, the group has done research to support Chapin's activities as a member of the president's commission. "This is not a normal commission whose report will be issued and then forgotten," said an FPC researcher. "After they come out with the report they will go on the road to disseminate their findings and sell their proposals to the public."

Similarly, Marjorie Guthrie did not desire to be merely the legatee of a famous name in music. She suffered with her husband Woody through fifteen years of off-and-on hospitalization, as he slowly died of Huntington's disease. Determined to help others with similar illnesses, she established the Committee to Combat Huntington's Disease to seek funds to combat not only Huntington's disease but other genetic and neurologic disorders.

In Washington, where secretaries are well trained to filter out as many calls to congressmen as possible, Marjorie Guthrie found a way to get through. "When I speak to a secretary, I ask her age. When she asks why, I tell her that if she is under 30, I'm Arlo Guthrie's mother and that if she is over 30, I'm Woody Guthrie's wife. . . . It is Woody's name that gets me in the door, but once I get in, I'm on my own."

Guthrie worked closely with the chairman of the House Health Subcommittee, Rep. Paul Rogers (D.-Fla.). It was Chairman Rogers who helped get the Congress to move to establish a commission to study Huntington's and related diseases. Rogers, Senator Kennedy (D.-Mass.), and Rep. Andrew Maguire (D.-N.J.) worked with Guthrie and other members to replace funds removed from the budget of the National Institute of Mental Health.

With a $150,000 budget, she can't support research, but does attempt to promote federal support for scientific research and to lobby constituents as well. "For the last several years I have testified on behalf of 50 million people with diseases of the brain and central nervous system who don't really have a voice. I am very angry at this moment. I'm the only one who refuses to testify for only one disease," she said in a 1979 interview. She has attempted to build a coalition of groups interested in related health issues, though many of them seem wedded to the "disease of the month" approach. Despite the frustrations, she compares her building of a grass-roots support for federal support for research to one of Woody's favorite stories. "There were two rabbits trapped by foxes in a hollow tree. One rabbit turned to the other and said, 'We'll just stay in here until we outnumber them.' "

What Motivates Members?

However a case is presented, and whatever tactics are employed, it is advisable to understand initially that, above all else, *votes* motivate congressmen. A large part of their job is staying in their job, and appeals which suggest their continued tenure—such as "labor has endorsed it" or "a poll showed consumers favor it"—will be favorably received by most members.

But pure politics is only one approach. Abe Bergman in part based his appeal, quite simply, on the homily that "it was right." Contrary to myth, appeals to justice and fairness can ignite some kindling among the wet logs of Congress. A related appeal can be made to a member's self-esteem—that by doing right, he'll do good. A con-

gressman likes to be known as a good guy, as a defender
of democracy, rather than as a "tool of special interests."
Even those who service only corporate enterprise drape
their arguments with appeals to the commonweal; it simply
would not do for Exxon's management to argue that they
need a reduction in the corporate income tax because
they want to earn even *more* exorbitant profits.

If exhortations to morality and self-esteem are attempted without the prop of actual or potential publicity,
they may fail. Congressmen respond to publicity—both adverse and complimentary. For example, favorable press
coverage may ease your path to a member happy to be
identified with a good cause. GASP (Group Against Smog
and Pollution), a local citizens' group, conducted a vigorous publicity campaign against the belching smokestacks
of one of Pittsburgh's prime polluters, United States Steel's
Clairton Coke Works. At one point, Pennsylvania air pollution commissioner Dr. William Hunt attempted to dis-
miss Mrs. Michelle Madoff, GASP's leader, as an "asth-
matic paranoid." When a government lawsuit to stop the
pollution was stalled by U.S. Steel's assertion that no adequate filter technology existed, GASP issued a thoroughly
documented, expert report demolishing the claim. The
press extensively reported GASP's activity, and U.S. Steel
read the headlines. The firm eventually capitulated by entering negotiations for a long-range plan for air pollution
abatement. Not surprisingly, Mrs. Madoff's first call to the
Washington office of Rep. Joe Gaydos met a warm reception. Congressmen, like bookies, favor winners. With Gaydos's active assistance, GASP, in the early 1970s, mobilized Pennsylvania's entire congressional delegation to
intervene with state and federal air pollution officials on
behalf of cleaner air in Pittsburgh.

Campaign contributions. Votes. Morality. Self-esteem.
Publicity. What else motivates a congressman to act on an
issue, or hide from it?

Congressmen, like most of us, also listen to reason—but
they hear many reasons. One effective way to bolster your
logical argument is to cite support from a "disinterested
source"—another congressman, a respected columnist, or
experts. Almost universally, congressmen refused to seriously consider hazards of smoking and the need to restrict

cigarette advertising until the authoritative Surgeon General's Committee on Smoking and Health delivered its grim verdict, in 1964, that cigarette smoking was tied to lung cancer and other diseases.

Serious citizen action, with all these various approaches attempted in tandem, can succeed, even against the usual formidable odds. In 1970 and 1971, for example, the 1,800-mile-per-hour supersonic transport appeared certain to fly unhindered through Congress. Ten years of federally funded investment and $1.1 billion already lay behind it. Three presidents (Kennedy, Johnson, and Nixon) had supported it. Its prime contractors were two giant corporations, General Electric and Boeing, and they had scattered $335 million in subcontracts across the home states of eighty-eight senators during 1967 to 1970 alone. Labor, viewing the issue as jobs, joined forces with big business to form a National Committee for the SST, headed by George Meany, president of the AFL-CIO, and Karl Harr, president of the Aerospace Industries Association. Forty-one corporations and several large unions amassed a war chest with an announced goal of $350,000 to save the SST in Congress. Big government, big business, and big labor—all combined into one giant coalition.

Opposing this colossus of economic and political power were ordinary citizens organized as the Citizens League against the Sonic Boom—concerned about the environment and "reordering priorities." The SST, they argued, endangered the atmosphere and our health, promised noise pollution and destructive sonic booms, and diverted federal tax dollars from more pressing and job-intensive areas, like housing, health, and education. They won the endorsement of such groups as Common Cause, Environmental Action, the activist Federation of American Scientists, the National Taxpayers' Union, and the Sierra Club.

In April, 1970, twenty-nine of these national and local organizations joined in a Coalition against the SST. Over the next fourteen months, their congressional effort was coordinated by George Alderson and Louise Dunlap of Friends of the Earth, a Washington-based registered lobbying group. Enlisting the support of sympathetic scientists and economists, they prepared a thoroughly researched case, concentrating on "swing" votes: the new members of Congress, members who voted "inconsistently" on SST the previous year, and undecided congressmen. They recruited constituents to visit their congressmen in the districts and in Washington and brought experts to testify at hearings.

Member organizations, like the Sierra Club, obtained a list of the campaign contributors to key members, calling, writing, and visiting them to urge their opposition to the SST. Common Cause compiled and mailed a press kit of information about the SST to three thousand editorial writers; anti-SST editorials soon sprouted up all across the country. Newspaper advertisements, TV talk shows—every possible opportunity was taken to arouse public opinion and Congress against the SST.

No fewer than four times between December, 1970, and March, 1971, the citizens' coalition won votes on the floor of Congress—only to have each victory nullified afterward by political and parliamentary maneuvers. On one vote, Senator Clinton Anderson, chairman of the Aeronautical and Space Sciences Committee, surprised all by voting against the appropriations. He explained simply, "I read my mail"; that morning his letters and telegrams had opposed the SST by a lopsided 78–8 margin. Such citizen action persisted until a final and decisive vote in May, 1971, when manufacture of the SST in the U.S. was grounded for good. Their odds had been long, but a disparate group of interested citizens working—in walkup offices and with used mimeographs—had prevailed.

How to Do It

1. LEARN ABOUT CONGRESS. You begin with a problem. Your daughter is seriously ill and you've discovered that hospital care costs $150 a day, and no person of your $10,000-a-year income could possibly afford full medical insurance—unless Congress steps in. Or a gripe: Why are utility prices so high? Or an idea: Why not serve nutritional food instead of glop in your child's school lunch program? You're black, Chicano, or native American—and your state commission against discrimination drags its feet for two years before acting on complaints. Or you wonder why you can't buy a washing machine that works, or a safe car. You're a tenant in a neighborhood about to be run over by another highway or "rehabilitated"

out of your price range by urban "renewal." Or you're a human being who breathes the foul exhaust of Chevrolets and Consolidated Edison plants ten miles away.

There are many ways to start acting to solve your problem. One is to write your senator or representative.

Your senator:

> The Honorable ———
> United States Senate
> Washington, D.C. 20510

Your representative:

> The Honorable ———
> House of Representatives
> Washington, D.C. 20515

Ask what laws Congress has passed or is considering to meet your community's needs. Ask which members of what congressional committees and which federal agencies handle such laws. In fact, ask your congressman what you can do. For example:

> Dear Senator or Representative ————,
>
> We are two of your constituents who are concerned about hospital insurance, federal income taxes, and school lunch programs. It is important that we learn better how to be assisted by the services of Congress and how to influence and participate in congressional decisions. Although we have been doing some thinking, it seems to us that you should have a great deal more knowledge, experience, and interchange with citizens on just these issues. Would you kindly give us *guidelines* and *details* on how we can more effectively present our concerns to you and to other legislators—local, state, and federal.
>
> This request may take some of your time, but, if you have not already prepared such a package of advice, we are sure that many other citizens would similarly benefit from your insights and pointers. You're the expert on these matters. We look forward to your help.
>
> > Sincerely,
> > Fred and Martha

But you don't need a "letter of introduction" from your congressman to "meet" Congress. You can begin with free government publications. For free copies of all House and Senate documents, including bills, resolutions, presidential messages to Congress, most committee reports, and public laws, write as follows.

For House documents:

> House Documents Room
> H 226
> United States Capitol
> Washington, D.C. 20515

For Senate documents:

> Senate Documents Room
> S 325
> United States Capitol
> Washington, D.C. 20510

Bills, resolutions, and laws are written in unfathomable legalese. But committee reports usually contain readable and informative descriptions of bills, presenting facts and arguments for and against, though often slanted toward the committee viewpoint.

Printed hearings contain copies of all testimony offered at committee hearings on a bill. Fact-filled and often even readable (but often a thousand pages thick), they also can be purchased by writing to the U.S. Government Printing Office.

The *Congressional Record* is printed daily while Congress is in session and purports to be a transcript of all speeches and proceedings on the floor of the House and Senate. Despite the fact that many members hurriedly revise their speeches just before the *Record* goes to the printer, it is the most useful source of congressional activity: of roll-call votes; of committee hearings and meetings; and of the floor and committee schedule for the following week, printed every Friday. It can also provide educational insight into congressional attitudes. The *Record* can be ordered for $75 a year from the Superintendent of Documents, Government Printing Office,

Washington, D.C. 20402; it is also located at many public and university libraries.*

2. RESEARCH. The first response many congressmen make to any in-person citizen request is a barrage of questions: How much will it cost, next year and five years from now? What kind of tax do we use to raise the money? What does labor think about it? Who benefits? Couldn't the program be better run by the states, and wouldn't loan guarantees be more effective than subsidies? Have you talked to the Banking and Currency Committee? These can wither the unprepared citizen lobbyist. To avoid trouble, first be informed; then lobby.

You can begin, of course, with information from Congress: hearings and committee reports. You can ask your congressman for information from the Congressional Research Service on important issues. The CRS, drawing on the 60-million-piece collection of the Library of Congress, answers specific questions, compiles reading lists, and discusses the pros and cons of policy issues. You can also directly contact a governmental agency which administers federal programs that affect your community. If you seek information or help from it, your congressman can be of assistance: congressional inquiries to agencies are usually answered more promptly than your own unassisted letters, which may molder for months.

If your probing of an agency leads you to question seriously its responsiveness or performance, you can ask your congressman to call in the investigative branch of Congress, the General Accounting Office. With a staff of five thousand, led by accountants, lawyers, and other skilled professionals, the GAO has published revealing and authoritative reports on such topics as defense waste, nuclear power, energy policy, health care waste, inadequate enforcement of sanitary meat and poultry inspection, nonenforcement of pesticide safety regulations and state strip mining laws, and the financial irregularities of national political parties. Potentially one of the greatest tools for citizens and Congress, the GAO is little known. It receives only a few hundred requests for action each year by members of Congress, who alone can request a GAO investigation on your behalf.

---

*See appendix 1 for a list of groups and publications with information on Congress.

You should also be aware of the Freedom of Information Act, which requires public access to all "identifiable records" in federal agency files (but not Congress's), with certain listed exceptions. The exceptions—for national security, corporate trade secrets, internal agency memoranda, and six others—along with delaying tactics and duplicating charges are often purposefully used by agencies to deny information that the public has a right to know. Amendments to the Freedom of Information Act, passed over President Gerald Ford's veto in 1974, strengthened the act and made it somewhat easier for citizens to obtain information; agencies must now respond to an information request within ten days, unresponsive bureaucrats can be sanctioned for their obstruction, and successful litigants can get attorney's fees from the government.*

Nor should you shrink from your own investigations. In April, 1972, a group of New York City neighbors, calling themselves the Upper West Side Air Pollution Campaign, conducted a building-by-building search of their community to track down polluters. Careful documentation by Citizens Action Program (CAP) in Chicago of how U.S. Steel underpaid its property taxes was a major factor in its plant tax reassessment and consequent higher taxes. CAP has also pressured local savings and loan associates to help stop inner-city deterioration by increasing house mortgage and improvement loans to local residents. An equally striking citizen action was the Connecticut Citizen Action Group's study of occupational health hazards, begun in the summer of 1971. During interviews at a Connecticut plant of Colt's Firearms, a student investigator was told by outraged workers that Colt was manufacturing bent-barreled M-16's, under contract with the Department of Defense, for use by GI's in Vietnam. Not only was Colt neglecting to straighten the barrels properly, but the company was also switching parts after performance tests of the rifles, inserting untested and perhaps defective equipment. The Citizen Action Group's headline-captur-

---

*If you cannot obtain the desired records, you can contact one of the groups which specializes in freedom of information problems. Among them are the Freedom of Information Clearing House, P.O. Box 19367, Washington, D.C. 20036, and the University of Missouri Freedom of Information Center, P.O. Box 858, Columbia, Mo. 65201. They will supply you with advice and information.

ing report, including sworn affidavits from the workers, was turned over to the Justice Department for further investigation.

Congressmen can also help obtain information from the private sector, especially giant corporations, who are far more reluctant than even government agencies to let the public peer through their screen of secrecy. At the urging of a citizen, Rep. Benjamin Rosenthal of New York sent out a letter to all domestic auto companies asking how they handle consumer complaints. The companies replied in some detail, and the letter may have stimulated them to formalize their complaint and review procedures; consumers can now at least point to these standards when they are violated. In 1966, when the information was treated like a trade secret, Connecticut Senator Abe Ribicoff successfully wrote the auto companies for a list of all models recalled for defects since 1960. A year or two later, when the National Highway Safety Administration neglected to continue gathering this data, Minnesota's Senator Walter Mondale wrote again and got more information about defective vehicle recalls by the auto firms, and he in addition stimulated the agency to issue regulations and set up a complete information system open to the public.

3. ORGANIZE. There are several reasons why it is worth taking the time to organize a citizen action group. A group can commit more energy and resources than even the most dedicated individual. An Abe Bergman could not have stopped the SST individually. A group is more likely to have the resources and endurance to carry a seemingly interminable project through to completion; and the results of group projects are also usually more respected than an individual's efforts.

Ordinary citizens have the capacity to organize a rudimentary group, which can grow into a powerful citizens' lobby. Take, for example, the late Ed Koupal, a former car salesman, and his wife Joyce. Aroused when highway incursion threatened the Sacramento, California, suburb where they lived, their concern spread to a range of issues. "We believe in the system, but that fools are operating it, that it can work," said Ed. He and Joyce formed the People's Lobby in 1969, whose purpose was summarized by the "Smash Smog!" on its letterhead, and which was financed by a $10 membership for adults, $2 for students. "We're radical, we're militant, and we're constitutional," he explained. "Radical because we believe there's got to be a big change in this country. Militant because we want the law implemented. And constitutional because we operate basically through the initiative process" (a means by which citizens propose laws to be placed on a statewide ballot). "The organization," says Joyce, "is based on survival of the fittest. All these people came in, did junk work, and gradually carved out areas of responsibility. This took three or four months. Now they're department heads."

Another highly successful organizing effort is the New York Public Interest Research Group's "Bank on Brooklyn" campaign, a well-coordinated drive attacking the redlining practices of major New York banks.

The effort began in 1975 with a study by several Brooklyn College students—titled "Take the Money and Run"—which illustrated the failure of banks to reinvest in the communities of their depositors. Specifically, seven banks surveyed in Brooklyn had invested less than one-half of 1% of their total assets in the communities where they received the bulk of their deposits.

Using this survey as an organizing tool, a NYPIRG staffer, in the fall of 1976, began organizing citizen groups in Brooklyn to oppose the banks' redlining practices. Negative publicity campaigns, including picketing, leafletting and rallies were aimed at recalcitrant banks. Throughout the campaign community groups have used data available under state and federal disclosure laws to determine how much of the depositors' money was going to depositors' credit needs. To date, the Bank on Brooklyn campaign has reached signed agreements with more than 10 banks, who have agreed to reinvest specific amounts of money—in the form of mortgage and home improvement loans—in the communities.

If you decide to form a group, you should first draft a tentative but clear statement of the scope of the group's proposed activities (such as lobbying Congress) and your purpose (such as obtaining federal mass transit development funds). Next, bring together a number of friends, acquaintances, or people in the community known for involvement in civic affairs. They might include the president of your neighborhood association, the lawyer who headed the fundraising drive for the reform candidate, or the ex-director of the free breakfast program.

The structure of your group is important. To be successful, you should emphasize *action* rather than organization. Minimize such typical club activities as regular meetings, titles, and minutes. Otherwise the purpose of the group becomes the group, rather than the substantive issue.

Funding is, of course, essential to organizing—and ultimate success. You can get by on little money by holding meetings in homes and similar skimping. Initial expenses can be paid by out-of-pocket $5 or $10 contributions from the organizers. Later, money can be raised by dues, if your membership is large, or by special fundraising events.

But serious citizen lobbying of Congress can well drain your coffers faster than $2 dues or bake sales can fill them. The Coalition against the SST spent more than $20,-000 for staff salaries, newspaper ads, research, phone calls, duplicating, and mailing—not counting expenses by individual member organizations. One way to raise necessary money is to appeal to sympathetic wealthy individuals who can underwrite you with thousands of dollars. For many years, philanthropist Mary Lasker has been a one-woman bank for public health lobbyists. Her efforts deserve much of the credit for the bills which established the National Institutes of Health and Regional Medical Centers. But at the same time be careful not to be bought off: fit available funds to your goals, not your goals to the funds. Another way to raise money is by public subscription, as do GASP in Pittsburgh and Public Citizen in Washington. Finally, if your citizen effort involves merely research and organizing, not lobbying, you may be able to obtain the support of foundations, which typically dole out $5,000 to $20,000 per worthy project.*

---

*To learn about foundations, you can buy for $35 the *Foundation Directory*, published by the Russell Sage Foundation (most recently in 1977) for the Foundation Library Center, 444 Madison Avenue, New York, N.Y. 10022. Information about more activist fundraising can be obtained from *Action for a Change*, by Ralph Nader and Donald Ross (1972, Viking-Grossman paperback), which de-

Once organized, your group's first project should be small, relatively easy to accomplish, cheap, and likely to arouse maximum interest and publicity. In 1969, for example, after Senator Everett Dirksen appealed on television for congressional pay hikes by arguing that "senators have to eat too," Mrs. George Cook of Idaho organized her friends to "send beans to the Senate," and received national press coverage. Other good projects are petition drives and preparing "congressional scoreboards," described below.

To be effective citizen lobbyists, group organizing should not stop at the local level. Whatever your interest, there is probably some national citizens' lobby in Washington that shares it.* Contacting, joining, or forming a nationwide citizens' lobby with a Washington office can help you in three ways.

First, it can serve as an early warning system to keep you informed well enough and quickly enough to make your lobbying in Congress timely and effective. Newsletters and word of mouth from Washington offices can give you a head start in developing personal contacts with congressmen and their staffs. The Environmental Policy Center has hosted lobbying conferences in Washington for citizens concerned about issues like strip mining; after in-depth briefings, the citizen lobbyists from "back home" fan out to communicate with their congressmen.

Second, these Washington offices can also speed the flow of information from you *to* Congress. Dealing daily with congressmen and staff, Washington lobbyists can pass on the right information at the right time and become

---

scribes how university students fund and organize public interest research groups by levies of a few dollars per student. It and *A Public Citizen's Action Manual* (1973), also by Donald Ross, provide illustrative consumer, environmental, and other projects that citizens can undertake. *For the People, A Consumer Action Handbook*, by Joanne Manning Anderson (1977, Addison-Wesley paperback), lists more than a dozen action-oriented consumer projects that citizens can carry out in their local communities—from health care and food marketing practices to energy use. *Fundraising in the Public Interest*, by David Grubb and David Zwick (1977, Public Citizen), and *The Grassroots Fundraising Book*, by Joan Flanagan (1977, The Youth Project), are valuable guides to activist fundraising, describing everything from canvassing and direct mail fundraising to marathons and benefits.

*See appendix 1 for list of national citizens' lobby groups.

trusted advisers. This is hard to do from a purely local base.

Third, national affiliations give you at least the opportunity to lobby congressional committees. As a single local group, you can have some effect on your representative—or, if you are powerful enough, on your senators or entire state delegation. But the members of one committee come from districts all over the country. Without a base as wide as their own, your lobbying may be ineffectual.

As a last organizing step, you may want to align your group or national affiliation with other sympathetic organizations. Coalition building is one of the most important tasks of citizen lobbyists, as long as it doesn't become a form of mutual, bureaucratic dependence. Coalitions increase the voters and geographic base represented, as well as improve the chances that at least some members of the coalition can command the congressman's attention. Look for allies in the home states and the districts of the congressmen—particularly the ranking ones—who sit on the committee you care about. A group from another state lobbying on a tax bill once startled then House Ways and Means chairman Wilbur Mills by encouraging picketing at his district office in Arkansas.

Thus, you have now moved from a person, to a group, to a network of groups. This path is the same progressive accumulation of citizen power that impressed Alexis de Tocqueville over a century ago. "As soon as several of the inhabitants of the United States have taken up an opinion or a feeling which they wish to promote in the world," he said, "they look out for mutual assistance; and as soon as they have found each other out, they combine; from that moment they are no longer isolated men, but a power seen from afar, whose actions serve for an example, and whose language is listened to."

4. LOBBYING. Whatever the connotation, to "lobby" means nothing more than to try to have an impact on the votes of lawmakers. You have a right to lobby under the Constitution, which guarantees "the right of the people peaceably . . . to petition the government for redress of grievances."

Facing you, of course, are the organized lobbies—

from the Chamber of Commerce to the American Medical Association—discussed in chapter 2. Citizen lobbyists, however, have often confounded the "pros" by breaking logjams of inertia and overcoming heavyweight opposition to achieve reform. Like Dr. Isadore Buff, who carried the bitter image of black lung from the coal fields of West Virginia to the corridors of Congress; Fred Lang, a solitary engineer who repeatedly protested the weakness of gas pipeline safety standards to no avail, until Congress listened and enacted the Gas Pipeline Safety Law; Jeremy Stone and Jerome Wiesner and other scientists, who launched a citizen critique of our nuclear armaments policy; Warren Braren, who resigned his position in 1969 as director of the National Association of Broadcasters' code office in New York—created to regulate deceptive advertising—and appeared before a hostile House Commerce Committee to document broadcasters' lip service to self-regulation.

Given such issues and such personal determination, a number of steps can be followed by the citizen lobbyist who is interested not only in making a stand but winning the point:*

• Planning. A serious lobbying organization working on a legislative effort begins with an analysis of the legislative forum in which it must do combat. Who are the key players? To answer this question, the National Right to Life Committee, an antiabortion group, in 1973 began compiling what its newsletter called "an elaborate profile" on each member of the House and Senate. "We need . . . to know his position on human life issues, his voting record, his committees, his friends, his source of campaign funds, his basis of political support, his family, his constituency, his district and anything else that will give us an advantage in influencing his vote."

What committee or subcommittee will consider the legislation? Who chairs it? Who are the important staff mem-

---

*For some, an initial, procedural step will be to file as a registered lobbyist under the 1946 Federal Registration of Lobbying Act. Registering should be as routine as renewing a driver's license. The reason for the act is not to prevent lobbying, but to keep track of who's doing it and how much is spent. (Since this is a technical area, with each situation turning on its particular facts, it is best to consult a lawyer.)

bers? Are there legislative assistants on the staffs of congressmen who have shown an interest in similar issues in the past? Early in the process, you should project a likely timetable of events, ranging from generating public support through introducing the bill, on to the hearing stage, committee markup sessions, floor consideration, Senate-House conference, and finally the possibility of veto by the president. Thoughtful consideration of substance and strategy at this early stage can avoid telling delays or outright failures later.

• Timing. Assuming you are lobbying on a specific piece of legislation rather than trying generally to educate, your lobbying should begin early, before the legislation concerning you is introduced or is still at the committee or subcommittee level. Since most bills are passed by the House and Senate exactly as reported by the committee, an ounce of lobbying in committee is worth a pound of lobbying on the floor.

Lobbying in Congress can pivot around someone else's bill *or* your own bill. Do not be surprised that you can ask your congressman to introduce a bill—that's part of his job.

Write up what you want to do in plain language. You can present your proposal directly to your congressman, who can refer it to the Office of Legislative Counsel for drafting. But it's better to have your bill drafted by an attorney who advocates your point of view. One good place to look is a law-student organization at a local law school. Even better may be one of the public interest law firms springing up around the country. Public Interest Research Groups, staffed by lawyers and other professionals, and funded by college students who guide overall policy, already exist in twenty-five states and the District of Columbia.

Your own congressman is probably not the best person to introduce your bill, for any bill introduced by a congressman not a member of the relevant committee is routinely passed over. Find out, therefore, which committee handles bills on your subject. And beware of the token bill, introduced by the congressman to get you off his back and then left to die in a committee he doesn't belong to. Most citizens are so excited by the introduction of their bill that they are easily fooled by this ploy. Ask your congressman to speak to members from your state on the committee; to write a letter to the chairman requesting hearings and to send you a copy; and to testify in favor of your bill at the hearings.

If the legislation concerning you doesn't get out of committee, chances are it will never be seriously considered. When Emanuel Celler, chairman of the House Judiciary Committee, was asked in 1958 for his stand on a certain bill, he replied, "I don't stand on it. I am sitting on it. It rests four-square under my fanny and will never see the light of day." Sometimes even the committee stage may be too late, because, as one committee staffer said, "Given an active subcommittee chairman, working in a specialized field with a staff of his own, the parent committee can do no more than change the grammar of a subcommittee report."

• Testimony and Hearings. Citizens have their best access to committees during the public hearings held on most major bills. When citizens are permitted through the large oaken doors into the hearing rooms, what they usually discover are plodding exercises in the compilation of information, views, and recommendations. Occasionally, the hearings are extravaganzas staged for publicity and the press. In either case, most experienced Capitol lobbyists find hearings serious enough—after all, they are making a public record that will last for years—so they rarely miss an opportunity to testify.

Testimony is an important way to educate committee members, committee staff, and the press. To ensure that your position gets a fair airing, you should help recruit relevant witnesses. One good pool to tap is experts. Many experts respond to calls from lay citizens, but a request from your congressman can help. Former Georgia representative Jim Mackay once contacted fifty experts, many of whom peppered the House Commerce Committee with requests to testify on an auto safety bill, and the points of view they expressed prevented the hearings from being a mere whitewash. Witness recruiting is especially important on subjects so arcane—bank and tax bills, complicated housing finance laws—that only private interests directly affected know about the hearings. Only systematic monitoring and continuous presence in Washington can prevent defeat by default.

Yet one needn't be a professional "expert" in order to testify effectively. Often personal experience and passion count far more than learning or polish. An 11-year-old Florida schoolgirl testified in 1972 before the Senate Commerce Committee on a study she had done of the impact of television advertising on her classmates. When Joseph ("Chip") Yablonski, son of murdered United Mine Workers insurgent Jock Yablonski, testified on UMW election irregularities before a Senate Labor and Public Welfare subcommittee, his intense and touching manner etched his words onto everyone present. After the Farmington, West Virginia, mine disasters, the stricken widows of the victimized miners retained enough composure to convey the lesson of their sadness to a congressional committee. Union rank and file on a labor bill, migrant workers on a bill to give them minimum wages, mechanics on car repairability, housewives on consumer purchases: firsthand knowledge counts.

Dramatizing your testimony with personal narration may not only stave off committee members' boredom, but can also attract press attention. During hearings on the coal mine health and safety bill, miners with severe black lung gripped the attention of congressmen by showing how they collapsed from lack of breath after jumping up and down just a few times. In the underground natural-gas pipeline hearings, Tony Mazzocchi, Washington lobbyist for the Oil, Chemical, and Atomic Workers Union, brought in the workers who repair and inspect underground pipelines in St. Louis. They showed the riddled pipe and demonstrated sloppy repairs to the members of Congress. In hearings on national health insurance, physicians performed a kidney dialysis before wide-eyed committee members.

Citizen groups can also ask members of Congress to hold hearings where the problem is—in your community. Rep. John Brademas took his subcommittee of the House Education and Labor Committee to Chicago, New York, Boston, and Miami to hear testimony on the problems of the aging. Senator Edmund Muskie trooped his subcommittee out to Gary, Indiana, to hear about alleged corporate under-payment of property taxes. Back in the fifties, former representative John Blatnik toured the country with his Public Works subcommittee looking into corruption in interstate highway construction, accumulating volumes of evidence.

You can also ask your representative to bring unofficial hearings to your district. In the fall of 1969 representatives from New York City held unofficial hometown hearings on one of the world's biggest air pollution problem areas. Former representative Jim Mackay of Georgia topped them all: he set up a Grass-Roots Congress in Atlanta, with citizens' committees organized along the lines of actual congressional committees. His constituents met and proposed and discussed bills on regular schedules. He also brought cabinet officials and agency heads who discussed key legislation—and agency implementation of it—directly with affected citizens.

• The "Markup" Sessions. After official hearings are held, staff typically prepare a draft committee bill. Committee members then meet to go over the draft bill and to propose amendments. Because it is here that the contours and details of legislation are ironed out, markup sessions are crucial for citizen lobbyists. If they cannot gain access to the markup session—most are now open to the public, but not all—they should at least contact the committee staff, who have direct substantive authority over the developing legislation. One can gain a reputation for giving honest, informative, and accurate answers, and staffers and congressmen may come to rely on your expertise. "The key point of contact is usually between a highly specialized lobbyist and the specialized staff people of the standing committee," said Rep. Bob Eckhardt of Texas. "Intimate friendships spring up there—it's the rivet point. Friendships that outlast terms. They probably have a greater influence on legislation, especially if it's technical."

• Lobbying for Votes. After all the legislative foreplay, legislation must come down to a simple head count. Eventually, the interested citizen will attempt to persuade a member to vote a certain way. How can you personally sway votes?

You can try to *meet your congressman.* In 1965, congressmen interviewed said they spent 7 percent of their work week meeting with constituents. When you visit your congressman, write ahead to arrange an appointment. You then have a better chance of seeing him or her and it is a courtesy appreciated by busy members. Also, it can make your visit far more effective. If you state in your letter the precise issue you wish to discuss, the congressman can have his staff research the problem and "brief" him before your visit. Groups are even more welcome than individuals, for obvious electoral reasons.

You can also call the district office to find out when your representative will be in town, and try to arrange an appointment to see him or her then. Most representatives have full-time district offices, and most members are there during weekends or congressional recesses. Some Eastern representatives, members of the so-called Tuesday-Thursday Club, are often in their districts Friday through Monday. Failing that, you should try to meet with a member of the representative's staff.

Or you can ask a congressman *to visit you and your group,* either in informal session or to give a speech followed by a question-and-answer session. Such gatherings can impress a member with your information, your issue, or your clout. Consider, for one example, Rep. Dan Rostenkowski, a Democrat from the Chicago machine. Formerly prowar, he was persuaded by persistent and passionate high school students to break with President Nixon's troop withdrawal approach. "I make a lot of speeches at high schools in my district," he explained, "and the kids ask damn penetrating questions about what useful purpose we are serving in Vietnam. As this thing has gone on, I've had more and more trouble answering them."

In personal lobbying, it is also essential *to get exact commitments.* An experienced labor lobbyist tells of the citizen group which visited its local representative to solicit federal money for schools. The representative's response: "Why, yes, I've always been in favor of education and when the pending legislation comes up I'll certainly vote pro-education." They walked away satisfied they had a "firm commitment." In fact, the congressman was free to vote any way he pleased when the specific provisions of the education bill came up; each side could claim to be "pro" education. The lesson: spell out exactly what you want your congressman to do.

Even if you are specific, your request may be met by a smokescreen of diversionary actions. Don't be fooled by camouflages like a public yes vote on the floor after the member has already added a crippling amendment in the privacy of committee; the introduction of a token bill which will be safely tucked away in a committee of which your congressman is not a member; or a nice speech inserted in the extensions section of the *Congressional Record.*

Writing your congressman can have an impact. It is true that most letters from constituents never reach the congressman's desk, but they all reach his office. Although most mail gets little more than a glance from a busy clerk, there are letters that electrify, that counter false information, that change votes. These very often reach the congressman's attention. In the mid-sixties, when Congress had barely begun to look at unsafe automobiles, several members of the Senate Commerce Committee began to receive letters that shared common characteristics. They were written carefully, many by engineers and professional people. They were precise. Each told a similar story of the shoddy performance of tires. The committee members probably received, in all, fewer than fifty of these letters. But they had a profound impact on the members, whose staffs decided that they were unique enough and significant enough to be read by the senators themselves. Indeed, the committee cited these letters as a significant part of the evidence convincing it that tire safety legislation was needed.

Even letters which are not seen by policymaking staff or the congressman can have an important impact if there are enough of them. On important issues, many members have their clerks count their mail the way geologists read seismographs. (Recall, for example, the labor law reform battle described in chapter 2.) The sample may be statistically inaccurate, but it offers understandable and numerical guidance to a member who faces conflicting views and who wants to be reelected. Form letters flooding an office will not have this impact. Many individual letters will.

Letters which demonstrate familiarity with the congressman and his record immediately evoke respectful interest. "I strongly support your efforts to amend the Housing Act by requiring the FHA inspectors to be responsible for the quality as well as the value of housing, and I was pleased to see you vote for the Morehead Amendment which would have strengthened the consumer protection bill. However, I am very much concerned . . ."

This kind of opening is particularly effective because it conveys to the reader a number of facts. First, he is dealing with an informed voter, probably an opinion leader in his community. Second, this is a potential supporter, not an ideological opponent who would complain if the member voted for Washington's visage on the one-dollar bill.*

Two alternatives to direct mail are *telegrams and telephone calls*. Early in the legislative life of a bill, when there is time to write and mail a letter, telegrams make little sense. Telegrams are attention-getters, however, and can be effective when sent just before a vote: to ask a yea or nay, and to urge the member to be present for the vote. Ducking a vote is easier when the congressman thinks no one is watching. By calling Western Union, a fifteen-word "Public Opinion Message" can be sent to Congress from anywhere in the country for two dollars. It usually arrives one day after being sent.

The idea of sending something other than a letter, something symbolic of the issue that concerns you, can have a much greater impact in a congressional office than the hundreds of letters that are received every day. For example, over 40.000 citizens joined the "Consumer Nickel Brigade" in the summer of 1977. They mailed nickels to 83 wavering members of Congress urging them to support an Agency for Consumer Representation—a nickel representing the average cost per American to create the $15 million advocacy office. As a result of a "Cans to Carter" campaign organized by environmental groups seeking mandatory deposits on beverage containers, over 30,000 tin cans were received by the White House during the first two months of 1978. And in a third campaign, people sent obituaries and automobile crash stories to their representatives to convince them to support passenger crash protection systems in automobiles.

On occasion, when an issue is emotional and well-publicized, great masses of telegrams flood into Washington. Within six days of former president Richard Nixon's firing of Special Prosecutor Archibald Cox in October,

---

*Rep. Mo Udall has put together a useful summary on the fundamentals of writing a letter to a Representative. It can be obtained by writing him to ask for a copy of "The Right to Write," (U.S. House of Representatives, Washington, D.C.)

1973, a total of *350,000 telegrams* were sent to Capitol Hill and the White House from concerned citizens and groups across the country. This upwelling of public sentiment played a major role in persuading Majority Leader Carl Albert and House Judiciary Chairman Peter Rodino to initiate the dreaded impeachment process.

5. PUBLIC COMMUNICATIONS. The news media are the most visible and efficient voice to disseminate your purpose and activities. You may have appealed to the press in getting your bill introduced; or in the hearings; or before the markup session. At some point, however, before a floor vote, public support becomes essential.

The basic tool in your press kit is the *press release*. This is nothing more than a written statement by any person or group issued to the press—i.e., mailed or hand-delivered to every newspaper and broadcaster in your community. It should consist of accurate, newsworthy information. The photogenic, the unusual, an event, a charge, testimony—all may be newsworthy.

A second tool, the *press conference,* must be used with more restraint. It may involve a public reading of a statement, a question-and-answer session, or both. To make the immediate issue interesting and concrete, you might try to accompany it with some symbolic act, such as the presentation of your voting scorecard (described below) to the congressman. Because they take newsmen's time, press conferences should be called only when there is important news. To help assure that the press will come to your conference, consider asking some community figure, such as a former elected official, to participate.

Your opponent's paid political advertisements on TV and radio may help you get *free broadcast time* to rebut them. Under the FCC's fairness doctrine, when a station presents commentary on one side of a "controversial issue of public importance," it must present the other side as well. The doctrine doesn't guarantee equal time, but it can give you free time if the station itself fails to broadcast your side. When you see materials you think require rebuttal, write the station manager, identify your group as having membership in the area, refer to the ads, and offer to provide or help the station prepare counterstatements. If you get no reply in a week, or if the station rejects your offer, you can send a written complaint to Chief, Complaints and Compliance Division, Federal Communications Commission, 1919 M Street, N.W., Washington, D.C. 20036. Many radio stations (and some TV stations) devote program time for citizens to air their views. Whatever it is called—"Point of View" or "The Voice of the People"—local radio or television time is invaluable exposure.

The print media require a somewhat different approach. Letters to the editor of local newspapers can be effective. Studies have shown that the "Letters to the Editor" column is one of the most widely read sections of a newspaper.

A more direct press approach is also possible. Often citizens complain about press apathy or favoritism. Most people don't realize that it is possible if not helpful to visit unresponsive editors, look them in the eye, and ask them why they haven't covered an important story.* If you try to educate, rather than manipulate, and are candid and informed, you may well affect the policy of previously inattentive local media. Develop personal contacts and information exchanges with reporters, photographers, broadcasters, and editors, just as you might with congressional staff. They can be valuable sources of information to you, and you to them.

Recalcitrant local press may also be jarred into action by national media coverage of a problem in your community. With the exception of the *Louisville Courier,* Appalachian media in the coal mining states did little or no reporting (except for covering disasters) on unsafe mines and black lung disease, until miners' marches and work stoppages caught the attention of NBC, CBS, ABC, the *Washington Post,* and the *New York Times.* This technique of appealing to national press to stimulate local reporting can be especially important for citizens of one-company communities, like textile and paper mill towns around the country.

---

*For an informative guide on how to prod local papers to be more accountable, see David Bollier's *How to Appraise and Approve Your Daily Newspaper: A Manual for Readers* (1978). (Copies can be obtained from Center for Study of Responsive Law, P.O. Box 19367, Washington, D.C.; $5 for individuals and $10 for institutions.)

Finally, groups can communicate with the public by more *direct action*. Although some picketing and sit-ins aim more to intimidate than to inform their targets, most forms of public demonstrations are quite simply to demonstrate a point to the public. "The rich can buy advertisements in newspapers, purchase radio or television time, and rent billboard space," said Justice William O. Douglas in dissent to a Supreme Court decision involving Dr. Martin Luther King's 1963 marches through Birmingham, Alabama. "The less affluent are restricted to the use of handbills . . . or petitions, or parades, or mass meetings." Public demonstrations, often resorted to by those lacking formal access to the established media, can be a part of an overall campaign to awaken Congress to their concerns and convictions. It can help give them conscience, in H. L. Mencken's definition of that word as "the inner voice which warns us that someone may be looking."

Beyond Congress

"The biggest mistake I ever made," reports Dr. Bergman, "was thinking I had won the victory just by getting a bill through Congress. That was only the beginning."

First, the president may veto your bill.

Second, even if he signs it, he may refuse to spend all the money appropriated by Congress.

Finally, the federal agency that is supposed to carry out the program may write ineffective regulations within the broad congressional guidelines or may simply not enforce the law's provisions.

Ultimately then, lobbying must focus on the agency and the White House. Tactics may have to change since, for example, appointed bureaucrats are generally less sensitive than elected congressmen to voters. Remember also that the agencies are beholden to the congressional committees which write laws governing their programs and which pass their annual budget. These committees (but not Appropriations committees) are now required by law to act as watchdogs over executive agencies, and, beginning in 1973, must issue reports every two years on their progress.

One important tactic beyond legislation is purely legal: going to court. NAACP lobbyists, for example, work arm in arm with their lawyer litigators, ready to file suit on the constitutionality of such bills as the antibusing act. In 1972, Ralph Nader's Congress Project filed suit against ex-representative Edward Garmatz, patriarch and sole proprietor of the House Merchant Marine and Fisheries Committee, and two of its clerks, for refusing to make records of committee votes available at committee offices as required by a 1970 reform law. Eight days later, Garmatz, through his chief counsel, opened the records.

Friendly congressmen can be of great assistance to you in bringing lawsuits, especially against hard-shelled executive agencies. A new and potentially powerful course of action—direct resort to the courts to tame the bureaucracy—is being pursued by more members of Congress. Twenty-eight congressmen successfully sued the Civil Aeronautics Board (CAB) eight years ago, challenging an airline rate increase approval as illegal. In 1972, Rep. Ronald Dellums of California and James Ridgeway, then an editor of *Ramparts,* sued to compel HEW to release information on Medicare and Medicaid; in 1973, Senators Williams, Pell, and Mondale were among the plaintiffs who successfully brought a lawsuit to remove Howard Phillips as acting head of the Office of Economic Opportunity.

A different step beyond the Capitol corridors is to compete with Congress. For example, if you suspect that a bill you favor will not get a fair hearing in the official committee, hold your own hearings. The National Welfare Rights Organization did just that, conducting hearings at the Capitol on President Nixon's welfare program two days before scheduled Senate Finance Committee action in November, 1970. Senator Fred Harris, when a member of the Finance Committee, was so impressed by testimony at the hearings that when the "real" committee met shortly afterward, he gave NWRO a one-vote margin of victory over the Nixon plan.

You can also competitively stimulate Congress by getting a state law passed which it can imitate. Then, Congress will have a proven model from which to build national legislation. After Massachusetts, for example, enacted a no-fault auto insurance plan, Congress gave serious consideration to a national no-fault plan for the first time.

How do you do it? In Michigan, a citizen campaign passed a bill to give individual citizens the legal right to file suits to protect the environment. They obtained an attentive press by attending hearings and numerous strategy meetings, flooding the governor's office with phone calls, concentrating on key legislators and the state's attorney general, and recruiting students to counter overblown charges made against the bill by the Chamber of Commerce. Joseph Sax, the Michigan law professor who drafted the bill, met with staff people working for Senators McGovern and Hart and Rep. Udall to draft a national bill, which was then introduced. When industrial polluters argued that the bill would choke the courts with too many lawsuits, its supporters could point to Michigan, where an average of only two suits a month have been filed since the law was passed. In addition, five other states have acted on Michigan's example to pass similar laws.

During the 1972 primary elections, the People's Lobby in California collected several hundred thousand signatures to put a sweeping environmental control bill on the ballot. Although the People's Lobby initiative went down to defeat, buried by a costly public relations campaign funded by industrial interests, it had already forced some state legislators to take a more concerned stand on environmental questions.* In 1974, it scored its greatest success. The People's Lobby was a major force behind Proposition 9, a tough campaign spending and lobbying reform measure. Working with Common Cause, the People's Lobby had volunteers collect over 500,000 signatures in fifty-three of fifty-eight California counties. In November, 1974, it became the law of the state. Nor can anyone blink at the success of Howard Jarvis, who after years of failure finally got his Proposition 13 (to lower property taxes) on the California ballot. In 1978, it passed by a 2 to 1 margin.

Election Year

Your ultimate resort against unresponsive congressmen is to "throw the rascals out." But regardless of whether

---

*The states that permit initiatives are Alaska, Arizona, Arkansas, California, Colorado, Idaho, Maine, Massachusetts, Michigan, Missouri, Montana, Nebraska, Nevada, North Carolina, North Dakota, Ohio, Oklahoma, Oregon, South Dakota, Utah, Washington, and Wyoming.

your congressman is vulnerable at the polls, election years and campaign months are the best times to press your issue upon congressmen, who seem not uncoincidentally more interested in their constituents at these moments of job insecurity. There exist, moreover, several low-cost and little-used techniques by which citizens can change votes and views during critical campaign years.

A congressional scorecard, to take a key approach, is a chart showing how your congressman has performed over the years on a specific issue—consumer protection, tax reform, civil rights, defense spending, environmental protection, or any other. Used creatively, this rating system can have a considerable impact in an election year. In election years since 1970, for example, Environmental Action prepared environmental scorecards for members of Congress. The twelve worst performers each year were labeled the "Dirty Dozen," whom Environmental Action then worked to defeat. In 1970, seven of them lost; in 1972, eight lost; and in 1974, eight lost—though the number defeated fell to three and two in the last two elections. In one such instance in the 1974 primary in Kentucky's first district, Dirty Dozen incumbent Frank Stubblefield was opposed by a candidate who proclaimed, "If elected, I will never be listed on the Dirty Dozen." Stubblefield lost the primary race.

In preparing your scorecards, it is best to concentrate on one area. Select perhaps ten votes in which the lines between support and opposition are clearly drawn, and make sure that you choose the important stage of the voting on each bill. (Sometimes a vote on an amendment or on a procedural motion may be more important than the vote on the final bill.) Publicize the results as widely as possible within the district.

Interested citizens can go beyond a voting scorecard to do profiles of representatives. Utilizing library research and field interviews, writers could evaluate a local congressman's campaign contributions, campaign tactics, constituent services, committee and floor actions, and relationships to his or her colleagues.

In 1972 Ralph Nader's Congress Project compiled 15-20 page profiles of all Members of Congress running for reelection, and in 1978 they updated the project by profiling a dozen more members who had entered office after 1972. Local citizen groups have also been involved in profile efforts. In 1972, 1974, and 1976, the Connecticut Citizen Action Group did profiles of all state representatives running for reelection—approximately 150 in all. And in the fall of 1974 the New York Public Interest Research Group profiled the 190 members of the New York Senate and Assembly who were seeking a return to office. Accurate and insightful profiles can educate the electorate in ways that self-lauding newsletters by members cannot.

What use can you make of campaign finance reports filed by candidates with the secretary of state in the home state and the clerk of the House or secretary of the Senate? Check especially for (1) failures to comply with the reporting requirements of the election laws, (2) potential conflicts of interest in the areas the candidate would cover as a legislator, (3) reported spending that is much greater than reported contributions—which suggests that some donors have secretly given cash, or (4) contributions "in kind," such as the loan of consultants, still on salary, from a corporation or labor union, or a free public opinion poll. The most important part of the laws to a citizen action group is the opportunity they provide—before the election —to find out who a candidate's supporters are, what interests they represent, and how much they are contributing. The laws provide one other "plus" for citizens' groups: any individual who believes the campaign finance laws have been violated may file a complaint with the Federal Election Commission.

Other areas of a candidate's background can also be investigated by the citizen. Members of Congress are required to file annual financial disclosure statements. These describe outside income and gifts over $100, and outside property and investments (excluding one's home) over $1,000, and liabilities over $10,000.† Other sources would include the public ownership files at television and radio

---

†House members' reports are available from the Committee on Standards of Official Conduct, Room 2360, Rayburn Building, Washington, D.C. 20515. Senators' reports are available from the Office of Public Records, ST-2 Capitol Building, Washington, D.C. 20510.

stations showing if the candidate is affiliated with broadcasting interests, county property tax records showing what properties the candidate owns, reports on file at the Securities and Exchange Commission listing major ownership of stock (10 percent) in one company, and Standard and Poor's Register of Corporations for corporate directorships.

During an election year, one of the most fruitful issues to raise with candidates is reform of Congress itself. Who goes to Congress is, of course, a critical question. But so is the question: What kind of institution should Congress be? Reform and creativity cannot flourish in an unresponsive institution, no matter how good its members. In letters, in visits, or during speeches, constituents can put their representatives on record about the rules which govern their work and our Congress. What follows are suggested questions, which can hopefully trigger a dialogue on congressional reform; each is merely a door to a roomful of detailed, follow-up inquiries. The candidate's replies to these questions (plus related newsletters, campaign literature, and newspaper clippings) should be kept handy so that the candidate can be reminded of his commitments if and when he or she wins the election and takes office. Will the candidate or congressman—

• Support public financing of a substantial portion of congressional campaign costs?

• Promote legislation to eliminate all existing loopholes (described in chapter 1) in the campaign finance disclosure laws?

• Back legislation requiring the reasonable disclosure of organized lobbying activity, including disclosure of the major sources of funds used in lobbying, the amounts spent and received, the way the funds are spent, and the specific issues involved?

• Support rules forbidding members to serve on committees having jurisdiction over any subjects affecting them financially?

• Work to further eliminate the secrecy that serves special interests by backing legislation to open all committee and subcommittee markup and House-Senate conference sessions to the public (limited only by national security considerations), to require the taking of transcripts to be available immediately to the public in unedited form, and to publish all roll-call committee votes?

● Support televised floor proceedings of the Senate?

Finally, there is the election process itself. Interested citizens can turn their efforts to old-fashioned political organizing techniques to get out the vote. As a citizen action group organized for nonelectoral purposes—for conservation or child care—you can often rally many people who would ignore the normal appeals of the political parties. Particularly since the surprise showing of Eugene McCarthy in the 1968 New Hampshire presidential primary, congressional candidates have respected the power of citizen groups and their volunteer workers.

Especially in the primaries, where a challenger's main problem may be to battle his way out of obscurity, door-to-door canvassers and street-corner leafleters can make the margin of difference. Canvassers are also needed for the all-important voter registration drives. New voters, of all ages, often poor or from minority groups, usually lean against the status quo. Later, volunteers can help man telephones, staple newsletters, lick envelopes, and mail literature from campaign headquarters. On election day, thousands of phone calls must go out to voters from sympathetic districts, to remind them to vote; carpools are needed to take house-bound voters to the polls; and leafleters should be at every nearby polling location. All these are within the capacity of a well-organized citizen action group.

Such an effort met with success on a county government level in Arkansas. In Pulaski County, seventeen local affiliates of a statewide community organizing group called ACORN set out in 1974 to have their members run for all 467 seats on the county legislative body, a body which controls the county's $6.5 million budget. The results of the election: ACORN-affiliated citizens won at least 195 of the seats.

But don't consider winning the election as your only goal. Your chances of losing are too great to risk such single-mindedness. If a few losses seem to thoroughly discourage your members, remind them that your long-range objective is not superior numbers in November, but favorable votes

in Congress. If you gain new access to your representative
or senator, or change his or her emphasis or views, your
citizen action has won a victory. For the goal realistically
is to obtain the attention and respect of those who represent you in Washington—and to give them conscience,
which H. L. Mencken defined as "the inner voice which
warns us that someone may be looking."

Appendix 1

Sources of Information on Congress

In addition to reading the government publications described in the epilogue, a good way for citizens to learn about current happenings is to draw on the research of Washington lobbies. Some distribute pocket-size directories listing members of Congress and their committee assignments: Common Cause, a leading citizens' lobby, at 2030 M Street, N.W., Washington, D.C. 20036 (free); the Chamber of Commerce of the United States, Legislative Dept., 1615 H Street, N.W., Washington, D.C. 20006 ($1.50); the American Gas Association, 1515 Wilson Blvd., Arlington, Va. 22209 ($2.25); the American Medical Association, 1776 K Street, N.W., Washington, D.C. 20006 (free).

Others publish scorecards on how every member of Congress voted on dozens of major bills, selected and scored from the political perspective of each organization. The most prominent are AFL-CIO, Legislative Department, 815 Sixteenth Street, N.W., Washington, D.C. 20006 (labor and social welfare votes); Americans for Constitutional Action, 955 L'Enfant Plaza North, S.W., Washington, D.C. 20024 ("conservative"); Americans for Democratic Action, 1411 K Street, N.W., Washington, D.C. 20005 ("liberal").

Groups with other perspectives which publish scorecards are Public Citizen, P.O. Box 19367, Washington, D.C. 20036 (consumer reform issues); National Associated Businessmen, 1000 Connecticut Avenue, N.W., Washington, D.C. 20036 (business); Consumer Federation of America, 1012 Fourteenth Street, N.W., Suite 901, Washington, D.C. 20005 (consumer); League of Conservation Voters, 317 Pennsylvania Avenue, S.E., Washington, D.C. 20003 (environmental); National Farmers Union, 1012 Fourteenth Street, N.W., Washington, D.C. 20005 (farming and agriculture); American Security Council, 1101 Seventeenth Street, N.W., Suite 803, Washington, D.C. 20036 (national security); Friends Committee on National Legisla-

319

tion, 245 Second Street, N.W., Washington, D.C. 20003 (peace issues).

Several sources offer more summarized, detailed, and comprehensive information. *Congressional Quarterly's Guide to the Congress of the United States* is an expensive ($55.00) but extremely thorough and fascinating tome on the history and workings of Congress, first published in 1971. *The Almanac of American Politics*, by Barone, Ujifusa, and Matthews (first published in 1972 and updated every two years), is a 1,200-page volume (one or two pages per member of Congress), available at bookstores for $8.95. *Ralph Nader's Congress Project* has 20–40-page profiles of all incumbents who ran in the 1972 election ($1 per incumbent profile, Congress Watch, 133 C Street, S.E., Washington, D.C. 20003). In-depth studies of major congressional committees, plus an examination of Senate and House rules were published beginning in 1975. (Major libraries should have these materials.)

The *Congressional Directory*, often available free from your congressman, is otherwise a $7.25 paperback from the U.S. Government Printing Office, North Capitol Street, N.W., Washington, D.C. 20001; it lists all congressmen and their committee (but not subcommittee) assignments, and most congressional staff. More complete information about staff is contained in the *Congressional Staff Directory*, available at $22.00 from P.O. Box 62, Mount Vernon, Va. 22121.

By writing most committee offices (same address as your congressman), you can obtain at no cost their 100–300-page committee Legislative Calendars. They list every bill referred to the committee and what action has been taken, as well as descriptions of committee work, members, history, rules, etc. They are typically issued from one to six times a year, depending on the committee, and are therefore usually weeks or months out of date.

Two periodicals are especially informative on current legislation and, though expensive, are available in some large public and college libraries. The $558.00-per-year *Congressional Quarterly Weekly Report* is mailed every Friday from 1414 Twenty-second Street, N.W., Washington, D.C. 20037, and is indexed by subject. The *National Journal*, a $345.00-per-year subscription, is published weekly by the Government Research Co., 1730 M Street, N.W., Washington, D.C. 20036. Each issue includes behind-the-scenes reports on legislative progress, pressures, and personal profiles, indexed every three months.

Finally, thousands of documents, directories, and reports can be obtained from the U.S. Government Printing Office. You can find out what may be helpful in the *Monthly Catalogue of U.S. Government Publications*, carried in many major public and university libraries; periodic GPO catalogues are mailed free on request.

As mentioned in the epilogue, there are numerous citizens' lobby groups with offices in Washington, D.C.—and many have local chapters. Each group centers its lobbying on one or more related topics, so you should be able to find an organization which represents your specific interests. Groups include Consumer Federation of America (address above); League of Conservation Voters (address above) and Friends of the Earth, 620 C Street, S.E., Washington, D.C. 20003 (conservation/environmental issues); National Taxpayers' Union, 153 E Street, S.E., Washington, D.C. 20003 (tax); Common Cause (address above); National Women's Political Caucus, 1411 K Street, N.W., Washington, D.C. 20005 (women's issues); Coalition for a New Foreign and Military Policy, 120 Maryland Avenue, N.E., Washington, D.C. 20002 (defense spending); Public Citizens' Congress Watch, 133 C Street, S.E., Washington, D.C. 20003 (consumer issues); Zero Population Growth, 1346 Connecticut Avenue, N.W., Washington, D.C. 20036 (population control); League of Women Voters, 1730 M Street, N.W., Washington, D.C. 20036 (women's issues, and election issues in general); National Association for the Advancement of Colored People (NAACP), 733 Fifteenth Street, N.W., Washington, D.C. 20005 (racial issues); National Farmers Union (address above); American Association of Retired Persons, 1909 K Street, N.W., Washington, D.C. 20006 and National Council of Senior Citizens, 1511 K Street, N.W., Washington, D.C. 20005 (issues pertaining to the retired and elderly); and the American Civil Liberties Union, 600 Pennsylvania Avenue, S.E., Washington, D.C. 20003 (legal and civil liberties issues).

Appendix 2

Senate

Member: Democrats in roman; Republicans in *italics;*
Independents in SMALL CAPS

Vice Pres. Mondale, Walter F. (Minn.)
Armstrong, William L. (Colo.)
Baker, Howard H., Jr. (Tenn.)
Baucus, Max (Mont.)
Bayh, Birch (Ind.)
Bellmon, Henry (Okla.)
Bentsen, Lloyd (Tex.)
Biden, Joseph R., Jr. (Del.)
Boren, David L. (Okla.)
Boschwitz, Rudolph E. (Minn.)
Bradley, Bill (N.J.)
Bumpers, Dale (Ark.)
Burdick, Quentin N. (N. Dak.)
BYRD, HARRY F., JR. (Va.)
Byrd, Robert C. (W. Va.)
Cannon, Howard W. (Nev.)
Chafee, John H. (R.I.)
Chiles, Lawton (Fla.)
Church, Frank (Idaho)
Cochran, Thad (Miss.)
Cohen, William S. (Maine)
Cranston, Alan (Calif.)
Culver, John C. (Iowa)
Danforth, John C. (Mo.)
DeConcini, Dennis (Ariz.)
Dole, Robert (Kans.)
Domenici, Pete V. (N. Mex.)
Durenberger, David (Minn.)
Durkin, John A. (N.H.)
Eagleton, Thomas F. (Mo.)
Exon, J. James (Nebr.)
Ford, Wendell H. (Ky.)
Garn, Jake (Utah)
Glenn, John (Ohio)

Goldwater, Barry (Ariz.)
Gravel, Mike (Alaska)
Hart, Gary (Colo.)
Hatch, Orrin G. (Utah)
Hatfield, Mark O. (Oreg.)
Hayakawa, S. I. (Sam) (Calif.)
Heflin, Howell (Ala.)
Heinz, H. John, III (Pa.)
Helms, Jesse (N.C.)
Hollings, Ernest F. (S.C.)
Huddleston, Walter D. (Ky.)
Humphrey, Gordon J. (N.H.)
Inouye, Daniel K. (Hawaii)
Jackson, Henry M. (Wash.)
Javits, Jacob K. (N.Y.)
Jepsen, Roger W. (Iowa)
Johnston, J. Bennett (La.)
Kassebaum, Nancy Landon (Kans.)
Kennedy, Edward M. (Mass.)
Laxalt, Paul (Nev.)
Leahy, Patrick J. (Vt.)
Levin, Carl (Mich.)
Long, Russell B. (La.)
Lugar, Richard G. (Ind.)
McClure, James A. (Idaho)
McGovern, George (S. Dak.)
Magnuson, Warren G. (Wash.)
Mathias, Charles McC., Jr. (Md.)
Matsunaga, Spark M. (Hawaii)
Melcher, John (Mont.)
Metzenbaum, Howard M. (Ohio)
Morgan, Robert (N.C.)

322

Moynihan, Daniel Patrick
(N.Y.)
Muskie, Edmund S. (Maine)
Nelson, Gaylord (Wis.)
Nunn, Sam (Ga.)
Packwood, Bob (Oreg.)
Pell, Claiborne (R.I.)
Percy, Charles H. (Ill.)
Pressler, Larry (S. Dak.)
Proxmire, William (Wis.)
Pryor, David (Ark.)
Randolph, Jennings (W. Va.)
Ribicoff, Abraham (Conn.)
Riegle, Donald W., Jr. (Mich.)
Roth, William V., Jr. (Del.)
Sarbanes, Paul S. (Md.)
Sasser, Jim (Tenn.)
Schmitt, Harrison "Jack"
(N. Mex.)
Schweiker, Richard S. (Pa.)
Simpson, Alan K. (Wyo.)
Stafford, Robert T. (Vt.)
Stennis, John C. (Miss.)
Stevens, Ted (Alaska)
Stevenson, Adlai E. (Ill.)
Stewart, Donald (Ala.)
Stone, Richard (Dick) (Fla.)
Talmadge, Herman E. (Ga.)
Thurmond, Strom (S.C.)
Tower, John (Tex.)
Tsongas, Paul E. (Mass.)
Wallop, Malcolm (Wyo.)
Warner, John W. (Va.)
Weicker, Lowell P., Jr. (Conn.)
Williams, Harrison A., Jr.
(N.J.)

Young, Milton R. (N. Dak.)
Zorinsky, Edward (Nebr.)

SENATE COMMITTEES

Agriculture, Nutrition, and
Forestry
Appropriations
Armed Services
Banking, Housing, and Urban
Affairs
Budget
Commerce, Science, and
Transportation
Energy and Natural Resources
Environment and Public Works
Finance
Foreign Relations
Governmental Affairs
Human Resources
Judiciary
Rules and Administration
Veterans Affairs
Select-Ethics
Select-Indian Affairs
Select-Intelligence
Select-Small Business
Special-Aging

LIAISON OFFICES

Air Force
Army
Civil Service
Navy
Veterans' Administration

House of Representatives

Members: Democrats in roman; Republicans in *italics;* nonvoting in SMALL CAPS; deceased in brackets

A

Abdnor, James (S. Dak.)
Addabbo, Joseph P. (N.Y.)
Akaka, Daniel K. (Hawaii)
Albosta, Donald Joseph (Mich.)
Alexander, Bill (Ark.)
Ambro, Jerome A. (N.Y.)
Anderson, Glenn M. (Calif.)
Anderson, John B. (Ill.)
Andrews, Ike F. (N.C.)
Andrews, Mark (N. Dak.)
Annunzio, Frank (Ill.)
Anthony, Beryl, Jr. (Ark.)
Applegate, Douglas (Ohio)
Archer, Bill (Tex.)
Ashbrook, John M. (Ohio)
Ashley, Thomas L.(Ohio)
Aspin, Les (Wis.)
Atkinson, Eugene V. (Pa.)
AuCoin, Les (Oreg.)

B

Badham, Robert E. (Calif.)
Bafalis, L. A. (Skip) (Fla.)
Bailey, Don (Pa.)
Baldus, Alvin (Wis.)
Barnard, Doug (Ga.)
Barnes, Michael D. (Md.)
Bauman, Robert E. (Md.)
Beard, Edward P. (R.I.)
Beard, Robin L. (Tenn.)

Bedell, Berkley (Iowa)
Beilenson, Anthony C. (Calif.)
Benjamin, Adam, Jr. (Ind.)
Bennett, Charles E. (Fla.)
Bereuter, Douglas K. (Nebr.)
Bethune, Edwin R., Jr. (Ark.)
Bevill, Tom (Ala.)
Biaggi, Mario (N.Y.)
Bingham, Jonathan B. (N.Y.)
Blanchard, James J. (Mich.)
Boggs, Lindy (Mrs. Hale) (La.)
Boland, Edward P. (Mass.)
Bolling, Richard (Mo.)
Boner, William Hill (Tenn.)
Bonior, David E. (Mich.)
Bonker, Don (Wash.)
Bouquard, Marilyn Lloyd (Tenn.)
Bowen, David R. (Miss.)
Brademas, John (Ind.)
Breaux, John B. (La.)
Brinkley, Jack (Ga.)
Brodhead, William M. (Mich.)
Brooks, Jack (Tex.)
Broomfield, Wm. S. (Mich.)
Brown, Clarence J. (Ohio)
Brown, George E., Jr. (Calif.)
Broyhill, James T. (N.C.)
Buchanan, John (Ala.)
Burgener, Clair W. (Calif.)
Burlison, Bill D. (Mo.)
Burton, John L. (Calif.)
Burton, Phillip (Calif.)

324

Butler, M. Caldwell (Va.)
Byron, Beverly B. (Md.)

C

Campbell, Carroll A., Jr. (S.C.)
Carney, William (N.Y.)
Carr, Bob (Mich.)
Carter, Tim Lee (Ky.)
Cavanaugh, John J. (Nebr.)
Chappell, Bill, Jr. (Fla.)
Cheney, Richard Bruce (Wyo.)
Chisholm, Shirley (N.Y.)
Clausen, Don H. (Calif.)
Clay, William (Bill) (Mo.)
Cleveland, James C. (N.H.)
Clinger, William F., Jr. (Pa.)
Coelho, Tony (Calif.)
Coleman, E. Thomas (Mo.)
Collins, Cardiss (Ill.)
Collins, James M. (Tex.)
Conable, Barber B., Jr. (N.Y.)
Conte, Silvio O. (Mass.)
Conyers, John, Jr. (Mich.)
Corcoran, Tom (Ill.)
Corman, James C. (Calif.)
CORRADA, BALTASAR (P.R.)
Cotter, William R. (Conn.)
Coughlin, Lawrence (Pa.)
Courter, James A. (N.J.)
Crane, Daniel B. (Ill.)
Crane, Philip M. (Ill.)

D

D'Amours, Norman E. (N.H.)
Daniel, Dan (Va.)
Daniel, Robert W., Jr. (Va.)
Danielson, George E. (Calif.)
Dannemeyer, William E. (Calif.)
Daschle, Thomas A. (S. Dak.)
Davis, Mendel J. (S.C.)
Davis, Robert W. (Mich.)
Deckard, H. Joel (Ind.)
de la Garza, E. (Tex.)
Dellums, Ronald V. (Calif.)
Derrick, Butler (S.C.)
Derwinski, Edward J. (Ill.)
Devine, Samuel L. (Ohio)
Dickinson, William L. (Ala.)
Dicks, Norman D. (Wash.)
Diggs, Charles C., Jr. (Mich.)

Dingell, John D. (Mich.)
Dixon, Julian C. (Calif.)
Dodd, Christopher J. (Conn.)
Donnelly, Brian J. (Mass.)
Dornan, Robert K. (Calif.)
Dougherty, Charles F. (Pa.)
Downey, Thomas J. (N.Y.)
Drinan, Robert F. (Mass.)
Duncan, John J. (Tenn.)
Duncan, Robert (Oreg.)

E

Early, Joseph D. (Mass.)
Eckhardt, Bob (Tex.)
Edgar, Robert W. (Pa.)
Edwards, Don (Calif.)
Edwards, Jack (Ala.)
Edwards, Mickey (Okla.)
Emery, David F. (Maine)
English, Glenn (Okla.)
Erdahl, Arlen (Minn.)
Erlenborn, John N. (Ill.)
Ertel, Allen E. (Pa.)
Evans, Billy Lee (Ga.)
Evans, David W. (Ind.)
EVANS, MELVIN H. (V.I.)
Evans, Thomas B., Jr. (Del.)

F

Fary, John G. (Ill.)
Fascell, Dante B. (Fla.)
FAUNTROY, WALTER E. (D.C).
Fazio, Vic (Calif.)
Fenwick, Millicent (N.J.)
Ferraro,Geraldine A. (N.Y.)
Findley, Paul (Ill.)
Fish, Hamilton, Jr. (N.Y.)
Fisher, Joseph L. (Va.)
Fithian, Floyd J. (Ind.)
Flippo, Ronnie G. (Ala.)
Flood, Daniel J. (Pa.)
Florio, James J. (N.J.)
Foley, Thomas S. (Wash.)
Ford, Harold E. (Tenn.)
Ford, William D. (Mich.)
Forsythe, Edwin B. (N.J.)
Fountain, L. H. (N.C.)
Fowler, Wyche, Jr. (Ga.)
Frenzel, Bill (Minn.)
Frost, Martin (Tex.)
Fuqua, Don (Fla.)

Levitas, Elliott H. (Ga.)
Lewis, Jerry (Calif.)
Livingston, Bob (La.)
Lloyd, Jim (Calif.)
Loeffler, Thomas G. (Tex.)
Long, Clarence D. (Md.)
Long, Gillis W. (La.)
Lott, Trent (Miss.)
Lowry, Michael E. (Wash.)
Lujan, Manuel, Jr. (N. Mex.)
Luken, Thomas A. (Ohio)
Lundine, Stanley N. (N.Y.)
Lungren, Dan (Calif.)

M

McClory, Robert (Ill.)
McCloskey, Paul N., Jr. (Calif.)
McCormack, Mike (Wash.)
McDade, Joseph M. (Pa.)
McDonald, Larry (Ga.)
McEwen, Robert C. (N.Y.)
McHugh, Matthew F. (N.Y.)
McKay, Gunn (Utah)
McKinney, Stewart B. (Conn.)
Madigan, Edward R. (Ill.)
Maguire, Andrew (N.J.)
Markey, Edward J. (Mass.)
Marks, Marc L. (Pa.)
Marlenee, Ron (Mont.)
Marriott, Dan (Utah)
Martin, James G. (N.C.)
Mathis, Dawson (Ga.)
Matsui, Robert T. (Calif.)
Mattox, Jim (Tex.)
Mavroules, Nicholas (Mass.)
Mazzoli, Romano L. (Ky.)
Mica, Dan (Fla.)
Michel, Robert H. (Ill.)
Mikulski, Barbara A. (Md.)
Mikva, Abner J. (Ill.)
Miller, Clarence E. (Ohio)
Miller, George (Calif.)
Mineta, Norman Y. (Calif.)
Minish, Joseph G. (N.J.)
Mitchell, Donald J. (N.Y.)
Mitchell, Parren J. (Md.)
Moakley, Joe (Mass.)
Moffett, Anthony Toby (Conn.)
Mollohan, Robert H. (W. Va.)
Montgomery, G. V. (Sonny) (Miss.)
Moore, W. Henson (La.)

Moorhead, Carlos J. (Calif.)
Moorhead, William S. (Pa.)
Mottl, Ronald M. (Ohio)
Murphy, Austin J. (Pa.)
Murphy, John M. (N.Y.)
Murphy, Morgan F. (Ill.)
Murtha, John P. (Pa.)
Myers, John T. (Ind.)
Myers, Michael O. (Pa.)

N

Natcher, William H. (Ky.)
Neal, Stephen L. (N.C.)
Nedzi, Lucien N. (Mich.)
Nelson, Bill (Fla.)
Nichols, Bill (Ala.)
Nolan, Richard (Minn.)
Nowak, Henry J. (N.Y.)

O

Oakar, Mary Rose (Ohio)
Oberstar, James L. (Minn.)
Obey, David R. (Wis.)
O'Brien, George M. (Ill.)
O'Neill, Thomas P., Jr. (Mass.)
Ottinger, Richard L. (N.Y.)

P

Panetta, Leon E. (Calif.)
Pashayan, Charles, Jr. (Calif.)
Patten, Edward J. (N.J.)
Patterson, Jerry M. (Calif.)
Paul, Ron (Tex.)
Pease, Donald J. (Ohio)
Pepper, Claude (Fla.)
Perkins, Carl D. (Ky.)
Peyser, Peter A. (N.Y.)
Pickle, J. J. (Tex.)
Preyer, Richardson (N.C.)
Price, Melvin (Ill.)
Pritchard, Joel (Wash.)
Pursell, Carl D. (Mich.)

Q

Quayle, Dan (Ind.)
Quillen, James H. (Jimmy) (Tenn.)

R

Rahall, Nick Joe, II (W. Va.)
Railsback, Tom (Ill.)
Rangel, Charles B. (N.Y.)
Ratchford, William R. (Conn.)
Regula, Ralph S. (Ohio)
Reuss, Henry S. (Wis.)
Rhodes, John J. (Ariz.)
Richmond, Frederick W.
  (N.Y.)
Rinaldo, Matthew J. (N.J.)
Ritter, Donald Lawrence (Pa.)
Roberts, Ray (Tex.)
Robinson, J. Kenneth (Va.)
Rodino, Peter W., Jr. (N.J.)
Roe, Robert A. (N.J.)
Rose, Charles (N.C.)
Rosenthal, Benjamin S. (N.Y.)
Rostenkowski, Dan (Ill.)
Roth, Toby (Wis.)
Rousselot, John H. (Calif.)
Roybal, Edward R. (Calif.)
Rudd, Eldon (Ariz.)
Runnels, Harold (N. Mex.)
Russo, Marty (Ill.)
[Ryan, Leo J. (Calif.)]

S

Sabo, Martin Olav (Minn.)
St. Germain, Fernand J. (R.I.)
Santini, Jim (Nev.)
Satterfield, David E., III (Va.)
Sawyer, Harold S. (Mich.)
Scheuer, James H. (N.Y.)
Schroeder, Patricia (Colo.)
Schulze, Richard T. (Pa.)
Sebelius, Keith G. (Kans.)
Seiberling, John F. (Ohio)
Sensenbrenner, F. James, Jr.
  (Wis.)
Shannon, James M. (Mass.)
Sharp, Philip R. (Ind.)
Shelby, Richard C. (Ala.)
Shumway, Norman D. (Calif.)
Shuster, Bud (Pa.)
Simon, Paul (Ill.)
Skelton, Ike (Mo.)
Slack, John M. (W. Va.)
Smith, Neal (Iowa)
Smith, Virginia (Nebr.)
Snowe, Olympia J. (Maine)

Snyder, Gene (Ky.)
Solarz, Stephen J. (N.Y.)
Solomon, Gerald B. H. (N.Y.)
Spellman, Gladys Noon (Md.)
Spence, Floyd (S.C.)
Stack, Edward J. (Fla.)
Staggers, Harley O. (W. Va.)
Stangeland, Arlan (Minn.)
Stanton, J. William (Ohio)
Stark, Fortney H. (Pete)
  (Calif.)
Steed, Tom (Okla.)
[Steiger, William A. (Wis.)]
Stenholm, Charles W. (Tex.)
Stewart, Bennett M. (Ill.)
Stockman, Dave (Mich.)
Stokes, Louis (Ohio)
Stratton, Samuel S. (N.Y.)
Studds, Gerry E. (Mass.)
Stump, Bob (Ariz.)
Swift, Allan Byron (Wash.)
Symms, Steven D. (Idaho)
Synar, Michael Lynn (Okla.)

T

Tauke, Thomas J. (Iowa)
Taylor, Gene (Mo.)
Thomas, William M. (Calif.)
Thompson, Frank, Jr. (N.J.)
Traxler, Bob (Mich.)
Treen, David C. (La.)
Trible, Paul S., Jr. (Va.)

U

Udall, Morris K. (Ariz.)
Ullman, Al (Oreg.)

V

Van Deerlin, Lionel (Calif.)
Vander Jagt, Guy (Mich.)
Vanik, Charles A. (Ohio)
Vento, Bruce F. (Minn.)
Volkmer, Harold L. (Mo.)

W

Walgren, Doug (Pa.)
Walker, Robert S. (Pa.)
Wampler, William C. (Va.)

Watkins, Wes (Okla.)
Waxman, Henry A. (Calif.)
Weaver, James (Oreg.)
Weiss, Ted (N.Y.)
White, Richard C. (Tex.)
Whitehurst, G. William (Va.)
Whitley, Charles (N.C.)
Whittaker, Robert (Bob)
  (Kans.)
Whitten, Jamie L. (Miss.)
Williams, Lyle (Ohio)
Williams, Pat (Mont.)
Wilson, Bob (Calif.)
Wilson, Charles (Tex.)
Wilson, Charles H. (Calif.)
Winn, Larry, Jr. (Kans.)
Wirth, Timothy E. (Colo.)
Wolff, Lester L. (N.Y.)
Wolpe, Howard (Mich.)
WON PAT, ANTONIO BORJA
  (Guam)
Wright, Jim (Tex.)
Wyatt, Joe, Jr. (Tex.)
Wydler, John W. (N.Y.)
Wylie, Chalmers P. (Ohio)

Y

Yates, Sidney R. (Ill.)
Yatron, Gus (Pa.)
Young, C. W. Bill (Fla.)
Young, Don (Alaska)
Young, Robert A. (Mo.)

Z

Zablocki, Clement J. (Wis.)
Zeferetti, Leo C. (N.Y.)

HOUSE COMMITTEES

Agriculture
Appropriations
Armed Services
Banking, Finance and
  Urban Affairs

Budget
District of Columbia
Education and Labor
Government Operations
House Administration
Interior and Insular Affairs
International Relations
Interstate and Foreign
  Commerce
Judiciary
Merchant Marine and Fisheries
Post Office and Civil Service
  Franking Commission
Public Works and
  Transportation
Rules
  Minority
Science and Technology
Small Business
Standards of Official Conduct
Veterans' Affairs
Ways and Means

SELECT COMMITTEES

Aging
Assassinations
Congressional Operations
Intelligence, Permanent
Narcotics Abuse and Control
Outer Continental Shelf
Population

JOINT COMMITTEES

Economic
Printing
Taxation

LIAISON OFFICES

Air Force
Army
Civil Service
Navy
Veterans' Administration

Index

cities' lobby, 41–42
Citizens Action Program, 295–296
citizens' groups
  coalitions of, 300
  funding, 298
  lobby for, 42–45
  and media, 309–10
  see also Consumer Protection Agency; specific groups
Citizens League against the Sonic Boom, 290–91
Civic Trust 80, 7
Civil Aeronautics Board, 312
Civil War, 108
Clark, Dick, 33
Clark, Frank, 61, 171, 268n
Clark, Joseph, 48, 243, 271
Clark, Ramsey, 270
Clay, Henry, 92
Clay, William, 172, 219
Clifford, Clark, 39, 120
Clifford, Thomas, 123
coal industry, 5
coalitions, citizen, 300
Coca-Cola Company, 7, 46
Cohen, David, 78
Colby, William, 145
Cole, Joseph, 3
Collins, Cardiss, 172
Colmer, William, 69
Colt's Firearms Company, 295–296
Common Cause, 313
  campaign contributions, 21–22, 269
  and H. Jackson, 77–78
  and House reform, 88
Conable, Barber, Jr., 198
conflicts of interest, congressmen's, 163–68, 199
Congress
  appropriations to, 121–25
  budget committees, 123–24
  committee chairmen, 72–91
  Committees, 61–64
  vs. Executive branch, 107–55
  and Executive impoundment of funds, 126–27
  and Executive lobbying, 116–121
  filibuster, 69–72
  General Accounting Office, 141–43, 294

and impeachment of Nixon, 148–53
information resources, 142–44
investigation of, 194
investigation of CIA and FBI, 144–45
and J. Carter, 153–55
and Koreagate, 193–94
leadership of, 91–106
legislation, 137–39, 264–65
legislative veto, 134–37
lobbyists, 116–21
log-rolling, 110–16
office and staff allowance, 225
ombudsmen, 243–44
parliamentary procedure, 261–262
pomp of, 219–23
quorum calls, 262
reform, 216
rules of, 64–72
secrecy, 66–68
seniority, 64–66
and special days and weeks, 220–21
sunset legislation, 137–39
War Powers Act, 132–33
and Watergate, 148–53
see also congressmen; House; Senate
Congressional Action, 28
Congressional Budget Office, 124–25
Congressional Record, 221–23, 256, 276–77, 293–94
Congressional Research Service, 294
Congress: Keystone of the Washington Establishment (Fiorina), 244
congressmen
  alcoholism of, 231–32
  attendance, 262–63
  and banking interests, 164–65
  casework of, 241–42, 243–44
  cliques of, 217–19
  clubs, 217–18
  conflicts of interest, 163–68, 199
  constituent servicing, 239–44, 305–7
  criminal conduct by, 156–205
  debating by, 244–46
  districters, 256–57